THE FRENCH COLONIAL MIND

VOLUME I

FRANCE OVERSEAS
Studies in Empire and Decolonization
....
SERIES EDITORS:
A. J. B. Johnston, James D. Le Sueur,
and Tyler Stovall

THE FRENCH COLONIAL MIND

VOLUME I

Mental Maps of Empire and Colonial Encounters

Edited and with an introduction by Martin Thomas

UNIVERSITY OF NEBRASKA PRESS : LINCOLN AND LONDON

© 2011 by the Board of Regents of the University of Nebraska

Portions of chapter 6, "Anticlericalism, French Language Policy, and the Conflicted Colonial Mind in Cameroon, 1923–1939," by Kenneth J. Orosz originally appeared in Kenneth J. Orosz, *Religious Conflict and the Evolution of Language Policy in German and French Cameroon, 1885–1939* (New York: Peter Lang, 2008). Portions of chapter 8, "Religious Rivalry and Cultural Policymaking in Lebanon under the French Mandate," by Jennifer M. Dueck originally appeared in Jennifer M. Dueck, *The Claims of Culture at Empire's End: Syria and Lebanon under French Rule* (Oxford: Oxford University Press, 2010).

All rights reserved. Manufactured in the United States of America

Library of Congress Cataloging-in-Publication Data

The French colonial mind, volume 1 : mental maps of empire and colonial encounters / edited and with an introduction by Martin Thomas.
p. cm. — (France overseas : studies in empire and decolonization)
Includes bibliographical references and index.
ISBN 978-0-8032-2093-5 (paperback : alkaline paper)
ISBN (set) 978-0-8032-3815-2 (paperback : alkaline paper)
1. France—Colonies—Africa—History. 2. France—Colonies—Africa—Administration—History. 3. Africa, French-speaking West—Colonization—History. 4. Africa, French-speaking Equatorial—Colonization—History. I. Thomas, Martin, 1964–

DT33.F73 2011   325'.344—dc23   2011024159

Set in Sabon by Bob Reitz. Designed by A. Shahan.

Contents

Preface and Acknowledgments — ix

Introduction:
Mapping the French Colonial Mind — xi
MARTIN THOMAS

PART 1
Colonial Encounters and Imaginings of Empire

1. Reflections on the French Colonial Mind — 3
   PATRICIA M. E. LORCIN

2. Intellectuals for Empire? The Imperial Training of Félicien Challaye, 1899–1914 — 26
   EMMANUELLE SIBEUD

3. Colonial Minds and African Witchcraft: Interpretations of Murder as Seen in Cases from French West Africa in the Interwar Era — 49
   RUTH GINIO

4. The Colonial Cosmology of Fernand Braudel — 72
   JOHN STRACHAN

5. Mental Maps of Modernity in Colonial Indochina during World War II: Mobilizing Sport to Combat Threats to French Rule — 96
   ANNE RAFFIN

PART 2
Language, Culture, and Communities of the Colonial Mind

6 Anticlericalism, French Language Policy, and the Conflicted Colonial Mind in Cameroon, 1923–1939   121
   KENNETH J. OROSZ

7 Information and Intelligence Collection among Imperial Subjects Abroad: The Case of Syrians and Lebanese in Latin America, 1915–1930   144
   MARÍA DEL MAR LOGROÑO NARBONA

8 Religious Rivalry and Cultural Policymaking in Lebanon under the French Mandate   168
   JENNIFER M. DUECK

9 France's Arabic Educational Reforms in Algeria during the Colonial Era: Language Instruction in Colonial and Anticolonial Minds before and after Algerian Independence   194
   JAMES D. LE SUEUR

PART 3
Administrators and the Colonial Mind after World War II

10 Thinking Like an Empire: Governor Henri Laurentie and Postwar Plans for the Late Colonial French "Empire-State"   219
    MARTIN SHIPWAY

11 Recycling Empire: French Colonial Administrators at the Heart of European Development Policy   251
    VÉRONIQUE DIMIER

12 Friend or Foe? Competing Visions of Empire in French West Africa in the Run-up to Independence   275
TONY CHAFER

13 Thinking between Metropole and Colony: The French Republic, "Exceptional Promotion," and the "Integration" of Algerians, 1955–1962   298
TODD SHEPARD

14 Rigged Elections? Democracy and Manipulation in the Late Colonial State in French West Africa and Togo, 1944–1958   324
ALEXANDER KEESE

List of Contributors   347
Index   351

Preface and Acknowledgments

Historical inquiry is often predicated on deceptively simple questions, one of which is "Why did people do that?" Answers are typically formulated around a combination of internal motivations and external factors: prevailing socioeconomic conditions, calculations of personal or political advantage, national security requirements, ethnic loyalties, or other cultural norms. The question of the objective sought becomes more urgent when the action taken appears, at least to the contemporary observer, hard to justify. Thus we tend to be more engaged by the actions of history's wrongdoers than by those of the well intentioned, who remain, for many, historically dull. Does the work of European colonialists fall into that category of historical wrongdoing? Superficially at least, the answer must surely be "yes." Imperial conquest and a colonial domination founded on racial differentiation and exclusion is indefensible on numerous grounds. Yet to scratch the surface of colonial history is to reveal countless ardent imperialists for whom colonialism was self-evidently virtuous, morally unimpeachable, even ethically imperative. Thus we return to our opening question: "Why?"

The external factors mentioned above provide answers, but not a comprehensive explanation of imperialists' motivations. To reach that, we need to think about the components of their cultural outlook, the sources of their attitudes toward such issues as nation, race, ethnicity, gender, and religion. In short, we have to look deeper into the colonizers' minds. It is the purpose of this book and its companion volume, *The French Colonial Mind, Volume 2: Violence, Military Encounters, and Colonialism*, to explore these questions.

The two linked volumes of *The French Colonial Mind* originated in a conference held at the University of Exeter's Institute of Arab and Islamic Studies over a sunny spring weekend in April 2007. Hosted by the Centre for the Study of War, State, and Society, the conference was generously supported by the Leverhulme Trust and the University of Exeter's Department of History. It is a pleasure to acknowledge their support here. The two anonymous readers who each read the manuscripts for each volume did a wonderful job in pointing us to additional lines of enquiry. Robert Aldrich helped clarify the conference's organizing theme, and his outstanding work over many years was a key inspiration for it. Ruth Ginio also kindly read my introductions to both volumes and, as usual, made incisive suggestions about how to improve them. As editor, I would also like to thank Claire Keyte and Andrew Thorpe at Exeter and Heather Lundine, Bridget Barry, Joeth Zucco, and Jim Le Sueur at the University of Nebraska Press for their invaluable help in bringing the project to fruition. Editing is sometimes regarded as a rather thankless task. That has certainly not been the case for me, for which I thank all of the contributors to *The French Colonial Mind*, as well as our outstanding copyeditor, Jane Curran. Producing the volumes has been a real pleasure and a rich source of insight into the many facets of French colonialism. I've learned a lot and enjoyed myself doing so. I hope that readers will derive something similar from the chapters that follow.

Introduction

Mapping the French Colonial Mind

MARTIN THOMAS

What is the French colonial mind? The proposition that there existed a collective conscious, or unconscious, thought process—a universal mind of French colonialism—that influenced, determined, or otherwise affected key decisions in the colonial encounter may appear ambitious to the credulous, ludicrous to the skeptic. There were, of course, countless supporters of imperialism, thousands of empire administrators, seemingly endless colonial minds. Yet, whether treated in the singular or the plural, investigating the mind—or minds—of colonialism promises valuable results. Why?

Historians typically search for links between extraneous factors and personal motivations in seeking to explain why individuals, groups, institutions, or governments acted in particular ways. Central to this is the mental universe—the outlook or worldview—of those involved in the events or decisions analyzed. The challenge facing scholars of empire is to study the commonalities among colonial minds while acknowledging the dangers of oversimplification. Attitudinal formation and the derivation of shared ideas are critical, often revealing more subtleties than stereotypes. As Susan Bayly has argued in relation to Paul Mus, one of France's most reflective and influential thinkers on the cultures of the Indochinese peninsula, careful interrogation of the idea of "colonial minds" challenges the generic applicability of the stock terminology familiar to scholars of colonial history, from "civilizing mission" to

"Orientalism" and notions of the Other.[1] Even in the case of the other turn-of-the-century Francophone empire, King Leopold's Congo Free State, the once widely accepted notion that the early paths of Belgian imperialism were reducible to the beliefs and desires of a single royal mind has now been exploded. Confronted with diverse peoples and practices, Belgium's imperialists, like their French cousins, "had multiple 'others' against which to define [their] identity."[2] Their responses were as multifaceted as the cultures they encountered. As in the Belgian case, so in the French, the suggestion that the connections between mental processes and identity formation could be precisely mapped or, more ambitious still, reduced to singular generic characteristics, might also raise scholarly eyebrows. Yet, strip these ideas down to their essentials, to their individual components, and the colonial mind quickly becomes an essential and familiar analytical tool. For colonial mind-sets, individual or collective, were products of their cultural environment and their historical moment. Seen in this light, study of the colonial mind—or minds—builds on the body of work regarding cultures of empire, which ranks among the fastest growing and the most dynamic in the field of colonial history.[3]

It has, for instance, become almost inconceivable that a general history of empire and its rulers could be written without consideration of social mores and cultural practices, of habit, tradition, and custom, as well as politics and economics.[4] Colonial minds made possible what Ann Stoler has termed the "imperial formations" on which the legal, institutional, and cultural bases of colonial discrimination were built. The legitimization of discrimination and coercive extraction derived from commonplace ideas among imperialists of the late nineteenth and twentieth centuries who, as Stoler puts it, justified "imperial guardianship, trusteeships, delayed autonomy, temporary intervention, conditional tutelage, military takeover in the name of humanitarian works, violent intervention in the name of human rights, and security measures in the name of peace."[5] Imperial formations, the product of shared presumptions and cultural norms, determined the forms of knowledge production regarding colonial societies within European imperial states.[6] As a result these formations provided the building blocks with which to construct what Roland Barthes termed "the myth of French imperiality."

This rhetoric of order from chaos, of cultural elevation within the fabric of "greater France," achieved widespread currency among politicians, intellectuals, and the wider public in twentieth-century France.[7] The underlying anxieties and unspoken fears of colonial officials only too aware of the actual fragility of their colonial presence, were rarely articulated in bureaucratic reports and government correspondence. And yet, as Stoler has again shown, such insecurity was deeply embedded in the very processes of reportage, surveillance, and segregation that helped make colonial rule inherently exclusionary and repressive. Investigating colonial attitudes helps us decode the bombast so common in official colonial documentation.[8] They reveal the gaps between the self-assurance with which empire was represented as a force for good on paper and the persistent doubts and fears among officials daily confronted with a majority population unremittingly hostile or, at best, indifferent to their claims of imperial improvement.

The few individuals, largely at the extreme left of the political spectrum or among the literary and artistic avant-garde, who opposed such representations of empire resorted to shock tactics in their efforts to persuade French opinion that colonialism was anything but benevolent.[9] Initially, at least, few took notice. Far more influential were the changing patterns of academic engagement with empire, which lent intellectual weight to the belief that France pursued a higher imperial purpose than mere strategic, economic, or political advantage. The role of such empire-oriented disciplines as social anthropology, psychology, and ethnography is now placed squarely alongside the perhaps better-known academic specialties—classical history, geography, and Darwinian biology—as determinants of European imperialist credos.[10] Understandings of the physical challenges of living and working in arid, tropical, or otherwise forbidding colonial climates were shaped by the belief, increasingly prevalent in France and Britain from the mid-nineteenth century, that successful colonization demanded mastery of the science of acclimatization. Focused primarily on the exploitation of unfamiliar flora and fauna and on conquering the physiological problems, diseases, and other maladies encountered by Europeans in the colonial world, an underlying assumption behind acclimatization's scientific precepts was that Western science could tame the colonial environment, harnessing it to European ends.[11]

Yet, while such scientific colonialism emboldened French colonizers to persist in the face of physical adversity, it was widely accepted that the unfamiliarity and daily hardships of life in the colonies could destabilize the European mind. Empire was dangerous, not just physically but also psychologically. Fears were stoked in the realms of the imagination, fueled by both penny-press scaremongering and academic treatises produced on both sides of the English Channel in which a strong tendency developed, particularly evident in the medical context, to "sensationalize" the pathological threats inherent to Africa especially. Prolonged exposure to life in the colonies could wreck the mind as much as the body, producing that quintessentially colonial malady, "tropical neurasthenia."[12] Aside from the menace of disease and mental breakdown, as one of our contributors, Emmanuelle Sibeud, has argued elsewhere, the social dangers that colonies and empire service presented were very much constructed by the colonizers. The colonial officials, doctors, missionaries, and other quasi-professional ethnographers who tried to codify the cultures with which they came into contact are now rightly seen not merely as the observers of colonial society but also as its creators.[13] Yet colonialism was a complex process, often dependent as much on collaboration as on conquest. The legal codes, customary practices, and economic transactions it generated rested on cultural borrowing. Only through the co-option of traditional elites and the compliance of thousands of local clerks, translators, and other adjuncts did colonial "administration" become possible at all.[14] A sustained colonial presence rested more on hybridity—cultural and administrative—than ruling officials cared to admit. Little wonder then that nineteenth-century racial theorists, Gustave Le Bon and Arthur Gobineau prominent among them, depicted colonial expansion and the resultant intercultural contacts not just as transformative but also as corruptive of the innate superiority of the French.[15]

If Le Bon and Gobineau represented one, particularly ugly, extreme of French reflections on colonialism, the administrators, soldiers, artists, and academics who viewed empire in more positive terms were no less prone to misconception. Whether anthropological, sociological, or ethnographic, their observations were necessarily artificial.[16] Their attempts to make sense of the unfamiliar drew on preexisting ideas, often on comparisons with other, foreign examples of phenomena that appeared in some way similar to what now confronted them. All were exterior points of reference, a reminder that colonial minds, like any others, came laden with presumptions. Moreover, those being observed were not just abstract "subjects" of enquiry but living subjects of colonial rule.[17] How, then, could they be considered dispassionately on their own terms? All this is to suggest that concepts of modernity and cultural authenticity, of state formation and capitalist economic organization in dependent territories, each of them central to our understanding of what colonialism involved, require prior consideration of the intellectual and attitudinal basis of European imperialism. As historian Frederick Cooper has recently observed in the context of French imperialist opinion after World War II, to comprehend colonialism, one must address how European imperial nations began "thinking like an empire."[18] Colonial minds, French or otherwise, are now integral to the study of empires, nations, and "natives."[19]

Identifiable commonalities of outlook—the product of education, career background, or lived experience—help us to grasp why those in positions of colonial power acted as they did, whether as governors, as economic overseers, as missionaries, or, conversely, as critics of empire. Certain aspects of imperialist thinking will always be integral to such analysis. Examples include attitudes toward an imperial "*mission civilisatrice*" or a "white man's burden," the changing philosophical and ideological justifications advanced for colonial rule, the borrowing of administrative practice and juridical form from other colonial environs or from other imperial rivals, and the intellectualization of race theory.[20] As Robert Nye has pointed out, racist ideas, anxiety about ethnic mixing, and dire eugenicist predictions of societal degeneration were not confined to the extremist margins of European intellectual thought in the nineteenth and early twentieth centuries. Quite the reverse: such ideas featured in a whole raft of scientific, medical, and political writing, gradually transferring into the mainstream current of ideas in France and elsewhere.[21]

Nowhere was this more apparent than in the minutiae of colonial codes of practice, whether administrative or commercial, military or legal. As Emmanuelle Saada has argued, just as colonial law made French prestige an inviolable concept, so it provided new legal frameworks to help police racial boundaries. Such restrictions cut both ways: on the one hand, sleights on the honor of colonial officials were a serious criminal offense; on the other, French officials were increasingly expected to exercise sexual self-restraint to conserve their "dignity" as members of the ruling elite.[22] Parallels might be drawn here with their brethren in the business community, although European traders and managers rarely faced the same level of sanction for "misconduct" toward their contacts and employees.[23] If the sexual preoccupations of certain *fonctionnaires* are now well known, other recesses of the colonial mind remain less explored. Beneath the horizon of landmark decisions of policy and principle the professional, social, and familial milieus inhabited by colonial officials, soldiers, educators, religious orders, or settlers also molded responses to the workaday challenges of colonial life, whether at the level of high policy or at that of personal interaction with indigenous peoples.[24] Understood as the study of attitudes, presumptions, and expectations, investigating the colonial mind thus becomes something achievable and useful: an attempt to unpick the constituent parts of imperialist (and to a degree anti-imperialist) thought and daily practice.

So is this really a collection of essays about colonial *mentalities*? Building on the Annales School's approach to histories of the everyday, historians of mentalities have tried to codify the formative influences of social customs, religious observance, education, the use of language, and other behavioral norms in configuring habits of mind. Theirs is a view of history that considers cultural practice one of the key determinants of social action. What people do reflects how they have been conditioned to think, whether at an intellectual or an emotive level, and this process is in turn driven by identifiable influences such as those referred to above. Cultural outlooks, or mentalities, imperceptibly formed over the long term, are thus judged to have a greater bearing on human action than the more episodic and transient political events that have typically predominated in historical enquiry.[25]

Does it follow that a study of colonial minds must take mentalities and the antipolitical history leanings of the Annales as its starting point? Not necessarily. Several of the chapters in both this volume and its partner, *Violence, Military Encounters, and Colonialism*, combine appreciation for socioeconomic change and formative cultural influences with abiding concern for the political "event history" disparaged by the Annales School. If anything, the essays in both volumes demonstrate the interactions between the two, between patterns of behavior and individual agency within the events described.[26] Taking a cue from international history's obsession with the mutually reinforcing presumptions of bureaucratic elites, several contributors here look beyond the politicians and colonial governors supposedly at the apex of French imperial rule to consider the derivation of their ideas and policy choices. The "unspoken assumptions" of colonial actors are every bit as important as those of the high political actors that James Joll examined so carefully in tracing the attitudes of mind—the "worldview"—that drove them into taking fateful decisions for war in 1914.[27]

Mary Lewis called recently for historians of empire to look beyond the binary oppositions of metropole and colony, colonizer and colonized, to recognize the connections between internal societal dynamics and wider international rivalries. It is a welcome rallying cry that several of the chapters in this and its partner volume take up, acknowledging that French colonial attitudes and practices were neither entirely forged in French-ruled territory nor solely with French geopolitical interests in mind.[28] Put differently, as Lewis herself has demonstrated, the local and the international were always linked. French colonial bureaucrats, wherever they were posted, usually acted in ways that were recognizably French, but that often displayed other inflections—perhaps born of their earlier career paths in different countries, perhaps derived from rulings, treaties, or other limitations imposed by international organizations such as the League of Nations. Equally, colonial subjects were just as likely to respond to the colonial presence in ways that mirrored their own experiences of the foreign. These experiences were as many as they were varied but include such dislocating factors as intermarriage, slaving, itinerant trading, seasonal movements to different pasturage, and economic migration. The colonial world, in other words, was in some ways more cosmopolitan than some depictions of predominantly sedentary peasant societies allow. Rulers and ruled were, moreover, aware of the disruptive potential of rival imperial powers, whose presence across a nearby frontier or, closer to home, within the consulates, missions, and commercial premises of the colony posed discrete challenges to untrammeled French domination.[29] Whether at the international level of competition between states or at the transnational level of economic, cultural, and political ties between communities across imperial boundaries, colonial rule could never shut out extraneous influences. Indeed, as Frederick Cooper and Jane Burbank have convincingly demonstrated, one of the things that made empires such durable political units was their capacity to accommodate diverse peoples, traditions, and practices.[30] Foreign experiences, foreign presences: both affected colonial minds.

If not uniquely French in its derivation, colonialist thinking was, first and foremost, elitist in its most fundamental presumption that hierarchy and the uneven distribution of power were both politically essential and ethically defensible. While French colonial minds provide our focus here, the contributors accept that these elite figures and the decisions they reached were subject to multiple influences, domestic, colonial, and foreign. The goal then is to connect cultural assumptions with political outcomes, the origins of prevalent colonialist ideas with the practical consequences of such thinking.

Another consideration comes into play here. Perhaps, as with international systems, so with colonial empires; political actors, whether backroom officials or leading politicians, do not begin from the proposition that they can bend the system/empire to their will but start from a recognition that the system/empire sets narrow limits to what could realistically be achieved.[31] And constraints on action could be financial, economic, or technological rather than narrowly political or military. As this implies, ruling empire was not simply a matter of bilateral relations between metropolitan center and colonial periphery. Several contributors in both of the *Colonial Mind* volumes have more to say about the transnational, about substate interactions across political (or colonial) frontiers than the high politics of French colonial policy. Theirs is a view of empire in which rigid divides between mother country and colony, between individual colonies, or between governors and governed cannot be sustained. The model of a honeycomb recently proposed by Patricia Clavin to help define transnational relationships is useful here. Bounded and interlinked, but with discrete spaces in which particular activities were performed, the honeycomb view of transnational imperial relations has much to commend it.[32] Yet at the risk of stretching a point, just as in a beehive, so within an empire, the colony is ultimately bound together by service to a single authority. As other contributors in this volume make plain, studying the queen bees can be rewarding. High-policy initiatives sometimes provided the clearest—and most significant—evidence of the material impact of attitudes and presumptions. Whether investigating those in high office or those working on the peripheries of empire, colonial minds, it seems, are not easily confined within any of history's subdisciplinary boundaries.

Set in the context of the French colonial empire, this analysis of intellectual *formation* inevitably engages with debates about the nature and purpose of empire, about the real and the imaginary in French colonialism. Some of these arguments—regarding the relationship between republicanism and imperialism, about the place of Christian religion in colonial settings, about the social consequences of economic development—are of long standing. All were central to colonial policies and actions from at least the early nineteenth century onward. Their centrality to the study of colonial history, rightly, persists.[33] Other debates—about the social construction of ethnic difference, about the exploitative aspects of colonial gender relations, about the forms of violence (physical, psychological, cultural) inherent to colonial domination, about memories of empire and the commemoration or memorialization of decisive colonial events—are more contemporary, demarcating and sometimes dividing scholars of the "new imperial history."[34]

To be sure, thinking about what put the "colonial" into French minds cannot alone provide a comprehensive understanding of empire. The very term "colonial minds" suggests an analytical preoccupation with the derivations of attitude and the connections between underlying assumptions and colonial actions among the insiders within various imperial projects, whether official, military, corporate, or cultural. Such a precise focus has potential pitfalls. Perhaps the most obvious is, almost by definition, less engagement with the minds of colonial subjects than with the rulers of empire. But maybe such rigid distinctions are misleading anyway. Consider, for a moment, an example from another empire—the British. In 1960, three years before Uganda's independence from Britain, Murray Carlin, an instructor at Makerere College, wrote the following:

> What we are practising at Makerere, day in and day out, . . . is the subversion . . . of the African *mind*; the breaking down of mental tissues; their reconstruction in the Western mode; the reordering of thoughts, feelings, habits, responses, of every aspect of the mind and personality. This is what *we are doing*, and cannot avoid doing—that is the core of our activity.[35]

At the time, Makerere College was the sole establishment of higher education in British-ruled East Africa. The implication in Carlin's words that the capacity of Makerere staff to reorder African minds was a one-way process was hardly remarkable. Yet here as elsewhere, it was not just the colonized whose outlook was transformed by colonial encounters. Those theoretically charged with molding or monitoring African opinion were profoundly influenced by the subjects of their gaze.[36]

As in the British Empire, so in the French, colonizers' ways of thinking were fluid, subject to change in response to colonial experience. But what of those with little direct exposure to life in the colonies? Numerous French ministers, senior officials, influential business figures, soldiers, or intellectuals had important things to say about empire even if their personal encounters with it were limited. Theirs could still be "colonial minds," colonialist in outlook because of the apparent ease with which they dismissed the opinions of dependent peoples. Except for those moments of crisis when insurrection threatened the colonial state, there was, for example, little appreciation among leading metropolitan policymakers of the "everyday forms of resistance"—the go-slows, noncompliance, verbal opposition, and tax avoidance, among numerous other things—by which peasant agriculturalists or industrial workers registered their hostility to colonial rule in a middle ground between outright rebellion and functional acquiescence.[37]

Awareness that numerous colonial minds condemned the overwhelming majority of unrepresented Africans, Asians, and others to silence, to bear mute witness as mere pawns in a grand imperial design, is therefore critical to any reading of colonialist attitudes, presumptions, or prejudice. And as Greg Mann has warned us, to forget this one-sidedness is to risk reproducing the very colonialist presumptions about African practices that the analysis of colonial minds should expose.[38] Another potential limitation of any work centered on the study of individuals and the roots of their ideas is that the impersonal, the structural forces driving processes of colonial change may also be overlooked. Attaching greater weight to plans, projects, and the origins of imperialist thinking risks leaving in the shadows long-term social change, economic transformation, international pressures, and other "macro" factors that perhaps played as great a role in making empire what it was. Perhaps—but as many of the essays collected here indicate, it need not be this way. Studying the ideas of French imperialists does not suggest that cultural diffusion—the spread of ideas and normative standards—was purely a one-way process. Looking at the French side of the colonial equation and taking individual agency seriously in doing so does not imply disregard for dependent peoples. Nor does it indicate a rejection of structural approaches to social change, political economy, or the impact of the prevailing international system of the day. To take but one example, it is surely impossible to understand French concerns about the productivity, the cost, and the insurrectionary potential of workers on the rubber plantations of southern Vietnam without appreciating the underlying economic processes that led to their proletarianization.[39] In this case, the cultural meets the political at a fundamental level.

Investigations of the cultures that produced colonial minds may complement structural approaches, not supplant them. Moreover, as Joachim Görlich has noted in the context of recent ethnographic analyses of colonial Oceania:

> These studies concentrate mainly on the cultural practices of colonized groups. The colonial authorities are frequently represented as undifferentiated, as a homogeneous, hegemonic power block, and characterized only as instigators of transformations. However, this perception is too one-sided and does not do justice to the complexity and dynamism of the colonial encounter.[40]

Görlich is surely right. Just as the colonized defy simple categorization, so colonial minds were never entirely monolithic, nor did they come to colonial situations or economic relationships with ideas fully formed. To borrow Andrew Zimmerman's telling Bourdieu-like phrase in relation to colonial anthropologists, "the field constructs the anthropologist" as much as the anthropologist constructs his or her field.[41] Put differently, ethnographic knowledge, much like other forms of knowledge about colonial societies, combined presumption and experience, subjective expectations and real encounters.[42] Broadly speaking, such is the finding of George Trumball, whose incisive analysis of French ethnographers at work in Algeria after 1871 pinpoints the limitations of such encounters:

> Defined through relations of participant-observation enmeshed in unequal power relations, colonial ethnographies trace the histories, above all, of interactions. The behaviors and beliefs of many Algerians remained occluded, outside of the purview of ethnographers. Hence, colonial ethnographies, like all administrative archives, perhaps overemphasize zones of contact and interaction.[43]

Nor were such interactions confined to academic fieldworkers observing colonial societies. Officials and settlers were also marked by their colonial surroundings, by the political situations they confronted. They were subject to conflicting ideas and emotions about what they saw or what they did.

Moreover, imperial decision makers, like any other individuals, were also affected by social relations within the particular professional milieus in which they operated. Elites have their own internal hierarchies, whether within government, within the armed forces, or within religious orders and educational organizations. Pause for a moment to think about the apex of French colonial hierarchy: the Ministry of Colonies. How did the permanent staff of that ministry relate to other, more senior departments of government with far larger budgets and more influential personnel, and how did this change over time? Without a formal ranking of ministries or a binding system of British-style "collective responsibility" by which it was expected that all ministers should support government decisions, how was consensus reached—and by whom—about the direction of colonial policy? If there was no common agreement at all, then which individuals or groups became the final arbiters of state—and colonial-state decision making? Sometimes these decisions did not stem from elected representatives, but from within state bureaucracy or from elite lobby groups collectively described as the "Parti Colonial." Sometimes colonial governments habitually defied central authority in Paris. What clearer evidence of dissentient colonial minds could there be than the notorious, disastrous insubordination of the so-called Saigon clique of senior officials and military officers grouped around High Commissioner Georges Thierry d'Argenlieu that sped headlong into war with the Vietminh in 1946 in open defiance of their nominal political masters in Paris.[44]

Another question we have to ask is thus how politicians related to permanent officials whose specialist expertise could be both intimidating and excluding? And beyond the walls of government, how did business elites interact with bankers and major overseas investors? How significant was the common ground between these commercial figures in shaping ideas about empire, particularly within the highly sectarian and yet oddly cohesive interest groups of the Parti Colonial?[45] Finally, beyond the boundaries of elite interest, was there room for the general public either in France or in the colonies to make their collective presence felt in the mental worlds of the powerful? If so, are we talking, at least before 1945, about the mobilization of predominantly male, predominantly bourgeois opinion, or about something more intangible: French society and what it would, or would not, tolerate being done overseas in its name, but without its express consent?

Most colonial encounters between Europeans and local populations were, of course, ostensibly remote from state action. These, too, could reverberate beyond those immediately involved, influencing wider attitudes to empire and the *purposes* it served. For increasing numbers of well-to-do French families of the early twentieth century, the empire was not only a source of national pride but also an exotic tourist playground, a tapestry of colorful places to visit and different cultures to "sample." For the less affluent, the heroic, the exotic, and the titillating were recurrent features of the empire-themed films that pervaded French cinema from the early 1920s to the last days of decolonization. In these recreational realms, too, colonial minds were at work. To take one telling example, the colonial authorities employed leading illusionist Jean-Eugène Robert-Houdin in the 1850s to tour Algeria. Beguiling local notables with mesmerizing tricks, Robert-Houdin was also employed to demonstrate the chicanery of sufi marabouts whose claims to mystical powers were thrown into question by the magician's sleight of hand. Here were colonial minds at work. The presumption that Algerians were peculiarly susceptible to supposedly supernatural, miraculous sights meshed with the official determination to prove the superiority of French rationality and the hollowness of Muslim alternatives by playing with the magician's art.[46] Deeply rooted—and deeply flawed—cultural presumptions rendered such bizarre methods normal. The use of Robert-Houdin pointed to what would become a common pattern. Whether in the production of official guidebooks that depicted colonial subjects and imperialist achievements in particular ways, in the exploitation of commercial opportunities to generate new sources of revenue from tourist encounters between French visitors and colonial populations, or in the distinct racial and economic taxonomies that differentiated the French from their fictionalized colonial subjects on the cinema screen, colonial subjects were rendered explicable to imperialist minds through two-dimensional stereotypes.[47] And these stereotypes were crudest of all in the sphere of popular leisure. These changing forms of recreation and popular "consumption" of imperialist ideas also influenced—and were influenced by—the promotion of empire in mainland France, something that required the engagement of French metropolitan minds with the colonial project.[48]

A final element to consider here is the national aspect of colonial minds. That changing forms of popular imperialism were connected with the development of imperialist attitudes may seem self-evident, but were the forms or the processes involved uniquely French? As Matthew Stanard has recently observed, such were the commonalities in attitude toward colonial peoples, dreams of colonial riches, and imperial obligation to "civilize" colonized groups across nineteenth- and early twentieth-century Europe that it is perhaps impossible to discern uniquely national imperialisms. These were viral ideas, fast spreading and seemingly irresistible; their original source was difficult to trace. In this sense the French colonial minds studied in this volume may offer scholars some means to hold a mirror to their equivalents in other European imperial states.[49]

These multifarious and unquantifiable composite elements of attitude formation make our task complicated enough, but there is another level of analysis entirely. Perhaps the minds of political leaders were largely made up before they faced the countervailing pressures of ministerial responsibility, party interest, financial market pressure, or voter verdicts. Should we see the agglomeration of competing external demands on decision makers as secondary to the preexistent attitudes of mind with which they approached colonial issues? A lofty politician or colonial governor, even a lowly police officer or missionary educator, might be subject to local political pressure to act in certain ways, but more influential still might be their underlying outlook in regard to the actions they were expected to take. To use the most obvious example, few questioned the notion that in colonial societies white Europeans and nonwhite indigenous populations would—and should—be treated differently. Such attitudes were often the product of ingrained prejudices and racial assumptions that owed more to family background, cultural milieus, educational experience, religious dogma, contemporary writings, and—conversely—to ignorance of any alternative way of thinking, than to specific instructions from higher authorities that could be located in time and place. Long years of reinforcement of such assumptions through social, familial, and professional contact with like-minded individuals carried greater weight than the more sporadic, unorthodox suggestions of a minority that such attitudes might, perhaps, be misguided. Thus we return to the importance of studying colonial minds to help us unravel the ways in which material alternatives were understood and approached. Actions, choices, and decisions rooted in culturally derived attitudes and practices had lasting political consequences.

These consequences, moreover, lasted beyond the formal end of colonial rule and in some ways endure still. Consider for a moment the recent struggles between politicians, media commentators, and academics over the ways in which the French colonial past should or should not be represented in French schools.[50] Or witness the contretemps between former French president Jacques Chirac and his Senegalese counterpart Abdoulaye Wade over the past contributions and present-day pension rights of West African former servicemen of the French colonial army.[51] Or simply look no further than the paternalist language still commonplace in French official pronouncements about former dependencies, of which French president Nicolas Sarkozy's otherwise conciliatory speech to Senegalese students at the University of Dakar on 27 July 2007 was but one among many.[52] All of these examples remind us that studying colonial minds is not just history, but a matter of current affairs.

This collection of essays and its partner volume on colonial violence take as their starting point the proposition that thought precedes action, its multiple forms notwithstanding. In certain circumstances—for instance, prior to the launch of a crucial policy initiative or the establishment of a trading company, a mission school, or a hospital—this reflective process could run to months and years, its twists and turns traceable in the archival record. In other cases—from decisions about where to settle, with whom to socialize, and how to behave in the company of different ethnic groups or in different communal settings—the "thought" involved requires more delicate unpicking. These were decisions more likely to be recorded in personal correspondence, in diaries, or in intimate conversation; often they were not recorded at all. Yet the importance of such decision making is hard to dispute. Collectively, these patterns of social behavior among the French communities of empire—the settlers, officials, and others who asserted their pride of place within colonial society—molded the ways in which empire developed politically, economically, and culturally.

Aside from this concern with the connections between thoughts and patterns of behavior, the chapters that follow suggest that thought is, to varying degrees, conditioned by habits of mind. Such habits were—and are—strongly affected by familial upbringing, educational background, or the social or professional networks in the context of which the actions discussed took place. What unites them is their concentration on what lay behind the decisions or the actions investigated, what made them possible, indeed probable, and, in some cases, even inevitable. Some of the events discussed are well known, others far less so. But in their focus on the derivation of ideas and the often unspoken assumptions of colonial elites, the essays cast new light on themes familiar to scholars of colonialism in general, and French colonialism in particular.

Chapter Content: Volume 1

In the opening chapter of volume 1 Patricia Lorcin reflects on the interpretive slants that might be applied to the term "colonial mind" or its collective equivalent, "colonial minds." She reviews the themes that emerge strongly across the two volumes, picking out points of convergence and divergence, as well as other aspects of imperialist attitude formation that might be further explored. Her chapter is also the prelude to the four essays in the first section of volume 1, all of which examine various facets of "Colonial Encounters and Imaginings of Empire."

Picking up from Patricia Lorcin, in her contribution Emmanuelle Sibeud revisits the issue central to the entire volume: was there ever a definitive French colonial mind? Her questioning goes further. If, indeed, there was an identifiable, collective "colonial mind," how far were intellectuals a part of it? How far, indeed, did they shape it? She answers these questions by focusing on an individual career, that of Félicien Challaye. Born in 1875, Challaye came to public attention after returning from Savorgnan de Brazza's mission to the French Congo. His ferocious criticism of colonial abuses in Central Africa and the sensational impact of his writings give the lie to a kind of "absent-minded" imperialism in the early Third Republic, suggesting that there was no lack of enthusiasm for empire, no lack of contested debate over its human costs, among the country's political and intellectual elite. Challaye was certainly no thoughtless imperialist inured to the cruelties of colonial rule. Yet he accepted the principle, even the inevitability, of colonial expansion, seeing it as a process that could not be resisted, only controlled. His attitude to empire was conditioned by the need, as he saw it, to regulate relations between exploiters and exploited. This led him to place empires and individual colonies in a hierarchy covering the spectrum from good to bad colonial governance. These ideas would become central to liberal and eventually Socialist thinking about the possibilities of "humanist" imperialism, marking him out as an intellectual architect of the French imperial mind.[53]

Ruth Ginio explores the imagination of colonial minds run wild in her examination of French colonial perceptions of African witchcraft.[54] She does so by focusing on allegations of ritual murder and consequent criminal trials in French West African criminal courts during the 1920s and 1930s. As she points out, colonial obsession with African witchcraft revealed far more about French fears and stereotypes than about the African societies being observed. Witchcraft, and especially what were defined as "witchcraft-related crimes," elicited a stream of inquiries, some official, others quasi-scholastic, which brought administrators and academics together as amateur ethnographers.

Ginio's chapter considers two instances of this process at work. It focuses first on Lucien Lévy-Bruhl (1857–1938), a French philosopher who wrote extensively on what he defined as the "primitive mind," and second on Marcel Prouteaux, a future governor whose interwar career began as a serving *commandant de cercle* in Côte d'Ivoire. Prouteaux mounted the largest official investigation hitherto attempted of witches' secret societies within his territory. It emerges that these two men thought very differently about African religion, African social organization, and African minds. Examining their writings comparatively, Ginio reduces their opposing viewpoints to two core differences: the capacity of Africans to think and act according to French precepts of logic, and the utility of prosecuting witchcraft cases in enhancing colonial state control. Where Lévy-Bruhl accepted the former and dismissed the latter, Prouteaux did the reverse. His more apocalyptic vision of West African witchcraft as a twentieth-century echo of Europe's premodern witch crazes proved the more influential—and damaging—as more alleged cases of ritual murder went through the colonial legal system.[55]

John Strachan's essay revisits the place of empire, in this case, Algeria, in the intellectual formation—the colonial minds—of two of France's most preeminent historians of the twentieth century: Fernand Braudel and Charles-André Julien.[56] Braudel spent most of the 1920s and early 1930s in the colony, taking teaching posts at lycées in Algiers and Constantine to help fund the completion of his doctoral research.[57] Julien's family had moved to Algeria from Caen in 1906, and their liberal, Dreyfusard leanings helped define his critical outlook toward the iniquities of colonialism that he saw around him. If Julien was always the academic heretic, drawing the hostile attention of the security services for his persistent attacks on colonial government, Braudel was slower to appreciate the social injustices of colonial rule. He did, however, take issue with the study of history at the University of Algiers, which during the interwar years was dominated by an ethnocentric, Latin perspective on the history of North Africa and the Mediterranean. In his adoption of the *longue durée* perspective on the history of Mediterranean cultures, Braudel marginalized—and thus implicitly criticized—the French colonial presence, which he identified as but a fleeting moment in historical time.

Focusing on wartime Indochina under Vichy rule, Anne Raffin demonstrates another side to the colonial encounter and its effects on official minds. She discusses the place of administrative inspection visits as intelligence-gathering exercises in which the potential for a transfer of knowledge between governors and governed was all too often missed. The papers of Governor-General Admiral Jean Decoux reveal remarkably little interaction with Vietnamese, whether members of the indigenous elites or not. Indeed, his accounts of inspection tours recount his impatience with the subtleties of indigenous cultures and traditions. Raffin takes this as her starting point for a broader consideration of Vichy's "official mind" in Indochina. She posits that there was a classic administrator "type," an official class prone to misperception about the peoples of Indochina. The recurrence of stereotype and the enduring reluctance to accord value to indigenous forms of social organization suggest that at certain times and in certain locales such "types" often came to prominence. Raffin proves the point by focusing on the relationship between Governor Decoux and his fellow naval officer, Maurice Ducoroy, appointed head of the Vichy-style youth organization in Indochina. By mobilizing Vietnamese youth into Vichyite organizations and attempting to foster a new style colonial patriotism through sport and other "character-building" activities, Ducoroy's policies rapidly backfired.[58] Far from providing a safe, apolitical outlet for youthful energies and so retarding the development of political consciousness among the young, mobilization sharpened the very sense of national belonging that the colonial authorities were anxious to prevent.

The second section of Volume 1, "Language, Culture, and Communities of the Colonial Mind," contains four essays that address the parts played by education, media of instruction, and bonds of community in forging colonial minds.[59] Kenneth J. Orosz's assessment of conflict and competition between state and missionary educators in the Cameroon mandate exposes the bitter disagreements over suitable educational practice for colonized minds. He begins from the proposition that however one chooses to define such a constituency, the language of instruction was uniquely influential in transforming those to be educated. He proves the point by focusing on the Mandate's early years, during which an intense, sectarian war was fought over language policy between the dominant missionary groups in the territory: the Catholic Spiritains and their Protestant missionary group rivals. Many of the latter established their schools during the preceding German colonial era, although they were largely staffed by British and Americans.

The central argument that divided these groups concerned the medium of instruction in primary school teaching. Determined to recast the minds of young Camerounais in a French Catholic image, the Spiritains' espousal of French instruction clashed with Protestant mission groups, which insisted that progress could be achieved only by teaching in the African vernacular languages of Cameroon. In spite of French state backing for French language instruction, the Spiritains underwent a fundamental change of mind in the mid-1920s, accepting that their spiritual and political message was more effectively delivered in vernacular form. As Orosz shows, these language wars and their effects, both on missionary minds and on those of the children to pass through mission schools, compel us to think about the very basis of colonial implantation, specifically about how colonial ideas were composed and transmitted.

María del Mar Logroño Narbona's contribution analyzes neglected, but substantial, communities of colonial minds: the thousands of Syrians and Lebanese settlers, mainly commercial traders, living across Latin America in the interwar years. French acquisition of the Syria and Lebanon Mandates in 1920 engaged these communities directly. Furthermore, the fact that some 20 percent of all Syrians and Lebanese lived outside the Levant aroused deep concern in the French security services, stirring fears that these emigrants would become focal points for anticolonial sedition, nationalist ideas, and hostile propaganda.[60] Concentrating on Latin America, Logroño charts the efforts of French diplomatic and police agencies to monitor these overseas Levantine communities and their links with families and acquaintances "back home." The French thereby sought to control the movement of knowledge between the mandates and their emigrant communities as well as the movement of people, money, and goods between the two. Logroño's examination of this French preoccupation with emigrant opinion suggests that we should conceptualize the Levant mandates in demographic terms—as peoples—rather than in merely geographical terms as distinct territorial locations.

The Levant mandates are also the focal point for Jennifer Dueck's chapter, which highlights differential state treatment of confessional groups in Lebanon, something that helped determine patterns of social and political change in the mandate. She analyzes the connections, professional and personal, between leading French and Lebanese educators and political actors, the cumulative result of which was to reinforce the power of the Maronite Patriarchy. Importantly, however, Dueck points to growing friction between Jesuit, Catholic, and Maronite religious and educational institutions as their minds became fixated on the prospect of Lebanese independence in the years immediately preceding World War II. Catholic, especially Jesuit, institutions were, above all, anxious to conserve the status and privileges of their religious and educational institutions whereas the Maronite Patriarchy was more broadly animated by the consolidation of Maronite dominance within the political elite of an independent Lebanese nation state. In her discussion of these mounting rivalries and differing political and cultural priorities, Dueck argues that French efforts to build consensus—a shared colonial mind—between Lebanon's French Catholic and Maronite hierarchies was doomed to failure.[61]

Algeria is the site for the last essay in this second section. James D. Le Sueur echoes the preceding essays in arguing that issues of language and identity were both inseparable and paramount in Algeria's colonial and postcolonial politics. Propagating the use of French, imposing strict language requirements, and denigrating local languages as inferior or obsolete were all weapons used by officials in the centralization of colonial power and the marginalization of precolonial cultures. Favoring certain languages over others was also integral to the practices of divide and rule, not least between Berber and Arabic-speaking populations in North Africa.[62] Conversely, as Le Sueur points out, for nationalists in numerous colonial and postcolonial locations an urgent political priority was to supplant the inauthentic language of the colonizer—English, French, Portuguese, Afrikaans—with the authentic, local indigenous languages that had for years been marginalized, even prohibited. Algeria's Front de Libération Nationale considered this task pivotal to the rediscovery of the country's Arabic and Arabo-Islamic civilization. Arabization began under Ahmed Ben Bella in 1964 but was pursued with greater intensity under Houari Boumediene when a process of what Le Sueur dubs "de-frenchification" gathered pace.

Matters did not run smoothly. Le Sueur detects a disjuncture between the Arabophones who had been trained and educated according to the tenets of the Arabization program, but who nonetheless could not secure the same level of administrative posts or other employments next to those who were fluent French speakers. Le Sueur then turns his attention to the colonial authorities in the last days of French Algeria. Ironically, they too turned to Arabization from 1959 onward, hoping that by doing so they might reconcile Algerians to a continuing French presence. It was also hoped that widespread adoption of a distinct Maghreb Arabic, as opposed to standard Arabic, would render Algerians immune to the attractions of pan-Arabism and Egyptian-style radicalism. These goals proved unrealistic. Thwarted by the practical obstacles and political barriers to such a program, French-controlled Arabization did not get far. It nonetheless tells us much about colonial minds in the final years of French Algeria as the pursuit of linguistic and cultural integration acquired greater urgency in the face of the apparent radicalization of the Arab world.

The five essays in the third and final section of volume 1 discuss what might be termed "official minds."[63] Each examines changing forms of imperialist thinking among French colonial administrators after 1945. Martin Shipway investigates one of the most influential actors in the reconfiguration of the French Empire as French Union between 1944 and 1947.[64] His subject, Henri Laurentie, director of political affairs in the Ministry for Overseas France, was a key figure in the postwar reconstruction of empire and the immediate origins of the Franco-Vietnam War. Yet, as Shipway indicates, while Laurentie was a central actor in these events, he remained strangely detached from them. Apparently an administrative insider, Laurentie was more the outsider intellectually—too liberal, too radical, and, in some ways, not enough of a "colonial" mind to secure acceptance of his ideas. His position was, in this sense, analogous to that of the minister who would build on many of Laurentie's ideas, the veteran Socialist Marius Moutet, who would, in turn, find himself marginalized once the scope for radical reform in the Indochina Federation diminished as the territory edged closer to war with France in 1946.[65] As Shipway makes clear, Laurentie's brief ascendancy during the late war years came to an abrupt halt even earlier, in September 1945. It was then that Laurentie dared to suggest that government reform plans, such as the March 1945 colonial declaration that he had helped draw up, were unfit for their purpose.

What lay behind this spectacular change of colonial mind? Shipway demonstrates that the answer lies in Laurentie's distinctive administrative background. He was neither a career colonial official with years of field service nor a graduate of the administrators' training college, the École Coloniale. As a result, Laurentie's view of empire was always more cosmopolitan and comparative than specialist and local. Laurentie's case was more typical in other ways, however. For one, he exemplified the dichotomy between administrative insider and political outsider that so often marked out colonial officials. Close to the center—even at the center—of power in their own locale, the empire's senior administrators found it harder to influence elite political opinion in metropolitan France. Sometimes, as in Indochina, this impelled them to backstairs intrigue.[66] In other instances it left officials feeling overlooked and ignored. In this sense, Laurentie offers a model of a certain sort of official: high-minded and farsighted certainly, but frustrated by the mundane realities of French coalition politics, inter-agency wrangling, and the scheming of lesser officials in Saigon. His was a frustrated colonial mind, its insights squandered by the political actors and governing officials to whom Laurentie reported.

Véronique Dimier's contribution puts a different perspective on the "official mind" of French imperialism by investigating the part played by former colonial administrators in the overseas aid agencies of the European Community.[67] She points out that, while such officials had rarely applied indirect rule in practice while serving in the empire, some of them eventually did so while administering European Economic Community (EEC) development aid. As Louis Sicking, another student of colonial influences on the EEC, has recently pointed out, "France thus joined two different communities in 1958: the EEC and the Community with its overseas territories. There was no question of a divorce yet. In the perception of some, this was more a case of bigamy."[68] That France was able to sustain this bigamous relationship with the EEC and its fast decolonizing black African territories was largely thanks to the former colonial officials that populated key offices of the EEC. As Dimier makes plain, it is thus possible to read the work of colonial minds even in the founding constitutional documents of European integration and European development aid to Africa. Her analysis ranges from the provisions of the Treaty of Rome to those of the Yaoundé Convention and, later still, the Lomé Convention of 1975. This date marks the endpoint of her analysis, as it was at Lomé that British officials wrested control of development aid from their French counterparts.

The picture was much different beforehand, as Dimier demonstrates. Initial European economic development provisions were entirely modeled on the French postwar colonial development scheme. Hence the recourse to colonial terminology and associationist precepts, styles, and practices that continued into the 1960s and even into the 1970s. Aid policy was therefore couched in a paternalist language of European support for emergent former dependencies. This was not, of course, a purely African phenomenon; witness, for example, the continuities in "developmentalist" thinking across the European colonial territories of Southeast Asia from the 1920s to the 1960s.[69] But it was certainly in black Africa that the EEC presence was strongest. Echoing the work of Christophe Bonneuil, Dimier illustrates that European aid to several newly independent African countries repackaged a string of state-driven development schemes informed by colonial era presumptions about the supremacy of western scientific rationalism and the continuing African requirement for European guidance.[70]

In another replication of erstwhile colonial practice, development aid administrators toured former colonial territories in order to cement relationships with client rulers and politicians. In Dimier's words, not only was the European Community's early aid policy colonial in origin, but it also was implemented by "colonial administrators at a distance." The result of this domination of administrative offices by colonial minds was what Dimier terms a new "sedimentation of empire."

Where Dimier traces French colonial thinking forward from the immediate postwar period, Tony Chafer's essay begins by looking backward from the perspective of the early Fourth Republic to colonial policymaking in Francophone West Africa immediately before World War II. He notes the extent to which pre-1939 precedents remained central to the delineation and implementation of post-1945 colonial reform. That said, the postwar period brought to the fore a host of factors that reconfigured colonial administrative practice. Among the most important were the new bureaucratic agencies, both governmental and nongovernmental, created to administer economic development, to monitor labor conditions, and to supervise political reform. Like Dimier, Chafer highlights the significance of the 1946 French colonial development program, the FIDES. Its implementation led to the emergence of a whole new raft of colonial bureaucracy. So, too, did the establishment of the colonial Labor Inspectorate (Inspection du travail), studied by Frederick Cooper.[71]

These new bureaucracies remolded official attitudes toward long-term structural change across French West Africa. For example, whereas before 1939 the African worker was typically depicted as a transient phenomenon to be tolerated but not encouraged, after 1945 state agencies and nongovernmental organizations (NGOs) presupposed that increasing industrialization and proletarianization were inevitable. But if colonial minds were changing, Chafer also argues that colonial policy became less coherent as the proliferation of groups with a stake in governmental decisions, not to mention the emergence of stronger, more cohesive nationalist groups, introduced greater complexity to the policymaking process. There was, for instance, intense rivalry between the Inspection du travail's universalist ethos, which posited that French and African workers should eventually be treated comparably, and the majority of colonial government officials who adhered to associationist thinking, preferring traditional solutions to local problems. Implicit in this argument is that the new institutional mechanisms devised after 1945, which were meant to achieve policy coordination, were inadequate to the task—that the official mind of French imperialism had broken down into fragmentary elements.

Todd Shepard's essay also connects past precedents to changing conceptualizations of empire. He does so by analyzing political debate in Paris and Algiers over the scope and purpose of "integrationism" in postwar Algeria.[72] As Shepard notes, although formal French adoption of the term "integration" is usually traced back to Interior Minister François Mitterrand's January 1955 announcement of French policy in North Africa, both the idea and the terminology had longer antecedents. In a fascinating discussion, he links integrationist thinking, most famously and most doggedly espoused by anthropologist-turned-Algerian governor Jacques Soustelle, to earlier variants of the policy in mainland France, in the United States, and, most notably in Soustelle's case, in Latin America. Central to the integrationists' argument was the contention that France did not *possess* an empire. Rather, it *was* an empire: hence their preference for the term *France mondiale*, "global France." Shepard's forensic exploration of the intellectual roots of integrationism, and the increasingly tortuous thinking of its proponents as the Algerian revolution proceeded, reveals how certain of the brightest colonial minds within France's governing elite struggled to devise viable institutional practices and citizenship reforms, the avowed, if unfulfilled, purpose of which was a "deracialized imperialism."

Alexander Keese's contribution, the final essay of volume 1, moves us south of the Sahara once more. He investigates the French colonial mind through the prism of elections and electoral procedures in the postwar years preceding decolonization's perhaps artificial 1960 endpoint in French West Africa. Elections took place with remarkable regularity in the final years of colonial rule throughout this vast region, widening the circle of African populations able to participate in differing levels of territorial representation. The process culminated in 1956–58 as votes took place, first over the French enabling law (*Loi Cadre*), and then in referenda on membership of the French "Community" of Francophone African states.[73] Superficially at least, this might be construed as a triumph of gradualism and democratic inclusion—a vindication of reformist colonial minds. Not so. Keese makes plain that the reality of electoral practice was altogether different. As fears of organized nationalist opposition intensified, so the rigging of elections assumed new forms. Keese reflects upon what this indicates, taking issue with British imperial historian Kenneth Robinson's identification of a "French style" of dealing with "natives" wishing to vote. In analyzing the methods by which colonial authorities sought to control the outcome of elections, Keese's judgment is subtler. While he highlights the prevalence of state coercion, financial corruption, and manipulation of opinion, he also concedes that in certain instances officials were prepared to countenance a free vote. His essay demonstrates that detailed study of these colonial elections is an excellent vehicle for analysis of the gradual alteration of official minds as resistance to decolonization diminished over time. With the curtain fast descending on France's empire in Africa, it is also a fitting point to close this first volume of essays on facets of French colonial minds at work.

Notes

1. Susan Bayly, "Conceptualizing Resistance and Revolution in Vietnam: Paul Mus' Understanding of Colonialism in Crisis," *Journal of Vietnamese Studies* 4:1 (2009), 192–205.

2. Vincent Viaene, "King Leopold's Imperialism and the Origins of the Belgian Colonial Party, 1860–1905," *Journal of Modern History* 80:4 (2008), 732, 763–80, quote at p. 763.

3. As examples, see Nicholas Thomas, *Colonialism's Culture: Anthropology, Travel and Government* (Cambridge UK: Polity, 1994); Frances Gouda, *Dutch Culture Overseas: Colonial Practice in the Netherlands Indies, 1900–1942* (Amsterdam: Amsterdam University Press, 1995); Frederick Cooper and Ann Laura Stoler, eds., *Tensions of Empire: Colonial Cultures in a Bourgeois World* (Berkeley: University of California Press, 1997); Catherine Hall, ed., *Cultures of Empire: Colonizers in Britain and the Empire in the Nineteenth and Twentieth Centuries* (Manchester: Manchester University Press, 2000); Catherine Hall, *Civilising Subjects: Metropole and Colony in the English Imagination, 1830–1867* (Cambridge: Cambridge University Press, 2002); David Cannadine, *Ornamentalism: How the British Saw Their Empire* (London: Allen Lane, 2001); Andrew S. Thompson, *The Empire Strikes Back? The Impact of Imperialism on Britain from the Mid-Nineteenth Century* (Harlow UK: Longman, 2005); Pascal Blanchard and Sandrine Lemaire, eds., *Culture coloniale: La France conquise par son empire, 1871–1931* (Paris: Editions

Autrement, 2003); Martin J. Evans, ed., *Empire and Culture: The French Experience, 1830–1940* (London: Palgrave-Macmillan, 2004).

4. Indeed, David Cannadine's *Ornamentalism*, one of the most innovative and popular such histories, discusses traditions and imaginings of empire to the virtual exclusion of "high politics." Catherine Hall and Sonya Rose also privilege cultural understandings in assessing empire's impact on British society and identity in their recent edited collection, *At Home with the Empire: Metropolitan Culture and the Imperial World* (Cambridge: Cambridge University Press, 2006), 2–3, 18–25.

5. Ann Laura Stoler, "Imperial Debris: Reflections on Ruins and Ruination," *Cultural Anthropology* 23:2 (2008), 193.

6. Ann Laura Stoler with David Bond, "Refractions Off Empire: Untimely Comparisons in Harsh Times," *Radical History Review* 95 (Spring 2006), 93–97.

7. Sophie Leclercq, "Le colonialisme mis à nu: Quand les surréalistes démythiaient la France coloniale (1919–1962)," *Revue Historique* 310:2 (2008), 315.

8. Ann Laura Stoler, *Along the Archival Grain: Epistemic Anxieties and Colonial Common Sense* (Princeton NJ: Princeton University Press, 2009), especially chap. 2 and part 1.

9. Claude Liauzu, *Histoire de l'anticolonialisme en France du XVIe siècle à nos jours* (Paris: Armand Colin, 2007), 96–121; Leclercq, "Le colonialism mis à nu," 317–24.

10. For the French empire, key work includes Jean-Loup Amselle and Emmanuelle Sibeud, eds., *Maurice Delafosse: Entre orientalisme et ethnographie: L'itinéraire d'un africaniste (1870–1926)* (Paris: Maisonneuve et Larose, 1998); Susan Bayly, "French Anthropology and the Durkheimians in Colonial Indochina," *Modern Asian Studies* 34:3 (2000), 581–622; Emmanuelle Sibeud, *Une science impériale pour l'Afrique? La construction des savoirs africanistes en France, 1878–1930* (Paris: EHESS, 2002); Alice L. Conklin, "The New 'Ethnology' and 'la situation coloniale' in Interwar France," *French Politics, Culture and Society* 20:2 (2002); Daniel J. Sherman, "'Peoples Ethnographic': Objects, Museums, and the Colonial Inheritance of French Ethnography," *French Historical Studies* 27:3 (2004), 669–703; Benoît de l'Estoile, "Rationalizing Colonial Domination: Anthropology and Native Policy in French-Ruled Africa," in *Empires, Nations, and Natives: Anthropology and State-Making*, ed. Benoît de l'Estoile, Federico Neiburg, and Lygia Sigaud (Durham NC: Duke University Press, 2005), 30–57; Andrew Apter, "Africa, Empire, and Anthropology: A Philological Exploration of Anthropology's Heart of Darkness," *Annual Review of Anthropology* 28 (1999), 577–81;

Spencer D. Segalla, "Georges Hardy and Educational Ethnology in French Morocco, 1920–26," *French Colonial History* 4 (2003), 171–90.

11. Michael A. Osborne, "Acclimatizing the World: A History of the Paradigmatic Colonial Science," *Osiris* 15 (2000), 135, 139–45, 151.

12. Anna Crozier, "Sensationalising Africa: British Medical Impressions of Sub-Saharan Africa, 1890–1939," *Journal of Imperial and Commonwealth History* 35:3 (2007), 399–408; Crozier, "What Was Tropical about Tropical Neurasthenia? The Utility of the Diagnosis in the Management of British East Africa," *Journal of the History of Medicine and Allied Sciences* 64:4 (2009), 518–23, 539–43; Crozier, *Practicing Colonial Medicine: The Colonial Medical Service in British East Africa* (London: I. B. Tauris, 2008), 93–95.

13. Emmanuelle Sibeud, "Ethnographie Africaniste et 'Inauthenticité' Coloniale," *French Politics, Culture, and Society* 20:2 (2002), 11–28.

14. Benjamin N. Lawrance, Emily Lynn Osborn, and Richard L. Roberts, "African Intermediaries and the 'Bargain' of Collaboration" in *Intermediaries, Interpreters, and Clerks: African Employees in the Making of Colonial Africa*, ed. Lawrance, Osborn, and Roberts (Madison: University of Wisconsin Press, 2006), 4–10.

15. Gustave Le Bon, *Lois psychologiques de l'évolution des peuples*, chaps. 1 and 2 (1889; reprint, Paris: Les Amis de Gustave Le Bon, 1978); Olivier Le Cour Grandmaison, *Coloniser, Exterminer: Sur la guerre et l'État colonial* (Paris: Fayard, 2005), 288–89.

16. Emmanuelle Sibeud, "'Negrophilia,' 'Negrology' or 'Africanism'? Colonial Ethnography and Racism in France around 1900," in *Promoting the Colonial Idea: Propaganda and Visions of Empire in France*, ed. Tony Chafer and Amanda Sackur (Basingstoke UK: Palgrave, 2002), 156–66.

17. Sibeud, "Ethnographie Africaniste," 11–12.

18. These comments draw on Frederick Cooper's indispensable *Colonialism in Question: Theory, Knowledge, History* (Berkeley: University of California Press, 2005), especially chap. 5, "Modernity," which contains by far the most comprehensive survey of social science, subaltern studies, and colonial history writing on the interrelationship between colonialism and modernity. For the "thinking like an empire" discussion, see Cooper *Colonialism in Question*, 153–54.

19. The phrase here derives from a key work on facets of intellectual formation and colonial rule: Benoît de L'Estoile, Federico Neiburg, and Lygia Sigaud, eds., *Empire, Nations and Natives: Anthropology and State-Making* (Durham NC: Duke University Press, 2005).

20. See, for example, Alice L. Conklin, *A Mission to Civilize: The Republican Idea of Empire in France and West Africa, 1895–1930* (Stanford:

Stanford University Press, 1997); Eric Savarese, *L'Ordre colonial et sa légitimation en France métropolitaine* (Paris: Harmattan, 1998); James E. Genova, *Colonial Ambivalence, Cultural Authenticity, and the Limits of Mimicry in French-Ruled West Africa, 1914–1956* (New York: Peter Lang, 2004); Gary Wilder, *The French Imperial Nation-State: Negritude and Colonial Humanism between the Two World Wars* (Chicago: University of Chicago Press, 2005); Romain Bertrand, "Histoire d'une 'réforme morale' de la politique coloniale des Pays-Bas: Les Éthicistes et l'Insulinde (vers 1880–1930)," *Revue d'Histoire Moderne et Contemporaine* 54:4 (2007), 109–11.

21. Robert A. Nye, "The Rise and Fall of the Eugenics Empire: Recent Perspectives on the Impact of Biomedical Thought on Modern Society," *Historical Journal* 36:3 (1993), 687; Nye, "Degeneration, Neurasthenia and the Culture of Sport in Belle Epoque France," *Journal of Contemporary History* 17:1 (1982), 52–55. See also Nye, *Crime, Madness, and Politics in Modern France: The Medical Concept of National Decline* (Princeton NJ: Princeton University Press, 1984).

22. Emmanuelle Saada, "The Empire of Law: Dignity, Prestige, and the 'Colonial Situation,'" *French Politics, Culture, and Society* 20:2 (2002), 98–100.

23. The abuses committed by estate managers on Michelin's rubber plantations in southern Vietnam come to mind here: see Stephen L. Harp, "Marketing in the Metropole: French Rubber Plantations and French Consumerism in the Early Twentieth Century," in *Views from the Margins: Creating Identities in Modern France*, ed. Kevin J. Callahan and Sarah A. Curtis (Lincoln: University of Nebraska Press, 2008), 89–92.

24. The pioneering work into the education and intellectual formation of colonial administrators, French and British, was done by the late William C. Cohen in his *Rulers of Empire*; and by Anthony Kirk-Greene, "Scholastic Attainment and Scholarly Achievement in Britain's Imperial Civil Services: The Case of the African Governors," *Oxford Review of Education* 7:1 (1981), 11–22; and Kirk-Greene, "The Sudan Political Service: A Profile in the Sociology of Imperialism," *International Journal of African Historical Studies* 15:1 (1982), 21–48.

25. Patrick H. Hutton, "The History of Mentalities: The New Map of Cultural History," *History and Theory* 20 (1981), 237–40. For insights into the connections between the postwar development of French cultural history and the study of French mentalities, see Hutton, "The Post-War Politics of Philippe Ariès," *Journal of Contemporary History* 34:3 (1999), 365–81.

26. Regarding this tension between long-term social processes and individual agency in key political events, see Zara Steiner, "On Writing International

History: Chaps, Maps, and Much More," *International Affairs* 73 (1997), 531–32.

27. The study of "unspoken assumptions" was pioneered by James Joll, who coined the term at his inaugural lecture as professor of international history at the London School of Economics; see Joll, *1914: The Unspoken Assumptions* (London: Weidenfeld & Nicolson, 1968).

28. Mary Dewhurst Lewis, "Geographies of Power: The Tunisian Civic Order, Jurisdictional Politics, and Imperial Rivalry in the Mediterranean, 1881–1935," *Journal of Modern History* 80:4 (2008), 791–99.

29. The ways in which Tunisians exploited these foreign presences to mitigate the effects of French rule are expertly dissected in Mary Dewhurst Lewis, *Divided Rule: Sovereignty and Empire in French Tunisia* (Berkeley: University of California Press, forthcoming).

30. Frederick Cooper and Jane Burbank, *Empires in World History: Power and the Politics of Difference* (Princeton NJ: Princeton University Press, 2010), 1–22.

31. Steiner, "On Writing International History," 533–34.

32. Patricia Clavin, "Defining Transnationalism," *Contemporary European History* 14:4 (2005), 421–39.

33. In addition to Conklin, Genova, and Wilder cited in note 20, see J. P. Daughton, *An Empire Divided: Religion, Republicanism and the Making of French Colonialism, 1880–1914* (Oxford: Oxford University Press, 2006); Martin Thomas, *The French Empire between the Wars: Imperialism, Politics and Society* (Manchester: Manchester University Press, 2005).

34. The literature on these questions is very extensive. Essential work includes the following. On difference: Ann Laura Stoler, *Carnal Knowledge and Imperial Power: Race and the Intimate in Colonial Rule* (Berkeley: University of California Press, 2002); Patricia M. E. Lorcin, *Imperial Identities: Stereotyping, Prejudice and Race in Colonial Algeria* (London: I. B. Tauris, 1995); Dipesh Chakrabarty, *Provincializing Europe: Postcolonial Thought and Historical Difference* (Princeton NJ: Princeton University Press, 2000); Sue Peabody and Tyler Stovall, eds., *The Color of Liberty: Histories of Race in France* (Durham NC: Duke University Press, 2003). On gender relations: Anne McLintock, *Imperial Leather: Race, Gender, and Sexuality in a Colonial Context* (London: Routledge, 1995); Julia Clancy-Smith and Frances Gouda, eds., *Domesticating the Empire: Race, Gender, and Family Life in French and Dutch Colonialism* (Charlottesville: University Press of Virginia, 1998); Margaret L. Meriwether and Judith E. Tucker, eds., *Women and Gender in the Modern Middle East* (Boulder CO: Westview Press, 1999); Elizabeth Thompson, *Colonial Citizens: Republican Rights, Paternal Privilege*

and Gender in French Syria and Lebanon (New York: Columbia University Press, 2000); Mary A. Procida, *Married to the Empire: Gender, Politics and Imperialism in India, 1883–1947* (Manchester: Manchester University Press, 2002); Philippa Levine, ed., *Gender and Empire* (Oxford: Oxford University Press, 2004). On violence and the colonial state: Mahmood Mamdani, *Citizen and Subject: Contemporary Africa and the Legacy of Late Colonialism* (Princeton NJ: Princeton University Press, 1996); and two works by David M. Anderson and David Killingray, eds., *Policing the Empire: Government, Authority and Control, 1830–1940* (Manchester: Manchester University Press, 1991), and *Policing and Decolonisation: Nationalism, Politics and the Police, 1917–65* (Manchester: Manchester University Press, 1992). On French colonial memory and the empire's lasting impact on French political culture: Benjamin Stora, *La gangrène et l'oubli: La mémoire de la guerre d'Algérie* (Paris: Editions La Découverte, 1991); Herman Lebovics, *Bringing the Empire Back Home: France in the Global Age* (Durham NC: Duke University Press, 2004); Robert Aldrich, *Vestiges of Colonial Empire in France: Monuments, Museums and Colonial Memories* (London: Palgrave-Macmillan, 2004).

35. Cited in Carol Sicherman, "Ngugi's Colonial Education: 'The Subversion . . . of the African Mind,'" *African Studies Review* 38:3 (1995), 11.

36. For details, see Carol Sicherman, *Becoming an African University: Makerere, 1922–2000* (Trenton NJ: Africa World Press, 2005).

37. James C. Scott, "Everyday Forms of Peasant Resistance," *Journal of Peasant Studies* 13:2 (1986), 5–8; Andrew Turton, "Patrolling the Middle-Ground: Methodological Perspectives on 'Everyday Peasant Resistance,'" *Journal of Peasant Studies* 13:2 (1986), 36–42.

38. See Gregory Mann, "Locating Colonial Histories: Between France and West Africa," *American Historical Review* 110:2 (2005), 409–34.

39. For examples of such structural, Marxian approaches, see Tom Brass and Henry Bernstein, "Proletarianisation and Deproletarianisation on the Colonial Plantation," *Journal of Peasant Studies* 19:3–4 (1992), 1–9; and, for a French case study, Martin J. Murray, "'White Gold' or 'White Blood'? The Rubber Plantations of Colonial Indochina, 1910–40," *Journal of Peasant Studies* 19:3–4 (1992), 42–63.

40. Joachim Görlich, "The Transformation of Violence in the Colonial Encounter: Intercultural Discourses and Practices in Papua New Guinea," *Ethnology* 38:2 (1999), 151.

41. Andrew Zimmerman, "'What Do You Really Want in German East Africa, *Herr Professor*?' Counterinsurgency and the Science Effect in Colonial Tanzania," *Comparative Studies of Society and History* 48:2 (2006), 422.

42. See Oscar Salemink, "Introduction: Locating the Colonial Subjects of Anthropology,' in *Colonial Subjects: Essays on the Practical History of Anthropology*, ed. Peter Pels and Oscar Salemink, 1–52 (Ann Arbor: University of Michigan Press, 1999); also cited in Zimmerman, "'What Do You Really Want,'" 422 n. 12.

43. George Trumball IV, *An Empire of Facts: Colonial Power, Cultural Knowledge and Islam in Algeria, 1870–1914* (Cambridge: Cambridge University Press, 2009), 4. I am grateful to the author for the opportunity to see an advance manuscript copy of this book.

44. The most recent damning historical verdict on d'Argenlieu's clique is James I. Lewis, "The Tragic Career of Marius Moutet," *European History Quarterly* 38:1 (2008), 78–81. Among the first was Alexander Werth, *France, 1940–1955* (New York: Henry Holt, 1956), chaps. 7–8.

45. Now classic studies of the *Parti Colonial* divided over its composition and methods, less so over its influence; see C. M. Andrew and A. S. Kanya-Forstner, "The French 'Colonial Party': Its Composition, Aims and Influence, 1885–1914," *Historical Journal* 14:1 (1971), 99–128; L. Abrams and D. J. Miller, "Who Were the French Colonialists? A Reassessment of the *Parti Colonial*, 1890–1914," *Historical Journal* 19:3 (1976), 685–725.

46. Graham M. Jones, "Modern Magic and the War on Miracles in French Colonial Culture," *Comparative Studies in Society and History* 52:1 (2010), 66–68, 72–79.

47. Ellen Furlough, "*Une leçon des choses*: Tourism, Empire, and the Nation in Interwar France," *French Historical Studies* 25:3 (2002), 441–73; F. Robert Hunter, "Promoting Empire: The Hachette Tourist in French Morocco 1919–36," *Middle Eastern Studies* 43:4 (2007), 579–91. For cinema, see David Slavin, "French Cinema's Other First Wave: Political and Racial Economies of 'Cinéma Colonial,' 1918 to 1934," *Cinema Journal* 37:1 (1997), 23–46; and for a specific case study, Slavin, "French Colonial Film before and after *Itto*: From Berber Myth to Race War," *French Historical Studies* 21:1 (1998), 125–55.

48. This theme is explored in Thomas G. August, *The Selling of the Empire: British and French Imperialist Propaganda, 1890–1940* (Westport CT: Greenwood Press, 1985); Chafer and Sackur, *Promoting the Colonial Idea*; Emmanuel Godin, "Greater France and the Provinces: Representations of Empire and Colonial Interests in the Rennes Region, 1880–1905," *French History* 21:1 (2007), 65–84.

49. Matthew G. Stanard, "Interwar Pro-Empire Propaganda and European Colonial Culture: Toward a Comparative Research Agenda," *Journal of Contemporary History* 44:1 (2009), 30–34.

50. Claude Liauzu, "At War with France's Past," *Le Monde Diplomatique*, English ed., June 2005, available online at *http://mondediplo.com/_Claude-Liauzu*.

51. Ferdinand De Jong, "The Monument as Objet Trouvé of the Postcolony," *Journal of Material Culture* 13 (2008), 197–200. The incident occurred during the 15 August 2004 commemoration aboard the aircraft carrier *Charles de Gaulle* of the Allied landings in Provence sixty years earlier in which troops of the *Armée d'Afrique* and *la Coloniale* had taken part.

52. The full text of President Sarkozy's Dakar speech is available at http://www.afrik.com/article12199.html. For thoughtful discussions of the persistence of such colonialist thinking and African reactions to it, see Gregory Mann, "Colonialism Now: Contemporary Anti-colonialism and the *facture coloniale*," *Politique Africaine* 105 (2007), 181–200; Abdoulaye Gueye, "The Colony Strikes Back: African Protest Movements in Postcolonial France," *Comparative Studies of South Asia, Africa and the Middle East* 26:2 (2006), 225–42.

53. Sibeud goes much further here than Eric Savarese's influential *L'Ordre colonial et sa légitimation en France métropolitaine* (Paris: L'Harmattan, 1998), which does not focus squarely on these connections.

54. Ginio's chapter helps redress the imbalance toward British Africa evident in studies of colonial responses to witchcraft. The most recent addition to this literature is David Pratten, *The Man-Leopard Murders: History and Society in Colonial Nigeria* (Edinburgh: Edinburgh University Press, 2007). For an Africanist perspective on indigenous fears of the colonizer, see Luise White, *Speaking with Vampires: Rumor and History in Colonial Africa* (Berkeley: University of California Press, 2000). For a perspective on witchcraft in postcolonial Francophone Africa, see Peter Geschiere, *The Modernity of Witchcraft: Politics and the Occult in Postcolonial Africa* (Charlottesville: University Press of Virginia, 1997).

55. Again, there are parallels with trends in British Africa here; see Alan R. Booth, "'European Courts Protect Women and Witches': Colonial Courts as Redistributers of Power in Swaziland, 1920–1950," *Journal of Southern African Studies* 18:2 (1992), 253–75; Richard D. Waller, "Witchcraft and Colonial Law in Kenya," *Past and Present* 180 (2003), 241–75.

56. Founder of the *Annales* School, Braudel perhaps needs no introduction. Charles-André Julien's most celebrated historical work remains *L'Afrique du Nord en marche: Algérie-Tunisie-Maroc, 1880–1952* (Paris: Julliard, 1952; reprint, Paris: Omnibus, 2002). Julien also came to prominence in French political circles as secretary to the Haut Comité Méditerranéen (Mediterranean High Committee), a strategic advisory committee on French policy

in its Arab dependencies, set up in 1935 and run, from 1937 to 1939, by Albert Sarraut; see William A. Hoisington Jr., "The Mediterranean Committee and French North Africa, 1935–1940," *Historian* 53:2 (1991), 255–66.

57. Fernand Braudel, "Personal Testimony," *Journal of Modern History* 44 (1972), 448–67.

58. Here, Raffin refines arguments she put forward in *Youth Mobilization in Vichy Indochina and Its Legacies, 1940 to 1970* (Lanham MD: Lexington, 2005).

59. It bears emphasis that relatively little English language scholarship has focused on the related issues of colonial education, missionary activity, and language transmission in the French African empire next to its British and Belgian neighbors and, especially, British India. Important work on the latter empires includes Seppo Sivonen, *White-Collar or Hoe Handle? African Education under British Colonial Policy, 1920–1945* (Helsinki: Finnish Academy of Sciences, 1995); James P. Hubbard, *Education under Colonial Rule: A History of Katsina College, 1921–1942* (Washington DC: University Press of America, 2000); Carol L. Summers, *Colonial Lessons: Africans' Education in Southern Rhodesia, 1918–1940* (Oxford: James Currey, 2002); Dan O'Brien, *The Struggle for Control of Education in Zambia: From the Colonial Period to the Present* (Lampeter: Edwin Mellon Press, 2006); Johannes Fabian, *Language and Colonial Power: The Appropriation of Swahili in the Former Belgian Congo, 1880–1938* (Berkeley: University of California Press, 1991). There has been an explosion of recent work on British India: Margrit Pernau, *The Delhi College: Traditional Elites, the Colonial State, and Education before 1857* (Oxford: Oxford University Press, 2006); Tim Allender, *Ruling through Education: The Politics of Schooling in the Colonial Punjab* (New Delhi: New Dawn Press, 2006); Hayden Bellnoit, *Missionary Education and Empire in Late Colonial India, 1860–1920* (London: Chatto, 2007); Sanjay Seth, *Subject Lessons: The Western Education of Colonial India* (Durham NC: Duke University Press, 2007).

60. French fears were sharpened by the fact that Muslim emigrant returnees might undermine official efforts to rig census results in Lebanon in order to contrive a Christian majority in the territory; see Rania Maktabi, "The Lebanese Census of 1932 Revisited: Who Are the Lebanese?" *British Journal of Middle Eastern Studies* 26:2 (1999), 219–41.

61. Dueck's argument here differs fundamentally from that of the two best-known works on Mandate Lebanon: Gérard Khoury, *La France et l'Orient Arabe: Naissance du Liban moderne* (Paris: Armand Colin, 1993); and Meir Zamir, *Lebanon's Quest: The Road to Statehood, 1926–1939* (London: I. B. Tauris, 1997).

Introduction

62. For a North African comparison, see Katherine E. Hoffman, "Purity and Contamination: Language Ideologies in French Colonial Native Policies in Morocco," *Comparative Studies in Society and History* 50:3 (2008), 724–52.

63. More common in the terminology of international history, the idea of an "official mind," of an identifiable bureaucratic consensus derived from shared cultural background and educational training, has also been a staple of French colonial history since the publication of William B. Cohen's landmark book, *Rulers of Empire: The French Colonial Service in Africa* (Stanford: Stanford University Press, 1971).

64. Shipway sees Laurentie's role in the colonial service very differently from James I. Lewis, "The French Colonial Service and the Issues of Reform, 1944–48," *Contemporary European History* 4:2 (1995), 153–88.

65. See James I. Lewis, "The Tragic Career of Marius Moutet," *European History Quarterly* 38:1 (2008), 66–92.

66. This process of collusion between the Saigon administration and its allies in the French political establishment before the start of the first Indochina War is meticulously dissected in Stein Tønnesson, *Vietnam 1946: How the War Began* (Berkeley: University of California Press, 2010). See also Lewis, "Tragic Career," 71–72, 78–85.

67. Work on this subject remains scanty. A rare exception is Louis Sicking, "A Colonial Echo: France and the Colonial Dimension of the European Economic Community," *French Colonial History* 5:1 (2004), 207–28.

68. Sicking, "Colonial Echo," 208. Sicking borrows here from the title of French economic historian Jacques Marseille's landmark analysis of French colonial trade, *Empire colonial et capitalisme français: Histoire d'un divorce* (Paris: Albin Michel, 1984).

69. Marc Frey, "Control, Legitimacy, and the Securing of Interests: European Development Policy in South-East Asia from the Late Colonial Period to the Early 1960s," *Contemporary European History* 12:4 (2003), 395–412; on French Indochina especially, see pp. 400–408.

70. Christophe Bonneuil, "Development as Experiment: Science and State Building in Late Colonial and Postcolonial Africa, 1930–1970," *Osiris* 15 (2000), 258–81, especially 265–68.

71. Frederick Cooper, "Labor, Politics, and the End of Empire in French Africa," *Colonialism in Question*, 204–30; and *Decolonization and African Society: The Labor Question in French and British Africa* (Cambridge: Cambridge University Press, 1996).

72. Todd Shepard here expands on arguments he put forward in *The In-*

vention of Decolonization: The Algerian War and the Remaking of France (Ithaca NY: Cornell University Press, 2006), 45–57, 157–68.

73. Catherine Atlan, "Demain la balkanisation? Les députés africains et le vote de la Loi-cadre (1956)," in AOF: *Réalités et héritages: Sociétés ouest-africaines et ordre colonial, 1895–1960*, ed. Charles Becker, Saliou Mbaye, and Ibrahima Thioub (Dakar: Direction des Archives du Sénégal, 1997), 358–75.

THE FRENCH COLONIAL MIND

VOLUME I

PART 1

*Colonial Encounters and
Imaginings of Empire*

1

Reflections on the French Colonial Mind

PATRICIA M. E. LORCIN

"What is the French colonial mind?" Martin Thomas asks in the introduction to this two-volume collection of conference papers. If the answer in the colonial context is elusive, or it might be better to say complicated, the question of what exactly the term "mind" signifies, without the tag of "French colonial," is even more so. Should we interpret it as a faculty of memory, which heads both the OED's and Merriam-Webster's long list of definitions, or, dipping into some of the other interpretations, as a mental state, as an expression of intent or desire, or more simply as a state of being? But the term "mind" can also mean caring for or caring about, connoting protectorship in the first instance and emotional response in the second. From a Freudian perspective, the term signifies the intellectual dimensions that constitute personality. Whereas the individuality suggested by this perspective certainly factors into any consideration of a "colonial mind," the concept of a "French colonial mind" is more collective and encompassing. Just how can the former be teased out from the latter? It is this complexity that makes it such a useful concept to frame a conference on French colonial practices and encounters and, for my purposes, to discuss the historiographical issues and themes raised in that conference.

Taking the lead from the dictionaries by linking mind to memory, the striking feature of the intense three days of discussion and the chapters that resulted was the underscoring of what is now almost a truism, namely that the historiography of French imperialism/colonialism is both rich and enriching. Historical writing is, of course, a type of memory, and the shifts of approach to the history of French imperialism and colonialism inevitably reflect contemporary issues and concerns, which in turn shape the themes chosen and the methods used to analyze the sources. The demise of the French empire in the mid-twentieth century, at the height of the Cold War, produced a methodological mind-set concerned with politics, economics, and diplomacy.[1] Only a few voices suggested that there might be alternative ways of framing the overall picture.[2] It was, however, the aftermath of decolonization and the easing and eventual end of the Cold War that led to the paradigmatic changes that shape much of the historiography of French imperialism and colonialism as we know it today. Decolonization brought France face to face with multiculturalism in an unprecedented way as large numbers of different ethnicities and religions from the ex-colonies flooded into the former metropole. The preoccupations and issues engendered by their displacement and their distinctive memory work provided the scholarly community with new angles from which to view the colonial and imperial past and encouraged its members to think in cultural and social as well as economic and political ways.[3] More obliquely, the post–Cold War era helped to push the historiographical mind-set in new directions by dissipating the Manichean worldview of two distinctive camps. In the context of colonial historiography this encouraged a questioning of the boundaries between colonizer and colonized, complicity and resistance, political and cultural.

Today imperialism has again reared its ugly head—if indeed it ever went away—and we are embroiled in conflicts that have few boundaries and no clear conception of distinctive camps, unless one adheres to the simplistic view of "good" and "evil," as some of our recent imperial administrators have been inclined to do. Militarism in a variety of forms, violence as torture or retribution, and language as spin or as a tool for the distortions of propaganda are, at present, the staples of our daily lives. How will they shape our historiographical mind-set and the direction the history of French colonialism/imperialism will take? And can the French experience and its "colonial minds" tell us anything about the patterns and frameworks of imperialism today? Attempting to answer the first question is not possible at present, but by laying out the overarching themes of the conference and trying to tease out some of the finer points from what are a stimulating set of papers I hope to trigger reflection on the way the past is echoed in the present and the present shapes the stories of the past.

Whereas the "colonial mind," as the framework around which to construct the contents of both conference and volume, helps to emphasize the ways in which conceptual and analytical boundaries have been and can be fudged, the multiplicity of spaces, be they geographical, chronological, or thematic, with which scholars can work, occasions the very difficulty of pinpointing what that mind is. What can be asserted from a perusal of the following chapters in this and its partner volume, subtitled *Violence, Military Encounters, and Colonialism*, is that the colonial mind is not just about the thought processes of policymakers, administrators, and intellectuals. It is also bound up with abstractions such as militarism, violence, mythmaking, and language, with ideological binaries such as modern (republican, democratic) and archaic (feudal, nondemocratic), and, of course, with notions of influence and power.

If the various contributions to these two volumes may be considered representative, it seems that Africa—and in particular Algeria—cast the longest shadow over the varying definitions of the colonial mind. Unlike the Southeast Asian colonies, their relative geographic proximity to France provides easier access for Africans and Maghrebis wishing to emigrate north. As a result they form the largest ethnic minorities in present-day France and receive the highest profile when social tensions erupt.[4] Inevitably this makes them, and the ex-colonies from which they came, of great topical and analytical interest. Indochina, although by no means neglected by scholars, is more remote both geographically and chronologically. As a site for imperial activity, scholarly interest has tended to focus on its role in the Cold War. The fact that the Vietnam War was a key moment in the U.S. transition from seemingly anti-imperialist to overtly imperialist power has overshadowed the French colonial era and complicated the analyses of France's role and legacy. The historiographical "division of labor" into geographical units, and the preponderance of chapters on Africa and Algeria in these two volumes, points to the structure that approaches to French imperialism or colonialism have hitherto taken.[5] Although a number of recent works have adopted a comparative approach between colonies, on the whole scholars have tended to center their research on one geographical area, echoing the administrative divisions of the colonial period and of the way space shaped colonial activities or the scholarly interpretation of them.⁶ A focus on the "colonial mind," which suggests the circulation of ideas as much as their development, leads the way to expanding and advancing our knowledge of how French colonialism functioned across space and time.

Focusing for a moment on some of the chapters in this volume, the influence of contemporary circumstances upon historians' approaches to their subject is the focus of John Strachen's chapter on Ferdinand Braudel and Charles-André Julien. He demonstrates how concerns about French colonialism shaped their work. Both historians were closely connected to Algeria in the interwar period when French colonialism was at its height, but far from espousing the colonial canon, they undermined it by pointing out the ephemeral nature of colonialism and unsettling its ideologies and mythologies. Strachan's suggestion that their work points in the direction of postcolonial theory is a reminder that clean breaks seldom occur in history. Decolonization certainly led to new political and social frameworks, but the critique of colonialism by postcolonial writers is the expression of the newly acquired agency of the colonized that was stifled during the colonial period but that French critics of colonialism in that period tried to express.

The importance of the French Empire—and especially Algeria—to France in both the colonial and postcolonial periods is well known, but what of their relevance to other colonies and states? Mathilde von Bülow raises this issue in volume 2 of this collection in her discussion of Franco-German tensions caused by the presence of Algerians in Germany during the Algerian War. The triangular relationship between French and German officialdom and the Algerian migrants was complicated by the fact the Germans registered the Algerians as French nationals and not as French Muslims, as they were registered in Algeria, thus undermining the official policy of the colony. French officials, furthermore, were fearful of the consequences of Algerians in Germany, fearing both a regrouping of an FLN (Front de Libération Nationale) contingent and possible German sympathy for Algerian independence. These fears prompted French officials to encourage the Germans to cooperate by acting in a colonial manner. Citizenship—who was and was not French—and the desire to control its benefits have already been explored in the context of the colony.[7] The surfacing of similar dynamics for French colonial subjects in noncolonial territories is not only an indication of the porous nature of political and social boundaries between imperial and non-imperial powers and colonial and noncolonial territories, but it also points to the way the colonial mind is appropriated and used for noncolonial political ends.

María Del Mar Logroño, in this volume, extends the geographical orbit of French imperialism from Europe to South America in her analysis of the French Syrian and Lebanese mandates' influence in Latin America. Logroño's chapter is a reminder of the desire of imperial powers to map the activities of the expatriate communities of their colonial "subjects" and underlines the tentacular impact of imperialism. The political, social, and cultural boundaries of colonialism may be restricted to the territories of the colonial power, but those of imperialism extend far beyond. Is this the essential difference between the imperial and colonial "minds"? Véronique Dimier's chapter in this volume would suggest not. Moving to the postcolonial period, Dimier discusses the postcolonial legacy of the French colonial mind in the European Union. The second careers of imperial or colonial personnel, once they have moved on to other spheres, is an essential way in which the imperial mind-set is perpetuated. Dimier's focus on the way in which former imperial and colonial administrators shaped the European Union's aid and development policies as of the 1960s demonstrates that economic and political patterns of behavior, learned in the colonies, were not broken at decolonization. Rather, the authority of experience acquired during the colonial period was reformulated as expertise of the developing world. The continuities she demonstrates between colonial and postcolonial practice assume added importance in light of the constitutional and electoral manipulation practiced in Francophone West Africa on the eve of decolonization, as discussed by Alexander Keese in this volume's final chapter.

The bureaucratic legacy of colonial mind-set, which Dimier's contribution highlights, is but one aspect of the *longue durée* of colonial and imperial ideas. An equally significant, if much more ominous, legacy is that of the military, whose officers serving in Algeria during the War of Independence (1954–62) subsequently fanned out in the Americas in the 1970s to teach their counter-insurgency "skills" to their counterparts at Fort Bragg, in the United States, and in the South American military dictatorships.[8] An edifying example of how the colonial past can be appropriated by the present is the Bush administration's interest in Gillo Pontecorvo's film *La battaglie di Algeri* (*The Battle of Algiers*). Filmed in 1966, and originally banned in France, it was intended as a documentary-type exposé of the iniquities of the war but was viewed by the Pentagon as a study in the way to combat terrorism.[9] It serves as a reminder not only of the manipulation of interpretations over time but also of how models of imperialism are inadvertently perpetuated. That the influence of French imperial and colonial activities across both time and space was widespread and in many cases profound should be no surprise. Not only do colonial administrators have second careers in diplomacy, commerce, state bureaucracies, or the arts both during and after the colonial period, but the colonized peoples also carry that influence forward through the assimilation of projections of the colonial mind. The two most obvious examples of this are the politics of language and the discourses and practices of violence.

The importance of language to French imperialism was institutionalized during the Third Republic in 1883 when Pierre Foncin, secretary of education, encouraged by Paul Cambon, French minister plenipotentiary at Tunis, created the Alliance française "to propagate the French language in the colonies and abroad."[10] As one of the early members of the Alliance put it: "Arabes d'Afrique noire, noirs du Niger et du Congo, Annamites du Tonkin, races barbares, nous vous frapperons à notre image; nous vous apprendrons notre langue (Arabs from Black Africa, blacks from Niger and the Congo, Annamites from Tonkin, barbaric races, we shall stamp you with our image; we shall teach you our language")."[11] The French language became an essential element of colonial ideology. Acquiring a high degree of French culture and a perfect command of its language became the path for the colonized peoples to acceptance into the French fold.[12] Although the majority of these peoples never attained this status, the Francophone elites could and did acquire citizenship or, failing that, the facility to move to and from the metropole without undue hindrance. French was, of course, also a passport to improved economic conditions as it opened the door to better-paying jobs. Although local populations often had ambiguous feelings about the use of French, as the language of the occupier, its practical necessity for economic, political, and social reasons often trumped the spontaneous reaction of resistance to its acquisition. The divisiveness of French language policies was not just a question of resistance or complicity to the colonial power. Cultural or religious differences among the local population of a given colony were often reflected in their attitudes to such policies, exacerbating existing tensions within the population. In Lebanon, as Jennifer Dueck's chapter in this volume indicates, the acquisition of French language and education symbolized oppression for the Muslims but privilege for the Maronites, many of whom were Jesuit trained. Whether the French had an official policy of divide and rule—in Lebanon or elsewhere—becomes immaterial. French culture became the wedge that drove communities apart, due to the different degrees of validity attached to it by the groups in question.

The importance attached to spreading the French language in the colonies varied according to circumstance and the beliefs and policies of colonial officials. In Cameroon, as Kenneth Orosz demonstrates in this volume, the French colonial administration's desire to Gallicize the local population in the period 1923–39, following the takeover of the colony from the Germans, led them to try to accelerate a process that usually spread slowly, if at all, from urban to rural areas. It was the colonial follow-up of a much more aggressive process that took place in Alsace-Lorraine from 1918 to 1923, when the French attempted to extirpate the German influence after reclaiming the territory at the war's end.[13] The backlash to the Gallicization policy in the Cameroon came not so much from the local population but from French missionaries, who championed the vernacular language as a more suitable vehicle for their evangelical activities. But outside imperial influences play a role in this story too, as the head of the Spiritan mission in Cameroon was motivated by the example of missionary activity in British Kenya, where education was conducted in vernacular languages. What had once seemed the laudable idea of promoting French civilization became undesirable as the acquisition of French language was seen as an open door to activism and discontent. Language, therefore, could be a contentious issue in the ranks of the colonial power, and as the Cameroonian case demonstrates, divisions of the "colonial mind" could and did occur. The questions that remain are whether the local population internalized these tensions and how they then played themselves out in interracial politics.

Where administrators and educators were not at loggerheads, the tension between French and vernacular language was most acute in areas with fewer languages or dialects. In sub-Saharan Africa, with its multitude of local languages, it was practical for French to become the lingua franca as it enabled communication across space and allowed for economic exchange between Africans of different ethnicities. In the North African colonies, where Arabic was the universal language of religion and culture, the tension between Arabic and French was ever present in spite of the near universal acquisition of some degree of French by the local populations in cities, large towns, and areas within easy reach of urban centers. In Algeria, where the French worried about the subversive nature of Islam and were wary of the centers of Arabic instruction, French fears reached their peak during the War of Independence. As James Le Sueur demonstrates in his contribution, language policies were not unique to the colonial period but were reshaped and promoted after independence. As tension mounted in the colony between the Algerians and the settlers as early as 1938, French officials started to campaign for the introduction of Arabic into the school curriculum. Although it was only in 1959 that an official program was finally created, immediately after World War II the debates about how to reduce German influences in Alsace were echoed in Algeria as the French sought to take Arabic out of the hands of the Koranic schools and assuage fears of the promotion of Islamicization and hence what they feared would be the subversion of the French secular state through language. After independence the process of Arabization continued as Houari Boumediene and subsequent leaders used the process as a way to rid the country of its colonial legacies and establish a feeling of nationhood.[14]

The close linkage of language and culture and the desire to root out influences that counteracted the colonial mission was, of course, a feature of all colonial societies. What varied from place to place, or at any given time, was the way in which colonial administrators and officials interpreted the society in which they were operating and acted on those interpretations. As Anne Raffin demonstrates in this volume in the case of sports policies in Vichy French Indochina, intercultural misunderstandings stemmed from the way reality was imagined. The loss of parts of Cambodia and Laos to the Japanese during World War II again produced imagined parallels to the French provinces of Alsace-Lorraine. Rather than respond to a Southeast Asian set of particulars, leading members of the administration, headed by Admiral Jean Decoux, interpreted the situation in essentially French terms. The importance to the local population of the family, ancestor worship, and hard work was equated with similar Vichy values encapsulated in their motto, *Famille, Travail, Patrie*. And although the third part of the motto appeared to be missing to the French colonials, they hoped to create it as a Franco-Indochinese relationship, albeit a decidedly unequal one whose hierarchies were encapsulated in the administration's approach to the physical education of the subject population.

In all the chapters discussed above, the constant is that imperial or colonial behavioral patterns, once acquired, are not easily shed. To be sure, the desire to impose French cultural, social, and political values stemmed from the belief in its superiority over those of its colonial subjects, but as Dimier's chapter demonstrates, it is more complicated than that. The inability of the majority of colonial personnel to step out of their educational and bureaucratic frameworks is also an indication of the quality of the frameworks as bulwarks against unfamiliarity and anxiety caused by the dislocations of expatriation, the confrontations of "other" societies, and, in cases as elaborated by Dimier, the need to adapt to practices of transnational exchanges outside the colonial situation. Functioning within known parameters is easier than trying to venture outside them. Indeed, one of the questions that emerges from an examination of the colonial mind and its legacies is whether the contemporary impulse to dismantle the nation state and its borders—shaped by ideologies of balance of power, spheres of influence, and economic regulations—to make way for globalization, is propelled by a desire to promote an imperialism whose lack of colonial borders makes it able to function with relative impunity on a world stage still accustomed to viewing national imperialisms with suspicion. Taking the lead from

Dimier's chapter, to what extent is the "global mind" the "colonial mind" writ large?

If teasing out the thematic content of the papers in this volume especially is a useful way of understanding the convolutions of the "colonial mind," thinking about its development over time adds a further dimension to its complexity. Of the many issues that preoccupied colonial minds, labor and forms of violence were among the most enduring as each concerned both economic prerogatives and racial relations. Labor issues in particular defined colonial societies. Whether these issues were about local or indentured labor, or the need for plantation labor or for workers in the service sector, the social and political structures of colonial society rested on its economic base defining whether it was a settler or an exploitation colony and complicating the class structure with a hierarchy of race. The abolition of slavery in French colonies in 1848 rekindled the question of colonial labor and signaled the beginning of a long-lasting debate on migrant labor. Should post-abolition labor be indentured, as in the case of British Caribbean colonies, or settler based? In the same year that the French abolished slavery in their colonies, French-occupied Algeria was converted into three departments, thus making it administratively an extension of the metropole. By that point the violence of colonization was still very much to the forefront of Algerian lives and colonial minds, as William Gallois's opening chapter in the second volume of this collection indicates. Gallois connects this violence with a disordering of colonial minds as violent acts came to be normalized, even made integral to ideas of what it meant to "serve" France in Algeria. This theme of violence entrenched in colonial minds unifies the contributions to volume 2.

By the beginning of the twentieth century the adventurers, missionaries, traders, and military officers (whose excesses Bertrand Taithe documents with such shocking clarity in volume 2), who had been the vanguard of French imperialism were joined by intellectuals whose prominence on the political and social scene in the metropole led to their involvement in debates on the colonies. Intellectuals were important in the colonial arena not just for their contributions to colonial policies but also for the stance they took against methods of colonial governance. Most of the scholarship on French intellectuals' challenges to colonialism has concentrated on the era of decolonization and in particular on the Algerian War of Independence.[15] Of course, the reaction of intellectuals to the colonial mind-set was not a straightforward binary division of resistance or complicity. The relationship was ambiguous and often paradoxical. As Emmanuelle Sibeud demonstrates in this volume, the pro-colonial training of organic intellectuals did not mean that they endorsed imperial or colonial activity wholeheartedly. The practical experience of the colonies could as easily serve as a catalyst to move away from previously held ideological convictions as it could serve to endorse them.[16] Colonial reformism characterized much of pre–World War I anticolonialism, reaching its height in the interwar period before morphing into the more radical pro-independence stances.

Colonial reformism came in many forms. It could lead to redefinitions of "indigenous" cultural practices, as Ruth Ginio's discussion in this volume of the changes in Lévy-Bruhl's responses to witchcraft in sub-Saharan Africa suggests, or to attempts to implement actual policies to accord with political developments, such as the 1936 Blum-Viollette bill in Algeria.[17] Colonial reformism was one response to the interwar rise of nationalism among the colonized peoples; another was the emergence of a more strident form of racism triggered by fears of the unbalanced demographics of colonial society where a French minority held sway over "indigenous" majorities. Two chapters in volume 2, by Samuel Kalman and Neil MacMaster, illustrate the grim consequences of this embattled settler racism, while other chapters, by Joshua Cole and Martin Thomas, situate major instances of Algerian colonial violence, in 1934 and 1945, in the context of chronic misinterpretations by colonial officials of Algeria's fraught internal politics. Kalman's examination of the tensions in interwar Algeria highlights the cynicism of French political parties in the manipulation of intercommunal relations. Given the racial and exclusionary tactics of the Front National today, the political practices of French far-right parties such as the Croix-de-Feu, later the Parti Social Français, appear as prototypes motivated by the same fears of intrusion of "foreign" elements. The violent discourses and practices of extreme right-wing parties are merely the political expression of colonial violence. But as Neil MacMaster so rightly pointed out during the conference—and as his own contribution in volume 2 demonstrates—a fixation on violence can obscure the subtleties and complexities that surround it. An avenue of research that has not been explored to any real extent is the "mind" of the PCF (Parti Communiste Français) in relation to the colonies. Although PCF reaction to the Algerian War of Independence has received some attention, no monograph has been produced on PCF attitudes and policies toward the colonies in the interwar period. Nor have the connections and divergences between Communist parties in the metropole and those of colonies been explored, to say nothing of the post–World War II era, when the "wind of change" started to sweep through the colonial empires in earnest.[18] Colonial reformism was certainly the main trend of the parties of the French Left, but a detailed examination of the PCF's "colonial mind" will lead to a better understanding of what the PCF believed was at stake politically, economically, and even socially.

Although the French were among the last to realize it, the twilight of their empire started immediately after World War II, but the seeds of its demise had been sown long before. The treatment of colonial troops was an important vector of changing attitudes to empire, most notably during the two world wars, and is the subject of the contributions by Joe Lunn and Martin Alexander in volume 2. If they take matters to the eve of World War I and the calamitous fall of France in 1940, Martin Shipway considers civilian efforts to refashion the empire in the wake of World War II in his chapter in the final section of this volume. The decade following the end of the war witnessed last-ditch French efforts to maintain control over dependent territories. And as Shipway demonstrates in his examination of the liberal-minded Henri Laurentie, even at this late stage, attempts to step outside the colonial straitjacket by introducing limited flexibility into colonial policies were resisted by hard-line colonialists and were thus unsuccessful. But even "acceptable" reformist policies geared to counteract the rising tide of nationalist feeling came too late. Alexander Keese explains how promises of increased democracy in post–World War II French West Africa were short-circuited by the fear of what an enlarged franchise might do to upset the colonial power balance. The constraining perimeters of the colonial mind are evident in both Keese's and Tony Chafer's chapters, each of which demonstrates that prewar misconceptions and perceptions of African societies in the sub-Saharan colonies persisted in spite of a rapidly evolving political situation when a radical rethinking of the situation was necessary.

The first image that usually springs to mind when broaching the subject of the decolonization of French colonies is Algeria. The Algerian War of Independence, which produced two new regimes and had such a profound impact on Algerian and French societies and cultures, has spawned an enormous output.[19] In spite of the prodigious amount of energy that has been expended on the topic, interest in the war continues. To be sure, the presence in France of the progeny of the groups caught up in the war, the Algerians, the *harkis*, and the *pieds-noirs*, creates an interest among scholars of postcolonialism whose focus is immigration or diaspora with its subthemes of identity, memory, and nostalgia. But it is the appeal of trying to unravel the paradoxes of French republicanism in its relation to France's colonies that underlies much of the recent scholarship. In his contribution to this volume Todd Shepard considers the political discourse on (and in) Algeria during the Fourth Republic, demonstrating in the process the postwar confusion in colonial/imperial "minds" when faced with the changing expectations of their colonial subjects and the realization that colonial hierarchies of race would have to be tempered if France was to maintain its hold on its overseas territories. Although a succession of laws and decrees attempted to redefine the relationship France had with its colonies, world events were moving too fast and the colonial mind moved too slowly for the results to be anything but flawed.[20]

By way of conclusion I should like to highlight a few of the spaces into which the colonial mind, at this conference at least, did not stray and on themes that were hinted at in some of the chapters. Although gender and empire in the French context is now receiving some of the attention it deserves, a stranger to French imperialism reading these chapters would conclude that the French colonial mind was masculine and that the female colonial mind—if it did exist—was a mere appendage. Gender, women, and imperialism have been the focus of extensive research in the British context, and the excellent works published as a result have stimulated interest in these questions in other colonial territories.[21] But to date works on women in the French empire have tended to focus on travelers, missionaries, and literary women and, with few exceptions, have restricted their analyses to colonial Algeria.[22] Gendering is, of course, a process closely associated with the colonial mind; something ably demonstrated in Owen White's discussion in volume 2 of French men's relationships with West African women in the 1890s and 1900s. Colonial spaces were gendered, as were the colonized peoples. The colonies and their inhabitants were imagined as feminine. Masculinity, sexuality, citizenship, and issues related to figures on the margins of colonial society such as prostitutes, métis, and "mixed-race" children have been analyzed in terms of gender.[23] But there has been little or no research on women's involvement in French colonial administrations or of the way in which such administrations were gendered. Was the female colonial mind merely confined to the *coulisses de pouvoir*, or did it make itself felt in other ways? Professions such as nursing and teaching were certainly gendered. What did the female colonial mind have to contribute in these and other professions where colonial women were present?

Another noticeable absence was the "mind" of science and technology; a reflection of the way the historiography of French colonialism is compartmentalized. The social sciences have, of course, been the focus of research, but the exact sciences and medicine have lagged behind.[24] Works on the exact sciences have tended to view science as a tool of expansion, whereas until recently much of the work devoted to colonial medicine has concentrated on straightforward narratives of its development or has pointed to the innovations introduced by French colonial physicians.[25] In thinking about the colonial mind in terms of medicine it is well to remember that it could also be a diseased mind. When posted to the psychiatric hospital in colonial Algeria, Frantz Fanon discovered its ramification by treating both torturers and the tortured. Colonial psychiatrists and their mentally ill patients, whether colonized or colonizer, tell us much about both the clinical and related social practices in the colonies. Recent scholarship on madness and psychiatry elucidates this dual aspect of the colonial mind and its importance to understanding colonial social and medical structures.[26] Tropical medicine was, of course, born of colonialism, but in the French context most of the early works dealing with the subject have tended to focus on epidemiology rather than its social and cultural significance.[27] The colonial physicians' minds were involved with more than epidemiology and upholding the civilizing mission through their clinical practices. Physicians were well-respected members of colonial society. Many held positions of scholarly or political significance, while others actively participated in the administration.[28] In many places and ways they helped shape colonial structures and in some cases left a significant scientific legacy where they had practiced. How has this legacy developed in the ex-colonies, and how does it shape relations to France today? But the legacy was not only scientific. Humanitarianism, which motivated some colonial and missionary physicians, has its counterpart in today's nongovernmental organizations (NGOs). The connections between humanitarianism as a discursive component of the civilizing mission and as the motivating discourse of today's NGOs are, like the legacy of the "colonial mind" in the European Economic Community (EEC), another manifestation of the often nebulous, but genuine, links between the frameworks of the colonial past and the present.[29] Scholarship on French colonial medicine has moved away from the older narrative approaches and has begun to explore the ambiguities and complexities of colonial medicine in its relationship to both the colonial state and to the institutions of the metropole, but, racial analysis apart, the interaction between French and indigenous medical practices has been largely overlooked.[30]

Finally, I want to mention two themes that have been touched on in passing but are not the focus of any one chapter. Both concern the French colonial mind in relation to global developments and its responses to pressures exerted from outside the French territorial arena. The first theme, competition with Great Britain, was a significant factor in French imperial developments in the nineteenth and early twentieth centuries, a fact no historian would contest. Beyond the larger territorial and political implications of the rivalry, as expressed in incidents such as Fashoda or the debates about the pros and cons of direct or indirect rule, the circumstances and contexts — economic, social, political — in which rivalry or tensions flared up in individual colonies have been largely ignored. The second theme, the Cold War, was the backdrop to decolonization. As a number of scholars have shown in the case of the Algerian War, the Cold War was an important factor in the final unraveling of the French empire.[31] Whereas the rise of nationalism among the colonized peoples in the interwar period has been the subject of extensive study focusing on developments both in the metropole and in the colonies, little attention has been paid to their significance to what some historians have called the "long Cold War," or indeed to the colonial ideologies that developed as a result. In other words, over and above the role of the colonies as pawns in Cold War politics, how did the early twentieth-century emergence and rise of Communism, and non-Communist reactions to it, affect the social and political structures of the colonies or reshape colonial discourses?

The chapters in these two volumes, which emerged from the conference on the French colonial mind, have provided the basis for an exciting way to reexamine the history of French imperialism and colonialism, with its many paradoxes and ambiguities. Following on this path will no doubt provide new surprises and challenges, but it will also enrich our knowledge of the history of France in the process.

Notes

1. For example: Jean Suret-Canale, *French Colonialism in Tropical Africa, 1900–1945*, trans. Till Gottheiner, (New York: Pica Press, 1971; French ed., 1964); Charles-Robert Ageron, *Les Algériens musulmans et la France, 1871–1919*, 2 vols., (Paris: P.U.F., 1968); Ageron, *Politiques coloniales au Maghreb* (Paris: P.U.F., 1972).

2. Henri Brunschwig, *Mythes et réalités de l'imperialisme française, 1871–1914* (Paris: Armand Colin, 1960); A. S. Kanya-Forstner, *The Conquest of the Western Sudan: A Study in French Military Imperialism* (London: Cambridge University Press, 1969); William Cohen, *The French Encounter with Africains: White Response to Blacks, 1530–1880* (Bloomington: Indiana University Press, 1980).

3. A few recent examples: Alec Hargreaves, *Immigration, "Race" and Ethnicity in Contemporary France* (London: Routledge, 1995); Mary Dewhurst Lewis, *The Boundaries of the Republic: Migrant Rights and the Limits of Universalism* (Stanford: Stanford University Press, 2007); Philippe Dewitte, *Les mouvements nègres en France, 1919–1920* (Paris: L'Harmattan, 1985); Todd Shepard, *The Invention of Decolonization: The Algerian War and the Remaking of France* (Ithaca NY: Cornell University Press, 2006); Neil MacMaster, *Colonial Migrants and Racism: Algerians in France, 1900–1962* (New York: St. Martin's Press, 1997); Paul Silverstein, *Algeria in France:*

Transpolitics, Race and Nation (Bloomington: Indiana University Press, 2004).

4. A case in point is the affaire du foulard (Head Scarf Affair), which started in 1989 and led to the law of March 15, 2004, banning the use of conspicuous religious symbols in public places. The "head scarf" has become the signifier for the law and the responses to this law, be it in the media or in the academy. The focus on the head scarf has led to ignoring or lightly passing over the comparable dilemma posed by the law for Sikhs or orthodox Jews. Some recent examples: John R. Bowen, *Why the French Don't Like Head scarves* (Princeton NJ: Princeton University Press, 2007); Trica Keaton, *Muslim Girls and the Other France* (Bloomington: Indiana University Press, 2006); Tariq Modood, "French Secularism and Islam: France's Headscarf Affair," in *Multiculturalism, Muslims and Citizenship*, ed. Tariq Modood (London: Routledge, 2006). Perhaps in reaction to this inclination, in 2005 the Singh Legal Foundation (Chandigarh) published a work by M. R. Rahi entitled *Removal of Turban in France: Sikhs' Struggle for Human Dignity*.

5. Martin Thomas, ed., *The French Colonial Mind: Violence, Military Encounters, and Colonialism*, vol. 2 (Lincoln NE: University of Nebraska Press, 2011).

6. For some comparative approaches see Eric T. Jennings, *Vichy in the Tropics: Petain's National Revolution in Madagascar, Guadeloupe, and Indochina, 1940–1944* (Stanford CA: Stanford University Press, 2001); Jennings, *Curing the Colonizers: Hydrotherapy, Climatology, and French Colonial Spas* (Durham NC: Duke University Press, 2006); J. P. Daughton, *An Empire Divided: Religion, Republicanism and the Making of French Colonialism, 1840–1914* (Oxford: Oxford University Press, 2006); Gary Wilder, *The French Imperial Nation-State: Negritude and Colonial Humanism between the Two World Wars* (Chicago: University of Chicago Press, 2005).

7. On citizenship and the significance of being French in the colonies see, for example, Emmanuelle Saada, *Les enfants de la colonie: Les métis de l'empire français entre sujétion et citoyenneté* (Paris: Découverte, 2007); Owen White, *Children of the French Empire: Miscegenation and Colonial Society in French West Africa, 1895–1960* (Oxford: Oxford University Press, 1999); John Garrigus, *Before Haiti: Race and Citizenship in French Saint-Domingue* (New York: Palgrave Macmillan, 2006); Jonathan Gosnell, *The Politics of Frenchness in Colonial Algeria, 1930–1954* (Rochester NY: University of Rochester Press, 2002); David Prochaska, *Making Algeria French: Colonialism in Bone, 1870–1920* (Cambridge: Cambridge University Press, 1990; rev. ed., 2002). On recent issues of immigration and citizenship see Maxim Silverman, *Deconstructing the Nation: Immigration, Racism and Citi-*

zenship in Modern France (London: Routledge, 1992); Elisa Camiscioli, "Producing Citizens, Reproducing the 'French Race': Immigration, Demography, and Pronatalism in Early Twentieth-Century France," *Gender and History* 13:2 (2001), 593–621; Camiscioli, *Reproducing the French Race: Immigration, Intimacy, and Embodiment in the Early Twentieth Century* (Durham NC: Duke University Press, 2009); Clifford Rosenberg, *Policing Paris: The Origins of Modern Immigration Control between the Wars* (Ithaca NY: Cornell University Press, 2006).

8. See, for example, Marie-Monique Robin, *Escadrons de la mort: L'école française* (Paris: Découverte, 2004), and the English translation of her film by the same name: *Death Squadrons: The French School* (Brooklyn NY, Icarus Films, 2004). See also Marnia Lazreg, *Torture and the Twilight of Empire: From Algiers to Baghdad* (Princeton NJ: Princeton University Press, 2008).

9. For a discussion of the use of the film by the Pentagon see Sheila K. Johnson, "The Battle of Algiers and Its Lessons," TomDispatch.com, September 7, 2003, http://www.commondreams.org/views03/0907-07.htm.

10. Since decolonization the Alliance française has assumed a new role as a promoter of *Francophonie*. Whereas during the colonial period the emphasis was on the spread of French metropolitan culture, today the overseas alliances, particularly those in Francophone countries, promote cultural exchange between the host country and France.

11. Charles Gide, quoted by François Chaubet, *La politique culturelle française et la diplomatie de la langue: L'Alliance française, 1883–1940* (Paris: L'Harmattan, 2006), 36. All translations are by the author unless otherwise noted.

12. See Chaubet, *La politique culturelle française*. Chaubet emphasizes the overseas rather than the colonial side of its history. For a dimension of colonial cultural politics see Randi Deguilhem, "Turning Syrians into Frenchmen: The Cultural Politics of a French Non-governmental Organization in Mandate Syria (1920–67)," *Islam and Christian-Muslim Relations* 13:4 (2002), 449–60.

13. Laird Boswell, "From Liberation to Purge Trials in the 'Mythic Provinces': Recasting French Identities in Alsace Lorraine, 1918–1923," *French Historical Studies* 23:1 (2000), 129–62.

14. On another aspect of Algerian language policies see Habiba Deming, "Language and Politics: A New Revisionism," in Lorcin, *Algeria and France*; Gilbert Grandguillaume, "Language and Legitimacy in the Maghreb," in *Language Policy and Political Development*, ed. Brian Weinstein (Norwood NJ: Ablex, 1990); Dubravko Skiljan, "L'arabisation en Algérie: Une négation de soi?" in *Politiques de la langue*, ed. Antonio Santamaria et al. (Paris: Transeuropéennes, 1999).

15. Eric Levine, *The French Intellectual and the Algerian War* (New York: Columbia University Press, 1962); Jean-Pierre Rioux and Jean-François Sirinelli, eds., *La Guerre d'Algérie et les intellectuals français* (Brussels: Editions Complexe, 1991); David Schalk, *War and the Ivory Tower: Algeria and Vietnam* (Lincoln: University of Nebraska Press, 1991); James Le Sueur, *An Uncivil War: Intellectuals and Identity Politics during the Algerian War of Independence* (Philadelphia: University of Pennsylvania Press, 2001); David Drake, "Colonialism and Anti-Colonialism: Indochina and Algeria," in *Intellectuals and Politics in Post-War France* (New York: Palgrave, 2001); Paul Clay Sorum, *Intellectuals and Decolonization in France* (Chapel Hill: University of North Carolina Press, 1977).

16. The two most striking examples are Jacques Soustelle's shift from left to right after his experience in Algeria and the development of Andé Gide's anticolonialism after his travels in the French Equatorial Africa.

17. The bill, which was introduced by Maurice Viollette, a former governor of Algeria from 1925 to 1927 under the Blum government, sought to grant 21,000 Algerians equal voting rights with the French. The bill was blocked by the settler lobby and was never passed. During the Popular Front hope for reform in the colonies was broached but dashed; see Tony Chafer and Amanda Sacker, *French Colonial Empire and the Popular Front: Hope and Disillusion* (New York: St. Martin's Press, 1999).

18. Danièle Joly, *The French Communist Party and the Algerian War* (Basingstoke UK: Macmillan, 1991); Jacques Jurquet, *La révolution nationale Algérienne et le Parti Communiste Français* (Paris: Éditions du centenaire, 1979); Robert E. O'Melia, "French Communists and Colonial Revolutionaries: The Colonial Section of the French Communist Party, 1921–1926," PhD thesis, City University of New York, 1980. For the Popular Front, see Chafer and Sackur, *French Colonial Empire*, and Martin Thomas, *The French Empire between the Wars: Imperialism, Politics and Society* (Manchester: Manchester University Press, 2005), chap. 9.

19. Typing in "Algerian War of Independence" on WorldCat produced 1,941 hits (1,766 books); "French decolonization" generated only 277. Even if half of these references are marginally related, or not related at all as sometimes happens in such searches, it still demonstrates the scholarly interest in the event and its impact. A sampling of recent works: Matthew Connelly, *A Diplomatic Revolution: Algeria's Fight for Independence and the Origins of the Cold War* (Oxford: Oxford University Press, 2002); Irwin W. Wall, *France, the United States and the Algerian War* (Berkeley: University of California Press, 2001); Alistair Horne, *A Savage War of Peace* (reprint, New York: New York Review of Books, 2006); Le Sueur, *Uncivil War*; Shepard, *In-*

vention of Decolonization; Philip C. Naylor, *France and Algeria: A History of Decolonization and Transformation* (Gainesville: University of Florida Press, 2000); Martin S. Alexander and Martin Evans, *The Algerian War and the French Army: Experiences, Images, Testimonies* (New York: Palgrave Macmillan, 2002); Jim House and Neil MacMaster, *Paris 1961: Algerians, State Terror and Memory* (Oxford: Oxford University Press, 2006); Martin Alexander and John Keiger, *France and the Algerian War, 1954–1962: Strategy, Operations and Diplomacy* (London: Frank Cass, 2002); Raphaëlle Branche, *La Torture et l'Armée pendant la Guerre d'Algérie, 1954–1962* (Paris: Gallimard, 2001); Benjamin Stora and Mohammed Harbi, *La guerre d'Algérie: 1954–2004, la fin le l'amnésie* (Paris: Robert Laffont, 2004); Philip Dine, *Images of the Algerian War: French Fiction and Film, 1954–1992* (Oxford: Clarendon Press, 1994).

20. The 1946 Constitution of the Fourth Republic created the Union française, a French equivalent to the British Commonwealth, and abolished the Code d'Indigénat. In April 1946 the Loi Lamine Guèye granted citizenship to all colonial subjects. The 1956 Loi Cadre created advisory committees in African colonies and tried to introduce decentralization. The Constitution of the Fifth Republic transformed the Union française into the Communauté française.

21. See, for example, Ann Laura Stoler, *Carnal Knowledge and Imperial Power, Race and the Intimate in Colonial Rule* (Berkeley: University of California Press, 2002); Elizabeth Locher-Scholten, *Women and the Colonial State: Essays on Gender and Modernity in the Netherlands Indies, 1900–1942* (Amsterdam: Amsterdam University Press, 2000); Lora Widenthal, *German Women for Empire, 1884–1945* (Durham NC: Duke University Press, 2001).

22. See Yvonne Knibiehler and Régine Goutalier, *La femme au temps des colonies* (Paris: Stock, 1985); Julia Clancy-Smith and Frances Gouda, eds., *Domesticating the Empire: Race and Gender in French and Dutch Colonialism* (Charlottesville: University Press of Virginia, 1998); Pamela A. Pears, *Remnants of Empire in Algeria and Vietnam: Women, Words, and War* (Lanham MD: Lexington Books, 2004); Victoria Thompson, "'I Went Pale with Pleasure': The Body, Sexuality and National Identity among French Travelers to Algiers in the Nineteenth Century," in Lorcin, *Algeria and France*; Sarah Curtis, "Emilie de Vialar and the Religious Reconquest of Algeria," *French Historical Studies* 29:2 (2006), 261–92; Phyllis M. Martin, "Celebrating the Ordinary: Church, Empire and Gender in the life of Mère Marie-Michelle Dédié (Senegal, Congo, 1882–1931)," *Gender and History* 16:2 (2004); Patricia M. E. Lorcin, "Women, Gender and Nation in Colonial Novels of

Inter-War Algeria," *Historical Reflections/Reflexions Historiques* 28:2 (2002), 163–84; Lorcin, "Teaching the Women of the French Empire," *French Historical Studies* 27:2 (2004), 293–310; Lorcin, "Mediating Gender; Mediating Race: Women Writers in Colonial Algeria," *Culture, Theory and Critique* 45:1 (2004), 45–61; Lim-Hing and Sharon Julie, "Vietnamese Novels in French: Rewriting Self, Gender and Nation," PhD thesis, Harvard University, 1993.

23. Robert Aldrich, *Colonialism and Homosexuality* (London: Routledge, 2003); David H. Slavin, *Colonial Cinema and Imperial France, 1919–1939: White Blind Spots, Male Fantasies, Settler Myths* (Baltimore: Johns Hopkins University Press, 2001); Elizabeth Thompson, *Colonial Citizens: Republican Rights, Paternal Privilege, and Gender in French Syria and Lebanon* (New York: Columbia University Press, 1999); Christelle Taraud, *La Prostitution Coloniale: Algérie, Tunisie, Maroc (1830–1962)* (Paris: Payot, 2003): Elisa Camiscioli, "Gender, Colonialism and Citizenship in the Modern Middle East," *Gender and History* 26:1 (2004), 205–8; Saada, *Les enfants de la colonie*; White, *Children of the French Empire*.

24. For the social sciences see Lucio Gambi, "The Science of Empire: The French Geographical Movement and the Forms of French Imperialism, 1870–1920," in *Geography and Empire*, ed. Anne Godlewska and Neil Smith (Oxford: Blackwell, 1994); Gwendolyn Wright, *The Politics of Design in French Colonialism* (Chicago: University of Chicago Press, 1991); Gérard Leclerc, *Anthropologie et Colonialism* (Paris: Fayard, 1972); Patricia M. E. Lorcin, *Imperial Identities: Stereotyping, Prejudice and Race in Nineteenth-Century Algeria* (London: I. B. Tauris, 1999); Michael A. Osborne, *Nature, the Exotic and the Science of French Colonialism* (Bloomington: Indiana University Press, 1994).

25. For the exact sciences see Lewis Pyenson, *Civilizing Mission: Exact Sciences and French Overseas Expansion, 1830–1940* (Baltimore: Johns Hopkins University Press, 1993); Michael Osborne, "Science and the French Empire," *Isis* 96:1 (2005), 80–87. For some examples of earlier approaches to colonial medicine see Simone Clapier-Valladon, *Les Médecins français d'outre-mer* (Lille, France: Anthropos, 1982); Yvonne Turin, *Affrontements culturels dans l'Algérie coloniale: Écoles, médecines, religion, 1830–1880* (Algiers: Entreprise nationale du livre, 1983); Léon Lapeyssonnie, *La médecine coloniale, mythes et réalités* (Paris: Seghers, 1988); Laurence Monnais-Rousselot, *Médecine et colonisation: L'aventure indochinoise* (Paris: CNRS, 1991); and Monnais-Rousselot, *Les médecins français au Maroc: Combats en urgence (1912–1956)* (Paris: L'Harmattan, 2000); Raymond Féry, *L'Œuvre médicale française en Algérie* (Calvisson, France: Gandini, 1994); Bernard

Brisou, "Les pionniers de la peste, médecins coloniaux et pasteuriens," *Histoire des sciences médicales* 29 (1995), 327–36.

26. Alice Bullard, "The Truth in Madness: Colonial Doctors and Insane Women in French North Africa," *South Atlantic Review* 66 (2001), 114–32; Richard Keller, *Colonial Madness: Psychiatry in French North Africa* (Chicago: University of Chicago Press, 2007). Keller has written numerous articles on psychiatry in France and the colonies. See, for example, "Taking Science to the Colonies: Psychiatric Innovation in France and North Africa," in *Psychiatry and Empire*, ed. Megan Vaughan and Sloan Mahone (London: Palgrave Macmillan, 2007); "Pinel in the Maghreb: Liberation, Confinement, and Psychiatric Reform in French North Africa," *Bulletin of the History of Medicine* 79:3 (2005): 459–99.

27. Michael A. Osborne has been working on the emergence of tropical medicine in France, and his research is soon to be published as *The Emergence of Tropical Medicine in France* (Berkeley: University of California Press, forthcoming); see also the chapter on tropical medicine in colonial prisons in Stephen A. Toth, *Beyond Papillon: The French Overseas Penal Colonies, 1854–1952* (Lincoln: University of Nebraska Press, 2006); Deborah Joy Neil, "Transnationalism in the Colonies: Cooperation, Rivalry and Race in German and French Tropical Medicine 1880–1930," PhD thesis, University of Toronto, 2005.

28. See Patricia M. E. Lorcin, "Imperialism, Colonial Identity, and Race in Algeria, 1830–1870: The Role of the French Medical Corps," *Isis* 90:4 (1999), 653–79.

29. On the question of humanitarianism past and present see Bertrand Taithe, "Algerian Orphans and Colonial Christianity in Algeria, 1866–1939," *French History* 20:3 (2006), 240–59, and Taithe, "Reinventing (French) Universalism: Religion, Humanitarianism and the 'French doctors,'" *Modern and Contemporary France* 12:2 (2004), 145–58.

30. See Nancy E. Gallagher, *Medicine and Power in Tunisia* (Cambridge: Cambridge University Press, 1983); Anne Marcovitch, "French Colonial Medicine and Colonial Rule: Algeria and Indochina," in *Disease, Medicine and Empire*, ed. Roy Macleod and Milton Lewis (London: Routledge, 1988); James E. McClellan III, "Science, Medicine and French Colonialism in Old Regime Haiti," in *Science, Medicine and Cultural Imperialism*, ed. Teresa Meade and Mark Walker (New York: St. Martin's Press, 1991): Osborne, *Emergence of Tropical Medicine*.

31. See, for example, Matthew Connelly, *A Diplomatic Revolution: Algeria's Fight for Independence and the Origins of the Post–Cold War Era* (Oxford: Oxford University Press, 2002); Irwin Wall, *France, the United*

States and the Algerian War (Berkeley: University of California Press, 2001); Martin Thomas, *The French North African Crisis: Colonial Breakdown and Anglo-French Relations, 1945–62* (Basingstoke UK: Macmillan, 2000); Robert Malley, *The Call from Algeria: Third Worldism, Revolution and the Turn to Islam* (Berkeley: University of California Press, 1996); Tony Chafer and Brian Jenkins, *France: From the Cold War to the New World Order* (Basingstoke UK: Macmillan, 1996).

2

Intellectuals for Empire?

*The Imperial Training of
Félicien Challaye, 1899–1914*

EMMANUELLE SIBEUD

The notion of an "imperial mentality," though often used by historians, demands a more nuanced approach to current debates about colonial culture and its legacy in France. The concept extends beyond simple commentary about the images and discourse of institutional propaganda to explore their social, political, and cultural reception.[1] At which moments, in which places, and for which players, both collective and individual, may we talk of an imperial mentality or mentalities in France? This chapter seeks answers to this question by examining how a young French intellectual, Félicien Challaye, received an imperial education during a trip around the world between 1899 and 1902. Several circumstantial elements lend further weight to this individual experience as a valuable case study of the formation of a colonial mind. For one thing, Challaye belonged to an intellectual circle that came of age during the Dreyfus Affair. For another, he was encouraged to visit both British and French colonies because at the time it seemed possible to teach intellectuals about the colonies in order to enhance their understanding of colonization, the better to defend it.

Challaye took full advantage of this opportunity to gain direct experience of colonial life and to open up other networks, closer to those of the Colonial Party. His travels were colored by his Socialist convictions nonetheless. Known for his dual political engagement as both an anticolonialist and a pacifist, in 1935 Challaye would publish *Un livre noir du colonialisme: Souvenirs sur la colonisation* (*A black book of colonialism: Memories of colonization*), a compendium of all his empire-related writings, following his return to France in 1902. It would, however, be a mistake to assume that there was an unwavering continuity from his first impressions of empire to this fierce indictment of its shortcomings. Returning to the context of his imperial education allows us to follow the rhythm and inflections of an intellectual journey that was neither preordained nor hopelessly convoluted. Several questions arise here. What made him eligible in 1899 for a fellowship to travel around the world? What transformed his simple visit to the colonies into a deeper reflection on colonization itself? And how did his reflections fit into the guiding precepts of these world travel fellowships? Finally, how was his report received amid the reformist debates of the 1910s about what a truly republican colonial policy should be?

An Intellectual Seeking Political Engagement

Born in 1875, Félicien Challaye was an outstanding candidate for one of the five world travel fellowships offered in 1899. He entered the École Normale Supérieure in 1894 at the same time as Charles Péguy to whom he was very close. The first-placed candidate in the 1897 philosophy *agrégation* examination, Challaye went on to complete a year's study abroad at the University of Berlin in 1899.[2] The signs were that he was destined for a glorious academic career. Georges Perrot, the head of the École Normale Supérieure who supported Challaye's application, commented that he did not know "a more generous mind nor someone with stronger moral fiber."[3] Yet, after returning from his travels in 1902 until his retirement in 1937, Challaye settled for a modest career as a high school teacher. He undoubtedly preferred to concentrate his energy on his political engagements, and these developed quickly. As early as 1909, he was nominated as a member of the central committee of the Ligue des droits de l'homme. He also flirted briefly with the Communist Party before moving on. Above all, he fought for pacifism and became the struggle's emblematic figure in France between 1920 and 1944.[4] Challaye was also a prolific author. During the 1910s he published works on Asia as well as articles challenging the boundaries of psychology and mapping out a distinct specialization between classical philosophy and the emerging social sciences. Despite moving further away from university research after World War I, Challaye continued to embody the engaged intellectual. When, in 1930, he was attacked by the right-wing press, which demanded the revocation of his *agrégation* as punishment for his anticolonialist and anti-French propaganda, the students of the École Normale Supérieure signed a petition to defend not only Challaye but through him the right to combine teaching, radical thinking, and free expression.[5] This discrepancy between his widely acknowledged position as an intellectual and his modest career, at least in comparison to those of his fellow graduates of the École Normale Supérieure,[6] underscores the acute tension that accompanied the appearance of new actors on France's public stage: intellectuals. If being an intellectual lies in one's capacity to translate academic legitimacy into political credibility, it is better to launch such a career either after having consolidated one's university career or having forever renounced it.

Challaye was certainly unaware of any such dilemma when he applied for a fellowship to travel around the world in June 1899. His military service, undertaken over the preceding two years in Romans, a small town in southeast France, followed by his overseas scholarship to study in Berlin during the 1898–99 school year, kept him far removed from the Dreyfus battle in which the majority of his graduating class were passionately engaged.[7] As it was, Challaye returned after the event eager to engage in a similar cause. This was confirmed in 1902 with his highly active involvement in the creation of the popular University of Laval, the place where he would begin his teaching career. He was reassigned the following September to high schools in Paris where it was thought he would have less scope to use his intellectual activism for political ends. As with several of his fellow graduates who came from families rapidly ascending the social ladder, he was drawn to Socialist ideas.[8] He defended his application for a world travel fellowship by explaining his interest in the expanding field of social research started in Germany "to obtain a global view of the universal battle between the workers and those of the aristocrats or bourgeois, between the forces of movement and progress and forces of conservatism and order."[9] He was clearly searching for a personal, albeit not an original, approach to the "social question," a common preoccupation among young intellectuals who had finished their political and academic education within the violent, highly charged atmosphere of the Dreyfus Affair. The world travel fellowship granted him in 1899 not only encouraged him to transform his study program but also gave him the means to do so.

World Travel Fellows: Intellectuals for Colonization?

The world travel fellowships ("Autour du monde"[10]) were founded in 1898 by the banker Albert Kahn. He hoped to offer teachers with the *agrégation* qualification the opportunity to see the world up close, the hope being that they would transplant the lessons of such "direct observation" to more open-minded and challenging classroom teaching.[11] Both the principle and the letter of his project are still today the stuff of dreams. Albert Kahn was a self-made man who built his fortune in part through risky speculation on Cecil Rhodes's De Beer Company. Very close to the philosopher Henri Bergson, he was as generous (each of the five fellowships offered 16,500 francs for a fifteen-month trip) as he was respectful of academic autonomy. Candidates were chosen by a commission that included Louis Liard, rector of the Academy of Paris and powerful director of higher education.[12] These fellowships were regularly granted from 1898 to 1930, at which point they succumbed—along with Kahn's fortune—to the stock market crash of 1929. As of 1905, two lesser grants, each of 7,500 francs, were added for female holders of the *agrégation*. These grants, however, stipulated that the recipients should travel together and limit themselves to the Western world: Europe, the Mediterranean basin, and North America. These constraints were quickly bypassed by the first grant holders, for Kahn willingly offered them supplementary funding to extend their trips.[13]

From 1898 to 1930, seventy-two recipients, forty-eight male and twenty-four female, were granted this extraordinary opportunity to see the world. Half of them were graduates of the École Normale Supérieure, something that Albert Kahn had explicitly requested. The fellowships had only two stipulations: the candidates had to be young, and they had to speak English.[14] The "Autour du monde" fellowships thus contributed to the turn away from the German intellectual model, dominant at the end of the nineteenth century, in favor of an Anglophone model. Almost all grantees began their trip with a stay in Great Britain to perfect their English and to gather information and any recommendation letters that they might need on their subsequent travels. The English-speaking world, of course, included the United States, and almost all recipients also opted for an extended stay there. Moreover, a study of the distribution of the fellows' majors points to an increasing interest in modern languages over time.[15] The recipients were free to choose their own travel itinerary so long as they took a trip around the world and did not try to turn the fellowship into a study grant for a prolonged stay, particularly at a North American university. Upon their return they were required to write a fifty-page report, a copy of which was sent to Albert Kahn. Technically, they were also forbidden to work as correspondents for the French or the local press during their trip, although in practice exceptional permissions were easy to come by; to describe an election campaign for French newspapers, for example. Once back, they were invited to describe their experiences either in writing or through a series of conferences, with all the reserve expected of a civil servant. As early as 1901, the grant winners founded an association, the Société autour du monde, which published a first volume of testimonials, *Autour du monde par les boursiers de voyage de l'Université de Paris*, in 1904. Starting in 1914, regular newsletters followed. The spirit of the project was respected; the majority of fellows upon their return to France resumed their former careers as high school teachers. Seventy-two individuals were certainly not going to transform their fellow citizens' notions of the wider world; nonetheless, their influence, though difficult to measure, was very real. Most notably, they constituted a group of voices and interlocutors with which official and quasi-official programs of colonial propaganda devised for French schools would have to contend.

The "Autour du monde" fellowships were not well adapted to the demands of scholarly research, not least because they had absolutely no ties with any academic institution. In 1898 Georges Perrot, the principal of the École Normale Supérieure, highlighted possible convergences with the rise of human geography and the social sciences whose key figures were Paul Vidal de la Blache and Emile Durkheim, each of whom was closely tied to the school.[16] Later on Perrot repeatedly favored historians and philosophers with links to the team of *L'Année sociologique*.[17] Results were nevertheless inconclusive. The geographers preferred to rely on the network of French high schools to travel to destinations within France's colonial empire, and the Durkheimiens were far too wary of empiricism to risk grasping this interesting opportunity unreservedly.[18] In the end it was those fellows who left behind academic careers or who became expatriates to take up positions in foreign universities or in the diplomatic corps, and especially the graduates of École Normale Supérieure, who made the most of the unique experiences acquired during their trips around the world.[19]

Colonization was integral to the world traveled by the recipients, and one can only speculate about the part it played in the initial project's design and itinerary. According to the initial project scheme, acknowledging social and political differences led logically to analyzing the domination—and particularly its colonial variant—that certain nations imposed upon others. The first candidates reserved a prominent place for the colonial world in their applications: they wanted to go to India, but also to Australia, New Zealand, though less often to the South African Union or Cuba. They were fascinated by the British dominions, all the while convinced that Western colonial domination was an established fact and an inevitable reality. America's end-of-century imperialist acquisitions seemed to confirm the latter, particularly with the takeover of Cuba and the Philippines in 1898. In the following year Lucien Bourgogne and Charles-Marie Garnier submitted travel projects with dual themes: the study of British colonial methods, presented as the most modern and most efficient, plus a critique of the institutionalization of state racism in the colonies.[20] It is clear, though, that not all the recipients were so interested in colonial matters. Yet these themes were closely tied to the world travel fellowships. In 1898 Ernest Lavisse published in the influential *Revue de Paris*, of which he was the lead editor, a long tribute to General Gallieni's "colonial methods" upon his return from Madagascar, citing Gallieni's *Rapport* and *Instructions*, which defined a "racial policy" resolutely hostile to any principle of assimilation. A member of the selection committee for "Autour du monde" fellows, Lavisse was quick to add that "our young travelers around the world will understand and appreciate General Gallieni's *Instructions* and *Rapport*" because they will have observed firsthand the superiority of English colonial methods.[21]

The award that same year of one of the five fellowships to Challaye demonstrates that Lavisse acted rather precipitously. Indeed, those recipients most interested in colonial matters consistently performed their roles as intellectual critics brilliantly, be it Challaye or Jacques Weulersse thirty years later.[22] It bears emphasis, however, that apart from the investment in these individuals, which remained the exception and not the rule, travel projects and letters sent by the fellows to the rector demonstrated a more diffuse curiosity that could be used as a basis for colonialist discourse such as that of Lavisse. However, they also laid the groundwork for discussions on "colonial questions" that gathered momentum in France in the decade preceding World War I. Challaye would become a key player in this debate upon his return.[23]

Imperial Tours

With the advantages of hindsight, it is tempting to view these debates as dead ends that contemporaries insisted on exploring, whether they were intent on maintaining the material benefits of domination or, in a less conscious manner, because they were led astray by their racism or their colonialist outlook. But this teleological perspective drastically simplifies the rationale of the participants, most significantly by omitting the actual interpretations and trajectories of the individuals and groups involved.[24] The file of "Autour du monde" fellows allows us to see a limited but nonetheless homogeneous selection of these trajectories. After the war a less regular attribution of funding and the emergence of an anticolonialism inspired by Communist thought profoundly modified the context in which such awards were made. So what possible interpretations of colonization can be culled from the group of recipients who travelled before 1914?

Two characteristics are notable: on the one hand, we are talking of interpretations that need to be viewed within the context of their day; on the other hand, the world travel recipients viewed colonization as an international phenomenon and were more interested in comparing systems rather than immersing themselves exclusively in the famous pink stain of the French colonial empire spreading across the global map.

In November 1899 one of the first world travel fellows, Albert Métin, told of his encounter, first in Cairo and then again in Luxor, with Major Marchand and Captain Baratier. Métin stated that he would have gladly accompanied them on their march toward Fashoda.[25] Twelve years later, in a contrary example, Paul Cornuel explained how he refused all letters of introduction offered to him in Great Britain for he did not want to visit one colonial official after another. Above all else he wanted to meet the natives.[26] In 1899 Métin had two topics he wanted to study: "First, several typical examples of colonies of exploitation; secondly, the societies and new states founded overseas by Europeans and whose social, democratic, industrial and agricultural developments are so interesting and so rife with controversy."[27] In 1912 Cornuel's letter of application mentioned his excitement at "the awakening of the races who strive, through political and social reforms, to achieve and maintain in English India as well as Indochina, in Persia or in Egypt, National Independence."[28] Both men took comparable trips in which India played a central role both in terms of the length of stay and its preponderance in their final report. Killed during World War I, Cornuel never published his report. Métin, by contrast, did publish his social study of India in 1903, a pivotal moment in his brilliant political career.[29]

The similarities between the itineraries of these two recipients also mirrored the constraints imposed by material considerations, particularly in relation to the travelers' ability to secure reduced prices when booking passage before their departure. The Thomas Cook travel agency effortlessly offered better terms than the Compagnie des Messageries Maritimes and other French agencies, whether in relation to the cost of the trip or to the decisive question of the availability of funds at the different destinations. The University of Paris recipients therefore set off on very British trips around the world, which most certainly influenced the choice of final destinations. While it was commonplace to decry the loss of French influence in Egypt, India remained the first and foremost colony to be visited; indeed, for those with only a passing interest in colonial matters, it was the only colony visited. This contrasted with Indochina, which was treated as a leg of the journey on a par with Ceylon and Java, rather than as a destination in and of itself. Even more telling was the fact that although the Mediterranean was nearly always crossed, an actual visit to Algeria or Tunisia remained an oddity almost always explained by family ties. Sub-Saharan Africa, apparently, seemed either inaccessible or otherwise unappealing, and the only recipient to venture there was the geographer Edmond Chassigneux, who, even so, chose to confine his 1906 visit to the Union of South Africa.[30] In order to complete their trips around the world in the allotted fifteen to twenty-four months, the fellows were obliged to stick to well-traveled routes. While they were not official visitors, they were taken in hand by the consular and colonial authorities and steered toward well-established tours. Even for someone like Paul Cornuel, who wanted to escape these accepted routes and restrictive chaperones, a two- or three-month stay was simply not enough time to establish sufficient ties to step through the looking glass held up by white colonial society.

Most recipients were conscious of these limits and remarked that they selected routes that were certainly a bit more exotic and off the beaten track, albeit, for the most part, well known and well trodden. They compared themselves rather willingly to globe-trotters who traveled the world for their own pleasure or made a living off the tales of their adventures.[31] However, it is precisely the conventional nature of their trips that makes them so interesting. As opposed to explorers, colonists, or other globe-trotters, whether professional or just wealthy amateurs, these young professors—proud recipients of world travel fellowships—were normal citizens of metropolitan France to whom access to the colonies had been momentarily granted. Upon their return their job was to share their reflections on colonial realities with their peers through their conferences and writings, as well as in the everyday work of teaching. They thus participated, albeit not necessarily consciously, in a banalization of the colonial experience, constructing a perspective that inextricably tied together the national and international dimension of colonial domination.

Challaye's conversion to the study of colonial paradigms lies at the heart of this desire to tie social issues both to a national and an international dimension in political debates. Upon his arrival in Japan in June 1901, with eighteen months of traveling behind him, he explained to Rector Liard that colonial concerns were the true revelation of his trip:

My point of view has probably not changed as much about any other subject: because this trip around the world is most especially aimed at reforming our general ideas, I would like to demonstrate through this example, how it has affected me. I left of the opinion that submitting one race to a stronger one was unjust and I condemned colonization as immoral; I now understand its inevitability. [. . .] Under these conditions, I have come to believe in what Kipling terms the burden of the white man and to wish that my country should shoulder its share of the burden. If the existence of colonies is inevitable, it is only right that our country should have its own colonies; it is just that it should enjoy the military and commercial benefits from its colonies that other great nations enjoy from theirs. From the standpoint of the nation and its workers, which to my mind is the true, concrete and equitable manner to judge all things, it is desirable that the product of labor here in France should be sold in far away regions as are the products of English or American workers. I felt stir in me a new interest in colonial concerns; I have devoted a large part of this second trip around the world to their study.[32]

If Challaye did not quite abandon his initial intention to study the "universal struggle" between working classes and the "bourgeois" classes, it was during his trip that he discovered that the colonies were fast becoming the primary theater of this struggle.

This change is even more interesting when one considers that Challaye was not one of the recipients originally interested in the colonies. He approached them in a very conventional fashion. After several days in Egypt, he spent two long stays of three months each in India and then Australia and New Zealand before touring the Far East. He lengthened the different intermediate legs into stays in their own right: a month in Java, three in Indochina. His growing interest in colonial concerns even led him to forego a visit to North America. Other problems intervened, however. Denied entry at Vladivostok by the Russian authorities, he had to re-embark for Japan, cross the Pacific, then to the United States, where he stayed barely a month—an extremely short stay when compared with those of other world travel fellows.

Challaye also changed his travel plans during his stays in Java and Indochina. However, he fared no better than his fellow grantees in evading the excursions proposed by his hosts. This was particularly true in Indochina, where tourism was almost nonexistent in 1901.[33] Challaye actively sought out members of colonial society there. He visited military barracks, schools, mines, plantations, and factories. He was also welcomed into colonial social milieus by well-placed colonial officials: most notably, he was invited by General Dodds, commander-in-chief of the colonial forces in Indochina, to the conclusion of large-scale troop maneuvers and the subsequent ceremonial military review at Bac Ninh. Challaye also met government officials within Governor Paul Doumer's inner circle of senior administrators. Among them were Jean Auvergne, "distinguished" resident-superior of Annam, and E. Dumoutier, head of the Hanoi educational service, who gave him a tour of the city's temples. His letter ended by describing his stay in Indochina with high praise for the new policies imposed by Governor Paul Doumer.[34]

As his writing indicated, in Indochina Challaye saw only what his hosts wanted to show him of colonial domination. He was probably not completely duped but believed that the simple circulation of information about local conditions could help transform the realities of domination by providing Parliament and public opinion in metropolitan France with the necessary arguments to wield influence over settlers and the local administration.[35] Paradoxically, he was arguing in favor of an open world just as the colonial empires tried to impose more rigid boundaries to their contiguous frontiers everywhere. He wavered between uneasy realism and internationalist enthusiasm. The first is evidenced when he analyzed the "exasperating imperialist chauvinism" of the Australians and the ways in which Great Britain's traditionally liberal empire had been undermined by the South African War and Colonial Secretary Joseph Chamberlain's jingoistic policies. The second mind-set is displayed in his statement that Western public opinion should demand that their governments pursue more equitable colonial policies or in his suggestion that there were lessons applicable to European social policy that could be learned from the Dutch approach to issues of ownership and tenure in colonial Java.[36] He considered the creation of fairer colonial policies a universal struggle: for those oppressed and exploited by colonization certainly, but also for the construction of international political and social peace. Challaye rightly believed that he had found a cause to champion that was perfectly suited to his intellectual vocation.

New Experts for a Democratic Debate?

Upon returning to France in the autumn of 1902, Challaye published widely using his travel notes. Péguy allowed him to publish the following articles one after the other in the *Cahiers de la quinzaine*: "Courrier d'Indo-Chine" (Letters from Indochina) in 1902, "La Russie vue de Vladivostock: Journal d'un expulsé" (Russia as seen from Vladivostok: Journal of a deportee), and impressions "of Japanese life" closely followed by "on Java" in 1903. In 1904 he focused on Indochina in a work the travel fellows edited together: *Autour du monde, par les boursiers de voyage de l'Université de Paris* (Around the world, by the University of Paris travel fellows). In the following year he gathered his essays together in a work entitled *Au Japon et en Extrême-Orient* (In Japan and the Far East).[37] His publications had a double aspect, comprised, on the one hand, of political testimony and, on the other hand, of more scientific erudition, much of it centered on Japan, which opened the pages to more scholarly publications such as the *Revue de Paris*.[38]

It should be noted that there was a marked change in tone between these early publications and their abridged second edition (including additional commentaries) in *Un livre noir du colonialisme: Souvenirs sur la colonisation* (A black book of colonialism: Memories of colonization). Challaye's 1935 text was an indictment of colonialism with any mitigating excuses for it expunged. Before 1914, however, he believed in his role as an intellectual successfully defending the cause of a colonial reformism capable of transforming imperial domination. This was neither youthful illusion nor egotistical infatuation. Challaye belonged to a political and intellectual network that from 1904 was buoyed up by the Dreyfusards' long sought-after victory, a network that had every reason to believe the conditions were right for a constructive contribution to colonial matters.[39] This atmosphere of optimistic anticipation is difficult to understand today. For one thing, we know how the story ends; for another, numerous analyses have systematically—and mistakenly—conflated colonial propaganda and colonial domination, overlooking the disjuncture between the ways in which empire was portrayed relative to how it was experienced.[40] Challaye has become a key target for these teleological endeavors: his *Souvenirs sur la colonisation* (republished in 1998) is held to exemplify a timeless truth about colonization. It supposedly defends the hypothesis that a majority of people were deliberately misled; out of guilt they willingly preferred to believe the more palatable propaganda rather than the truth about colonial exploitation. To counteract such a regressive and narrow reading of his work, it is important to focus more clearly on the different moments during which Challaye wrote. Closer examination of his early writings, written for various different audiences, coherent yet divergently influenced, allows us to understand the complex maturation of his colonial ideas.

It is vital here to take into account the context of his first, pre–World War I publications, which must attach due emphasis to his political engagement as protagonist in a debate on colonization that was just starting to crystallize between 1900 and 1914. Although increasingly critical, Challaye's viewpoints remained compatible with those of Liard, an influential civil servant on whom, among other things, Challaye's future career depended. Challaye also closely mirrored Péguy's standpoints and, via Péguy's editorship, those of the readers of the *Cahiers de la quinzaine*. Thus, to Liard, he praised the fairness and intelligence of the judges in Indochina fighting against the brutality and abuses committed by settlers against the native population.[41] But to Péguy he revealed that his first visit in Indochina was to a Dreyfusard judge and fellow subscriber to the *Cahiers*, and he concluded as follows: "So, my dear Péguy, when we work all together to deliver the innocent captain, to deliver the French people who[m] nationalist and clerical reactions were gearing up to crush, we are also working, without realizing it, to save the poor Annamites from inhuman punishment. There is a bond between all just and humane causes: by struggling for one of them, we help all of them progress."[42] In other words, colonial problems were accessible to committed viewpoints based on political principles and not just on technical expertise; they were therefore a matter of common interest for all those connected to intellectual networks. Far from being radically opposed to Lavisse and his passionate colonialism, Challaye shared his belief that their mutual networks must take a close interest in colonization.

The contrast is striking between the rather uninhibited dialogue between Liard, Lavisse, and Challaye concerning colonial matters and the outraged local response to Challaye's 1905 contribution to the work that he coedited with other world travel fellows. In Hanoi the journalist and explorer Alfred Raquez published a leaflet sharply critical of *Les boursiers de voyage de l'Université de Paris* and the unduly representative role that it ascribed to the "freshly graduated" *agrégation* holders.[43] Raquez singled out Challaye for vilifying colonists without having understood anything of what he had been told in Indochina.[44] The author's identity is even more interesting than his arguments. As of 1904 Raquez headed up the *Revue indochinoise*, the colony's scientific review. In 1906 he took charge of gathering ethnographic collections for the colonial exhibit at the Marseilles Exhibition and became a correspondent for the École française d'Extrême-Orient. But he felt his status as local expert sufficiently threatened by Challaye to set about obtaining from the *Petit Parisien* a right of reply that had wider public impact than his leaflet. He challenged the imperial perspective that both Lavisse and Challaye defended—though with vastly different orientations—with the classic argument of colonial difference, of the unique exceptionalism of colonial problems that disbarred any intrusion by metropolitan do-gooders.

In 1905, however, it seemed more sensible to make Challaye a colonial expert, and he was recognized as such by influential intellectual networks. He defended his own case to Liard by underlining the political pertinence of a psychologist's point of view: for only a psychologist has "a broad enough brow to appreciate different civilizations fairly."[45] Challaye's philosophy and his colonial travels allowed him to try his hand at colonial psychology, a newly emerging subdiscipline, which, although it had no qualified specialists as yet, was much in vogue within colonialist circles.[46] His short-lived interest in this field was distilled in his article "Les âges et les races" published in 1914 in the *Revue de Paris*. His colonial experiences and his ties with Célestin Bouglé and the rest of the production team behind *L'Année sociologique* inspired this attempt to contribute to the argument over the nature of racial inequalities that had gathered intensity since 1900. His one foray into this emerging discipline would later reappear in 1924 in his chapter "La psychologie génétique et ethnique" (Ethnic and genetic psychology) in the monumental *Traité de psychologie* edited by Georges Dumas.[47]

Using his knowledge of English, Dutch, and French colonial practices as an empirical foundation, Challaye criticized both assimilation and association, advocating in their stead a pragmatic position compatible with the opportunistic empiricism of French colonial administration. Both his arguments and his articles in the *Cahiers de la quinzaine* drew the attention of the writer and journalist Pierre Mille, who was at the time conducting a lonely struggle in France fighting against atrocities committed in the Congo Free State, as well as that of Paul Bourde, a prudent reformist who was also an influential member of the Colonial Party. In March 1905 both men ensured that Challaye would be assigned—as the special correspondent for *Le Temps*—to the inspection mission to French Congo led by Pierre Savorgnan de Brazza.[48] Even though he was officially recruited as Brazza's personal secretary, Challaye was responsible for only minor, secondary investigations. He visited missionary schools and closely followed the trial of the administrators Gaud and Toqué that opened in Brazzaville in August 1905. The two men were accused of a series of atrocities including the murders of local inhabitants and a number of other grotesque cruelties.[49] Meanwhile the bulk of the mission's work was conducted by Brazza, his right-hand man, Captain Mangin, and the trusted inspectors and administrators he had recruited. Yet Challaye was indispensable nonetheless. It was he who provided the link to intellectual networks back home, Péguy having promised the expeditious publication of Challaye's travelogue in the *Cahiers de la quinzaine*. Brazza's circle had already anticipated that both the French government and the colonial administrations concerned would seek to bury their findings, and in order to forestall this they took steps to ensure their diffusion through other means. Challaye was integral to this process. Brazza's death in Dakar in September 1905 further accentuated Challaye's role. The mission's members were immediately dispersed to the four corners of the empire and, aside from these transfers, were effectively muzzled by various promotions. Challaye therefore became the sole person capable of testifying when the inspection report was declared confidential by the parliamentary commission that drew it up in Brazza's stead. Challaye duly published his account in the *Cahiers de la quinzaine* in 1905 and completed it in 1909 with a work that delved further into the international aspects of the Congo question.

This second incursion into the colonies definitively sealed Challaye's political engagement in colonial affairs. He helped Pierre Mille spread the word in France about the intense international debate over the colonial abuses committed in the Congo Free State. He subsequently took the lead in 1908 by founding the Ligue française pour la défense des indigènes dans le bassin du Congo (French league for the protection of native inhabitants of the Congo basin), which in 1914 became the Ligue pour la défense des indigènes (League for the protection of natives). His involvement in the Ligue des droits de l'homme allowed him to organize conferences throughout France while his own intellectual networks closely tied to academia gave him access to a potentially more receptive audience. More significant still, he participated in the creation in 1908 of a new intellectual review, the *Revue du mois*, proposing a regular column associating colonial concerns and international matters. Here he mingled, not only with Mauss's students who defended the idea of a scientific ethnology capable of shedding light on native politics, but also with his classmates from the École Normale Superieure and other world travel fellows who had entered the political arena and were putting together a reformist program, notably Albert Métin and Albert Thomas.

In the decade following his return from the Congo Challaye remained actively engaged, resolutely reformist, and reasonably optimistic. Hope, though, was already tempered with bitter experience. In the Congo Challaye was forced to confront the banal violence of colonial domination more directly. Although he spent five months in the company of the experienced colonial administrators who made up the Brazza mission, the trust he had once placed in the good judges of Indochina was sorely tried by the mockery of a trial he witnessed in Brazzaville arising from the Gaud and Toqué affair. Challaye returned convinced that Toqué had been made a scapegoat.[50] Furthermore, the articles he sent to *Le Temps* were deftly cut and edited in such a way as to support the newspaper's campaign against the Brazza mission and in favor of Governor Émile Gentil, the key administrative official on whose watch the worst atrocities were committed in the French Congo. Challaye was thus a direct witness to the creation of a more virulent colonial propaganda in France. He was also its victim insofar as this propaganda, at once more assertive and therefore less amenable to challenge, precluded the kind of open debate for which Challaye had called.

Conclusion

The total societal mobilization demanded by World War I stifled the reformist drive that had framed Challaye's imperial training from 1900 to 1914. The Ministry of Colonies and the Colonial Party together concocted the publicity campaigns designed to educate the masses, especially children, about colonial questions, thereby shutting down more critical observations about empire. Indeed, their unspoken aim was to preclude any such political debate concerning the ethical justifications and practical implications of colonization. While such direct state action would not have been tenable before World War I, with the war effort and its associated propaganda well underway, a firmer strain of imperialist propaganda was legitimized. Instead of the more critical and reflective imperial consciousness that had been taking shape before the war, particularly among the grant fellows who had been sent around an entirely colonized world, the Ministry of Colonies and the Colonial Party supported a prefabricated, mass colonial culture whose proclamation was ultimately more important than its foundations. They invented a sterile alternative to either blind adhesion or absolute objection, which condemned any critical analysis of colonial policies to an impotent radicalization. Between the two world wars Challaye was hostage to this artificial choice. He tried to free himself by meeting colonized peoples living in metropolitan France or those who had managed to contact the Ligue des droits de l'homme, but he no longer had the means to spark debates with his contemporaries on colonial matters.[51] Colonial culture's fictitious facade glossed over elements of an emergent critical imperial consciousness. Even though scattered and diffuse, these elements became the substrata for a deeper and more reflective political understanding of colonization, something colonial propaganda had vainly tried to forbid at the time. Current confusion between colonial domination and its representation threatens to blur those limits once again.

Notes

1. Claude Blanckaert, "Note critique: Spectacles ethniques et culture de masse au temps des colonies," *Revue d'histoire des sciences humaines* 7 (2002), 223–32; Eric T. Jennings, "Visions and Representations of French Empire," *Journal of Modern History* 77:4 (2005), 701–21.

2. For details, see Nicole Racine, "Félicien Challaye," *Dictionnaire biographique du mouvement ouvrier français*, 47–49.

3. Archives Nationales, Paris, 16 AJ 7021, file Félicien Challaye, Georges Perrot letter to the Rector, Paris Academy, 22 June 1899. All translations are by the author unless otherwise noted.

4. His unconditional pacifism led him to defend the French-German collaboration during the occupation. He was accused during the autumn of 1944, his retirement pension was revoked for five years in November 1945, and his works were banned by the Comité national des écrivains. But his pension was reinstated in February 1946 after several resistance fighters, friends, and former students had testified in his favor; see Jean-François Sirinelli, *Génération intellectuelle: Khâgneux et normaliens dans l'entre-deux guerres* (Paris: Fayard, 1988), 453–60.

5. Sirinelli, *Génération intellectuelle*, 457.

6. The 1894 graduation class of Normaliens included twenty-eight literature majors, eight of whom were high school teachers, while thirteen taught at university level or at large research institutes, and two became general inspectors of public education. The remaining five included Péguy, the public intellectual and editor, a deputy, and three students whose careers are unknown. Challaye was, therefore, in a minority with neither a career in higher education nor a high-level government position nor an independent intellectual career.

7. Robert John Smith, "L'atmosphère politique à l'Ecole normale supérieure à la fin du XIXe siècle," *Revue d'histoire moderne et contemporaine* 29:2 (1982), 248–68.

8. Christophe Charle in *Naissance des "intellectuels," 1880–1900* (Paris: Les éditions de Minuit, 1990); Charle, "Les normaliens et le socialism," in *Jaurès et les intellectuels*, ed. Madeleine Rébérioux and Gilles Candar (Paris: Les éditions de l'atelier, 1994), 133–68; Christophe Prochasson, *Les intellectuels, le socialisme et la guerre, 1900–1938* (Paris: Le Seuil, "L'Univers historique," 1993).

9. AN, 16 AJ 7021, file Félicien Challaye, application letter, 22 June 1899, pp. 2–3.

10. A similar fellowship would be inaugurated in 1910 by the University of London and was known as the Albert Kahn Travelling Fellowship. To avoid

confusion between the two fellowships, in this chapter the French name of "Autour du monde" fellowship is maintained when not describing it simply as a world travel fellowship.

11. Nathalie Clet-Bonnet, "Les bourses 'Autour du monde,' la fondation française, 1898–1930" in *Albert Kahn, 1860–1940: Réalités d'une utopia*, ed. Jeanne Beausoleil and Pascal Ory (Boulogne: Musée Albert Kahn, 1995), 137–52.

12. The commission was composed of members of the bureau of the university council, including its five most senior members, the head of Advanced Teaching, and the presidents of the Paris and Lyon Chambers of Commerce, and it was open to all university council members. AN 16 AJ 7020 file 1899, decree of June 12, 1899. Its mixed composition, both academic and industrial/commercial, echoed that of the Ministry of Public Education commission that awarded funding for literary and scientific field trips and missions.

13. As of 1910, Rachel Allard planned to go all the way to Japan, Indochina, and Indonesia; see AN 16 AJ 7021, Rachel Allard file. In 1912 Jeanne Antoine obtained an extra 2,000 francs from Kahn by explaining that she too would like to travel to Asia; see AN 16 AJ 7021, Jeanne Antoine file.

14. Candidates had to have been teaching for fewer than ten years, and the commission regularly examined the "robustness" of the candidates, especially the females.

15. Only five grantees had not passed the *agrégation*: two lawyers who were allowed to apply in 1904, a painter, a journalist, and a graduate of the École Normale Supérieure. The largest group of fellows held *agrégations* in French literature, particularly the women (eleven out of a total of twenty-four female grantees). Almost as numerous were the eighteen with *agrégations* in English and German, followed by twelve qualified in history and geography, seven in the natural sciences, and five in philosophy. In only four cases was the type of *agrégation* not explicitly mentioned.

16. "It would seem to me that those with an *agrégation* in History or Philosophy are, without exception, better prepared than the others to benefit immediately from this trip, to understand what they will see. Of the historians, who have spent a large portion of their studies on Geography, I need say no more. Of the philosophers, I merely need to state that for the past several years, many of them, oftentimes the most distinguished, have left purely speculative research by the wayside, something that occupied them almost exclusively before, in favour of what we call today sociology." AN, 16 AJ 7020, file 1898, letter from Georges Perrot, 19 June 1898, p. 1.

17. Among the twenty-four grantees from Ecole Normale Supérieure, five were philosophers (no other candidate with a philosophy *agrégation* was recruited other than these five), and seven were historians or geographers.

18. Emmanuelle Sibeud, "Marcel Mauss: Projet de présentation d'un Bureau d'ethnologie (1913)," *Revue d'histoire des sciences humaines,* "Les sciences sociales en situation coloniale," 10 (mai 2004), 105–24.

19. As demonstrated by the careers of three members of Challaye's graduating class who also won grants in 1898 and 1899. Georges Weulersse (a 1898 grantee) ended his career as a history professor at the Ecole Normale Supérieure of Saint-Cloud, and in 1928 his son Jacques was one of the last candidates to obtain the grant. Désiré Roustan (a 1899 grantee and Challaye's traveling companion in India) became general inspector of public, instruction and Louis Allard (a 1900 grantee) made use of his stay in the United States to secure a job as a French professor at Harvard. On a more general note, of the twenty-four grantees from the Ecole Normale Superieure, ten went on to exceptional careers at the most prestigious of institutions: two became professors at the College de France, one a director of the École française d'Extrême-Orient. Three others taught at foreign universities, and four became diplomats. The success of such a high percentage is even more notable when considering that both world wars exacted the heavy toll of five premature deaths among the grantees.

20. Lucien Bourgogne was motivated by "a desire to know and understand fairly races and civilizations different from ours and to understand the English and French influence abroad." And Charles-Marie Garnier, explaining that he had many family and friends in the colonies, concluded by asking "how governments intend to strengthen public opinion against the individualism of race that is still exaggerated and transplanted in these new lands." See AN 16 AJ 7020, file 1899, letter from Lucien Bourgogne, 13 June 1899, p. 2; and Charles-Marie Garnier letter, 15 October 1900, p. 4.

21. Ernest Lavisse, "Une méthode coloniale," *Revue de Paris,* 1er juillet 1899, 61.

22. Jacques Weulersse, *Noirs et Blancs: A travers l'Afrique nouvelle: De Dakar au Cap* (Paris: Armand Colin, 1931).

23. Emmanuel Naquet, "Félicien Challaye (1875–1967): Itinéraire d'un recipient anticolonialiste et pacifiste," in *Albert Kahn, 1860–1940: Réalités d'une utopie,* ed. Jeanne Beausoleil and Pascal Ory (Boulogne: Musée Albert Kahn, 1995), 157–67.

24. Isabelle Merle and Emmanuelle Sibeud, "Histoire en marge ou histoire en marche? La colonisation entre repentance et patrimonialisation," in *Politiques du passé: Usages politiques du passé dans la France contemporaine,* vol. 2: *La concurrence des passés* (Aix-en-Provence: Presse Universitaire de Provence, 2006), 245–55.

25. AN 16 AJ 7023, file Albert Métin, letter sent from Assouan, 18 November 1898, p. 1.

26. AN 16 AJ 7021, file Paul Cornuel, letter sent from Lahore, 28 March 1912, p. 1.

27. AN 16 AJ 7023, file Albert Métin, undated note (probably written in 1899).

28. AN 16 AJ 7021, file Paul Cornuel, undated application letter, p. 2.

29. Albert Métin, *L'Inde d'aujourd'hui: Etude sociale* (Paris: Armand Colin, 1903). Elected deputy in 1909, he became minister of labor in 1913. Born in 1871, he died prematurely in 1918.

30. AN 16 AJ 7021, file Edmund Chassigneux.

31. AN 16 AJ 7020, file 1898, letter from Émile Hovelacque, sent from London in October 1898.

32. AN, 16 AJ 7021, Dossier Challaye, letter from Nagasaki, 17 June 1901, pp. 1–3. Like many other fellows, Challaye divided his trip into two, separated by a brief stay in France; hence, the allusion to his second trip.

33. This was still the period of failed projects such as the cruise that the *Revue générale des sciences pures et appliquées* hoped to organize in 1899 for two hundred chosen tourists: one hundred guests of the governor-general of Indochina and one hundred tourists chosen by the *revue* among "this middle class that furnishes our Grandes Ecoles with professors, engineers, chemists and our largest industries with directors." The project failed in part because it depended on a large grant from the Indochina budget (which was to pay for the guests' tickets plus those of some of the tourists). Quotation from CAOM, série L 80, carton 26787: "Tourisme, sport et chasse."

34. "M. Doumer's political programme, the systematic unification and decentralization of taxes, loans, public works, represents in my mind the best adaptation possible of these general ideas to the actual situation of Indochina," AN 16 AJ 7021, file Challaye, letter from Nagasaki, 17 June 1901, pp. 61–62.

35. "Should this gentle and patient population ever revolt, it will be because our compatriots' brutality will have pushed them beyond their limits. France must be made aware of this so that she may put a stop to it. The nation can act through its parliament on its ministers and, by this means, on government officials and colonists." Quote from AN 16 AJ 7021, file Challaye, letter from Nagasaki, 17 June 1901, p. 27.

36. AN 16 AJ 7021, file Challaye, letter from Nagasaki, 17 June 1901, pp. 6–9.

37. Challaye's key publications in this period were the following: "Impressions sur Java, fragments de journal," *Cahiers de la Quinzaine* 13e cahier, 4e série (1902), 3–40; "Lafcadio Hearn et le Japon," *Revue de Paris* (novembre 1904), 654–72; *Au Japon et en Extrême-Orient* (Paris: Armand Colin, 1905);

"Le Congo français," *Les Cahiers de la quinzaine* 12e cahier, 7e série (1905); *Le Congo français: La question internationale du Congo* (Paris: Félix Alcan, 1909).

38. The world travel fellowships were the subject of stiff competition. In 1904, besides Challaye's homage to Lafcadio Hearn and his work on Japan, the *Revue de Paris* also published two articles by Louis Aubert (a 1903 prize recipient) on Japan and the United States that were sent directly from the United States.

39. Thus, in 1906, the annual congress of the Ligue des droits de l'homme witnessed long debates about the atrocities committed in French Congo, and the Ligue demanded an appropriately republican response to such colonial activity; see *Bulletin de la Ligue des droits de l'homme*, no. 11, 15 June 1906, 885–91.

40. Nicolas Bancel, Pascal Blanchard, and Françoise Vergès, *La République coloniale?* (Paris: Albin Michel, 2003); Gilles Manceron, *Marianne et les colonies: Une introduction à l'histoire coloniale de la France* (Paris: Éditions La Découverte, 2003).

41. AN 16 AJ 7021, file Challaye, letter from Nagasaki, 17 June 1901, p. 28.

42. Félicien Challaye, "Courrier d'Indo-Chine," *Cahiers de la Quinzaine* 7e cahier, 3e série (1902), 53–70, quote at p. 61.

43. Alfred Raquez, *Les recipients de voyage de l'Université de Paris* (Hanoi: Imprimerie F. H. Schneider, 1905).

44. The tone is vicious: "Mr. Félicien Challaye Is the Traveling, Honest Solution [to the colonial problem]," Alfred Raquez, *Les recipients de voyage de l'Université de Paris* (Hanoi: Imprimerie F. H. Schneider, 1905), 4.

45. AN 16 AJ 7021, file Challaye, letter from Nagasaki, 17 June 1901, p. 23.

46. Emmanuelle Sibeud, *Une science impériale pour l'Afrique? La construction des savoirs africanistes en France (1878–1930)* (Paris: Éditions de l'EHESS, 2002).

47. Georges Dumas, ed., *Traité de psychologie* (Paris: Félix Alcan, 1924), vol. 2, 703–38. This work brought together the outstanding specialists in the field, but its publication was delayed by the war.

48. London School of Economics, Edmund D. Morel Papers, F 4: letter to Edmund D. Morel, 12 March 1905. As Pierre Mille told Morel, "Brazza is leaving. And he is taking with him as personal secretary, entrusted with sending correspondence to the *Temps*, even concerning the Free State, a very distinguished young writer, on my recommendation and approved by Bourde (who as you know is a very honest man!). This extremely sincere and talented

young man is Félicien Challaye. In regard to everyone, his sole condition was that he would leave only if he did not lie."

49. The two men were, for instance, accused of boiling a human head and of killing a native porter to celebrate Bastille Day in 1903 by igniting a stick of dynamite placed in his anus. Once leaked to the press, the contents of the trial caused outrage in France, exposing the hollowness of French claims to their civilizing influence and leading to calls for the Brazza mission to review the excessive powers of concessionary companies and their administrative auxiliaries in the Lower Congo.

50. Challaye urged the Ligue des droits de l'homme to take up Toqué's case.

51. Challaye struggled to secure the assent of the Ligue des droits de l'homme to dedicate one of its annual congresses to the question of colonization. The proposal was rejected on numerous occasions by the Ligue's local federations and sections until the central committee finally imposed it in 1931.

3

Colonial Minds and African Witchcraft

Interpretations of Murder as Seen in Cases from French West Africa in the Interwar Era

RUTH GINIO

Belief in witchcraft, "ritual" crimes, and witches' secret societies has always represented one of the primary images of Africa in the French colonial mind. It was certainly one of the continent's most disturbing and lurid images that colonial minds could conjure. The literature of the period further reinforced it. Paul Morand's descriptions of Africa, for example, in his novel *Magie Noire*, published in 1928, are filled with horrifying figures of witches and societies of *hommes-panthères* (leopard men).[1] This chapter argues, however, that the discussion of witchcraft in the colonial context offers us more than mere reflections of French colonial imagery. It sheds light, in addition, on the different forms of knowledge production about this cultural phenomenon, in turn revealing the ways in which use of this knowledge became bound up with the exercise of political power within the colonial arena.

Witchcraft, in fact, had two advantages for the colonizer. First, it supplied the ultimate justification for colonial rule—the eradication of primitive and barbaric beliefs. Second, it was a fascinating phenomenon that brought a whiff of interest and excitement to administrative service in Africa. These two advantages were, of course, rather contradictory, because for witchcraft to become truly fascinating it had to be more than just a barbaric superstition—it had to be real. As discussed, this is not the sole contradiction stemming from colonial inquiries into African witchcraft.

This chapter examines two kinds of knowledge about witchcraft that derived from the French colonial mind—academic knowledge and administrative knowledge.[2] These two forms of knowledge are represented by two figures: the French philosopher Lucien Lévy-Bruhl (1857–1939) and Maurice Prouteaux, a long-serving member of the colonial administration from 1908 to 1934 who was also an amateur ethnographer. The chapter first discusses the two very different perceptions of African witchcraft represented by Lévy-Bruhl and Prouteaux, before moving on to consider how the "knowledge" created by these two differing kinds of investigation shaped decisions taken within the colonial legal arena in response to alleged witchcraft-related crimes.

I have chosen to focus on ideas developed by Lévy-Bruhl and Prouteaux for two reasons. Each dealt excessively with questions related to witchcraft, and each left extensive reports explaining his analysis of African beliefs in witchcraft. Furthermore, the renowned British anthropologist Sir Edward Evans-Pritchard, professor of social anthropology at Oxford University, who was also deeply interested in African witchcraft, discussed Lévy-Bruhl's work at length, while several ethnographic journals published articles written by Prouteaux. Taken together, the writings of Lévy-Bruhl and Prouteaux represent two distinct ways in which African witchcraft was understood in the French colonial mind. The chapter shows that although their contrasting perceptions of witchcraft endured throughout the interwar era, only one—that represented by Prouteaux—prevailed in the colonial legal field. This arena consisted of a system of native courts (*tribunaux indigènes*) that was established in 1903 and began operating two years later. Supposedly adapted to African traditions and customs, this court system actually copied the hierarchical structure of the metropolitan legal system. It was subdivided into four tiers: the village, the province, the circle courts, and the *chambre d'homologation* that served as the highest appeal court.[3] A key drawback of this system was that its judgments incorporated and relied on a set of indigenous customs that the colonial authorities could not understand.

The Metropolitan Academic Mind and African Witchcraft: The Case of Lucien Lévy-Bruhl

In October 1937 Marcel de Coppet, governor-general of French West Africa (FWA), asked all governors of the federation's territories to send him reports on recent criminal cases brought before the native courts in their colonies that involved witchcraft, ritual cannibalism, or felonies committed by so-called secret societies. The motive for this request was to assist Lucien Lévy-Bruhl's scientific inquiries into what he referred to as "primitive mentality." Both de Coppet's instructions and the enthusiastic response to it emphasize the close relations between academic research in France and colonial administrative practice. On 4 February 1938, for example, the governor of Côte d'Ivoire submitted reports regarding forty-four such legal cases that had occurred between 1907 and 1929 and that were judged by circle courts. All crimes were classified according to a rudimentary list of definitions, such as cannibalism (*anthropophagie*), ritual poisoning (*empoisonnement rituelle*), and sorcery (*pratiques de sorcellerie*).[4] Lévy-Bruhl certainly made use of this copious material in his research, as can be gleaned from the *Carnets de Lévy-Bruhl*, notes he made in 1938 that were published posthumously by Maurice Leenhardt (1878–1954).[5] These notes are especially significant because within them he refuted some of his earlier, most controversial conclusions that had drawn hostile criticism from other academics, notably the assertion of the existence of a distinct "primitive mentality" that was essentially mystical and pre-logical.[6]

Born in 1857, Lévy-Bruhl studied philosophy at the École Normale Supérieure. Together with Jean Jaurès, Léon Blum, and Marcel Mauss he established the newspaper *L'humanité*, which was later to become the mouthpiece of the French Communist Party. In 1906 he was appointed professor of modern philosophy at the Sorbonne. Although a philosopher by training, he was drawn to the growing science of ethnography that took off alongside the European colonial expansion of the late nineteenth century. This attraction was probably fueled by his close relations with renowned anthropologists and ethnographers, among them Mauss, Emile Durkheim, Maurice Delafosse, and Paul Rivet. Together with the last two he founded the Institut français d'anthropologie in 1925.[7] As noted, Lévy-Bruhl's foremost interest was "primitive mentality" and its supposed differences from Western mentality. His first book, published in 1910, *Les fonctions mentales dans les sociétés inférieures*, aroused heated debates, especially as Durkheim and Mauss disagreed with some of his views. His next book, *La mentalité primitive*, published in 1922, stirred further controversy.[8] The main source of objection to Lévy-Bruhl's ideas was his definition of "primitive mentality" as being essentially pre-logical. In the conclusion to *La mentalité primitive* Lévy-Bruhl explained the core difference he discerned between Western and primitive mentalities, claiming that the two were foreign and therefore simply unintelligible to one another. While Western mentality was conceptual, its primitive namesake did not elevate to abstractions or to logical formulas. It did not raise the same questions but was essentially mystical and pre-logical, following different thought patterns entirely.[9] Lévy-Bruhl was particularly intrigued by beliefs in witchcraft, which he believed opened a window into the "native mind." He dedicated an entire chapter to this subject in his subsequent book, *Le surnaturel et la nature dans la mentalité primitive* (1931). Crucially, he now depicted witchcraft as an ingredient of the primitive mentality, which attributes every disaster, illness, or death to supernatural powers.[10]

This fascination with witchcraft probably lay behind the request to receive information regarding ritual crimes in FWA in 1937. Lévy-Bruhl died two years later, before publishing another book, but his notes, mentioned above, demonstrate the transformation of his basic ideas regarding the "African mind" following his exposure to these court cases. Lévy-Bruhl's notes indicate that he no longer considered "primitive mentality" fundamentally different from its Western equivalent. He rejected his own concept of "pre-logical mentality" and endeavored instead to demonstrate that, in fact, all humans think in logical terms.

In his notes Lévy-Bruhl describes four court cases that he found especially revealing, using them to prove that, contrary to his beliefs when he began writing about primitive mentality two decades earlier, this mentality could not be defined as pre-logical. In one case from Guinea in 1929 a father claimed that witches had eaten his daughter although he himself had buried her body. When the father was asked how these people could have eaten his daughter when her body was never in their possession, he answered that they did so "in the manner of witches." Lévy-Bruhl explained that the sudden unnatural death of the girl elicited the accusation of witchcraft. According to local tradition, he wrote, witches kill people by eating them. Therefore, when the father said that the witches had eaten his daughter, he actually meant that they had caused her death. Witches eat people when no one can see them. The "eaten" man continues to walk about, but he is already doomed and eventually will die. Lévy-Bruhl then raised the inevitable question: why did the African not explain all that to the puzzled administrator? The answer lay in the fact that unlike his colonial masters, he was uninterested in the double meaning of the concept of "eating." He might not deny this distinction if it were presented to him, but he himself would not make it. He was upset because his daughter had been eaten. The question of *how* she was eaten did not arise at all. Whether witches were cannibals, in the sense familiar to Western minds, or only spiritually—that did not interest the African. Lévy-Bruhl maintained that this apathy toward the precise operation of witchcraft was typical of the African attitude toward it. Once the witch had decided to kill someone, death would necessarily result; it did not matter how.

Another case Lévy-Bruhl examined occurred in 1927 in a suburb of Conakry, capital of French Guinea. A crocodile was alleged to have attacked and wounded a man. It was claimed that this was not normal and that a "witch doctor" (*sorcier*) should be consulted. The witch doctor duly identified the "real" culprits. They confessed in court and were found guilty. But the verdict was later revoked because it proved impossible to make sense of the confessions. The accused each gave three contradictory versions of how the crime was committed: a real crocodile attacked the victim; the accused turned himself into a crocodile so that he could attack the victim; and the accused hid under a crocodile skin, crawled in the mud, and wounded the victim with crocodile teeth and knives. The report noted that none of the accused grasped the incompatibility of the various versions, each of them insisting only that the attack took place "in the manner of witches" (*à la manière des sorciers*).[11]

The problem of inconsistent testimonies recurred in a case from the Boké circle in Guinea in 1935. A man walked out of a rice field, was attacked by a snake, and died shortly afterward. It did not seem natural, and the witch had to be found. A witch doctor identified the culprit, and he was brought to court. Here again, the witnesses gave three different versions: the accused shot the victim's leg with a "bingo" (a tiny pistol that shoots small poisonous wooden needles); the accused turned himself into a snake and bit his victim; the accused ordered a snake to bite the victim. Some of the witnesses provided all three versions in one testimony and could not be persuaded to choose one. To add to the confusion, some witnesses admitted that they actually saw nothing at all but were nonetheless convinced that their testimonies were correct.[12]

Lévy-Bruhl drew certain conclusions from these cases, which he claimed represented a much larger number of comparable accounts. He claimed that they proved that the Africans' logic was not inferior to Western logic. It was not that the Africans were indifferent to contradictions; they simply did not notice them. But this was not a result of weak logic. Rather, at certain moments they entered the sphere of mystical experience. While their logic was normally as solid as that of Western people, he argued, when the African mind left the ordinary sphere of experience and entered the mystical one of supernatural forces it began working in different ways.[13] It is important to note here that Lévy-Bruhl raised doubts about his ability to know exactly what the Africans involved in these cases actually said because it was impossible to be certain that the interpreter did his job well. But he emphasized that the questions colonial officials typically posed in such cases should not be asked at all. For the Africans, when witchcraft operated it did not matter which means were chosen. Obviously, the African could tell the difference between a snake bite and a hunting accident, but this difference was insignificant to him. The witch acts in "the manner of witches," meaning that ordinary people did not know how he or she operates. The important thing was to find the witch and rectify the damage he or she had caused.[14]

The process by which Lévy-Bruhl formulated his theories demonstrates that although colonial power depended on knowledge, it also molded knowledge. Lévy-Bruhl was interested in court cases that involved witchcraft because he wished to reexamine his own understanding of the "African mind." But the academic knowledge he created was thus shaped by colonial representations of the African reality, a problem of which he was aware. It is also important to bear in mind that Lévy-Bruhl's objective was to analyze the African mind and not to help colonial administrators solve murder mysteries. As is discussed below, for the colonial administration in FWA, this was the main disadvantage of the knowledge he produced.

Let us now turn to an example of another form of research conducted in the colonies by colonial officials on the ground. This type of knowledge production, formulated in long and detailed administrative reports, was generated with the specific aim of assisting the colonial administration in dealing with criminal cases associated with witchcraft.

The Administrative Mind and Witchcraft-Related Crimes: The Case of Maurice Prouteaux

Lévy-Bruhl was sensitive to the problems raised for colonial officials by criminal cases like those he analyzed. He claimed that officials' inability to understand seemingly illogical statements by African witnesses stemmed from their misperception of the mystical aspect of native mentality. They simply asked questions that were insignificant to the witnesses, questions that should have not been asked at all. This analysis, however, was not helpful for colonial officials; for them, witchcraft-related court cases presented practical problems that simply demanded resolution. They required another sort of research that would explain African witchcraft in a manner that would help them deal with it effectively. In pursuit of this aim, local administrators wrote reports and field studies based on their own ethnographical research. These reports, which often accompanied judicial documents regarding "ritual crimes," help illuminate perceptions of African witchcraft among French colonial administrators.

The science of social anthropology—and, within it, that of ethnography—gathered impetus in France during the late nineteenth and early twentieth centuries. Heightened overseas expansion advanced both professional and amateur fieldwork in newly acquired territories. Social anthropology acquired greater prominence following the establishment of the Paris École d'anthropologie in 1876 and the nearby Musée d'ethnographie du Trocadéro two years later. At the turn of the twentieth century there was a proliferation of ethnographic journals that differed from traditional anthropological journals in which ethnography was marginal. The close relationship between ethnography and French colonialism was reflected in the large number of colonial administrators who were also members of the Institut ethnographique international de Paris (45 out of 225 in 1914). In fact, according to Emmanuelle

Sibeud, until 1914 the term "colonial ethnography" was a pleonasm as all ethnographers were in some sense colonial: administrators, military officials, or doctors, as well as the relatively isolated group of missionaries and travelers. This imperialist community published a great number of ethnographic works in scientific journals.[15]

Although not all colonial administrators appreciated ethnography or believed that it might enhance their ability to rule their colonial subjects, some were captivated by it and spent at least part of their time investigating the societies under their sway. The phenomenon of the "scholar-administrator" who conducted research while fulfilling his administrative duties existed in other areas as well. At the beginning of the twentieth century, administrators in FWA, for example, studied African Islam and its ostensible differences from Arab Islam.[16] There were, of course, precedents for this spirit of enquiry. About two centuries before, for example, in Mauritius, administrators such as Pierre Poivre were fascinated by the study of local agriculture and the relationship between man and nature.[17]

Ethnographic research, however, was especially important as a tool of acquiring knowledge regarding local customs, which were not codified in any way but were to become part of the native legal system established in FWA in 1903. The native courts were supposed to rule according to local customs as long as these did not contradict the principles of French civilization. This meant that if the local administrator wished to retain any measure of control over the judicial process he had to familiarize himself with these customs. While systematic but largely fruitless attempts to codify customary law were made in the early twentieth century, administrators occasionally continued to pursue their own inquiries into local customary practices.[18]

Of all existing customs the phenomenon of witchcraft and magic attracted particular attention. This attraction might explain the exceptionally long and detailed reports that colonial administrators filed about issues such as ritual murders, anthropophagy, and secret societies. Another explanation for the special attention accorded to witchcraft is that crimes related to it, such as those that served Lévy-Bruhl in the construction of his theories, often left colonial officials helpless and confused about how such cases could be prosecuted in conformity with their own judicial procedures.

Maurice Prouteaux began his colonial career in 1908 as a native affairs assistant (*adjoint des affaires indigènes*) in Côte d'Ivoire. Between 1917 and 1921 he served as the *commandant de cercle* (district administrator) of Bas-Cavally in Côte d'Ivoire. Prouteaux was one of those administrators—ethnographers who wrote extensive reports about witchcraft and secret societies. He was a member of the Société d'anthropologie de Paris and published articles in social science journals such as *L'Anthropologie*.[19] In 1918, following a murder investigation undertaken in his *cercle* that concerned so-called ritual crimes of secret societies, Prouteaux put together an eighty-two-page report on the subject of "witches' societies." It seems that the views presented in this report to a large extent articulated the thoughts of many other colonial administrators in FWA at the time. Similar views were expressed in other administrators' notes regarding cases of witchcraft, albeit with less detail.[20]

Prouteaux began his report with an apology about its unusual bulk. He explained that it was impossible to evaluate the murderers' degree of responsibility without learning about the magical-religious rules of the region. His description of the secret meetings of African witches serves as an excellent example for the examination of an African phenomenon through a European prism. The vocabulary he used to describe the activity of these witches derived from sixteenth-century France. "I use the word 'witches,'" he writes, "because it seems to suit these people who gather in secrecy and whose rituals strangely remind us of our witches of the sixteenth century whose memory was conserved by Jean Bodin and others."[21] He then recounted the practices and behaviors of these centuries-old European witches. The African witches use sticks to fly to their meetings, which Prouteaux termed "Sabbaths," a word that applied to similar gatherings in sixteenth-century France.[22] According to Prouteaux, the society met every full moon in a remote corner of the forest after drinking a potion that rendered them invisible to regular people. They performed magic acts but also indulged in sexual activities, including orgies and incest. They also discussed their future victims. Every member in turn had to propose a victim whom he had to murder before the next meeting. The victim—unlike those of European witches who were usually their neighbors' young children—had to belong to the witch's immediate family—wife, brother, sister, father, or mother. After the murder, usually by poisoning, a feast took place at which the witches ate the victim's flesh. A look at the descriptions from which the *commandant* culled his vocabulary indicates that most of these elements recur time and again.[23]

In his book *Ecstasies: Deciphering the Witches' Sabbath* Carlo Ginzburg provides a vivid description of the stereotypical witches' gatherings or "Sabbaths." This description highlights the similarities between the way in which witchcraft was perceived in fifteenth- to seventeenth-century France and how Prouteaux described it in early twentieth-century Africa:

> Male and female witches met at night, generally in solitary places, in fields or on mountains. Sometimes, having anointed their bodies, they flew, arriving astride poles or broomsticks; sometimes they arrived on the backs of animals, or transformed into animals themselves. Those who came for the first time had to renounce the Christian faith, desecrate the sacrament and offer homage to the devil, who was present in human or (most often) animal or semi-animal form. There would follow banquets, dancing, sexual orgies. Before returning home the female and male witches received evil ointments made from children's fat and other ingredients.[24]

This view of African witchcraft entirely derived from early modern France signifies a very different interpretation than that of Lévy-Bruhl and other professional anthropologists in interwar France and Britain. Evans-Pritchard, for example, interpreted African witchcraft in his well-known study of the Azande in Sudan as a natural philosophy that explained the occurrence of unfortunate events and that was completely different from the notion that haunted and disgusted Europeans in the distant past.[25]

Administrators such as Prouteaux took no account of such explanations, either because they lacked the professional skill to appreciate them, or because their own perceptions of witchcraft fueled their imagination in a way that no professional anthropological inquiry could have done. Conducting serious inquiries about witchcraft was often impossible—sometimes, as in the region of Cassamanse in Senegal—because of local hostility toward colonial officials, but mostly because Africans were hardly enthusiastic about discussing such secret and dangerous matters with their colonizers. Instead, unable to conduct such inquiries, as Robert Baum suggests, "local administrators sat on the verandahs of their residence; they heard the sound of drums and singing penetrating the stillness of the night; and their imaginations filled in what their inquiries failed to yield."[26]

Aside from the excitement that writing such reports brought to administrators' lives, they served another important purpose: reports were explicitly designed to assist colonial rule. A key question arises in light of this: how did the perceptions of African witchcraft reflected in such ethnographic studies affect how the colonial officials who investigated witchcraft-related cases dealt with problems they encountered in the courtroom?

The Colonial Encounter with Witchcraft in the Legal Arena

Witchcraft was intrinsically a fascinating subject, and investigating it was a great way for bored colonial officials to pass the time. However, when murder was committed and witchcraft cases entered the colonial court system, the menacing potential of these beliefs became more manifest. Such cases were brought before the circle court, which served as a criminal tribunal. It was presided over by the circle commander, his deputy, or possibly some other European official designated by the governor.[27] The basic problem raised by witchcraft-related crimes was the following paradox: how could the French colonial authorities prosecute a person for a crime they did not believe he or she could have committed?[28] The solution, in most cases, was to ignore the main accusation against the defendant—that he or she was a witch—and to find other, ostensibly more realistic reasons for prosecution. But even then, several problems bedeviled court cases in which witchcraft was involved. This section focuses on three of these problems: the question of the missing motive, contradictory testimonies, and inadmissible confessions. These three judicial obstacles were difficult to overcome, and colonial administrators who presided over such trials had to decide how to tackle them. As is discussed, in many cases the unswerving French belief in the existence of cannibalism in their colonial territories helped resolve some of these judicial problems.

Cannibalism and the French Colonial Mind

Prouteaux's understanding of African witchcraft brought to the fore the issue of cannibalism, something believed to have featured in witchcraft practices in sixteenth-century France.[29] This view was reinforced by the popular image of Africa as a land where cannibalism was endemic. For centuries rumors about cannibalistic practices were commonplace within European colonial societies in Africa. Although Africans who claimed cannibalism existed always pointed to other societies and never to their own, Europeans were more than ready to believe these allegations. Some early ethnographers, such as Thomas Winterbottom (1766–1859), concluded that aside from occasional ritual cannibalism, there was no reliable proof that it existed. Nevertheless, European belief in the existence of such practices in Africa remained deeply embedded.[30] In the introduction to *Cannibalism and the Colonial World*, Peter Hulme speaks of the European obsession with cannibalism in the non-Western world and asks why Europeans were so eager to find confirmation of their suspicions. Part of the answer lies in the need to justify colonial rule and to civilize the peoples of the newly acquired territories. Europeans who wrote about cannibalism saw it as a clear marker between civilized Europe and the "non-civilized" world that existed beyond European knowledge.[31]

Lévy-Bruhl was unusual in this respect. He did not dwell on whether cannibalistic practices existed but only mentioned the subject to explain the inability of colonial officials to understand apparent contradictions in African witness accounts. As mentioned, his discussion of the father who claimed his daughter had been eaten—although he himself buried her body—explained the act of man-eating as a symbolic and spiritual process.[32] While this explanation implicitly precludes the possibility of actually eating—that is, consuming—the victims' flesh, French colonial administrators were more than ready to believe in the existence of cannibalism. Notwithstanding the fact that toward the end of the period discussed here, reports occasionally expressed greater skepticism about allegations of cannibalism in FWA, the colonial reflex was still to assume its existence despite the lack of tangible evidence.[33] When Prouteaux mentioned the cannibalistic practices of witches' secret societies he admitted both that there was no concrete evidence to bear this out and that the informants who claimed such practices existed were usually unreliable. As he conceded, he tended to believe it nevertheless.[34] Accepting the existence of cannibalism had become imperative for some colonial officials because it reinforced the perception of a barbaric African society, which had to be acculturated to European values. Belief in cannibalism also helped French administrators resolve the dilemma of prosecuting people for witchcraft. Where Lévy-Bruhl explained the relationship between witchcraft and "eating" as symbolic, these administrators chose to understand it literally. By equating witchcraft with cannibalism they could prosecute ostensible witches as cannibals. While witchcraft was imaginary—no more than a superstitious barbaric belief—cannibalism, according to the French colonial mind, was real and, therefore, could be considered a crime to be dealt with rationally through legal instruments. Hence, in the case of the French trials of Diola witches described by Baum, the administration interpreted the description of witchcraft literally as eating. Members of the Kussanga secret society were duly prosecuted for cannibalism. One of the interpreters who participated in these trials described this mistake in the following words: "It was not flesh . . . it was the soul . . . it was witchcraft that we transformed into cannibalism . . . in witchcraft, it is the soul that one eats."[35]

Yet, even after the prosecution's major dilemma of how to secure a conviction was resolved, other difficulties emerged during the legal process. This leads to the matter of how the firm belief in the existence of cannibalism helped the French colonial officials overcome the three principal problems posed in witchcraft-related trials.

The Question of the Missing Motive

The basic aim of every murder investigator has always been to find the motive. The answer to the question "who had the most to gain from the victim's disappearance?" often led to the crime's perpetrator. But for Prouteaux and other colonial officials who dealt with witchcraft-related crimes, such a question was useless because they believed that Africans who belonged to witches' societies did not kill for a reason but, rather, did so in fulfillment of their ritual duties. Prouteaux claimed that the absence of motive was the most fascinating and challenging aspect of ritual murders, complaining that as a result it was sometimes impossible to find the murderer.[36] However, during the lengthy questioning of witnesses in the 1918 trial on which his report focused, as well as that in a similar case from the same *cercle* at much the same time, various witnesses suggested motives that should have been considered perfectly "normal" in French eyes: a murdered relative was the lover of the wife of one of the murderers;[37] another victim had a dispute with his murderer over the payment of dowry; and so on.[38] In another case from 1922 a woman was brought before Conakry's circle court after murdering her grandson and her son. Motives for both crimes were mentioned in the investigation report. She killed her grandson because his mother (her daughter-in-law) had upset her, and she later killed her son because he returned from a long journey without bringing her a gift. These motives, admittedly dubious, were completely ignored in the verdict, which declared the murders a ritual and therefore motiveless. The woman, it was established, belonged to a *hommes-panthères* society that chose its victims from among its members' relatives.[39] The colonial administrator who reported this case could not accept that a grandmother murdered her grandson because she disliked his mother, but he was more than ready to believe she murdered him because she desired human flesh.

The allegation of anthropophagy that supposedly accompanied ritual crimes is evident in most of the reports, and in some of the cases this was held to be the actual motive for the crime. A report on the activities of the *hommes-panthères*, for example, lamented the fact that the convicted criminals were not accused of cannibalism, but only of murder because cannibalism was not mentioned in Islamic law or in the customary law of the region. Such an abominable offence, the report explained, was inconceivable to these two legal systems. Nevertheless, the administrator argued, this was, in general, the main motive for ritual crimes.[40]

The answer to the question of the missing motive thus becomes clear—appetite for human flesh. These ostensibly inexplicable crimes became very clear because cannibals did not need a motive. The perception that African witchcraft was equivalent to its counterpart in early modern France added further weight to the claim that cannibalism explained the absence of motive because the prevalent image of French witchcraft portrayed the devil's allies killing people at his command without rational motive after which the victims were often devoured.[41]

Contradictory or "Illogical" Testimonies

Lévy-Bruhl's fascination with the matter of contradictory testimonies has already been observed. Indeed, for him this was a key to understanding "primitive mentality." The problem, he explained, was not the supposed contradiction, but the questions that led to contradictory responses.

Nevertheless, in a murder investigation some questions simply have to be asked. When Lévy-Bruhl stated that for the witness it did not matter whether the victim was devoured by a crocodile (whether a transformed witch or the reptile sent by a witch) or was attacked by a man disguised as one—because both were just ways that a witch killed his or her victim—he offered no solution to the problem faced by the colonial murder investigator. The colonial legal system did not allow that the three possible scenarios offered by the witnesses in the cases Lévy-Bruhl analyzed could be considered the same. The first two described an accident while the third was clearly murder. According to Lévy-Bruhl, the contradiction ceases to exist when the witness entered the mystical sphere. But legal procedure, at least according to French officials, had nothing mystical about it. A person was killed, and a clear verdict was required. When faced with such contradictory testimonies, most colonial administrators were less understanding than Lévy-Bruhl. Prouteaux, for instance, described the individual accused in the case that inspired his report as an intelligent and sincere man because, unlike most other witnesses, he corrected his statements when his attention was drawn to inconsistencies in his testimony.[42] Prouteaux's interpretation for such contradictions, then, was that the people responsible for them were simply not intelligent or sincere enough to avoid them.

Just as with the problem of the missing motive, so belief in cannibalism could also help to resolve problems raised by contradictory or "illogical" testimonies. In the case Lévy-Bruhl described of the father who testified that his daughter had been eaten, the contradiction inherent in accusing a person of eating a girl whose untouched body was buried by the accusing father was completely overlooked. Indeed, the father's reference to "eating" helped the prosecutor to proceed with the trial, as the offence was now cannibalism and not witchcraft.

In another case from French Guinea in 1922, in which eight people were prosecuted for allegedly committing ritual crimes, the administrator described the defendants as "*sorciers simplement mangeurs d'hommes*" (sorcerers who were simply man-eaters). The administrator wrote that the accused beat their victim before eating imaginary bits of his flesh. The witches thus pretended to have eaten their victim but recognized that he could continue living for another two to five days. A short time later the victim died as a result of the beating he endured.[43] What we have here is a perfect example for Lévy-Bruhl's interpretation of "witches' cannibalism." The account described the witches' harmful actions as a symbolic eating. The administrator even used words such as "imaginary" and "pretend," which emphasized this symbolic notion. He nevertheless insisted on viewing this as a literal description of cannibalism, concluding that the witches had in fact physically eaten their victim. The "eating" described was not, after all, a symbolic description of the witches' actions, but the principal motive for their crime. So convinced of this version was the administrator that he was willing to believe that a man who had been partially devoured by others could remain mobile for a considerable time before finally dying. In this instance French colonial belief in cannibalism made sense of otherwise illogical testimonies that described partially eaten people and witches who ate others without leaving their house. Understanding these descriptions as merely symbolizing the act of witchcraft rather than as literal cannibalism might have done more to resolve ostensible contradictions. However, this kind of understanding required prior acceptance that the accused should be charged with witchcraft and not cannibalism—and this was something French administrators could not accept. By taking a literal view of witness accounts of cannibalism, the prosecution supposedly erased the illogical and contradictory aspects in these testimonies. In fact, the reverse was true: in most cases literal interpretation rendered these testimonies more illogical than they originally sounded.

It bears emphasis that symbolic cannibalism was not mentioned in all court cases that involved witchcraft. The following example exposes the difficulties French administrators faced when dealing with "illogical" testimonies in which the accusation of witchcraft did not involve any kind of "eating." Interrogation of a "witch doctor" who served as a kind of "expert witness" took place during the trial of a village chief in which he and his friends were accused of driving a slave to suicide in the region of Tivaoune, Senegal, in 1911. The investigator's questions first highlighted the material profits that the blind witch doctor stood to gain from identifying the witch before discrediting this witness's professional ability:

> Q: How do you know if someone is a witch?
> A: The Demon tells me so.
> Q: What is this Demon's name?
> A: Samarrossine.
> Q: Where does he live?
> A: Between the sky and the earth.
> Q: Could you call him now so that he might help us determine who among us is a witch?
> A: He does not always answer my call. He is an important person.[44]

While it is clear that the French colonial official tried to convince the court of the absurdity of the claim that this person could find witches, or even that witches actually existed, it is also quite obvious he had failed to do so. His arguments failed to undermine the witness's credibility in the eyes of those who believed in witchcraft.[45]

Inadmissible Confessions

Another judicial problem that witchcraft-related trials posed was the delicate issue of inadmissible confessions. Here again an insistence on cannibalism occasionally helped overcome this obstacle.

In the Diola trials mentioned above, eight of the thirteen defendants admitted that they have eaten human flesh in their distant past. In all cases they claimed that a relative gave them meat without telling them it was human. After they had eaten the meat they became sick—probably because it was spoiled—and therefore believed that they had eaten human flesh and were being punished for it. These confessions would probably not have held up in any French court, but in this case they were all accepted as true.⁴⁶ As before, reference to cannibalism overrode the weakness of inconsistent testimony. When cannibalism or anything that sounded like it was not mentioned, however, things become more complicated.

One such paradox that did not involve cannibalism and therefore could not be easily resolved emerged in a report about a pharmacist, Colonel Laffitte, who studied African medicines. A European living in an isolated area, Laffitte fell ill for no apparent reason. There was cause to suspect that one of his three servants had poisoned him. One of the servants soon confessed. Under further questioning, however, he explained that he had asked a *conrté-tigui*, meaning a witch who could kill from a distance, to murder his master. He was certain that the witch had acted when the European fell ill.⁴⁷ In this case the colonial court could not accept the confession, because the servant confessed to something that the French thought impossible.

French Colonial Minds and the Production of Knowledge about Witchcraft

Knowledge about African witchcraft, whether generated by metropolitan scholars, such as Lévy-Bruhl, or by colonial administrators, such as Prouteaux, could not help the French colonizers to resolve all, or even most, of the problems arising from the encounter between French colonial courts and witchcraft-related crimes. As discussed, substituting unrealistic witchcraft with supposedly realistic cannibalism in the African context was occasionally helpful in solving these legal dilemmas. For the most part, however, judicial administrators were simply helpless when facing the cultural world of witchcraft.

The two forms of understanding—of contrary colonial minds—presented in this chapter represent completely different attitudes to the cultural phenomenon of African witchcraft. Academics, such as Lévy-Bruhl, were principally interested in studying and understanding African beliefs for scholarly reasons, but local administrators, such as Prouteaux, had to deal with the practical outcomes of such beliefs. Officials' lack of professional anthropological knowledge and their difficulties in conducting serious fieldwork molded their perceptions. They interpreted the African world of witchcraft through the prism of the French historical past and their stereotypical image of Africa as the land of barbarism. These administrators tried to harness their interpretation of African witchcraft to the investigation and prosecution of crimes that seemed to relate to it. They did not make use of Lévy-Bruhl's alternative understanding of witchcraft perhaps because they were unaware of it, but probably because it offered no immediate resolution to their legal problems. Levy-Bruhl's complex evaluation of African beliefs in witchcraft did nothing to help the confused administrator in court. These encounters between the French colonial minds and African witchcraft remind us that although in many colonial contexts knowledge is power, sometimes power stems not from knowledge but rather from the ability to ignore it.

Notes

1. Paul Morand, *Magie Noire* (Paris: Grasset, 1928).

2. On the relations between academic and colonial logic in the context of the science of ethnography see Emmanuelle Sibeud, *Une science impériale pour l'Afrique? La construction des savoirs africanistes en France, 1878–1930* (Paris: EHESS, 2002), 185–89.

3. For more on the native legal system see Ruth Ginio, "Negotiating Legal Authority in French West Africa: The Colonial Administration and the African Assessors, 1903–1918," in *Intermediaries, Interpreters, and Clerks: African Employees in the Making of Colonial Africa*, ed. Benjamin Lawrance, Emily Osborn, and Richard Roberts (Madison: University of Wisconsin Press, 2006), 115–35; Alice L. Conklin, *A Mission to Civilize the Republican Idea of Empire in France and West Africa, 1895–1930* (Stanford CA: Stanford University Press, 1997), 86–87.

4. Unfortunately there are only lists of cases attached to the request.

5. Maurice Leenhardt was a French ethnologist who specialized in the Kanak, the people of New Caledonia.

6. See Lucian Lévy-Bruhl, *Les fonctions mentales dans les sociétés inférieures* (Paris: Librarie Félix Alcan, 1910); Lévy-Bruhl, *La mentalité primitive* (Paris: Librarie Félix Alcan, 1922); Lévy-Bruhl, *Le surnaturel et la nature dans la metalité primitive* (Paris: Librarie Félix Alcan, 1931).

7. Emmanuelle Sibeud, "La naissance de l'ethnographie africaniste en France avant 1914," *Cahiers d'études africaines* 34:4 (1994), 651.

8. Martine Balard, *Dahomey 1930: Mission Catholique et culte vodoun* (Paris: L'Harmattan, 1996), 68.

9. Lévy-Bruhl, *La mentalité*, 505–6, 516–17.

10. Lévy-Bruhl, *Le surnaturel*, 165–226.

11. Lévy-Bruhl, *Le surnaturel*, 51–52. All translations are by the author unless otherwise noted.

12. Lévy-Bruhl, *Le surnaturel*, 52–53. Lévy-Bruhl cites a very similar case in which the murder was committed by a shark, either real or not; see Lévy-Bruhl, *Le surnaturel*, 24–28. The problem of contradicting testimonies with regard to the identity of the killer as a person or an animal existed in the case of the leopard-men killings in Nigeria in the 1940s. In that case contradictions stemmed from a wish to accuse a certain person. David Pratten, *The Man-Leopard Murder Mysteries: History and Society in Colonial Nigeria* (Edinburg: Edinburgh University Press, 2007), 6.

13. Pratten, *Man-Leopard Murder Mysteries*, 53–56.

14. Pratten, *Man-Leopard Murder Mysteries*, 57–59.

15. Sibeud, "La naissance," 640, 645, 651.

16. Christopher Harrison, *France and Islam in West Africa, 1860–1960* (Cambridge: Cambridge University Press, 1988), 97–102.

17. Megan Vaghan, *Creating the Creole Island: Slavery in Eighteenth-Century Mauritius* (Durham NC: Duke University Press, 2005), 65–75.

18. On the attempts to use ethnographic research to understand and codify African customary law see David Robinson, "Ethnography and Customary Law in Senegal," *Cahiers d'études africaines* 32:126 (1992), 231–35. On this subject see also Ed Van Hoven, "Representing Social Hierarchy: Administrators-Ethnographers in the French Sudan—Delafosse, Monteil, and Labouret," *Cahiers d'études africaines* 30:118 (1990), 180–81. On the influence of ethnographic research on French colonial policy see also Ruth Ginio, "French Colonial Reading of Ethnographic Research—The Case of the 'Desertion' of the Abron King and Its Aftermath," *Cahiers d'études africaines* 42:166 (2002), 337–57.

19. For a short biography of Prouteaux see Sibeud, *Une science impériale*, 310–11. One of Prouteaux's key published articles is Maurice Prouteaux, "Notes sur certains rites magico-réligieux de la haute Côte d'Ivoire—Les Gbons," *L'Anthropologie* 29 (1918), 37–52.

20. Similar perceptions of witchcraft and cannibalism characterized the administrators who dealt with a series of crimes in the Diola region in Senegal around the same period. See Robert Baum, "Crimes of the Dream World: French Trials of Diola Witches in Colonial Senegal," *International Journal of African Historical Studies* 37:2 (2004), 201–28.

21. Jean Bodin (1530–96), a social and political philosopher of the renaissance, is best known for his chef-d'œuvre, *Six livres de la république*. In 1580 he also wrote *Démonomanie des sorciers*, in which he described witches

as Satan's agents. His treatment of the subject sparked a period of very intense witch hunts in France. On Bodin and on his book see Charlotte Wells, "Leeches on the Body Politic: Xenophobia and Witchcraft in Early Modern French Political Thought," *French Historical Studies* 22:3 (1999), 357–58. On Jean Bodin in general see George Holland Sabine, *A History of Political Theory*, 3rd ed. (New York: Holt, Rinehart and Winston, 1961), 399–414.

22. The term "Sabbath," like "Synagogue," was, of course, taken from the Jewish religion, which was traditionally regarded in Christian Europe as the quintessence of anti-Christianity, indeed as a form of devil worship. On "Sabbaths" and the witches' societies in fifteenth- to seventeenth-century Europe see Norman Cohn, *Europe's Inner Demons—An Enquiry Inspired by the Great Witch-Hunt* (New York: New York: New American Library, 1977), 99–125.

23. Archives Nationales (hereafter AN), Paris, 200mi/1238, M93/136, Tabou, 18 August 1918.

24. Carlo Ginzburg, *Ecstasies: Deciphering the Witches' Sabbath* (London: Hutchinson Radius, 1990), 1.

25. E. E. Evans-Pritchard, *Witchcraft, Oracles and Magic among the Azande* (Oxford: Clarendon Press, 1937), 1–32.

26. Robert M. Baum, "Crimes of the Dream World: French Trials of Diola Witches in Colonial Senegal," *International Journal of African Historical Studies* 37:2 (2004), 209.

27. Ginio, 'Negotiating Legal Authority," 118.

28. This dilemma did not characterize only the French colonial administration. Alan Booth shows how the British in Swaziland prosecuted people who accused others in witchcraft instead of prosecuting witches. Alan R. Booth, "'European Courts Protect Women and Witches': Colonial Courts as Redistributors of Power in Swaziland, 1920–1950," *Journal of Southern African Studies* 18:2 (1992), 253–75.

29. Bodin, who obviously greatly influenced Prouteaux's perspective on witchcraft, comments several times in his book on witches' appetite for human flesh; see Wells, "Leeches on the Body Politic," 357.

30. Baum, "Crimes of the Dream," 203.

31. Peter Hulme, "Introduction: The Cannibal Scene," in *Cannibalism and the Colonial World*, ed. Francis Barker, Peter Hulme, and Margaret Iversen (Cambridge: Cambridge University Press, 1998), 3–4.

32. Lévy-Bruhl, *Les Carnets*, 24–28.

33. An example of such a skeptical report is a colonial ethnographic study on "native paganism" from 1940. The author of the report (whose name is not noted) warns administrators about accepting at face value confessions to

cannibalistic acts. He explains that when a lamb was "witched" and transformed into a child and an African ate it, he might believe he had actually eaten a child. Centre des Archives d'Outre Mer (hereafter CAOM), Aix-en-Provence, 17/G92, 14mi/2304, 1940, "Le paganism indigène."

34. AN, 200mi/1238, M93/136, Tabou, 18 August 1918.

35. Baum, "Crimes of the Dream," 228.

36. AN, 200mi/1238, M93/136, Tabou, 18 August 1918.

37. AN, 200mi/1239, M96/66, Côte d'Ivoire, Cercle du Bas-Cavally, l'affaire Toubadé, June 1918. In this case a man was poisoned by two of his relatives. In the verdict the *commandant de cercle* insisted that this murder had no real motive but was committed only because it was the murderer's turn to offer one of his relatives as a victim. However, in the process of the inquiry one of the witnesses testified that the wife of one of the killers had had an affair with the victim. The commandant dismissed this testimony as immaterial.

38. AN, 200mi/1238 M93/136, 19 December 1917. After the lengthy report about the magical-religious rules of his circle, Prouteaux cites the protocol of the witnesses' investigations. One of the witnesses testified that the so-called ritual victim was actually murdered over a financial dispute regarding one of his wives. The *commandant* totally ignored this testimony, which was obviously too practical and boring to be integrated to his colorful description of African witchcraft.

39. CAOM, Aix-en-Provence, 17G/92, 14mi/2304, Guinée française, cercle de Conakry, "Rapport sur l' affaire de Dambi Bangoura et sept autres coupables de crimes rituels jugée par le tribunal de cercle de Conakry en son audience du 7 février 1922." In the Nigerian example of the leopard-men cases, as well as in other cases Pratten cites, the British investigators did not automatically deny the possibility of a "rational" motive for the murders, although they did consider "ritual" motives as well. See Pratten, *Man-Leopard Murder*, 6–7, 10.

40. CAOM, 17G/92, 14mi/2304, Guinée française, cercle de Conakry, "Rapport sur l' affaire de Dambi Bangoura."

41. According to Keith Thomas, who analyzed English seventeenth-century witchcraft in light of the work of social anthropologists in modern Africa, the main difference between continental and English witchcraft evolved around the question of motive. The religious issue of a pact with the devil was far more prevalent in continental Europe than in England. This form of diabolical witchcraft that harms people with no clear motive was rare in England, where witches always harmed people they knew and had a reason to resent; see Keith Thomas, "The Relevance of Social Anthropology to the Historical

Study of English Witchcraft," in *Witchcraft Confessions and Accusations*, ed. Mary Douglas (London: Tavistock, 1970), 49–50, 61.

42. AN, 200mi/1238, M93/136, 18 August, 1918.

43. CAOM, 17G/92, 14mi/2304, Guinée française, cercle de Conakry, 'Rapport sur l' affaire de Dambi Bangoura."

44. AN, 200mi/1241, M99/98, Tivaoune, 4 July 1911.

45. One has to bear in mind that there is some danger in relying too much on such transcripts because it is impossible to know whether the translation of the witnesses' declarations was accurate, especially with regard to terms such as "witch doctors" and "demons."

46. Baum, "Crimes of the Dream," 221.

47. CAOM, 17G/92, 14mi/2304, 26 juin 1936, Mission d' Etude de la pharmacopée indigène.

4

The Colonial Cosmology of Fernand Braudel

JOHN STRACHAN

The sunlight sinks over the golden buildings that tumble along the Malécon as it sweeps along the shoreline into La Habana Vieja. Sitting on the concrete wall, I stare out into the sea, towards Miami, thinking of the generations that have sailed into this harbor—the Spanish conquistadors, the shiploads of slaves from West Africa, British buccaneers arriving to capture the island in 1762, US troops arriving in 1898, US troops arriving in two thousand and . . . ? *Cette implacable blancheur*: wave after wave of white conquerors have rolled in on the surf, wanting this island, coveted object of imperial desire.

ROBERT J. C. YOUNG, "White Mythologies Revisited"

There exists an intimacy, as Robert Young points out, between empires, bodies of water, and the cyclical nature of history.[1] Throughout history imperial pretenders have risen and fallen, ebbed and flowed in time with the waves that carried them to their happy destinations. Of the many who have contemplated this tripartite relationship none was more eloquent than the French historian Fernand Braudel (1902–85). Mobilized, captured, and imprisoned in 1940, Braudel spent the war years in Germany, completing a project conceived in the 1920s and published as *The Mediterranean and the Mediterranean World in the Age of Philip II* in 1949.[2] This book, now considered his masterpiece, has enjoyed extensive influence in France and beyond, particularly among the Annales School of historians. Braudel's revolutionary approach to historical time is well documented and is discussed further below. What is less often remembered is that Braudel's *Mediterranean* was also, crucially, a work of imperial history, conceived in colonial Algeria and in the turbulent context of France's own imperial decline. The focus of this essay is the importance of this distinctively colonial genealogy of Braudelian and Annaliste thought.

Braudel's imperial imaginary has suffered from comparative neglect in the studies produced since his death.[3] The first and most obvious explanation for this lies in the structure of his text in which the sixteenth-century imperial machinations of Philip II of Spain occupy a relatively marginal place. A brief account of Braudel's methodology helps clarify this point and introduce the discussion that follows. The great innovation of the *Mediterranean* was to divide historical time into three—*longue*, *moyenne*, and *courte durées* (or what Braudel referred to as geographical, social, and individual time)—and to explore the relationship between these constituent parts. First and most important was the *longue durée*.[4] Here Braudel charts the history of humans' unequal relationship with their physical environment. Mountains, deserts, climate, and, of course, the Mediterranean Sea are the essential components in his *géohistoire*, setting the parameters for, and defining the possibilities of, human civilization and history. This *longue durée* moves slowly and cyclically.

Part two of the *Mediterranean* deals with "collective destinies and general trends." This is the *moyenne durée*—the history of economies, populations, and states—moving faster and more superficially, and always at the mercy of geographical considerations. Peter Burke has compared Braudel's rendering of the sixteenth-century Mediterranean to Edward Gibbon's classic account of ancient Rome—both empires operated within the constraints imposed upon them by geography; both were limited and doomed, ultimately, to a similar fate.[5] Finally, the *courte durée* of individual time is of least importance. Political and military events, championed as the essence of history in the work of Leopold von Ranke, appear as ephemera in the Braudelian cosmology.

The sea is both the subject of Braudel's *Mediterranean* and the most important actor in his drama. Changes in the *moyenne* and *courte durées* occur invariably within this framework and are seen to have little, if any, lasting impact upon geographical time. The sea is also a metaphor, in Braudel's imaginary, for the rhythm and the pace of history. The deep and unchanging Mediterranean is his *longue durée* personified. Change in the *moyenne durée* is described as the ebb and flow of tidal movement. Lastly events on the surface of things and of time stand for the flotsam and jetsam of history. Throughout the text, empires occupy the *moyenne* and *courte durées* and are condemned to all the frailties that such status demands. Least momentous of all are the wars and battles that fill the pages of conventional histories of empire. In terms of both its prose and its temporal arrangement, therefore, Braudel's *Mediterranean* may be seen to embody an implicitly negative, or perhaps dismissive, perspective on empire.

European Influences

There remains good cause, however, to caution against an exclusively colonial reading of Braudel's work. In many ways his historical methodology can be understood as part of the wider structuralist approach to the human sciences that dominated the academic world of twentieth-century France. Structuralism as a body of knowledge has its own complex set of genealogies.[6] In his *Le temps de l'histoire*, Philippe Ariès associates the maturation of French historiography in the twentieth century with historians' consciousness of, and implication in, the crises of European modernity. For Ariès, the founding fathers of the Annales School, Marc Bloch and Lucien Febvre, together with the Burgundian historian Gaston Roupnel, were at the heart of this developing *histoire existentielle*.[7] More broadly, the philosophical crisis of the *fin de siècle*, inaugurated by Nietzsche, had increasingly important implications for the role of time in historiography. At the beginning of the twentieth century, Henri Bergson played a crucial role in these developments. As one recent commentator suggests:

> [Bergson] proposes that discursive thought is itself a biological adaptation, one that overlays the real and gives the world to us in certain ways for pragmatic reasons. It presents an immobile world for us to master, projecting our thought through a grid of space, thrown out, Bergson says, like a net to collect and organize the

heterogeneous and dynamic real, so that we can better act upon it and take control of it.[8]

As Braudel was forming his historical ideas in the turbulent context of the interwar years, there emerged a growing intellectual reaction against the chaotic world of Nietzsche and Bergson. The lack of structures, or roots (as Simone Weil has it), in European thinking was held to have had profound effects on social cohesion and international relations. Looking back on the devastation wrought by the First World War, the German philosopher Eugen Rosenstock-Huessy lamented:

> such is the noble nature of man, that his heart will never wholly lose itself on one single passion or idol, or, as people call it apologetically, one idea. On it goes from one devotion to the next, not because it is ashamed of its first love, but because it must be on fire perpetually.[9]

A generation later, in the context of France's own *étrange défaite*, Bloch and Weil echoed Rosenstock-Huessy's sentiments. For these writers, ideological pessimism and short-termism were central to the Third Republic's weaknesses as a military power and cohesive society.[10] To this chorus were added the voices of numerous young scholars who saw in structuralism the opportunity to advance a new and more optimistic humanism. In his *Tristes Tropiques* Claude Lévi-Strauss explains his anthropological theory, in part, as a reaction against the dizzying uncertainties of Bergsonism.[11] And this context of uncertainty, defeat, and the desire for transcendence were no less important to Braudel as he was composing the *Mediterranean* in a German prisoner-of-war camp. In a rhythmic, cyclical, and structural understanding of history, Braudel found what he calls "a direct existential response to the tragic times I was passing through."[12]

If his structuralist influences were predominantly European in origin, Braudel was also working within an essentially European literary tradition.[13] His *longue durée* account of the Mediterranean, privileging as it does the role of geography in human activity, has important antecedents in the work of many historians, geographers, and novelists. The leading French historian of the nineteenth century, Jules Michelet, was a pioneer of the art of framing history within geography. His accounts of the French Revolution make much of the geographical context in which politics operates, always guiding the course of human actors in a nation that was slow to change in spite of its revolutionary infatuations.[14] And Michelet's work, more than that of any other historian, enjoyed a dramatic influence upon subsequent French historiography, particularly the work of the Annales School. Following Michelet, the historical geographers Paul Vidal de la Blache and André Siegfried would take up and develop this theme of framing human history within and, at times, subordinating it to its geographical setting.[15]

Turning to empire, European encounters with the exoticism of the East were commonly expressed in terms of geographical difference and wonder. One is reminded of E. M. Forster's bewitching description of the Marabar caves in his *Passage to India*. Without their dominant presence in the novel, all of the rest—friendships, marriages, imperial politics, race relations—are rendered hollow. There is also Camus' celebrated protagonist, Meursault, who is propelled into a fatal showdown with an Arab by the oppressive effects of the Algiers sun in *L'étranger*. For Forster and Camus, as for Braudel, geography structures, enables, and dominates.[16]

Even more striking convergences with the *Mediterranean* are to be found in the work of Roupnel, especially in his theoretical essay *Histoire et destin*, which Braudel later described as "that delirious, prophetic book, half lost in a world of dreams, but borne up by a wealth of compassion for the 'sorrows of men.'"[17] Roupnel corresponded with Braudel, although the strength of the relationship between the two men seems to have been played down in the context of postwar sensitivities to do with Roupnel's perceived proximity to the Vichy empire.[18] Nonetheless, the structural similarities between *Histoire et destin* and the *Mediterranean*, two works that were written almost simultaneously, are remarkable. Braudel and Roupnel share a tripartite conceptualization of historical time, and both use oceanic metaphors to describe the unimportance of events in comparison to the profound currents of history. At the beginning of a chapter entitled "Le rythme historique" Roupnel writes:

History now appears as a three-tiered structure. The more solid and deep-rooted elements are at the base. The least significant, and most fleeting, float on the surface.[19]

A final and major concern is Braudel's immense intellectual debt to Febvre. More explicitly influential than Roupnel, Febvre cofounded the Annales movement in 1929 and acted as mentor to Braudel from their definitive encounter in 1937 until the former's death in 1956. As editor of the Annales and an established and highly regarded academic, Febvre furthered Braudel's career in several ways. He spoke warmly of the *Mediterranean*, which, after all, was dedicated to him by Braudel *with affection*.[20] Together with a number of other leading historians like Henri Pirenne, Febvre can be seen as the gateway to a Paris-centered intellectual milieu that was arguably the single biggest influence on a young Braudel.

Febvre's influence, moreover, offered seemingly little to Braudel in terms of thinking critically about the relationship between empire and history. A 1932 article on the recently held Exposition coloniale at Vincennes showed Febvre's inability, or lack of desire, to challenge France's imperial status quo. As Jonathan Dewald observes, Febvre overlooked the left-wing anti-Exposition manifesto written by André Breton, Louis Aragon, and others and displayed a general insensitivity: "[He] did not praise colonialism, but he did not take seriously the ethnic, economic and cultural assumptions behind it."[21] Dewald's criticisms of Febvre hold some force, especially if they are compared to the insouciance that Braudel admitted in regard to his own view of colonialism:

> I believe that this spectacle, the Mediterranean as seen from the opposite shore, upside down had considerable impact on my vision of history. But the change in my viewpoint was slow. At any rate, at that point in my life I did not understand the colonial drama, which was, nevertheless, right before my eyes . . . in 1923, in 1926, and in the years which followed, French Algeria did not appear as a monster to my eyes. Some day perhaps a *pied noir* settler will write a book like *Gone with the Wind* about those lost years. At any rate, I did not personally feel any twinges of conscience. The bad conscience would be there twenty years later.[22]

It should be remembered that many of Braudel's seemingly European influences were tinged with aspects of this unfolding colonial drama. Roupnel's, for instance, was a vision steeped in the conflict between center and periphery that dominated the Third Republic—a conflict that has often been described in terms of the imperial ambitions of the nation-state.[23] Returning to Braudel's relationship with Febvre, their definitive encounter took place on a return journey from Brazil, an experience that was every bit as important for Braudel as it was for Lévi-Strauss. Braudel famously remarked that it was on a night in Bahia, watching the passing glow of the fireflies, that he realized the ephemeral nature of historical events.[24] Just as we are learning new and unexpected things about the development of the early Annales School, Braudel's formative years now appear equally complex.[25] Paris, Febvre, and the wider world of the Annales were undoubtedly an important part of the story. But so, too, was the imperial context and Braudel's many travels beyond the borders of *l'hexagone*. As Omar Carlier has stated:

> The quality of the work, as well as the character of the man, owe much to an experience that was simultaneously affective and effective, inseparably physical and intellectual, and dependent upon a sustained period of separation from both his mother country and the Parisian academic world.[26]

Empire and the Writing of History

The remainder of this essay addresses the North African origins of Braudel's *Mediterranean* and seeks to reposition his work in terms of the crucial relationship between empire and the writing of history. With this context firmly in mind, Braudel's Algerian *séjour* (1923–32) is considered in relation to the life and work of another major French historian of empire, Charles-André Julien (1891–1991). Julien is an important if underestimated figure in the history of French anticolonialism.[27] His groundbreaking work, *Histoire de l'Afrique du Nord*, displays a number of structural similarities to the *Mediterranean* and holds the key, I argue, to the important and unexpected colonial genealogies of Braudel's *longue durée* vision.[28]

For more than forty years, postcolonial critics have sought to understand historiography as an integral component of the process of colonization. Especially in the nineteenth century, historians portrayed space and time in such a way as to assert, justify, and legitimize imperial conquest. And historiography collaborated in the grand project of Orientalism insofar as it helped to construct categories of civilization, Self, and Other on which European empires depended for their epistemological and political integrity.[29] Appropriating the raw material of the colonized space was a task well suited to the historian. The French polymath Michel de Certeau sums this up neatly in the opening gambit of his *L'écriture de l'histoire*. Evoking the mythological moment of first contact with an alien civilization, Certeau writes:

> Amerigo Vespucci the voyager arrives from the sea. A crusader standing erect, his body in armor, he bears the European weapons of meaning. Behind him are the vessels that will bring back to the European West the spoils of a paradise. Before him is the Indian "America," a nude woman reclining in her hammock, an unnamed presence of difference, a body which awakens within a space of exotic fauna and flora . . . An inaugural scene: after a moment of stupor, on this threshold dotted with colonnades of trees, the conqueror will write the body of the other and trace there his own history. From her he will make a historized body—a blazon—of his labors and phantasms. She will be "Latin" America.[30]

Reflecting on her adolescence in colonial Algeria, the poststructuralist feminist critic Hélène Cixous makes a closely related point about the polarizing function of history as it relates to empire and race:

> I learned everything from this first spectacle: I saw how the white (French), superior, plutocratic, civilized world founded its power on the repression of populations who had suddenly become "invisible," like proletarians, immigrant workers, minorities, who are not the right "color." Women. Invisible as humans. But, of course, perceived as tools—dirty, stupid, lazy, underhanded, etc. Thanks to some annihilating dialectical magic. I saw that the great, noble,

"advanced" countries established themselves by expelling what was "strange"; excluding it but not dismissing it; enslaving it. A commonplace gesture of History: there have to be *two* races—the masters and the slaves.[31]

The reference to Cixous is taken from the opening pages of Robert Young's *White Mythologies: Writing History and the West.* Young describes how colonial Algeria played a fundamental role in the genealogy of poststructuralism and, more broadly, in the formative experiences of an entire generation of French intellectuals who were personally involved either by birth or by engagement in the Algerian War of Independence and the crises of France's decolonization.[32] Intellectuals who cut their polemical teeth in the context of late- or postcolonial Algeria included Albert Camus, Jean-Paul Sartre, Raymond Aron, Pierre Bourdieu, Louis Althusser, Jean-François Lyotard, and Pierre Nora. Julien and Braudel can equally be considered a part of this Franco-Algerian intellectual trajectory.

If the relationship between empire and the writing of history is firmly established, the potential for European historiographies to serve as forces of decolonization and postcolonial thinking is less remarked upon. The traditional histories and genealogies of postcolonialism have tended to focus on the work of a colonized elite, "writing back" against the hegemonic pretensions of Western culture.[33] In the late 1930s Aimé Césaire's *Cahier d'un retour au pays natal* and C. L. R. James's classic account of the Haitian Revolution, *The Black Jacobins*, were important, if very different, developments in the early history of postcolonialism's writing back against the West.[34] Julien and Braudel represent what might be considered an alternative genealogy of postcolonial thought, contemporary and in many ways related to the work of Césaire and James. In the colonial Algeria of the 1930s, anticolonial and increasingly postcolonial ideas were also starting to emerge in the writings of a European colonial elite. These developments were crucial to the formation of Braudel's *Mediterranean*.

The Algerian Séjour

A young Braudel left metropolitan France in 1923, having secured appointment to the French lycée in the city of Constantine in eastern Algeria. In 1924 he moved to Algiers, teaching and researching throughout the Mediterranean basin until his definitive return to Paris in 1932. It was in Algeria that Braudel met his future wife and lifelong research assistant, Paule Pradel. Whatever importance one attaches to his later Brazilian *séjour* (1935–37) and to the influence of the Paris-based Annalistes, the experience of Algeria was clearly revelatory in terms of Braudel's historical cosmology. He soon began to lose interest in the political and military history of sixteenth-century Spain that had been the original subject of his doctoral thesis in 1927. Slowly and fittingly, a new kind of historical vision began to emerge, one that owed much to the nexus of imperial history and lived colonial experience. The following year Braudel published an almost book-length article on his early research in the *Revue Africaine*.[35] In this piece, as Burke observes, there were already signs that Braudel was moving away from traditional event-centered history:

> a critique of his predecessors in the field for their overemphasis on battles and great men, a discussion of the "daily life" of the Spanish garrisons, and a demonstration of the close (if inverse) relation between African and European history. When war broke out in Europe, the African campaigns were halted, and vice versa.[36]

In 1929 Braudel wrote a long letter to his supervisors in Paris in support of his application for a research bursary. He detailed the extensive work he had already conducted in the Spanish State Archives in Simancas. Here, too, Braudel revealed an understanding that the documents he was using were part of a much broader, deeper history.[37] Later he would write of this period:

> Little by little, I grew more doubtful about the subject of my labors. Philip II the Prudent, the Sad, attracted me less and less, and the Mediterranean more and more. In 1931, Henri Pirenne spoke at Algiers about his ideas on the closure of the Mediterranean after the Moslem invasions. His lectures seemed prodigious to me; his hand opened and shut, and the entire Mediterranean was by turns free and locked in! It was during these years, between 1927 and

1933, when I lived in the archives without hurrying to choose my subject—that my decision ripened of its own accord. And so I chose the Mediterranean.[38]

The link to Pirenne was critical. Pirenne's *Mohammed and Charlemagne* had conceived of the Mediterranean as a site (and a means) of cultural exchange that persisted in this timeless role in spite of the ebb and flow of subsequent human civilizations.[39] The now-famous structure of Braudel's *Mediterranean* owed much to Pirenne's worldview. Febvre summarized this neatly:

> The book is a manifesto, a sign . . . a milestone. . . . The Mediterranean and the Mediterranean World in the Age of Philip II (two characters of unequal importance and the fact that the second does not take precedence over the first represents a great innovation).[40]

But Braudel's perspective was also closely related to the intellectual milieu of the Algiers of the 1920s and early 1930s in which his ideas coalesced. He was among a group of young scholars, working in Rabat and Algiers, that Henri Hauser referred to in 1932 as "an outstanding school of historians, already full of promise."[41] The preface to the original edition of the *Mediterranean* lists the author's intellectual debts to this Algerian milieu—Georges Yver and Gabriel Esquer, respectively of the University of Algiers and the Bibliothèque nationale d'Alger—together with the influential historical geographer Émile-Félix Gautier and Julien.[42]

Braudel met Julien for the first time in 1930, the year of the centenary celebrations of French Algeria. The centenary (together with the Exposition coloniale) served as an important site in the celebration, dissemination, and contestation of the mythology of France as an imperial power. Together, the centenary and the Exposition coloniale were meant to mark the apogee of French imperialism.[43] In Algeria, vast amounts were paid to popularize the celebrations through cinema, radio, books, and the press; banknotes, postcards, stamps, and medals carried the reality and symbolism of the centenary into the minutiae of everyday life.

On the surface of things, the centenary and the Exposition coloniale can be seen as uncomplicated expressions of a civilizing mission that had changed little in its ideology and means of operation since 1870. The organizers of the Exposition stressed France's commitment to health and education in the colonies, and emphasized familiar themes of progress, morality, and national identity.[44] For Raoul Girardet (a rather sympathetic observer, it should be noted), the centenary and Exposition became deeply embedded in the national (and colonial) consciousness, marking the apotheosis of the French empire:

> A quite extraordinary encounter of form, image and color, the vividness of which lives on in the memory of a whole generation of Frenchmen. The majestic vision of the Angkhor Temple, accurately reconstructed, the water-mirrors of the Moroccan Palace, the imposing red mass of the Sudanese Mosque, the twisting lanes of the Tunisian *souk*, the high tower of the Madagascan Pavilion, topped off with sculptures of animal skulls. Moorish camel-herders, Annamite embroiderers, Congolese canoe-makers, Berber weavers ... their juxtaposition under the skies of the *Île de France* marked an important moment in the history of modern France: that of its colonial apotheosis.[45]

Imperial historiography before 1930 echoed several motifs of the centenary and the Exposition. Certeau's critique of the relationship of history to colonization is borne out by works like Camille Rousset's *La Conquête d'Alger* that emphasized themes of civilization and transformation. Here the Algerian Other is at once defined and transformed by the actions of the colonizer:

> M. de Bourmant [first commander of the Armée d'Afrique] would have no sweeter memory than the sight of the Casbah, where he had had the honor of planting the first marker of French and Christian civilization in a Muslim and Berber land.[46]

The study of history in Algiers was dominated by an ethnocentric, Latinist perspective on the Mediterranean and the history of empire. Fluid boundaries between ancient and modern were later critical to the thinking of Julien and Braudel. In this earlier period, however, they were deployed to legitimize imperial conquest. The conceptual link between Roman and French settlement in North Africa was emphasized and served to bestow the French presence with a strong sense of historical inevitability.[47] The study of archaeology, popular in colonial Algeria, allowed the French to reiterate the Roman (and therefore European antecedents) of modern-day empire and to make what Edward Said calls "severe and ontologically prior claims" to the land.[48] Said takes the argument further in an essay on Freud and the paradoxes of Jewish identity, stressing the function of archaeology as a means of overcoming strangeness and dislocation by re-inscribing Israeli settlement of the West Bank within a European historical tradition.[49]

In the years prior to the publication of Julien's *Histoire de l'Afrique du Nord*, this celebratory and revivalist paradigm of imperial history began to be challenged by the writings of current and former members of the colonial elite. In many ways, these writers both anticipated the campaign of Breton and Aragon at Vincennes and laid the groundwork for Julien's own assault on colonialism. Jean Mélia, president of the Commission du centenaire that oversaw the centenary and one-time *chef de cabinet* to the governor-general of Algeria, complained that metropolitan journalists covering the centenary were some distance from the realities of the colonial world.[50] Mélia clearly saw the highly publicized centenary as an opportunity to restate his own liberal approach to empire that was now growing in popularity. He was heavily involved in Louis Massignon's efforts to secure electoral reforms in favor of indigenous Algerians—efforts that echoed Mélia's own concerns as expressed in his *La France et l'Algérie*.[51] In this text Mélia looked forward to political reforms as a continuation of the extension of French citizenship that had included the abolition of slavery, the Crémieux decree, and the naturalization of non-French European Algerians in 1889. By 1930, eleven years after Mélia wrote, the failures of assimilation were becoming all too evident for the liberals. Former governor-general Maurice Viollette wrote of his hope that France's charitable intentions toward indigenous Algeria would now take the form of republican solidarity and citizenship. The alternative, he argued, would be the increasingly untenable position of France in Algeria. Mélia himself appears to have given up hope of such a *rapprochement* in his *Le triste sort des indigènes musulmans d'Algérie*.[52] Thus, the centenary served as a battleground for the reworking of conflicts over assimilation and association and the legitimacy of France's continued presence in North Africa.

Already an established historian, and Braudel's elder by eleven years, Julien entered the historical and colonial debate forcefully with the 1931 publication of his *Histoire de l'Afrique du Nord*. Born in Caen in 1891, Julien was the son of a Dreyfusard *instituteur* whose work took him to Algeria around 1906. Julien attended lycée in Oran and went on to the increasingly important University of Algiers, studying under Jérôme Carcopino and Gautier.[53] From an early age, Julien combined scholarly enthusiasm with radical political persuasions. André Nouschi underscores Julien's contribution to *l'Algérie coloniale* in July 1914, at the age of twenty-three, as of a symbiosis between "the careful, objective historian and the militant."[54] Julien became highly active in the Ligue des droits de l'homme and the French Socialist Party.[55] His encounters in the 1920s included meetings with Lenin, Trotsky, and Ho Chi Minh. On his return to Algeria from Moscow in the summer of 1921, Julien was singled out by the colonial authorities' counter-espionage services. The Commissaire spécial d'Annemasse offered this (probably not exaggerated) account of his activities:

> Charles-André Julien has been entrusted with the dissemination of communist propaganda in the colonies. Julien has received total authority in North Africa to act and liaise with Spanish, Arabic, Italian and Egyptian communists.[56]

Elected *conseiller général* in Oran in 1921, Julien maintained both historical and political interests. He went on to become the leading North Africanist of his generation and editorial secretary of the *Revue historique*, and he published a number of significant works of colonial history.[57] In 1937 Léon Blum appointed him general secretary of the Haut comité méditerranéen, the recently created governmental advisory committee on North African and Middle Eastern affairs.

Magali Morsy describes Julien's life as "one long j'accuse," referring to him as the "Zola of decolonization."[58] The contrast with Braudel's low-key approach to the politics of empire is striking. In historiographical terms, however, Julien's writing anticipated many of the themes of the *Mediterranean*. Julien's thesis for the *licence* was a study of the 1830 conquest of Algeria. He published a series of articles and short works in the 1920s that dealt with various aspects of the conquest, particularly the role of the anticolonial opposition in France. Julien's studies of the early *colons* described the group as immoral speculators amid the chaos that was the early years of colonization. France had no consistent aim or policy in North Africa, he argued, and was pursuing a quixotic delusion to its inevitable conclusion.[59] Clearly, in his writings of the 1920s Julien was attempting to situate his own ideas within an established anticolonial tradition. Toward the end of *Histoire de l'Afrique du Nord* he remarks of the colonization of Algiers:

> A shady affair led by Jewish merchants in Algiers, acting in complicity with dishonored politicians in Paris; an incident provoked by a suspect diplomat; an expedition conducted with mediocrity by a discredited general; a victory treated with indifference by public opinion and followed by the fall of the dynasty which supported it—these were the inauspicious beginnings of the French conquest of North Africa.[60]

The publication of *Histoire de l'Afrique du Nord* marked a tipping point in colonial historiography. Most observers read Julien's text as a damning indictment of French practices. Contemporary reviews confirm the (sometimes baffling) originality of the argument. Reviewing Julien for the *Revue historique,* Hauser felt compelled to warn readers of the author's evident anger over dark episodes of colonial history such as the *Affaire des Grottes* (where French troops had "smoked out" Algerian combatants from caves used as hiding places).[61] Although Hauser applauded Julien's honesty, the tone of his comments reveals the extent to which *Histoire de l'Afrique du Nord* would challenge established sensibilities. For Hauser, the errors of the *colons* should not detract from France's contribution in North Africa to the progress of "Mediterranean humanity":

French peace, French justice—these are the values that have been introduced by the conqueror in North Africa—even if that justice has too often been rudimentary and unequal, even if the spread of education has been too sparing, even if an inadequate number of doctors have done still too little to tackle endemic Mediterranean diseases.[62]

Hauser felt that *Histoire de l'Afrique du Nord* should have been written with more "serenity."[63] Braudel would broadly agree with this judgment in the long review that he wrote for the *Revue Africaine* in 1933, arguing, somewhat disingenuously, that "French achievements, in North Africa, are not discredited in the text."[64] Julien's political agenda in writing *Histoire de l'Afrique du Nord* was (perhaps uncomfortably) unambiguous. He had cast himself in direct opposition to those historians who saw the centenary as an opportunity to celebrate empire. Some reviewers applauded the author's effective combination of professional and objective historiography with political militancy. Stéphane Gsell observed this in the short preface that he wrote for the book, and as we have seen, Nouschi suggests that a continual symbiosis of the two was at the core of Julien's being.[65] In an observation that could have anticipated the split between Albert Camus and Jean-Paul Sartre, an American reviewer remarked on Julien's almost native authenticity as a clear advantage over detached metropolitan academics.[66]

More important than the fact of Julien's anticolonialism was the way in which he structured the text so as to arrive at an inevitably anticolonial conclusion.[67] *Histoire de l'Afrique du Nord* begins with a consideration of the geography of the Maghreb that draws heavily on the work of Gautier. Julien then proceeds to discuss cultures, civilizations, and economic formations. Though these factors (and the relations between them) are not as developed as they are in the *Mediterranean*, Julien nonetheless displays a spatial and temporal understanding of history that is close to Braudel's. Gsell noted that Julien had been the first to write a history of the Maghreb as a single geographical entity.[68] And Hauser went on to explore the author's reasons for abandoning the traditional history of the nation-state, attributing these to illusory divisions, introduced into geography by history and sustained by politics and administrative routine, but which correspond very imperfectly to the realities of the past, and which will be swept away, no doubt, by the tide of history.[69]

Though Julien's work is not a perfect fit with the Braudelian mould of *milieu-conjoncture-événement*, his temporal working of North Africa seems especially close to early Annaliste thinking. Gsell applauded the ways in which *Histoire de l'Afrique du Nord* embraced interdisciplinary approaches, welding prehistory, ethnography, religion, archaeology, and more in a tour de force through three millennia of the Maghreb's history.[70] Some reviewers were left puzzled by the amount of time that the author devoted to climate, soil, topography, and natural resources.[71]

A holistic and interdisciplinary approach to the history of the Maghreb was not strikingly original in itself. But in Julien's case the consideration of geographies and economies is followed, in the last two hundred pages of the text, by a sustained indictment of empire. Latinist historiography had sought to establish a conceptual bridge between Roman and French occupation of North Africa. Julien makes a similar point but now inverts the purpose of the comparison. In his view North African history could best be represented as a succession of failed colonizations—Romans, Vandals, Almoravids, Almohads, Turks, the French—all attempting (and failing) to establish great civilizations. At its core, Julien suggests, North Africa was a Berber land. Repeated colonization had left little, if any, lasting impact on the natural environment, nor on the underlying structures of Berber civilization, the resilience of which Julien defined in the following terms:

> An historical singularity in which Arab Islam and French or, rather, Franco-Mediterranean civilization have grafted themselves onto the old, Berber trunk.[72]

Like Braudel's *Mediterranean*, Julien's *Histoire de l'Afrique du Nord* unfolds rhythmically. Imperial pretenders rise and fall. Situated at the very end of the text, "French" North Africa appears weak and transitory. Julien then asks a rhetorical question:

Should we not conclude from these failed attempts at colonization that they were bound to fail and, that being the case, are we not led to condemn all foreign occupation on the grounds that it, like its forebears, is destined to lead to catastrophe?[73]

Ultimately, Julien condemns France's shortcomings in Algeria in precisely the same terms as Braudel condemns Philip II. Both historians use a form of the *longue durée* to situate their human subjects on what Braudel called the "third level" of history. If Braudel's acknowledgment of Julien was not as explicit and generous as we might expect, this was at least partly the result of what Carlier identifies as an element of "personal rivalry" between the two men in the context of the opportunities provided to Algerian men of letters by the centenary celebrations of 1930.[74]

Subsequent editions of *Histoire de l'Afrique du Nord* were reprinted without the final, critical section dealing with the French period.[75] Whether or not Julien was invited to revise and update his text in the 1950s or 1960s remains unclear (although he did publish a major history of early colonial Algeria with Presses Universitaires de France in 1964[76]). In 1931, however, Julien had deployed his own embryonic version of the *longue durée* as a means of challenging the legitimacy and the conceptual underpinnings of the French presence. This radical and overtly anticolonial perspective was deeply problematic in the political and imperial context of 1931. Braudel's *Mediterranean* was, of course, fundamentally different from Julien's work. The tripartite division of the text represented an innovation, and probably a conceptual improvement, on what Julien had achieved. Nonetheless, Braudel's spatial and temporal cosmology together with his holistic and interdisciplinary approaches to the Mediterranean represented a revisiting and reworking of Julien's own themes in the far less politically problematic context of the sixteenth century.

European structuralists embraced aspects of the *longue durée* as an escape from the political and philosophical uncertainties of the *fin de siècle*. Structures provided a means of controlling, and making sense of, the enigmatic relationship between time and history. Julien's own *longue durée* was also envisaged as a means of escaping the chaos and injustice of the colonial world, and had the immediate political purpose of imagining and theorizing the end of empire.[77] Braudel, though not entirely immune from contemporary political developments, did not share Julien's overt and confrontational brand of political activism. It remains difficult, therefore, to make a firm and consistent case for Braudel's implicit anticolonialism on the evidence of his lack of direct engagement with contemporary colonial affairs. But as Braudel himself implies in his autobiographical essay in the *Journal of Modern History*, the *Mediterranean* can be seen both as historical escapism from the political uncertainties of twentieth-century Europe *and* as cathartic return to his own Algerian *séjour* of the 1920s and 1930s. Though the European context is perhaps more immediate (and certainly better documented), the *Mediterranean* reveals its colonial genealogies in subtle and understated ways. Braudel the *bricoleur* appropriated and adapted elements of Julien's structure for the purposes of his own historical cosmology. In doing so he established the *longue durée* at the heart of modern historiography but obscured the colonial and Algerian context that is a significant part of its history.

Notes

All translations are by the author unless indicated otherwise. The author thanks audiences at the Universities of Exeter, Leeds, and St. Andrews for their comments on early versions of this essay, parts of which appeared in the final chapter of "Reshaping the Mythologies of Frenchness: Culture, History and Identity in European Algeria, 1870–1930," unpublished PhD dissertation, University of Manchester, 2006.

1. Robert J. C. Young, *White Mythologies: Writing History and the West* (1990; 2nd ed., London: Routledge, 2004), 1.

2. Fernand Braudel, *La méditerranée et le monde méditerranéen à l'époque de Philippe II* (Paris: Armand Colin, 1949); English trans., *The Mediterranean and the Mediterranean World in the Age of Philip II*, trans. Sian Reynolds (London: Collins, 1972).

3. The literature on Braudel is extensive. Many of the best articles are collected in Jacques Revel, ed., *Fernand Braudel et l'histoire* (Paris: Hachette, 1999); Stuart Clark, ed., *The Annales School: Critical Assessments* (London: Routledge, 1999). See also Cheng-Chung Lai, *Braudel's Historiography Reconsidered* (Lanham MD: University Press of America, 2004). On his formative experiences and Algerian *séjour*, see Pierre Daix, *Braudel* (Paris: Flam-

marion, 1995); Erato Paris, *La genèse intellectuelle de l'œuvre de Fernand Braudel: La méditerranée et le monde méditerranéen à l'époque de Philippe II (1923–1947)* (Athens: Institut de recherches néohelléniques, 1999); Omar Carlier, "Braudel avant Braudel? Les années algériennes (1923–1932)," *Insaniyat* 19–20 (2003); Fernand Braudel, "Personal Testimony," *Journal of Modern History* 44:4 (1972), 448–67; Braudel, *Autour de la Méditerranée*, ed. Roselyne de Ayala and Paule Braudel, (Paris: Éditions de Fallois, 1996); Paule Braudel, "La genèse de *La Mediterranée* de Fernand Braudel," in *Rencontres intellectuelles franco-hongroises: Regards croisés sur l'histoire et la littérature*, ed. Péter Sahin-Tóth (Budapest: Collegium Budapest, Institute for Advanced Study, 2001). A wider treatment of the influences of empire on the Annales School has recently been offered by Carole Reynaud Paligot, "Les *Annales* de Lucien Febvre à Fernand Braudel: Entre épopée coloniale et opposition Orient/Occident," *French Historical Studies* 32:1 (2009), 121–44.

4. Braudel expanded upon his theory of the *longue durée* in "Histoire et sciences sociales: La longue durée," *Annales E. S. C.* 4 (October–December 1958), 725–53.

5. Peter Burke, *The French Historical Revolution: The Annales School, 1929–89* (London: Polity, 1990), 35.

6. See especially François Dosse, *Histoire du structuralisme*, vol. 1: *Le champ du signe* (Paris: Éditions la Découverte, 1991), and vol. 2: *Le chant du cygne* (Paris: Éditions la Découverte, 1992).

7. Philippe Ariès, *Le temps de l'histoire* (Monaco: Éditions du Rocher, 1954), 291–311.

8. Suzanne Guerlac, *Thinking in Time: An Introduction to Henri Bergson* (Ithaca NY: Cornell University Press, 2006), 2.

9. Eugen Rosenstock-Huessy, *Out of Revolution: Autobiography of Western Man* (1931; reprint, Oxford: Berg, 1993), 4.

10. Marc Bloch, *L'étrange défaite: Témoignage écrit en 1940* (Paris: Éditions Franc-Tireur, 1946); S. Weil, *L'énracinement: Prélude à une declaration des devoirs envers l'être humain* (Paris: Gallimard, 1949).

11. Claude Lévi-Strauss, *Tristes Tropiques* (Paris: Plon, 1955), 60.

12. Braudel, "Personal Testimony," 454.

13. For an interesting take on Braudel's eurocentrism, see Jack Goody, *The Theft of History* (Cambridge: Cambridge University Press, 2006), 180–211.

14. See especially Arthur Mitzman, *Michelet Historian: Rebirth and Romanticism in Nineteenth Century France* (New Haven CT: Yale University Press, 1990); John Strachan, "Romance, Religion and the Republic: Bruno's *Le tour de la France par deux enfants*," *French History* 18:1 (2004), 96–118.

15. See especially Paul Vidal de la Blache, *Tableau de la géographie de*

la France (Paris: Hachette, 1903); André Siegfried, *Tableau politique de la France de l'ouest sous la troisième république* (Paris: Armand Colin, 1913).

16. E. M. Forster, *A Passage to India* (London: E. Arnold, 1924).

17. Gaston Roupnel, *Histoire et destin* (Paris: Grasset, 1943); Fernand Braudel, *On History*, trans. Sarah Matthews (Chicago: University of Chicago Press, 1980), 7.

18. Philippe Poirrier, "L'oubli historiographique: La postérité historienne d'*Histoire et destin* de Gaston Roupnel," in *Le temps des sciences humaines: Gaston Roupnel et les années trente*, ed. Annie Bleton-Ruget and Philippe Poirrier (Paris: Éditions le Manuscrit-Maison des sciences de l'homme de Dijon, 2006), 237–56.

19. Roupnel, *Histoire et destin*, 321–22. All translations are by the author unless otherwise noted.

20. Lucien Febvre, *A New Kind of History: From the Writings of Lucien Febvre*, trans. K. Folca, ed. Peter Burke (London: Routledge and Kegan, 1973), 27–43.

21. Lucien Febvre, "L'histoire économique et la vie: Leçon d'une exposition," *Annales d'histoire économique et sociale* 13:1 (1932), 1–10; J. Dewald, *Lost Worlds: The Emergence of French Social History, 1815–1970* (University Park PA: Pennsylvania State University Press, 2006), 116–17.

22. Braudel, "Personal Testimony," 450–51.

23. The classic statement is Eugen Weber, *Peasants into Frenchmen: The Modernization of Rural France, 1870–1914* (Palo Alto CA: Stanford University Press, 1976), especially 485–96. For a recent take on the importance of empire in defining and redefining the republican nation-state see Gary Wilder, *The French Imperial Nation-State: Negritude and Colonial Humanism between the Two World Wars* (Chicago: University of Chicago Press, 2005).

24. Braudel, *On History*, 10–11; Lévi-Strauss, *Tristes Tropiques*. On their intellectual encounters with Brazil see Thomas Skidmore, "Lévi-Strauss, Braudel and Brazil: A Case of Mutual Influence," *Bulletin of Latin American Research* 22:3 (2003), 340–49.

25. Our understanding of Febvre's role in the development of the *Annales* has been enriched by Peter Schöttler, "Lucie Varga: A Central European Refugee in the Circle of the French 'Annales,' 1934–1941," *History Workshop Journal* 33:1 (1992), 100–120; Natalie Zemon Davis, "Women and the World of the *Annales*," *History Workshop Journal* 33:1 (1992), 121–37.

26. O. Carlier, "Braudel avant Braudel? Les années algériennes (1923–1932)," *Insaniyat* 19–20 (2003), 143.

27. A good collection of his explicitly anticolonial writings is Charles-André Julien, *Une pensée anticoloniale: Positions 1914–1979*, ed. Magali

Morsy (Paris: Sindbad, 1979). More recently, see Claude Liauzu, *Histoire de l'anticolonialisme en France du XVIe siècle à nos jours* (Paris: Armand Colin, 2007). Julien receives a brief mention in Edward Said's *Culture and Imperialism* (London; Chatto and Windus), 224–25.

28. Charles-André Julien, *Histoire de l'Afrique du Nord: Tunisie, Algérie, Maroc* (Paris: Payot, 1931).

29. The classic work is Edward Said, *Orientalism: Western Perceptions of the Orient* (1978; reprint, London: Penguin, 1995).

30. Michel de Certeau, *The Writing of History*, trans. Tom Conley (1975; reprint, New York: Columbia University Press, 1988), xxv.

31. Hélène Cixous and Catherine Clément, *The Newly Born Woman*, trans. Betsy Wing (Manchester: Manchester University Press, 1986), 70, cited in Young, *White Mythologies*, 32.

32. Young, *White Mythologies*, 32.

33. James Clifford makes this point, citing Michel Leiris, in "Orientalism," *History and Theory* 19:2 (1980), 204.

34. Aimé Césaire, *Cahier d'un retour au pays natal* (1939; reprint, Paris: Présence Africaine, 1960); C. L. R. James, *The Black Jacobins: Toussaint Louverture and the San Domingo Revolution* (London: Secker and Warburg, 1938).

35. Braudel, "Les Espagnols et l'Afrique du Nord de 1492 à 1577" (1928), in Braudel, *Autour de la Méditerranée*, 47–124.

36. Burke, *French Historical Revolution*, 32.

37. Braudel, "Premières recherches," in *Autour de la Méditerranée*, 23–43.

38. Braudel, "Personal Testimony," 452.

39. Henri Pirenne, *Mahomet et Charlemagne* (Paris: Alcan, 1937).

40. Febvre, *New Kind of History*, 37–38.

41. Henri Hauser, "Ch.-André Julien: Histoire de l'Afrique du Nord (Tunisie-Algérie-Maroc)," *Revue Historique* 169 (1932), 666.

42. Braudel, *La méditerranée*, 19.

43. On the centenary see Catherine Coquery-Vidrovitch, "L'Apogee: L'exposition coloniale internationale," in *Histoire de la France coloniale, 1914–1990*, ed. Jacques Thobie, Gilbert Meynier, Catherine Coquery-Vidrovitch, and Charles-Robert Ageron, 2 vols. (Paris: Armand Colin, 1990); Charles-Robert Ageron, "L'Exposition coloniale de 1931: Mythe républicain ou mythe impérial?" in *Les lieux de mémoire*, vol. 1: *La République*, ed. Pierre Nora (1984; reprint, Paris: Gallimard, 1997); Emmanuelle Sibeud, "Le centenaire raté de l'Algérie française," in *L'Algérie des français*, ed. Charles-Robert Ageron (Paris: Éditions du Seuil, 1993). On the Exposition coloniale see Patricia Morton, *Hybrid Modernities: Architecture and Representation at the 1931 Colonial Exposition, Paris* (Boston: MIT Press, 2000); Catherine

Hodeir, "Une journée à l'exposition coloniale internationale," *L'Histoire* 69 (July 1984), 41–48; Herman Lebovics, *True France: The Wars over Cultural Identity, 1900–1945* (Ithaca NY: Cornell University Press, 1992), 98–134.

44. Coquery-Vidrovitch, "L'Apogee: L'exposition coloniale internationale," 215–17.

45. Raoul Girardet, *L'idée coloniale en France de 1871 à 1962* (1972; reprint, Paris: Hachette, 2005), 175–76.

46. Rousset, *La Conquête d'Alger* (Paris: Plon, 1880), 272.

47. On the importance and uses of latinity see Patricia Lorcin, "Rome and France in Africa: Recovering Colonial Algeria's Latin Past," *French Historical Studies* 25:2 (2002), 295–329. For a literary perspective see Peter Dunwoodie, *Writing French Algeria* (Oxford: Clarendon Press, 1998).

48. Said, *Culture and Imperialism*, 217.

49. Said, *Freud and the Non-European* (London: Verso, 2003), 45–46.

50. Charles-Robert Ageron, *Histoire de l'Algérie contemporaine: De l'insurrection de 1871 au déclenchement de la guerre de libération* (Paris: Presses Universitaires de la France, 1979), 404.

51. Charles-Robert Ageron, "Un rapport inedit de Louis Massignon à la commission du centenaire de l'Algérie," *Cahiers de Tunisie* 22 (1985), 40; Jean Mélia, *La France et l'Algérie* (Paris: Plon, 1919).

52. M. Viollette, *L'Algérie vivra-t-elle? Notes d'un ancien gouverneur général* (Paris: Alcan, 1931); Jean Mélia, *Le triste sort des indigènes musulmans d'Algérie* (Paris: Mercure de France, 1935).

53. Charles-Robert Ageron, "Nécrologie: Charles-andré Julien (1891–1991)," *Revue Française d'Histoire d'Outre-Mer*, 79 (1992), 401–2.

54. André Nouschi, "Témoignages et éclairages sur la colonisation française," *Revue d'Histoire Moderne et Contemporaine* 28 (1981), 515.

55. On Julien's extensive political involvements, see Julien, *Une pensée anticoloniale*.

56. Centre des Archives d'Outre-Mer, *Fonds du département de Constantine*, 3, B, 329.

57. See Charles-André Julien, *L'Afrique du Nord en marche: Nationalismes musulmans et souveraineté française* (Paris: Julliard, 1952); Julien, *Histoire de l'Algérie contemporaine: La conquête et les débuts de la colonisation (1827–1871)* (Paris: Presses Universitaires de France, 1964).

58. Julien, *Une pensée anticoloniale*, back cover.

59. See, especially, [André] Julien, "Marseille et la question d'Alger à la veille de la conquête," *Revue Africaine* 60:298 (1919); [André] Julien, "L'opposition et la guerre d'Alger à la veille de la conquête," *Bulletin de la Société de Géographie et d'Archéologie de la Province d'Oran*, 41:1 (1921);

[André] Julien, "L'Avenir d'Alger et l'opposition des libéraux et des économistes en 1830," *Bulletin de la Société de Géographie et d'Archéologie de la Province d'Oran*, 42:1 (1922); Charles-André Julien, *La concession de Themistocle Lestiboudois* (Paris: F. Reider, 1924); Julien, "Un médecin romantique, interprète et professeur d'arabe: Eusèbe de Salles," *Revue Africaine* 65:320 (1924) and 66:323–24 (1925); Julien, "Le conflit entre les généraux et les préfets d'Algérie sous la deuxième République," *La révolution de 1848* 22:115 (1926); Hauser, "Ch.-André Julien," 668.

60. Julien, *Histoire de l'Afrique du Nord*, 574.

61. Hauser, "Ch.-André Julien," 667.

62. Hauser, "Ch.-André Julien," 667.

63. Hauser, "Ch.-André Julien," 667.

64. Fernand Braudel, "À propos de *L'Histoire de l'Afrique du Nord* de Charles-André Julien" (1933), in *Autour de la Méditerranée* (Paris: Éditions de Fallois, 1996), 164.

65. Nouschi, "Témoignages et éclairages," 515–16.

66. M. M. Knight, "Histoire de l'Afrique du Nord (Tunisie-Algérie-Maroc) par Ch. André Julien," *American Historical Review* 37:2 (1932), 380.

67. Erato Paris considers the influence of Julien on Braudel but does not, I think, push the argument far enough; see Paris, *La genèse intellectuelle de l'œuvre de Fernand Braudel*, 125–34.

68. Stéphane Gsell, "Préface" to Julien, *Histoire de l'Afrique du Nord*, ix–xi.

69. Hauser, "Ch.-André Julien," 665–66.

70. Gsell, "Préface" to Julien, *Histoire de l'Afrique du Nord*, Hauser, "Ch.-André Julien," 665.

71. Knight, "Histoire de l'Afrique du Nord," 381.

72. Hauser, "Ch.-André Julien," 666.

73. Julien, *Histoire de l'Afrique du Nord*, 23.

74. Carlier, "Braudel avant Braudel?" 165. On the Algerian *cahiers du centenaire* see André Lambelet, "Back to the Future: Politics, Propaganda and the Centennial of the Conquest of Algeria," *French History and Civilization: Papers from the George Rudé Seminar*, vol. 1 (Charleston IL: H-France, 2005), 62–72.

75. See, for instance, the 1951 edition (Paris: Payot).

76. Charles-André Julien, *Histoire de l'Algérie contemporaine: La conquête et les débuts de la colonisation (1827–1871)* (Paris: Presses Universitaires de France, 1964).

77. Recent commentators have testified to the longevity of the *longue durée* as a category of colonial and postcolonial historical analysis. See, for instance, Achille Mbembe, *On the Postcolony* (Berkeley: University of California Press, 2001), 14.

5

Mental Maps of Modernity in Colonial Indochina during World War II

*Mobilizing Sport to Combat
Threats to French Rule*

ANNE RAFFIN

Under the Vichy empire, French authorities at home and abroad introduced new policies that used sport and youth corps activities to mobilize physical education as a means to regulate cultural behavior and political loyalties. Such policies were motivated by the need to rejuvenate a population that had been defeated by Germany in France and by Japan in Indochina. Organized sporting events in the contiguous territories of the Indochina federation also provided a means to divert youngsters from joining subversive political movements by offering them socially oriented activities with an underlying message of loyalty to empire. This chapter argues that official interest in the physical condition of the colonized was also molded by the mind-sets of colonial officials and their more subjective perceptions of the locals. Hence, its main focus is on the mental perceptions—the colonial minds—of three French colonial figures, their constructions of the physicality of Indochinese societies during World War II, and, in turn, how these constructions were reflected in policy.

The specificity of this case study lies in the merging of values of rationality linked to modernity with a colonial ideology of racial superiority defined in relation to the supposed bodily fitness of the native peoples, all of which occurred within the particular historical context of a defeated French nation. The result was, as one might expect, a curious and paradoxical mix. On one hand, locals were encouraged to release energy through new kinds of physical exertion as a means to build strong bodies that could defend the empire against external and internal threats. At the same time, bodily activities were restrained by channeling youngsters' energy toward inoffensive sport activities while teaching them self-control and cultivating in them feelings of gratitude toward the French empire.

"Modernity" is a difficult term to grasp. Classical founders of sociology such as Max Weber and Emile Durkheim devised a typology that deliberately contrasted traditional societies with modern ones. In their construction, traditional societies were often portrayed as religious communities held together by mechanical solidarity. In contrast, their vision of a modern society is more flexible as it is predicated on the view that members of such societies have greater scope for formal and informal interaction. In addition, working life is organized around the division of labor while people's worldview is materialistic and their practical behaviors are utilitarian. The demands of rationality also have an impact on the conception of the human body in a manner that promotes bodily restraint and discipline.[1]

For Max Weber, modern discipline had its roots in two institutions: the monastery and the army. Likewise the three colonial officials under study here belonged either to the armed forces or to the Catholic Church.[2] Admiral Jean Decoux became governor-general of Indochina in 1940. Navy captain Maurice Ducoroy was the general commissioner for physical education, sports, and youth in Indochina from 1941 to 1945. Sister Durand arrived in Indochina in 1935. She later accepted Decoux's offer to establish physical educational programs for girls and schools to train female youth cadres wherever the order had a community.[3] Each of these colonial officials represented important facets of the youth and sports policies of the Vichy empire in Indochina.

Much of the theoretical literature connecting bodily and social discipline draws upon the work of Michel Foucault. He coined the term "bio-power" to express a particular form of power expressed within the self through introspection, inhibition, and regulation. The concept of "bio-power," in addition, connotes the rule and control of bodies by the state and other institutions, and it is on this facet of the theory that this essay focuses.[4] Both Foucault and Weber viewed modern rational practices as emanating from the monastery and the army and expanding outward toward the factory, the hospital, and the home.[5] For instance, exploring the nature of disciplinary power within colonial Egypt, Timothy Mitchell analyzes the attempt by the colonial order to control the mind and body through discipline and hard work. Microforms of power based on persuasion rather than coercion were instilled through the building of a new army or the creation of a model village.[6]

Within colonial studies several important works have been written on distinctly colonial constructions of the body—and, more particularly, of the bodies of colonized populations—as a site of illness.[7] Often the bodies of the colonized were seen as dirty and as a source of disease requiring regulation. One Vietnamese doctor, Bui, recounted the attitude of a French woman doctor who let slip a not untypical representation of French superiority toward locals in observing that "the Annamites are as dirty as pigs! Everywhere they spit betel!"[8] Controlling one's body was thought of as controlling one's morality; hence colonial subjects were perceived as not only a hygienic threat but also as a potential moral one by the Europeans. Similarly, Christian missionaries in colonial Zimbabwe perceived their task as not only to encourage physical cleanliness among the locals but to heal them spiritually as well.[9]

One key work that challenges Foucault's thesis on discipline and panoptics is Peter Zinoman's study of colonial French prisons in colonial Vietnam. As Zinoman demonstrates, rather than trying to reform the inmates' character and behaviors, harsh regimes of corporal punishment were not the exception, but the rule. Racist beliefs supported colonial officials' perceptions of locals who broke the law as "innately incorrigible."[10] Building on this earlier research into colonizers' presumptions about the colonized body, this chapter examines the interplay of three intersecting concerns: the physicality of the Indochinese population, the European bodily assessment of locals and its impact on colonial policy, and the concept of rationalization within the context of World War II. What follows is organized into two sections. The first discusses one map of modernity focused upon the rationalized control of the body in France through sport, and the more specific physical assessment of the natives by French colonials in Indochina. The second examines the ways in which colonial officials charted public places and routes that were intended to be used for new kinds of rationalized physicality across French-administrated Vietnam, Cambodia, and Laos.

Maps of Modernity: Rational Control of Bodily Hygiene and the Role of Physical Education in French Culture

Sport and politics first became intertwined in modern France in the wake of the military conflict of 1870. The country's defeat at the hands of a Prussian-led coalition of German states in 1870 was often explained by a lack of a proper military and physical training in schools. Such a view led to the creation of gymnastic clubs as a space where bodies could display their strength, discipline, and readiness to take on any future assault by the Prussians.

During this period, a growing influence of militarism and social Darwinism in France translated into racial nationalism. Many shared the common belief that men belonged to various competing races that struggled among themselves for domination. Such a perspective stressed the importance of the appropriate and calculated mental and physical adaptation of people to their environment, and the French empire was perceived as a place where such mental and physical abilities could be tested. The commingling of militarism, social Darwinism, and imperialism resulted in a bellicose core of values in the French sporting community on the eve of World War I. Physical activities in France, especially after World War I, became an arena that attracted politicians as a means to promote nationalist ideals, mental and physical health, and the politicization of gymnastics clubs along secular versus Catholic lines. Strength among Frenchmen was to be rebuilt in modern society as obedience, discipline, and readiness to serve any national cause.

In French history, state-sponsored sporting activities had been limited before the Popular Front administration's promotion of a state-backed leisure program in 1936–38. The arrival of Léon Blum's Socialist-led coalition government in 1936 resulted in a policy of "sport for all." Underlying this policy shift was the belief that all had the right to enjoy leisure activities regardless of class, as well as a more explicit linkage between national efficiency and sport, which was intended to promote "the welfare of the race." Slogans about racial health and national resurgence were no longer confined to the vocabulary of the Right but became part of the official rhetoric of the Left as well. Continuing the Popular Front's preoccupation with the links between leisure and national vitality, albeit as part of a completely different ideological vision, the Vichy empire saw sport as an efficient tool by which to mold faithful, cheerful, obedient, and active youngsters.[11] Nowhere was this more apparent in the overseas territories still under Vichy control than in Indochina. Committed Vichyites they may have been, but Decoux, Ducoroy, and Sister Durand's perception of the centrality of sport to the promotion of various ideologies was rooted in the interwar period, when authorities back home and abroad had begun to recognize the political potential of sport.[12] The Hanoi regime also tapped into other strands of Vichy colonialism, namely, the veneration of martial qualities and Catholic traditionalism. There was ready support for such policies among serving armed forces personnel in the Indochina federation. Gymnastics had always played an important role in French military training, and in Indochina military officers initiated sporting activities from the outset. Replicating their involvement in youth clubs in France after the disestablishment of the church in 1905, religious congregations were the other means by which Western sports were spread through the French empire.[13]

This historical legacy continued to influence the orientation of sport and youth policies throughout the duration of the French presence in Indochina, and each would be especially evident during Decoux's wartime governorship. The admiral invested tremendous faith in sporting activities and targeted youth policies in order to regulate and discipline the body of his young subjects during World War II. As discussed later in the chapter, others in influential positions within the Indochina federation's Vichyite hierarchy shared the governor-general's enthusiasm. Both Ducoroy and Sister Durand were socialized in the same French culture that shaped Decoux's thinking, and that normalized the role of armed forces and church personnel as devoted instructors molding strong and virtuous (industrious, responsible, committed) youngsters.

French Assessments of Colonial Subjects

The project of crafting youngsters in the colonies into disciplined and rational beings who would display exemplary self-control in matters political and moral was predicated on certain prevalent cultural presumptions about the ethnic hierarchies thought to exist in the Indochinese peninsula as well as elsewhere in the colonial empire. French colonial authorities shared a common belief in the demonstrable superiority of the French civilization and its people, in contrast to the "backwardness" of their colonial subjects. The Hanoi administration was no exception, and its personnel both assimilated and disseminated the pervasive colonial stereotyping regarding Indochinese populations. Colonial administrators' diagnoses of the physical capabilities of the Indochinese peoples were tied to their particular perceptions of various groups. From the outset of colonization, French officials repeatedly depicted Laotians and Cambodians as "lazy," "weak," and "moribund." These negative attributes seemed to underline the requirement to use physical education as a tool to "revive" them. The Vietnamese population, by contrast, was often portrayed as vigorous and dynamic, although supposedly lacking in "virility" nonetheless.[14] Once again, physical activities would help eradicate their residual "effeminate" qualities.

The review *Indochine*, the unofficial mouthpiece of the Vichy empire in Indochina, propagated the image of a Laos that had "overslept," lying culturally dormant for decades and, as a result, "like so many other things in Laos . . . lived only in the past."[15] In addition, according to Decoux, the previous colonial regimes tended to privilege a "su su regime,"[16] by which he implied the supposed indolence and infantilism of the locals. Likewise, both the colonial administration and French propaganda more generally constructed the Lao people in clichéd terms as carefree, uncorrupted by industrial modernity, and yet renowned for their Bacchynalian taste for celebrations and feasts. According to such official and semi-official rhetoric, blessed by a natural environment that could provide for their needs without arduous labor, Laotians had become endemically lazy; for them work had only "a relative attraction."[17]

If the particular characteristics of decadence ascribed by French officials to Indochina's various ethnic groups varied, all derived from similar, racially grounded assumptions about innate human qualities, capacity for advancement, and the connections between land and people. As Governor-General Decoux put it in regard to Cambodia, it was the job of the colonial regime to "improve" natives' well-being and economic potential by dragging them out of their "inertia" to better prepare them for "the necessities and requirements of modern life."[18] If this sentiment was reminiscent of Rudyard Kipling's "white man's burden," depictions of the Vietnamese in the French language press were rather different, tending to emphasize the population's "active, industrious, and hard-working" qualities.[19] The more robust qualities of the Vietnamese were, however, similarly ascribed to local topography and environment, the country's rugged natural terrain, and the hard labor required to exploit it, being seen as integral to the greater fortitude of Vietnam's people.[20]

In charge of Vichy's youth and sports projects in Indochina, and an accomplished sportsman himself, Maurice Ducoroy was preoccupied with the relative physical abilities of Indochinese people, as was apparent in his assessment of their behavior during organized sporting activities. Building on received colonial wisdom about local subject groups, he depicted Cambodians as

> solid, well-built, a little nonchalant, but very friendly. The crossbreeding, frequently found between Chinese and Cambodians, results in mixed-blood, handsome specimens who make excellent subjects.... Cambodians and Sino-Cambodians have a pleasant mood, and are intelligent and resilient.[21]

Similarly, Laotians were listed within Ducoroy's classification system as residing in an "appetizing country where all the inhabitants live only for flowers, music, dance, and love." His concluding summary was equally stereotypical; the Laotians, he thought, were "a gentle population, but not particularly active."[22] By contrast, Ducoroy's observations of young Vietnamese, or "Annamites" as he termed them, using the prevailing colonial moniker of the day, was much different:

> They like soccer and practice this game with passion. More easily than the Europeans, they can endure prolonged effort during a very hot day. Acclimatized from childhood by long journeys in the countryside, they often won out in the cross-country running and cross-country skiing [competitions]. [Yet] they affect to be over-

sensitive, they love to whine about insignificant maladies, and ask to be pampered. In adversity or defeat they fall apart and become morally crushed.

Ducoroy's observations were not confined to amateur anthropological musings about events on the sports field but extended to equally ill-informed physiological observations as well:

Their [the Vietnamese] heart is abnormal, very large, and placed toward the left. Is this the effect of the climate or the result of a very harsh life as a small child, or perhaps the after-effect of beri-beri? I don't know. Despite this organic deformity, rarely are any actual cardiac weaknesses noticed after tiring events. Perhaps it is simply a racial anomaly.[23]

Alan Petersen reminds us that judging an individual's personality and mental attributes based on body size and appearance was a practice deeply rooted in Western culture.[24] Seen in this light, perhaps Ducoroy's observations revealed rather more about his own cultural makeup than that of the colonial subjects he described. He was, after all, following long traditions among western European race theorists who associated body shapes and physical abilities with ethnic origins, and who thus claimed that particular groups displayed a propensity for specific sports. Consistently racist, Ducoroy was nonetheless inconsistent in his methodology, alternating between cultural and genetic explanations regarding the physical characteristics of the colonial subjects he scrutinized. Like the medical community, he codified the qualities of the "normal" body by reference to those of the "abnormal" body in his discussion of the anatomy of the Vietnamese. However, he did not perceive the peculiarities he claimed to discern as a pathological condition that would require medical treatment. While Ducoroy adopted a "medical/pseudo-anthropological gaze," his ambition was less to cure than to classify. Ordering Indochinese bodies in defined rankings was a means to gauge their energy levels and physical abilities. This, in turn, would guide their participation in sports and physical education for the utilitarian purpose of molding faithful and useful subjects.

Modernity, Gender Roles, and Morality

Let us return once more to the review *Indochine*, a pro-French publication certainly, and one in which local authors were encouraged to express their views about the benevolent impact of the French colonial presence in Southeast Asia, thereby demonstrating that contact between the best of French culture and Indochina would foster a new civilization in Indochina. Take Doctor Nguyen-Van-Luyen, for example, whose April 1941 contribution to the magazine dwelt on the beneficial effects of French-inspired modernity in Vietnam, from the rule of law to the dissemination of European scientific and industrial knowledge.[25] Clearly meant to chime with official thinking, with the colonial minds in and around Decoux's administration, it was but a small step to regard the development of the subject population's optimal physical abilities as in tune with such rational, benevolent colonial rule.

To build these strong subjects, state-sponsored summer camps were organized for French and local youngsters. Camp officials kept records about participants in the form of itemized index cards that registered weight gained or lost. Ducoroy personally inspected these cards when he visited the camps.[26] Likewise, in vacation camps run during 1943 educators tabulated more detailed records that, in addition to recording attendees' weight gained or lost, provided information about height gained, illnesses, and accidents.[27] Charting measurement and progress in terms of weight and height reflected the growth of rationalization thinking within the colonial bureaucracy. Greater official attention to the use of statistics in order to quantify, categorize, and predict was thus both a part of this process and a reflection of the particular racialist thinking epitomized under Decoux's regime by Ducoroy's work.[28] This interest was also consistent with the underlying concept of "bio-power" discussed earlier, with its concern with the regulation and control of bodies by state authorities.

Such regulation was, of course, also the product of longer-term trends in colonial administration that mirrored the spread of industrial capitalism and the increasing stress on the scientific understanding and rational organization of economic and social life in the colonies. Connections might, for instance, be made between the growing preoccupation with rational organization and early twentieth-century French discourses on Taylorism as a means to improve industrial efficiency. Taylorism also featured within broader debates among French elites nervous about relative industrial decline and resurgent social conflict. These ranged from crowd psychology and eugenics to French societal "degeneration," exemplified by pro-natalist anxieties over France's low birthrate after World War I.[29]

If Maurice Ducoroy was closer to the governor-general, another key figure in the manufacturing of healthy bodies was Sister Durand, who accepted Ducoroy's invitation to supervise the following two schools in Dalat created to train female instructors for sports and youth.[30] Opened in February 1942, the Indochina Advanced School of Female Instructors (École Supérieure des Monitrices d'Indochine, or ESMIC) sought to disseminate "appropriate" sports for girls, thereby developing greater propensity for these physical activities among the female subject population.[31] The work was also taken on in a partner institution, the Indochina Advanced School for Feminine Youth Cadres (École Supérieure des Cadres de la Jeunesse Féminine d'Indochine, or ESCJFIC) that also opened in Dalat a month later, in February 1943.

Both the summer camps and Sister Durand's Dalat schools drew on a specific training practice, known as Hébert's "natural method," which originated in France. Hébert was a French naval officer in the early 1900s whose eponymously named "natural method" used a prescribed set of activities to cultivate individuals' physical, moral, and virile qualities in an outdoor setting. Those activities he described as "natural and utilitarian exercises"—walking, running, jumping, climbing, lifting, throwing, defending, and swimming—formed the bedrock of his method, while his motto was "Be strong to be useful," an epithet with obvious colonial resonance. A more utilitarian and rational use of the body was at the core of this method, which was perceived as being naturally suited to people of all types and did not pose any threat to women's procreative functions. Perhaps unsurprisingly, then, before the opening of the ESMIC, educators received a one-week training session that focused on collective outdoor games performed by instructors trained in Hébertism. During the training, participants were told that the new knowledge they were about to acquire would serve the ultimate "vocation of the woman: maternity." Under Decoux's regime, Sister Durand kept her traditional function as the arbiter of women's morality and guardian of their appropriate role, drawing upon the Catholic traditionalism so much favored at Vichy, a regime that constantly reiterated its support for conservative family values and women's role as mothers.[32]

Sister Durand was also in charge of the Center for Feminine Youth in Saigon, which taught physical education, moral training, and domestic skills to Vietnamese and French youngsters of any religion between the ages of sixteen and twenty-five.[33] Other schools also promoted this traditional vision of female domesticity. For instance, the Advanced School of Homecrafts (École Supérieure des Arts Ménagers) trained young women for their future roles as wives and mothers by teaching home economics, morality, hygiene, and infant care.[34]

While Decoux, Ducoroy, and Sister Durand were at the cutting edge of Vichy's attempt to reform bodies and minds in colonial Vietnam, each embraced the project differently. Whereas the two navy men linked bodily self-control and mental training to wider defensive purposes, Sister Durand connected the body with spirituality. Drawing on her training as a nun, she took seriously her evangelical responsibility to discipline the inner self. Her actions as head of the various schools described above were guided by an overriding Christian resolve to resist people's growing alienation from spiritual values.[35] Hence, within the one-week orientation session for the female trainers were lectures on how to inculcate Christian morality and a sense of service and obedience toward the regime among their young charges.[36] Obedience to religious and political leaders was symbolically displayed when Decoux awarded the Legion of Honor to Sister Durand for her services to France in 1944. During the ceremony, students of the Dalat ESCJFIC and the Advanced School of Homecrafts formed a double guard of honor all dressed in white and giving the Athenian salute in the direction of the chapel where Sister Durand received her medal.[37]

Choreographing Bodies: Mass Entertainment Sports in the Colonial Mind

The vision of a white-clad Vietnamese honor guard saluting the moral achievements of an elderly French nun brings us naturally to the connections between attitudes and performance, between colonial minds and the choreography of colonial power. Decoux's staff designated prescribed meeting places with plotted access routes that were to be used for new kinds of rationalized physicality, such as bicycle races, athletics events and marches, and group exercise programs. Such outdoor programs represented the symbolic connection between the population and the colonial state, and assumed a near-religious quality in which a loyalist population publicly venerated the regime, demonstrating their unity in defense of the Vichy Empire. Ducoroy was certainly a fan of such events, which, he believed, resonated with the mentality of Indochina's subject populations who, his reports claimed, showed an "extraordinary taste of Orientals for huge spectacle"[38]:

> The Indochinese, be they monarchs or humble *nha-qués* [peasants] from the paddies, showed a strong interest in the new activities proposed to them by the General [Youth and Sport] Commissariat. They were particularly enthusiastic about the [sporting] "spectacles."[39]

Decoux's and Ducoroy's mental representations of the regime are evident in their orchestration of mass displays. They choreographed spectacles of power, with both muscular power and the power of unity visible to all. Part of the rationale behind such events was "to bring the crowd to the stadia to create an atmosphere, a favorable climate for developing the sporting movement among the masses."[40] Equally integral to this policy was the coordination of the festivities held, often at stadia, which usually followed a specific agenda: first the official speeches and flag salutes, then youth marches, songs, and physical exercises, followed in the afternoon by mass participation in a sports competition. Colonial officials in Vientiane, for instance, attended a stadium event to celebrate Joan of Arc Day during which the *résident supérieur* first reviewed a parade of local schoolchildren. After saluting the flag, officials watched parades of girls and boys, followed by athletic competitions based on discus throwing and races. These were followed by afternoon basketball and soccer competitions.[41]

From religious to secular celebrations, stadia were the sites of intricately choreographed crowd gatherings with allegories to the Vichy empire (the song "Chant du Maréchal," for instance) and parades of youngsters as well as competitive sports. Stadia were the preferred locations for these festivities, so much so that they became a discrete public space for glorification of the regime that propagated the illusion of grandeur and the myth of present and future unity between the colonized and the colonizers. As a political tool, such events were a means to assert a nationalized form of control over subjects' bodies.

Participants in these mass spectacles wore matching outfits that indicated the regime's interest in the details of dress. Not only bodily performance, but personal appearance had to be molded to display affiliation with the Vichy empire. All cadres taking part had to wear uniforms specific to their training and their school based on combinations of the colors of the French flag. Physical education instructors were dressed in white shorts with blue stripes and a white sports shirt emblazoned with the ESEPIC insignia and the victory sign, also in the French tricolors. The letters ESEPIC were written in blue on the back of the sports shirt as well. Those instructors who had not received their diploma at the ESCJFIC were dressed in white shorts with blue stripes, with the insignia of their school on the left side of the chest.[42]

These uniforms did not go unchallenged. For one thing, female cadres expressed their uneasiness about wearing shorts, a new vision of presenting the collective feminine self. For another, some young Vietnamese instructors refused to wear shorts in public and instead participated in physical activities in pants and long tunics that restricted their movements.[43] To encourage women to practice sports and reconsider their attitudes to displaying their bodies in public, Lao Princess Khamla formed a female basketball team in Luang-Prabang, and for the first time young women wore shorts during their training.[44]

Ducoroy linked the issue of clothing to the "inevitable" process of modernization, which he believed would replace tradition with discipline:

> There mustn't be a quarrel over whether "to wear or not to wear shorts." It is a question of discipline, and I do not believe the ones who refer to ancestral customs [and] oppose useful reforms;

modernization is inevitable.... [If] these people travel through the countries of the Union [Indochina], they will see that everywhere youth is on the move.[45]

A more modern way of dressing would allow women to perform sporting exercise more efficiently. In addition, clothing became a calculated display of one's ideological affiliation. Female instructors trained in Hébert's physical education methods at Sister Durand's educational centers also adopted modern dress, something that Sister Durand did not oppose.[46]

Mapping Routes for Bodily Displays of Unity and Rejuvenation

The annual Tour d'Indochine bike race, covering 3,900 kilometers, began in 1941. Triumphal arches and posters of Pétain were erected all along its route, representing the ideological altars of the homeland and celebrating a new consecration of the Indochinese population united behind the Vichy empire. Inspired by the Tour de France, these cycle races sought to reinforce political identity, whether national or imperial, and to reassure officials and the local populations of their physical fitness. Each race recreated an adult version of the French schoolbook *Le tour de France par deux enfants*, which told the story of two orphaned Alsatian children traveling through the French regions in search of their family members. Each race encapsulated the textbook's focus on teaching civic virtue and attachment to the motherland.[47]

Many Vietnamese had already developed a taste for cycling, and colonial officials harnessed this popular pastime to political ends. By the 1930s young Vietnamese, especially in the major towns, were already turning to cycling and hiking to historical landmarks as popular pastimes, a trend further encouraged by the Popular Front administration in 1936–37.[48] Writing to Decoux regarding the 1942 Hanoi-Saigon-Phnom Penh cycle race (the so-called Capital Circuit), Ducoroy noted that locals were supportive of such events and that he was opening stadia by the dozen. Such experiences reinforced Ducoroy's belief in Vietnamese love of grandiose festivities.[49]

Other popular events were organized, such as the "race of the torch" (*la course au flambeau*), a long-distance run from Angkor to Hanoi held in the fall of 1941. Dinners were held in villages along the race route.[50] Interestingly, such feasts were the founding instrument of French Republicanism's beliefs and practices, according to Girardet.[51] World War II colonial personnel were steeped in the Third Republic's ideology, and their political and social actions were partially molded by beliefs and practices that predated Vichy. Ducoroy, for one, encouraged such events as a means to celebrate an Indochinese and imperial identity and to encourage popular deference to colonial authority.

Organized dinners along the race route asserted the so-called masculine values of strength, resilience, virility, and above all discipline, which were required of the participants whose journeys often took place on unpaved roads and in rough weather. As Decoux stated, cycling and long-distance running taught locals the importance of discipline and obedience.[52] Ducoroy wrote to Decoux of how even Vietnamese countrymen wanted such masculine values to be developed among the young and thus supported the colonial administration since, as one put it, "the governor-general has decided to strengthen the Annamite race by taking care of its youth."[53]

In addition to races, other athletic events also embodied the regime's developing conception of its imperial mission to train a new loyalist generation. New cycle paths were, for instance, marked out to encourage adolescent men and women to take up cycling as a wholesome leisure activity. Signs were put up marking one such path, a sixty-five-kilometer route between Vientiane and Ban Keun in Laos. Such mixed-gender activities were designed to help foster the healthy rejuvenation of the Lao race in the face of a dangerously expansionist Thailand. They also meshed with more organized events in which recognition of the French empire was represented by salutes to the French flag, and the vitality of the previously "moribund" Lao identity was encouraged through performances of Lao dances, songs, and plays, combined with gymnastic exercises for the young and a basketball competition. Swimming competitions were also held and consisted of high diving followed by a fifty-meter race open to entrants of all ages.[54] These activities bore the imprint of Ducoroy's assumption that the Indochinese people, especially the Vietnamese, were talented swimmers—"a sport for which the Annamites are especially gifted"—due to the existence of many streams and ponds in their land.[55]

Mental Maps of Modernity in Colonial Indochina

The bicycle was a symbol of modernity. By the turn of the century, a series of technical improvements had altered what had been a dangerous novelty into a more comfortable and dependable machine. Like the Tour de France, the Tour d'Indochine stood for the alliance of modernity and progress. In both the metropolitan and Indochinese contexts, the very long distances involved and the difficulty of the competitions epitomized how modern sport and modern science fostered not only physical ability but also the moral resilience required for French imperial regeneration.[56] These objectives also underpinned the work of the Phanthiet schools that trained sports and youth instructors and that were strategically located some two hundred kilometers northeast of Saigon and hence were both easily reachable from Hue, the capital of Annam, and accessible from Hanoi thanks to the Mandarin road. Among their pupils were recently graduated local administrators, or mandarins, sometimes derided by colonial officials as physically deficient—displaying either "excessive thinness" or "precocious obesity"—due to their bookish lifestyle. Young mandarins were therefore sent to the Indochina Advanced School of Physical Education for three months to get in shape, and were required to take part in races and marches organized along various routes devised to develop their strength and endurance.[57] Some of these challenges consisted of 1,500 meter courses to be completed in only five or six minutes. Other, longer routes of between three and five kilometers were laid out as obstacle courses with sand pits or steep slopes that had to be negotiated in order to develop participants' stamina. Another, similar endurance test required the trainees to run nonstop for thirty minutes "like a machine." Two long-distance walks of twenty-five and thirty-five kilometers respectively were also mapped out. The young mandarins were ordered to navigate these at 2:00 a.m. to familiarize themselves with walking in complete darkness. According to one observer, the overall objective was to turn out

> beautiful athletes with a tanned skin, and a lithe body on which the biceps and pectoral muscles are clearly drawn. Whereas at the beginning they knew absolutely nothing, today they run, climb, and jump as if they had done those things all their lives.[58]

The muscular, modern Vietnamese was reinvented as a colonial variant of Vichy's "new man" ideal.

Conclusion

As this image of bookish mandarins transformed suggests, and as this study has indicated, sports and outdoor recreational policies in wartime colonial Indochina combined French officials' perceptions of the physicality of these indigenous societies with their understanding of their mission as colonial modernizers, but modernizers wedded to traditionalist hierarchies and rigid moral standards. Decoux and Ducoroy viewed Laotians and Cambodians as being physically weak and morally lazy; hence, the requirement to devise physical education techniques inspired by military precedents. Sister Durand saw sport and other physical activities as promoting moral values and obedience to political and religious authorities. The knowledge that these three leading colonial figures had acquired regarding Indochina was context-dependent, in the sense that they inherited and accepted the stereotyping of the native populations already existent in the colonial society they encountered on arrival in Vietnam. Some of this knowledge was also conveyed through the state administration and the Catholic Church; hence the three of them came to "know" their subjects through the distorted prism of their respective institutions.

This chapter has attempted to demonstrate how colonial minds were shaped by distinct visions of modernity in a particular colonial environment where values of rationality were blended with a colonialist ideology of racial superiority that was, in turn, mapped onto the bodily characteristics of the Indochinese. All of this transpired within a context of political emergency after France's defeat when the internal and external enemies of French rule in Indochina, most notably the Communist-led Vietminh and the Japanese military overseers who would eventually seize outright control in March 1945, were becoming an increasingly proximate danger to Decoux's regime. In these testing conditions, the physicality of the indigenous people had to be molded afresh to produce useful and faithful subjects. This was less a matter of training cadres to help defend the colonial state than of using physical training and moral education to steer the subject population away from the regime's opponents. To control one's body was to control one's personality; hence, the colonial administration's enthusiastic embrace of organized sporting activities, morality classes, and public displays of loyalty.

Colonial sports policies in Indochina thus echo Foucault's vision of the long-term breakdown, from the seventeenth century onward, of sovereign power into "micro-powers" such as schools and the army, just as penal reformers were advancing the notion that it was more humane to reform the mind than to punish the body. In Foucault's words, "there was an explosion of numerous and diverse techniques for achieving the subjugation of bodies and the control of the population."[59] In Indochina, for instance, those who had broken the law did not necessarily have to be coerced through corporal punishment or protracted confinement; rather, they could be reprogrammed to change their behavior by a combination of physical exercises, such as marching, camping, or singing, which, according to Ducoroy, offered "a discipline of cadence."[60] In addition, sporting activities had a performative role: they were "an exhibition" of support for the colonial authorities. The political rituals in which youngsters participated, such as marching, races, and parades, were an affirmation of colonial power albeit divorced from the actual condition of the regime.

Coubertin, who brought the Olympic Games back to life, favored the British practice of allowing the Indian elite to play polo and to compete with the colonizers, yet he would have disapproved of this Vichy colonial sports project during World War II. Coubertin did not believe that the victory of an indigenous team in a sporting contest necessarily constituted a political threat. Quite the reverse: sports were a disciplinary tool that taught "good social qualities, such as hygiene, order, and self-control." In colonial Indochina, however, sporting activity, whether team based or not, typically had a militaristic appearance that turned the activities into "official spectacles":

> The national flag, the presence of the authorities, stands, harangues, uniforms—... this is what would give to an indigenous victory a significance whose influence could diminish the authority of the governing [power]; it will not be the victory itself, but the pomp surrounding it that we would have to blame. In sum, sports

should not be a tool of government colonization policy, but an institution parallel to it.⁶¹

Just as Courbertin's assessment of the symbolic importance of colonial sport was inextricably tied to his vision of colonization itself, so, in a later era, the judgments of the Vichy officials studied here were skewed by their own colonialist outlook. Decoux and Ducoroy, for instance, sometimes confused the impressive scale of organized parades and the presence of large crowds with active popular support for the political regime. This was far from the truth. By 1941 the French authorities had to contend with two political competitors, the Japanese and the Vietminh. As the war proceeded, the presence and activities of the Vietminh became much more crucial in many areas of rural Tonkin, for instance, than any French-sponsored youth activities or sporting events, which remained primarily an urban phenomenon. Ultimately, examining French colonial sporting policies in Indochina during the politically unstable war years is instructive because it demonstrates how colonial officials' concern with indigenous bodies—their training, their form, their "discipline"—illuminates various aspects of a colonial mentality, of colonial minds at work, whatever the realities of declining Vichy political fortunes as the war proceeded.

Notes

1. Jens Ljungren, "The Masculine Road through Modernity: Ling Gymnastics and Male Socialization in Nineteenth-Century Sweden," in *Making European Masculinities: Sport, Europe, Gender*, ed. J. A. Mangan (London: Frank Cass, 2000), 86–87.

2. Bryan S. Turner, "The Rationalization of the Body: Reflections on Modernity and Discipline," in *The Body: Critical Concepts in Sociology*, ed. the Aberdeen Body Group (London: Routledge, 2004), vol. 3, 322.

3. "Soeur Durant, Visitatrice des Filles de la Charité en Indochine," *Indochine* 25 (November 1943), 11–13.

4. Michel Foucault, *The History of Sexuality*, vol. 1 (New York: Pantheon Books, 1978), 140; Timothy Burke, "Sunlight Soap Has Changed My Life: Hygiene, Commodification, and the Body in Colonial Zimbabwe," in *Clothing and Difference: Embodied Identities in Colonial and Post-Colonial*

Africa, ed. Hildi Hendrickson (Durham NC: Duke University Press, 1996), 189–90.

5. Turner, "Rationalization of the Body," 329.

6. Timothy Mitchell, *Colonizing Egypt* (Cambridge: Cambridge University Press, 1988).

7. See David Arnold, *Colonizing the Body: State Medicine and Epidemic Disease in Nineteenth-Century India* (Berkeley: University of California Press, 1993); Gyan Prakash, *Another Reason: Science and the Imagination of Modern India* (Princeton NJ: Princeton University Press, 1999); Alice L. Conklin, *A Mission to Civilize: The Republican Idea of Empire in France and West Africa, 1895–1930* (Stanford CA: Stanford University Press, 1997), 38–72; Megan Vaughan, *Curing Their Ills: Colonial Power and African Illness* (Cambridge UK: Polity Press, 1991).

8. Tran Thi Liên, "Henriette Bui: The Narrative of Vietnam's First Woman Doctor," in *Viêt-Nam Exposé: French Scholarship on Twentieth-Century Vietnamese Society*, ed. Gisèle L. Bousquet and Pierre Bourdieu (Ann Arbor: University of Michigan Press, 2002), 292. French colonizers often called Vietnamese people "Annamites."

9. Timothy Burke, *Lifebuoy Men, Lux Women: Commodification, Consumption and Cleanliness in Modern Zimbabwe* (Durham NC: Duke University Press, 1996).

10. Michel Foucault, *Discipline and Punish: The Birth of the Prison* ((New York: Vintage Books, 1979), 195–228; Peter Zinoman, *The Colonial Bastille: A History of Imprisonment in Vietnam, 1862–1940* (Berkeley: University of California Press, 2001), 13–17.

11. Richard Holt, *Sport and Society in Modern France* (Hamden CT: Archon Books, 1981), 190–211.

12. On the topic see Pierre Arnaud and James Riordan, *Sport and International Politics* (London: E & FN Spon, 1998).

13. See Centre des Archives d'Outre-Mer (hereafter CAOM), *L'Empire du sport: Les sports dans les anciennes colonies françaises* (Aix-en-Provence: CAOM, May–July 1992).

14. Mark Philip Bradley, *Imagining Vietnam and America: The Making of Postcolonial Vietnam, 1919–1950* (Chapel Hill: University of North Carolina Press, 2000), 49.

15. J. R. "Théatre Lao," *Indochine*, 18 February 1943, n. 129, p. II. All translations are by the author unless otherwise noted.

16. CAOM, Aix-en-Provence, 14 PA 6, letter from Rochet to Jean Decoux, Vientiane, 12 July 1944.

17. Thao Phoui, "Qui sommes-nous?" *Indochine*, n. 56, 25 September

1941, p. 5; see also Thao Kou, "Appel aux jeunes Lao," *Indochine*, n. 64, 20 November 1941, 3–7.

18. CAOM, HCI, carton 240, letter from Governor-General Jean Decoux, Hanoi, 11 December 1944.

19. Ton-That-Binh, "Patrie Française et Patrie Annamite," *Indochine*, 2 August 1941, 4.

20. Ourot Souvannavong, "Les Annamites et nous," *Indochine*, 2 October 1941, 3.

21. Maurice Ducoroy, *Ma Trahison en Indochine* (Paris: Les Editions Inter-Nationales, 1949), 76.

22. Ducoroy, *Ma Trahison en Indochine* 77, 82.

23. Ducoroy, *Ma Trahison en Indochine*, 165–66.

24. Alan Peterson, *The Body in Question: A Socio-Cultural Approach* (London: Routledge, 2007), 80.

25. Docteur Nguyen-Van-Luyen, "Visions d'Avenir," *Indochine*, n. 34, 24 April 1941, 3–4.

26. "Nha-Trang Inspection du Commissaire Général à l'Education Physique, aux Sports et à la Jeunesse,' *France-Annam*, 24 August 1944, 3.

27. CAOM, dossier L871(2), RSTNF, 6425, "Résultats physiques des camps de vacances de l'année 1943."

28. Peterson, *Body in Question*, 81.

29. On the topic see George G. Humphreys, *Taylorism, in France 1904–1920: The Impact of Scientific Management on Factory Relations and Society* (New York: Garland, 1986).

30. "Promotion de la légion d'Honneur Soeur Durand, Visitatrice des Filles de Charité en Indochine," *France-Annam*, 11 November 1943.

31. CAOM, GGI, 65296, Conseil Fédéral Indochinois, session de juillet 1942; National Archive of Vietnam, Archives #1, GI, D.271F.30, n. 1310, Conseil Fédéral Indochinois, in "Question d'éducation physique et de formation morale de la jeunesse indochinoise à la session de juillet 1942 du Conseil Fédéral Indochinois, 1942."

32. Francine Muel-Dreyfus, *Vichy et l'éternel féminin: Contribution à une sociologie politique de l'ordre du corps* (Paris: Editions du Seuil, 1996), 152.

33. "L'Œuvre des Filles de la Charité," *La Tribune Indochinoise*, 6 March 1942; "L'Indochine en marche Le centre de jeunesse féminin de Saïgon," *Indochine*, 22 July 1943, 14.

34. Ducoroy, *Ma trahison en Indochine*, 97.

35. Nigel Dodd, *Social Theory and Modernity* (Cambridge UK: Polity Press, 1999), 35.

36. CAOM, GGI, L. 837(43), "Soeur Durand, Programmes de la Semaine

des Dirigeantes," unindexed; "La jeunesse féminine à Dalat," *Indochine*, 6 May 1943, v–viii.

37. "Le 28 juin 1944 l'Amiral Decoux a remi à la Soeur Durand la Croix de la Légion d'honneur," *Indochine*, 27 July 1944.

38. CAOM, HCI, conspol 247, Annexes to report by Capitaine de Vaisseau Ducoroy, Saigon, 21 September 1945.

39. Ducoroy, *Ma Trahison en Indochine*, 117.

40. CAOM, GGI, 65296, Conseil fédéral indochinois, session de juillet 1942.

41. "La fête de Jeanne d'Arc à Vientiane," *Lao Nhay*, n. 32, 1 June 1942.

42. Circular no. 373-CGB, 3 September 42; Maurice Ducoroy, "Jeunesse d'empire français," *Sports-Jeunesse d'Indochine*, 12 March 1942, 3.

43. Lieutenant Tan-Hai, "Quelques remarques sur la tenue,' *Le Bulletin des Anciens Elèves de l'Ecole Supérieure d'Education Physique de l'Indochine*, 8 (May 1943), 4–5.

44. "Suivant l'exemple de la famille royale," *Sports-Jeunesse d'Indochine*, April 1942, 4.

45. Maurice Ducoroy, "Le Chef vous parle," *Sports-Jeunesse d'Indochine*, n. 15, 11 April 1942, 3.

46. CAOM, "Soeur Durand, Programmes de la Semaine."

47. Holt, *Sport and Society*, 100.

48. David G. Marr, *Vietnamese Tradition on Trial, 1920–1945* (Berkeley: University of California Press, 1981), 77–81.

49. CAOM, GGI, reference 83 11(42), unindexed, letter from Ducoroy to Decoux, Mhatrang, 5 January 1942.

50. Ducoroy, *Ma Trahison en Indochine*, 147.

51. Raoul Girardet, *Mythes et mythologies politiques* (Paris: Editions du Seuil, 1986), 148.

52. CAOM, GGI, 65289, dossier: Conseil du Gouvernement (session 1943), "Exposé de M. le Vice-Admiral d'Escade Jean Decoux Gouverneur-Général d'Indochine en conseil de gouvernement," 1 March 1944.

53. CAOM, GGI, 83 11(42), unindexed, letter from Ducoroy to Decoux, Mhatrang, 5 January 1942.

54. "La sortie cycliste Vientiane-Bankeun," *Le Nouveau Laos*, n. 25, 25 March 1944, 2.

55. "Nha-Trang, Inspection du Commissaire Général à l'Education Physique, aux Sports et à la Jeunesse," *France-Annam*, 24 August 1944, 3.

56. Christopher S. Thompson, *The Tour de France: A Cultural History* (Berkeley: University of California Press, 2006), 10.

57. Le-Van-Tuan, "Les Mandarins Tonkinois à Phan-Thiet," *Indochine*, n. 97, 9 July 1942.

58. Le-Van-Tuan, "Les Mandarins Tonkinois à Phan-Thiet," *Indochine*, n. 97, 9 July 1942.

59. Foucault, *Discipline and Punish*, 140.

60. "Le Commandant Ducoroy parle aux Sportifs d'Indochine," *Voix d'Empire*, 15 August 1942, 3.

61. Pierre de Coubertin, "Les sports et la colonisation," *Essais de Psychologie Sportive* (Lausanne, France: Librairie Payot, 1913), 233–41.

PART 2

*Language, Culture, and Communities
of the Colonial Mind*

6

Anticlericalism, French Language Policy, and the Conflicted Colonial Mind in Cameroon, 1923–1939

KENNETH J. OROSZ

Perhaps more so than for any other colonial power, the twin issues of language and education policy played a vitally important role in shaping and reflecting the French colonial mind. In interwar Cameroon that translated into a single-minded commitment on the part of colonial administrators to rapidly spread French language and culture as part of a campaign to bind their new possession to France, a determination that only intensified after the League of Nations 1922 decision to turn the former German colony into a mandate under French supervision rather than grant it outright to Paris as a colony. Despite official commitment to these ideals, however, chronic manpower shortages both during and immediately after the First World War meant that the actual implementation of this Gallicization policy was largely left in the hands of missionaries. Of the missions called into service, the Catholic Congregation du Saint Ésprit (also known as the Spiritain order) soon distinguished itself as the staunchest supporter of official French language and cultural policies, thereby earning it the surprised gratitude of colonial authorities, many of whom still harbored lingering anticlerical sentiments left over from the turn-of-the-century battles to secularize education.[1] By 1923, however, the Spiritains had reassessed their commitment to French language instruction and began instead to promote the use of local vernaculars, a reversal that colonial authorities viewed as tantamount to treason. In the eyes of most French officials only the spread of French language and culture would enable the economic and social transformation called for in the mandate. Since these colonial transformations would in turn promote French prestige and postwar reconstruction, government officials regarded the Spiritain decision to curtail French language instruction in favor of local vernaculars as a threat to national interests, resulting in a growing rift in church-state relations inside Cameroon that persisted right up until the outbreak of war in 1939.

Although it had moments of cohesion and clarity, events in interwar Cameroon also illustrate that the French colonial mind was often conflicted and ambivalent. Initially both the government and the Spiritain mission concurred on the need for patriotic support of the war effort, shared a sense of grievance at the lack of material compensation for French losses, and agreed that education was the key to fulfilling France's destiny to promote the development of its new territory. Beyond that, however, their common vision for Cameroon shattered. French colonial officials saw development primarily in terms of economic progress and felt that education, including French language instruction, should serve that end. Moreover, they hoped that rapid economic progress in Cameroon and improvement in the material lives of its native peoples would demonstrate the superiority of French civilization while simultaneously assisting with postwar reconstruction in France. The Spiritains, on the other hand, saw colonial development and French destiny in terms of salvation, evangelism, and social reform. While they did not dispute the need for economic progress in Cameroon, the missionaries felt that the primary purpose of education was to expose the indigenous peoples to Scripture and promote morality. Since they felt that these goals were best achieved by educating the masses in the vernacular, the Spiritains gradually began opposing overly academic curricula and the widespread diffusion of the French language in the belief that they undermined long-term national interests by generating resentment among natives whose elevated ambitions could not possibly be met. Ultimately, the inability to reconcile these competing visions of French destiny and how best to achieve it led to rising tensions among the white population serving in Cameroon during the interwar period and effectively illustrate some of the inherent internal conflicts within the French colonial mind.

While the tensions between missionaries and government officials in French Cameroon were by no means unique, until recently historians have generally ignored or misinterpreted the role of clergy in the French colonial empire. Prior to the 1960s scholars focused primarily on the issues of colonial conquest, administration, economic development, or the much vaunted *mission civilisatrice*.[2] Early studies of French Cameroon like Henri Labouret's *Le Cameroun* thus concentrated on the colonial administration's efforts to exploit the territory's resources, with all other topics treated either as unimportant side issues or seen purely in terms of their impact on economic development.[3] The onset of decolonization, however, led to major historiographical innovations as historians began studying African agency inside the colonial system with an eye toward understanding post–World War II nation building. Spurred by the booming subdiscipline of social history, in the mid-1970s scholarly focus shifted either to African resistance or the impact of colonial policies on native peoples. In the case of Cameroon this led Emmanuel Ghomsi and Ralph Austen to explore Duala efforts to regain expropriated lands, protest French policies, and maintain a measure of social autonomy and de facto political independence within the mandate.[4] Others, like Hugh Vernon-Jackson, Solomon Nfor Gwei, Rudolf Stumpf, Madiba Essiben, and Lucie Ewane, began looking at the development of the educational system and its impact on colonized peoples.[5] Since schools in the colonies were largely run by religious organizations, these early studies provided the first real efforts to analyze missionary activities in French Cameroon. Reflecting overall trends in French colonial historiography, the resultant view of missionary activities that emerged was primarily descriptive and tended to depict the various religious organizations as little more than an extension of the local administration designed to recruit and train African functionaries.[6]

Starting in the early 1980s a new round of studies emerged that began challenging existing historiographical conventions and interpretations of the missionary presence in the French empire. Focusing on Cameroon, Richard Joseph and Jonas Dah studied the impact of local conditions on the evolution of mission theology and practice, uncovering in the process fundamental disagreements between church and state regarding the value and purpose of educating the indigenous peoples.[7] More recently,

Frederick Cooper and Ann Stoler convincingly argued that rather than being monolithic, unified entities with a single coherent developmental vision, colonial regimes were instead made up of multiple groups, each seeking to enact their own unique agendas.[8] As these groups competed with one another to advance their own interests and visions for how best to administer the colonies, they created fundamental tensions that profoundly affected colonial culture, society, and government policy. Building on Cooper and Stoler's work, J. P. Daughton, Elizabeth Foster, Oissila Saaïda, and Charles Keith have reexamined the missionary presence in the French overseas empire. These scholars have shown that not only was metropolitan anticlericalism routinely exported to the colonies, but it also created many instances in which religious organizations found themselves at odds with colonial authorities over matters of government policy.[9] These conflicts, which took on many forms and varied widely in terms of degree and openness, proved instrumental in the evolution of French colonial theory and practice. Within this context the conflict between the Catholic Spiritain order and the colonial authorities in Cameroon during the interwar period constitutes an important and hitherto overlooked facet of examining the French colonial mind.

Gallicization and Spiritain Cooperation, 1916–1923

Efforts to Gallicize Cameroon began shortly after Anglo-French forces invaded and then divided the former German colony.[10] Faced with the need for French-speaking African clerical staff, in early 1916 military commanders began demobilizing chaplains with missionary experience and dispatched them to Cameroon to reopen schools and begin the all-important task of spreading the French language.[11] Spiritain missionaries played a key role in this process from the very beginning due to a combination of patriotic and petty motivations. While the Spiritains saw the task of aiding the government's plan to spread French as part of the wartime Union Sacrée in which personal ambitions were set aside for the good of the nation, they were equally motivated by a deep-seated hatred and jealousy of "heretical" Protestant missions that they feared might best them in the all-important race to convert native souls.[12] As much as they disliked the presence of French Protestants in the form of the Paris Evangelical Missionary Society, the Spiritains objected even more strongly to the continued presence of American Presbyterians who, as citizens of a neutral power, were not only allowed to remain when other missions that had operated in the German period were expelled but who had also taken advantage of the resultant religious vacuum to expand their base of operations.[13] Furthermore, with less than a dozen priests to promote Catholic initiatives in the territory, the Spiritains worried that the combination of greater numbers—the Presbyterians had nearly thirty missionaries in the field with another sixteen home on leave—superior financial resources, and greater familiarity with Cameroon gave the Americans an unfair evangelical advantage by allowing them to open more schools than any other mission society. Given that experience under German rule had taught the local African population that Western education and fluency in European languages were the keys to better-paying white-collar jobs with merchant firms or the colonial administration, the Spiritains made no secret of their fear that the proliferation of Presbyterian schools would give their American rivals an unassailable and unacceptable lead in terms of access to pupils and potential converts. However, since the French authorities were unlikely to respond to purely sectarian complaints about the nature and scope of Protestant operations, the Spiritains opted instead to play the patriotism card by throwing themselves wholeheartedly into the Gallicization campaign in a blatant attempt to solicit administrative favoritism on their own behalf.[14] Consequently, the Spiritains began reopening as many schools as possible with the aid of German-trained native catechists who had been taught the rudiments of French. Spiritain willingness to cooperate with government authorities and their policies was thus deeply ingrained in the mission's activities three years before the 1919 rise of the conservative Bloc National ushered in a brief period of reconciliation between church and state at home in France.[15]

These early Spiritain efforts paid immediate dividends in the form of rapidly expanding school enrollments and excellent relations with Lucien Fourneau, French Cameroon's first civilian governor. Fourneau, who was already well disposed toward the Catholics due to his long friendship with Alexandre Le Roy, head of the Paris-based Spiritain order, was very pleased with Catholic efforts on behalf of the Gallicization campaign, particularly when their commitment did not falter after his September

1917 decision to create parallel public and private school systems.[16] As part of this process Fourneau also created an examination system to test the ability of private schools to teach French and began encouraging the missions to open even more schools by providing them with subsidies in the form of payments to teaching staff. Fourneau's decision, which was prompted by the lingering problem of how to reconcile the missionary desire to evangelize with the secular character of public schools, thrilled the Spiritains since it meant that they could finally engage in a head-to-head race with the Protestants to convert and save native souls by reopening village-based catechism schools.[17] At the same time, the Catholics recognized both the government's ongoing critical shortage of French-speaking native personnel and the fact that access to French language instruction was often what drew pupils to mission schools in the first place; hence in addition to operating a handful of schools run by white missionaries who taught exclusively in French, the Spiritains also opted to create a parallel system of catechism schools that offered both rudimentary French lessons as well as vernacular-based religious instruction.

As a result of these efforts, which stood in stark contrast to those of the Protestants, the Spiritains' already warm relations with the local colonial regime appeared to solidify. Whereas Catholic participation in Gallicization tripled along with the number of their schools from 1917 to 1920, Protestants, including both the American Presbyterians and the Paris Evangelical Missionary Society, lagged behind.[18] In the wake of Fourneau's September 1917 decision to allow missions to open purely religious schools, the Paris Mission significantly reduced its commitment to French language schools in favor of reverting to traditional Protestant missionary methods, which mandated that evangelical work be done in the vernacular so as to ensure a true conversion process. As upsetting as this was to the French authorities, the Paris Mission's choice of the Duala language as the medium of instruction in its coastal schools was also deeply troubling since the Duala's political agitation and repeated petitions to the League of Nations for independence appeared subversive and consequently tainted the Protestants by association in the eyes of local administrators.[19] To make matters worse the Paris Mission developed close ties to the American Presbyterians, whose inability to teach, let alone communicate, in French served as a constant thorn in the side of the Fourneau administration and threatened to undermine the ongoing Gallicization campaign.[20]

The resultant souring of government-Protestant relations, to which the Spiritains responded with unrestrained glee, soon worsened after Fourneau's March 1919 replacement as governor by Jules Carde. Convinced that the policies of *mise en valeur*, or economic development, and the cultural transformations of the civilizing mission called for under the terms of the mandate could be achieved only through faster and more regular dissemination of the French language, in October 1920 Carde issued a decree to regulate the organization and function of private schools.[21] The new decree required missions to get permission before opening any new schools and drew a distinction between recognized and unrecognized schools. Recognized schools were defined as those that followed an official secular curriculum set by the colonial administration, taught exclusively in French, and employed only certified teaching staff. Furthermore, the new law revamped the subsidy system and linked payments to the number of recognized school graduates who passed an annual government exam in French. Finally, the law required all missions to comply within a year and threatened to punish any infractions with permanent closure of the offending school.

While Carde saw the October 1920 law as a compromise intended to enforce rigorous teaching standards and generate more cooperation in spreading French while simultaneously permitting the use of vernaculars in unrecognized catechism schools, the reactions of the various missions were decidedly mixed.[22] The Protestants saw the new law as punitive and began arguing that it represented an unacceptable intrusion into mission affairs. Both the Presbyterians and the Paris Mission also voiced concerns that overzealous application of its provisions by individual colonial administrators would result in the closure of both recognized and unrecognized schools.[23] In the case of the Presbyterians, whose efforts to recruit French-literate mission personnel continued to meet with very limited success, strict application of the law threatened to shut down their work entirely, leading to their disappearance from Cameroon altogether. Although a review of the educational data indicates that both Protestant missions reluctantly took steps to conform to the new law, they spent the remainder of the Carde administration continually and vociferously complaining about the nature and extent of government intrusion into mission school affairs.[24]

Catholic reactions to the October 1920 law, on the other hand, were nothing short of euphoric since they had long called for government intervention to reign in the activities of their Protestant rivals.[25] As for their own efforts, the Spiritains anticipated few problems since the law essentially codified existing mission practices while providing them with new opportunities to earn much-needed subsidies. Moreover, the mission's warm relations with the colonial administration ensured that their schools were unlikely to be closed by overzealous administrators misinformed about the law's provisions, as had repeatedly happened to their Presbyterian rivals.[26] When the new system was first put to the test in 1921, the exam results confirmed that the Spiritains were making a disproportionately large effort to promote the spread of French, earning them both sizeable subsidies and continued government goodwill.[27] Just as they were in a position to begin capitalizing on this arrangement, however, everything changed. The unexpected March 1922 death of Father Malessard, head of Spiritain operations in Cameroon and the mission's most influential local colonial mind, left the Catholics adrift without a leader or direction at the height of the busy exam preparation season, causing their exam results to plummet well below those of their hated Protestant rivals.[28] Although the Catholics could have recovered from this temporary setback, the arrival of both a new governor and a new apostolic vicar of Cameroon precipitated a fundamental shift in church-state relations in which the Catholics and colonial administrators soon found each other at odds over language policy.

Anticlericalism and Spiritain Rejection of Official Language Policies, 1923–1939

In many ways the 1923 appointment of Theodore Paul Marchand as Cameroon's new governor could not have come at a worse time. Although the League of Nations had decided the year before to confirm the French mandate over Cameroon, the Permanent Mandates Commission had recently blasted French authorities for their failure to make adequate progress in educating the natives, arguing that perhaps the Protestants were right and that education was best conducted in the vernacular.[29] Marchand, however, disagreed. Reflecting the beliefs of the official interwar colonial mind, as articulated by educational theorists such as Georges Hardy and André Davesne, he remained firmly convinced that the higher intellectual concepts inherent in French civilization and the technical skills necessary for colonial development could only be expressed in French.[30] Consequently his administration redoubled official efforts to promote the spread of French in an attempt to prove the commission wrong and live up to the spirit of the mandate by completing the *mission civilisatrice*. As part of this process he not only expanded the public school system, but he also increased the subsidy rates for private schools in an effort to elicit greater missionary interest in teaching French while simultaneously imposing maximum age limits on students so as to force missions to cut loose supposedly uneducable pupils.[31] The final component of Marchand's efforts to promote the diffusion of French entailed expanding educational opportunities for girls by opening *écoles ménagères* throughout the country. Echoing the courses in sewing, cooking, and home economics offered by the various missionary societies, these newly created institutions were designed to train girls to become better wives and mothers. At the same time, however, the administration explicitly hoped that pupils in the *écoles ménagères* would also pick up some French language skills that they could then pass on to their future children.[32]

Given the colonial administration's past warm relations with the Spiritains and their earlier willingness to assist with the implementation of official policies, Marchand expected the Catholics to adapt readily and easily to these new directives. After all, they were not particularly revolutionary, and even the Protestants, albeit with their usual grumbling and complaints, quickly fell in line with a minimum of fuss.[33] Marchand was therefore shocked and offended when F. X. Vogt, the newly appointed head of the Spiritains in Cameroon, chose instead to rebuff these overtures and reverse longstanding Spiritain policy by championing the use of vernaculars instead of French. After so many years of close church-state cooperation on language and education policy, Marchand inevitably saw this change of heart by the Spiritains as a betrayal and consequently became increasingly hostile toward the mission and its activities in the mandate. This hostility, which coincided with the emergence of Radical Party leader Édouard Herriot's short-lived anticlerical administration back in metropolitan France, ultimately soured government relations with the Spiritains for the remainder of the interwar period. Given rising worker militancy in the mid-1920s, the Herriot administration was intensely suspicious of the church's links to Catholic trade unions and sought to curtail their activities by extending the 1901–5 anticlerical laws to Alsace and Lorraine. The Catholic lobby, which had pushed unsuccessfully since the end of the war for the repeal of the anticlerical laws as reward for its support of the Union Sacrée, responded by working to restore moderate Republicans to power in the 1928 elections. Nevertheless, latent hostility to the church—and religious orders such as the Spiritains—remained a theme in French domestic politics until the start of World War II.[34]

What, then, were the motives behind Vogt's fundamental reversal of Spiritain educational policy? When the Vatican named Vogt as its choice to replace the deceased Malessard as apostolic vicar of Cameroon, it did so in belief that his years of experience as a missionary in East Africa made him ideally suited to take over the floundering Spiritain operations inside the French mandate.[35] On arrival in Cameroon Vogt quickly became concerned not only by the chaos that emerged among the Spiritains after Malessard's death, but also by what he considered inadequate evangelical work among the natives, particularly when compared to that of the Presbyterians.[36] Vogt attributed this failure to the mistaken preoccupation of his predecessors with aiding official efforts to spread French to the near exclusion of all other activities. In order to rectify the situation, Vogt argued for a reduction in the Spiritain commitment to French language instruction in favor of making schools and the catechism available in the vernacular. According to Vogt, this was not only good evangelical policy, but it also made sense in light of the postwar decline of the Union Sacrée and his own conviction that Catholics were bound to a higher calling.

Seeking to overhaul Catholic methodology in Cameroon, Vogt sent out a series of circulars in 1923 to all Spiritain personnel in which he insisted that the mission's primary goal was evangelism and explicitly stated that other considerations, including the teaching of French, were secondary.[37] In order to facilitate this new emphasis on evangelism, Vogt ordered all mission personnel to begin preaching in the local vernaculars and ordered that anyone unable to do so after a year of study be sent back to France. Marchand, already suspicious of Vogt's patriotism due to the latter's Alsatian background, was deeply distressed by these circulars as well as by Vogt's tendency to openly question the utility of teaching African pupils to speak French in his correspondence with local administrators.[38] According to Vogt, experience showed that most natives quit school in search of jobs with Europeans shortly after acquiring little more than a smattering of French. Worse yet, he argued that those who did acquire greater fluency lost their work ethic in the process. Most left their villages in order to avoid manual labor and turned into *deracinés* with delusions of racial equality. Not only were such people unlikely to make good converts, but they were also, in Vogt's opinion, downright harmful since they led other Africans astray. Over the next several years Vogt repeatedly returned to this theme and in the process became increasingly critical of official policy. He even went so far as to decline what Marchand felt was a generous offer to train future Catholic teachers in the government's École Supérieure on the grounds that the secular education provided was inferior and was either in the hands of Protestants and blasphemers or atheists and freemasons who used the classroom to denounce all missions.[39]

While these increasingly testy exchanges naturally led to a cooling of the Spiritains' previously warm relations with the colonial administration, it was not until 1929 that the situation erupted into open conflict. In response to yet another of Vogt's missives challenging the wisdom of spreading French among the natives, Marchand launched a series of attacks on the mission that quickly escalated beyond a mere war of words.[40] Marchand began with the argument that the Spiritain mission was subversive and incompetent as demonstrated by its yearly exam results, pointing out that even the Americans were doing a better job of spreading the French language. Marchand also began cracking down on the Spiritains for violating the age limits on their school pupils. When Vogt protested that they had done so in the interests of saving souls, Marchand observed that strict adherence to the age limits would focus the mission's limited energies on those who could still learn while simultaneously aiding the process of *mise en valeur* by forcing expelled pupils back into the workforce.[41] Although Marchand's rebuke was intended to induce the Spiritains to resume their earlier support of French language instruction, these jabs merely goaded Vogt into more accusations, recriminations, and complaints, including charges that government officials were helping Protestant pupils cheat on exams. The apostolic vicar also made the far more serious charge that the administration's decision to include women and children in the *corvée*, a form of labor tax used for public works projects, was a form of forced labor that ran contrary to the spirit of the mandate.[42]

As the ensuing claims and counterclaims took an increasingly nasty and bitter turn, the Marchand administration sought new leverage to force the Catholics back into the fold regarding government language and education policies. Since the text of the mandate included statements guaranteeing freedom of conscience, direct attacks on the Spiritains were out of the question. Nevertheless, in 1930 the Marchand administration struck back at Vogt and his followers by convicting two priests of slander for their antigovernment comments.[43] This was followed in short order by the so-called Affaire des Sixas in which Marchand attacked the mission's boarding schools for the fiancées of converts. The Sixas, which were designed to train women to be Christian wives and mothers, came to the governor's attention in the wake of a fatal accident while pupils were working in a brickyard owned by the Spiritains. According to Marchand this was proof that the mission was engaging in forced labor by requiring pupils to perform unpaid work in exchange for their tuition and living expenses.[44] Worse, the governor alleged that the Sixas were actually a threat to public order due to their tendency to harbor women fleeing polygamous marriages and toyed with the idea of closing them down altogether. Vogt heatedly denied Marchand's claims in a series of letters and leveled his own counter-accusations about official language, education, and labor policies.

In July 1930 Marchand added to the already poisonous atmosphere by claiming that in addition to being difficult and obstructionist regarding the diffusion of French and the *mission civilisatrice*, the Spiritains were also unpatriotic and were engaged in acts bordering on treason by harboring German agents inside their mission stations.[45] These allegations, which were prompted by the presence of a German filmmaker illegally squatting in abandoned Catholic mission stations and the fact that several Spiritains (including Vogt) were of Alsatian extraction, tapped into interwar French paranoia about German influence in their colonies. Not content with impugning the Spiritains' patriotism, Marchand began hitting the Catholics where it hurt most by targeting their ability to attract converts. As part of this process the governor repeatedly refused to grant adequate amounts of land for the creation of new mission stations and began working to undermine the power and authority of Catholic catechists. Rather than simply reject Spiritain requests for new land grants east of Yaounde to cater to some fifteen thousand potential converts, a move that arguably would have violated the freedom of conscience clause in the mandate, Marchand opted instead to grant a mere four hectares, knowing that it was insufficient for the church, school, gardens, and residence necessary for a functional mission outstation.[46]

Just as the Spiritains began to feel the bite of Marchand's refusal to grant sufficient land for new mission stations, the governor also increased his pressure on the Catholics by working to undermine the authority of their catechists. This new attack on the mission's operations came hard on the heels of a 1929 Duala petition to the League of Nations that criticized French policies and demanded the revocation of its mandate in Cameroon.[47] The combination of resurgent Duala political activism and their decision to write the petition in German made French colonial officials hypersensitive to all challenges to their authority. Given the anticlerical sentiments at home, Catholic reluctance to aid in the spread of French, and the tendency of catechists to replace both unbaptized traditional hereditary chiefs and local administrators as the nucleus of local authority, the Marchand administration became increasingly concerned that the church was gaining an unacceptable level of political influence in the mandate.[48] In particular, the governor and his staff were bothered by the public's willingness to turn to catechists rather than government officials when seeking advice, arbitration of disputes, or interpretations of policy. When initial efforts to weaken the influence of the catechists by appointing them to unpopular positions as regional government intermediaries failed, Marchand tried to reign in their burgeoning political power by passing an April 1930 law requiring catechists to submit an endless series of paperwork before being allowed to take up their duties, a process that affected nearly two thousand catechists and their parishioners.⁴⁹ Marchand also released a related circular that required the demolition of unregistered mission buildings and required new ones to be built at least five hundred meters from any towns. The effect of these measures was to cut off Catholic evangelical efforts by either preventing catechists from working or requiring potential converts to walk long distances in order to get vernacular-based religious instruction.

Marchand's actions proved too much for the Catholics to bear, prompting Vogt to write the Spiritain headquarters in Paris with a request for direct intervention from the minister of colonies and possibly the League of Nations.⁵⁰ When news of his request leaked to the press, it led in quick succession to a deeply embarrassing parliamentary enquiry, a March 1931 inspection tour by the French delegate to the League of Nations, and orders from the minister of colonies to repeal the April 1930 law.⁵¹ Less than a month later Marchand was recalled to Paris and replaced by the more conciliatory Paul Bonnecarrère.

Although generally eager to avoid further conflict with the missions, Bonnecarrère insisted that the government had the right to regulate the missions and could specifically require the use of French, Latin, or vernaculars for church-related activities. Consequently, he passed a new law in March 1933 that revived many of the same provisions as Marchand's controversial April 1930 legislation regarding the registration of property and the need for missions to obtain official permission before opening new stations.⁵² In response, the Spiritains defiantly reduced enrollments in their recognized schools by nearly 60 percent while more than doubling the number of pupils in their vernacular-based village and catechism schools in order to underscore their refusal to be pushed into following official language and education policies.⁵³

The Spiritains were equally unimpressed with Bonnecarrère's decision the following month to begin encouraging the use of regional lingua francas such as Ewondo, Duala, and Bamum among government employees by providing administrators with stipends for learning local languages. Bonnecarrère's decision came in the wake of a series of educational conferences that concluded that the rudimentary nature of the educational system and the extreme linguistic diversity in the colonies prevented French authorities from adequately providing the masses with training in hygiene and vocational skills.[54] While the Catholics welcomed the governor's apparent willingness to accept the utility of vernaculars, they were suspicious of Bonnecarrère's motives and remained hostile to the government's emphasis on secular education and its ongoing efforts to promote the spread of French. Consequently, through the mid-1930s Spiritain leaders continued to attack official schools in sermons and admonished parishioners for even considering enrolling their children in the territory's public school system.[55]

Stung by the constant criticism, the newly appointed governor Pierre François Boisson convened several meetings in March 1937 in an effort to resolve the situation definitively. After chastising the Catholic missions for their bellicose comments, Boisson reminded the Spiritains that freedom of conscience had to be met on their side with discretion when critiquing official policy so as to avoid the eruption of open conflict or the codification of anticlerical sentiments into law.[56] Despite the Spiritains' declaration that they were willing to resume their earlier collaboration on matters of education and language policy, Governor Boisson remained skeptical of their sincerity. The outbreak of war in September 1939, however, quickly rendered the point moot. When hostilities finally wound to a close, the evolution of the mandate into a United Nations trusteeship, which clearly called on France to prepare Cameroon for the acquisition of independence, effectively terminated the interwar debates about language policy and its place in the *mission civilisatrice*.

Conclusion

While these fiercely acrimonious debates came to an abrupt halt in 1939, their existence and the church-state conflicts that they created represent a significant contribution to the growing body of evidence that French missions were not mere extensions of the colonial regime as alleged in earlier scholarly interpretations, but that they instead actively pursued their own agendas regardless of the consequences. These debates also illustrate that far from being a unified entity, the French colonial mind in the interwar period was divided. While government officials and missionaries alike viewed the *mission civilisatrice* and development efforts in Cameroon as part of the French national destiny, they disagreed as to what that destiny actually was or how it should be achieved. Rather than the Spiritains unquestioningly assisting with the official focus on economic development to the near exclusion of other issues, despite their earlier willingness to cooperate in efforts to Gallicize Cameroon by spreading the French language, the Spiritains made evangelism and the need to defeat their hated Protestant rivals in the race to acquire converts ultimately more important than maintaining cordial relations with local administrators. The resultant tensions created by this reversal of Catholic policy and the inability to resolve the essential ambivalence of the French colonial mind not only disprove Léon Gambetta's assertion that anticlericalism was not for export; these tensions also remain very much at work in France as the driving force behind current debates about how to assimilate immigrant Muslim communities. Best represented by the 2004 decision to ban the wearing of veils and head scarves in official photos and public schools, at their core these debates revolve around the same unresolved question of how to reconcile religion, modernization, the role of African populations, and the needs of a secular state faced by the Spiritains and French colonial authorities in the 1920s and 1930s.

Notes

This essay is drawn from and includes with permission several short passages from chapters 5–6 of Kenneth J. Orosz, *Religious Conflict and the Evolution of Language Policy in German and French Cameroon, 1885–1939* (New York: Peter Lang, 2008).

1. For the history of the Spiritain order see Henry J. Koren, *To the Ends of the Earth: A General History of the Congregation of the Holy Ghost* (Pittsburgh: Duquesne University Press, 1983); and Jean Criaud, *La Geste des Spiritains: Histoire de l'Eglise au Cameroun, 1916–1990* (Paris: Maison des PP. du Saint Esprit, 1990). Details of turn-of-the-century French anticlericalism can be found in Maurice Larkin, *Religion, Politics and Preferment in France since 1890* (Cambridge: Cambridge University Press, 1995).

2. See David Gardinier, "French Colonial Rule in Africa: A Bibliographic Essay," in *France and Britain in Africa*, ed. Prosser Gifford and William Roger Louis (New Haven CT: Yale University Press, 1971), 787–950; and Andrew Porter, *European Imperialism, 1860–1914* (London: Macmillan, 1994).

3. Henri Labouret, *Le Cameroun* (Paris: Paul Hartman, 1937).

4. Emmanuel Ghomsi, "Résistance à l'imperialisme Européen: Le Cas des Douala du Cameroun," *Afrika Zamani* 4 (July 1975), 157–202; and Ralph Austen, "The Metamorphoses of Middlemen: The Duala, Europeans and the Cameroon Hinterland, 1800–1960," *International Journal of African Historical Studies* 16:1 (1983), 1–24.

5. H. O. H. Vernon-Jackson, "Schools and School Systems in Cameroon, 1884–1961" (EdD diss., Columbia University, 1968); Solomon Nfor Gwei, "Education in Cameroon: Western Pre-colonial and Colonial Antecedents and the Development of Higher Education" (PhD diss., University of Michigan, 1975); Rudolf Stumpf, *La Politique Linguistique au Cameroun de 1884 à 1960* (Berne: Peter Lang, 1979); Madiba Essiben, *Colonisation et Evangélisation en Afrique: L'héritage scolaire du Cameroun (1885–1956)* (Frankfurt: Peter Lang, 1980); Lucie Ewane, "L'enseignement au Cameroun (1920–1960)" (These de doctorat de 3ème Cycle, Université de Provence, 1983).

6. For an example of the larger trend in French colonial historiography see Jean Suret-Canale, *French Colonialism in Tropical Africa, 1900–1945* (New York: Pica Press, 1971); and Denise Bouche, *Histoire de la colonisation française*, 2 vols. (Paris: Fayard, 1991).

7. Richard A. Joseph, "Church, State and Society in Colonial Cameroon," *International Journal of African Historical Studies* 13:1 (1980), 5–32; Jonas N. Dah, *One Hundred Years: Roman Catholic Church in Cameroon (1890–1990)* (Owirri, Nigeria: Namdi Printing Press, 1989). Johannes Fabian and William Samarin have uncovered similar issues in their studies of language policy in central Africa. See Johannes Fabian, *Language and Colonial Power: The Appropriation of Swahili in the Former Belgian Congo, 1880–1938* (Berkeley: University of California Press, 1991); and William J. Samarin, "Language in the Colonization of Central Africa, 1880–1900," *Canadian Journal of African Studies* 23:2 (1989), 232–49.

8. Ann Laura Stoler and Frederick Cooper, "Between Metropole and Colony: Rethinking a Research Agenda," in *Tensions of Empire*, ed. Frederick Cooper and Ann Laura Stoler (Berkeley: University of California Press, 1997), 1–56.

9. J. P. Daughton, *An Empire Divided: Religion, Republicanism, and the Making of French Colonialism, 1880–1914* (Oxford: Oxford University Press, 2006); Elizabeth A. Foster, "Church and State in the Republic's Empire: Catholic Missionaries and the Colonial Administration in French Senegal, 1880–1936" (PhD diss., Princeton University, 2006); Oissila Saaïda, "L'anticléricalisme: Article d'exportation? Le cas de l'Algerie avant la Première Guerre Mondiale,' *Vingtième Siècle, Revue d'histoire* 87 (July–September 2005), 101–12; Charles P. Keith, "Catholicisme, Bouddhisme et lois

laïques au Tonkin (1899–1914)," *Vingtième Siècle, Revue d'histoire* 87 (July–September 2005): 113–28.

10. For an account of the hostilities in Cameroon see Hew Strachan, *The First World War in Africa* (Oxford: Oxford University Press, 2004), chap. 3; and Michael Crowder and Jide Osuntokun, "The First World War and West Africa 1914–1918," in *History of West Africa*, rev. ed., ed. J. F. A. Ajayi and Michael Crowder (New York: Longman, 1987), 2:546–77. The decision to partition Cameroon is discussed at length in Madiba Essiben, "La France et la Redistribution des Territoires du Cameroun (1914–1916)," *Afrika Zamani* 11–12 (December 1981), 36–52; and Brian Digre, *Imperialism's New Clothes: The Repartitioning of Tropical Africa, 1914–1919* (New York: Peter Lang, 1990).

11. Essiben, *Colonisation et Evangelisation*, 111–13; Joseph, "Church, State and Society," 11; and Barthélèmy Mvondo Nyina, "L'enseignement dans la politique coloniale française au Cameroun de 1916 à 1938," *Etudes d'histoire africaine* 8 (1976), 199–213.

12. For an introduction to French Catholic responses to the onset of war and the creation of the Union Sacrée see Larkin, *Religion, Politics and Preferment*, 148–51.

13. Details on Spiritain personnel and their quarrel with the Presbyterians are outlined in Congrégation du Saint Esprit Archive, Chevilly Larue, 2J1.2a (hereafter CSSP), Jules Douvry to Mgr. Alexandre Le Roy, 16 September 1916; see also Orosz, *Religious Conflict*, 202–4. For an overview of Presbyterian activities and personnel in Cameroon, see Henry T. Efesoa Mokosso, *American Evangelical Enterprise in Africa: The Case of the United Presbyterian Mission in Cameroon, 1879–1957* (New York: Peter Lang, 2007). Similar information on the Paris Mission, which had only four missionaries in the field during the war years, is covered in Elie Allégret, *La Mission du Cameroun* (Paris: Société des Missions Évangéliques, 1924).

14. Centre des Archives d'Outre-Mer, Aix-en-Provence (hereafter CAOM), 1 Aff Pol/29, "Missions au Cameroun et au Togo," untitled report by Jules Douvry, December 1916; and Criaud, *La Geste des Spiritains*, 42, 122–23.

15. For an introduction to the Bloc National and its politics see James F. McMillan, *Twentieth Century France: Politics and Society, 1898–1991* (London: Edward Arnold, 1992), chap. 9.

16. The Spiritains' relations with the Fourneau administration are documented in Louis Ngongo, *Histoire des Forces Religieuses au Cameroun* (Paris: Éditions Karthala, 1982), 47–57; and Criaud, *La Geste des Spiritains*, 122–23. For Fourneau's reorganization of the educational system in Cameroon see CAOM SG TGO/29, file 250, "Le Mandat français au Cameroun," and "Rap-

port sur l'administration du Cameroun de la conquête au 1er Juillet," Annexe de la *Journal Officiel de la République Française* 53:415 (7 September 1921), 430–31.

17. CSSP 2J1.5a1, Douvry to Le Roy, 29 December 1917; CSSP 2J1.2a, [Louis] Malessard to Le Roy, 5 April 1921; and Stumpf, *La Politique Linguistique*, 84–86.

18. Between 1917 and 1920 enrollments in Catholic schools went from 1,700 pupils in twenty-seven schools to 6,000 pupils in eighty-eight schools. During the same period enrollments in the ten schools run by the Paris Mission vacillated widely and actually dropped to a low of 260 pupils in 1919 before settling down to just over 1,000 students in 1922. By contrast the American Presbyterians increased their enrollments from 800 pupils in nine schools to 2,200 pupils in ninety schools between 1918 and 1920; see "Rapport sur l'administration des territoires occupés du Cameroun de la conquête au 1er Juillet 1921," 431; *Rapport au Ministre des Colonies sur l'administration des territoires occupés du Cameroun pendant l'anneé 1921*, 17; *Rapport annuel du Gouvernement Français sur l'administration sous mandat des territoires du Cameroun 1922*, 27.

19. The response of local colonial authorities to the Paris Mission's decision to work in the vernacular is outlined in "Cameroun Dernières Nouvelles," *Journal des Missions Évangéliques* (hereafter JME) 93:2 (1918), 57–63; and Département Évangélique Française d'Action Protestante (hereafter DEFAP), Paris 52.724 B.22, André Oechsner de Connick, "Au Jour le Jour 14 Juin 1919–31 Octobre 1920," entry for 15 May 1920. For the Duala's political activism and petitions to the League see Michael D. Callahan, *Mandates and Empire: The League of Nations and Africa, 1914–1931* (Brighton: Sussex Academic Press, 1999), 43–44; Ralph Austen and Jonathan Derrick, *Middlemen of the Cameroons Rivers: The Duala and Their Hinterland c. 1600–c. 1960* (Cambridge: Cambridge University Press, 1999), 144–48.

20. W. Reginald Wheeler, *The Words of God in an African Forest: The Story of an American Mission in West Africa* (New York: Fleming H. Revell, 1931), 41; "Cameroun Dernières Nouvelles," *JME* 92:2 (1917), 126–28; and CAOM 1 Aff Pol/3139 file 4: 68, Meray, Inspector of Colonies, to Governor Jules Carde, 1 February 1920.

21. "Arrêté reglement le fonctionnement des écoles privées d'enseignement primaire," 1 October 1920, *Journal Officiel du Cameroun* (hereafter JOC)5:51 (1 November 1920), 151.

22. "Rapport sur l'administration des territoires occupés du Cameroun de la conquête au 1er Juillet 1921," 430–31; and Gwei, "Education in Cameroon," 208.

23. Orosz, *Religious Conflict*, 224–34.

24. From 1921 to 1927 the French Protestants averaged 1,125 pupils in thirteen recognized schools compared to the Presbyterians' average of 1,990 pupils in ten schools. Despite their chronic lack of French-speaking personnel during the same period the Americans routinely had 35 or more pupils per year pass the official exam while the Paris Mission had only 10. See *Rapport sur l'administration des territoires occupés du Cameroun pendant l'anneé 1921*, 18; *Rapport annuel sur l'administration sous mandat des territoires du Cameroun*, 1922:28; 1923:37; 1924:28; 1925:14; 1926:20; *Rapport annuel addressé par le Gouvernement Français au Conseil de la Société des Nations sur l'administration sous mandat du territoire du Cameroun 1927*, 16.

25. Essiben, *Colonisation et Evangelisation*, 157; and Stumpf, *La Politique Linguistique*, 85–86.

26. The Presbyterians' problems with overzealous government officials are chronicled in Orosz, *Religious Conflict*, 227–31.

27. While the Catholics had only 1,820 pupils in their ten recognized schools, they had 35 students pass the first round of official exams in 1921 and earned 5,250 francs in subsidies. See *Rapport sur l'administration des territoires occupés du Cameroun pendant l'anneé 1921*, 17.

28. Louis Malessard had replaced Douvry in 1920 when the latter returned to France. For more on Malessard's death and its effect on Spiritain operations in Cameroon see Criaud, *La Geste des Spiritains*, 56; and Roger Dussercle, *Du Kilimanjaro au Cameroun: Mgr F. X. Vogt (1870–1943)* (Paris: La Colombe, 1954), 84.

29. League of Nations, Permanent Mandates Commission, *Report on the Work of the Third Session of the Commission*, Minutes of the Fourth Meeting, 1923, C.519, 28–29. For a discussion of the Permanent Mandates Commission's structure and function see Callahan, *Mandates and Empire*, chap. 4.

30. For the Marchand administration's attitude toward language and education see Marcel Jezouin, *Directions Pedagogiques* (Yaounde: Imprimerie du Gouvernement, 1930), 6–7. Regarding interwar French colonial educational theory see Gail P. Kelly, "Colonialism, Indigenous Society and School Practices: French West Africa and Indochina, 1918–1938," in *Education and the Colonial Experience*, 2nd ed., ed. Philip G. Altbach and Gail P. Kelly (New Brunswick NJ: Transaction Books, 1984), 9–32; and Alice L. Conklin, *A Mission to Civilize: The Republican Idea of Empire in France and West Africa, 1895–1930* (Stanford: Stanford University Press, 1997), chap. 2.

31. "Arrêté completant les dispositions des arrêtés de 1er Octobre 1920 et 25 Juillet 1921 sur l'enseignement," 26 December 1925, JOC 10:114 (1 February 1935), 52–53. Subsequent laws doubled the subsidies available in 1930

and again in 1936. "Arrêté réglementant le fonctionnement des écoles privées dans le Territoire," 19 March 1930, *JOC* 15:236 (1 April 1930), 209–10; and "Arrêté portant modification du taux des subventions scolaires," 29 August 1936, *JOC* 21:393 (15 September 1936), 710.

32. Only a handful of girls obtained admission to regular schools run by either the local administration or the various missionary societies since the European community in Cameroon shared the opinion that native girls had little need or use for an academic education. For the creation and purpose of the *écoles ménagères* see *Rapport annuel sur l'administration du Cameroun 1923*, 24–26, 31; and Ewane, "L'Enseignement au Cameroun," 103, 287–93.

33. For Protestant reactions to Marchand's policies see Orosz, *Religious Conflicts*, 265–76.

34. Nicholas Atkin, "The Politics of Legality: The Religious Orders in France 1901–1945," in *Religion, Society and Politics in France since 1789*, ed. Frank Tallett and Nicholas Atkin (London: Hambledown Press, 1991), 149–66; and Larkin, *Religion, Politics and Preferment*, 147–51.

35. Criaud, *La Geste des Spiritains*, 54–59. Vogt's life and work are chronicled in detail in Nicolas Ossama, *Monseigneur François-Xavier Vogt: Cinquante ans apres* (Yaounde: Imprimerie St Paul, 1993).

36. Vogt was bothered to note that the Presbyterians routinely outperformed the Catholics on government exams by a three to one margin and had triple the number of pupils in unrecognized village schools between 1921 and 1925. See *Rapport annuel sur l'administration sous mandat des territoires du Cameroun*, 1921:18; 1922:28; 1923:37; 1924:28; 1925:14. For Vogt's opinions concerning the need to reduce French language instruction see CSSP 2J1.5a1, Vogt to the Director General [Mgr Merio, Director General of the Sainte Enfance] 26 November 1922; and CSSP 2J1.4b1-2, Vogt to [Le Roy], 5 August 1924.

37. Circular 7 and 11–13, 1 June 1923, 21 and 28 November 1923, and 16 December 1923, in CSSP 2J1.12b4, Jean Criaud, ed., "Les Circulaires du Monseigneur François Xavier Vogt."

38. CSSP 2J1.2b2, Vogt to Marchand, "Rapport succinct sur l'œuvre des missions catholiques dans le Vicariat apostoliques du Cameroun," 3 September 1924. Marchand's reactions to Vogt's statements are contained in marginal notes on an accompanying letter sent with the report. See Archives Nationales, Yaounde (hereafter ANY), APA 10384, F. X. Vogt to Marchand, 3 September 1924. Also see CSSP 2J1.2b2, Marchand to Vogt, 20 October 1924.

39. CSSP 2J1.4b1-2, Vogt to [Le Roy], 5 August 1924; CSSP 2J1.2b, Vogt, "Rapport sur le Vicariat apostolique du Cameroun, 1 Octobre 1924"; CSSP

2J1.5a2, "Rapport à la Sainte Enfance 1927"; CSSP 2J1.5a3, "Rapport à la Sainte Enfance 1929"; and CSSP 2J1.5a4, Joseph Soul, "Rapport General sur la visite du District du Cameroun," January–July 1929.

40. See Marchand's response to Dimpault [Inspector General of Colonies], in CAOM 1 Aff Pol/3140, "Action des missions religieuses juin 1931," 27 June 1931.

41. CSSP 2J1.12b4, "Les Circulaires du Monseigneur François-Xavier Vogt," Circular 72, 20 April 1932; and ANYAPA 10559J, untitled circular to Missions, 25 February 1930.

42. CAOM 1 Aff Pol/3140, Marchand's response to Dimpault [Inspector General of Colonies], "Action des missions religieuses juin 1931," 27 June 1931; Criaud, *La Geste des Spiritains*, 131–39; and Ngongo, *Histoire des Forces Religieuses*, chap. 5.

43. Criaud, *La Geste des Spiritains*, 138; and CAOM 1 Aff Pol/3140, Dimpault to Minister of Colonies [François Piétri], 25 July 1931.

44. CAOM 1 Aff Pol/3140, Marchand's response to Dimpault [Inspector General of Colonies], "Action des missions religieuses juin 1931," 27 June 1931. For more on the Affaire des Sixas see Kenneth J. Orosz, "The *Affaire des Sixas* and Catholic Education of Women in French Colonial Cameroon, 1915–1939," *French Colonial History* 1:1 (2002), 33–49.

45. CSSP 2J1.2b3, Le Hunsec to Minister of Colonies, 11 July 1930. Louis Le Hunsec succeeded Alexandre Le Roy as head of the Spiritain Order in 1925. Koren, *To the Ends of the Earth*, 394–99.

46. CSSP 2J1.2b3, Le Hunsec to the Minister of Colonies, 11 July 1930.

47. CAOM 1 Aff Pol/615 file 1, Petition of the Douala tribe to the League of Nations, 11 August 1929. Richard A. Joseph, "The German Question in French Cameroon, 1919–1939," *Comparative Studies in Society and History* 17:1 (1975), 65–90; and Austen and Derrick, *Middlemen of the Cameroons Rivers*, 144–52.

48. CAOM 1 Aff Pol/3140, Dimpault to the Minister of Colonies, 25 July 1931; and Philippe Laburthe-Tolra, "Rôle des laïcs et des catechistes dans la conversion au catholicisme des Beti du Sud-Cameroun," in *Naitre et Grandir en Eglise: Le role des autocthones dans la premiere inculturation du christianisme hors Europe* (Lyon: Université Jean Moulin III, 1987), 132–46.

49. "Arrêté reglementant l'installation des postes secondaires des missions religiuses confiés à des indigènes," 24 April 1930, JOC 15:239 (15 May 1930), 301–2; and Ngongo, *Histoire des Forces Religieuses*, 59–61, 93–98, and appendix 2.

50. Criaud, *La Geste des Spiritains*, 142–44.

51. Laburthe-Tolra, "Rôle des laïcs," 140–41.

52. "Décret réglement le régime des cultes dans les territoires du Cameroun sous mandat français," 28 March 1933, *JOC* 18:274 (15 May 1933), 274–78.

53. While enrollments in recognized schools gradually increased over the next several years, they remained roughly half their 1932 value for the duration of the interwar period. *Rapport annuel addressé par le Gouvernement Français au Conseil de la Société des Nations sur l'administration sous mandat du territoire du Cameroun*, 1932:139; 1933:109–10; 1934:139; 1935:132; 1936:121; 1937:107–8; 1938:104.

54. "Circulaire à Messieurs des chefs de circonscription," 31 January 1933, *JOC* 18:306 (15 February 1933), 94–95; and Stumpf, *La Politique Linguistique*, 100; O. Louwers, "Native Education: General Report," in *L'Enseignement aux Indigènes*, Institut Colonial Internationale (Bruxelles: Établissements Généraux d'Imprimerie, 1931), 41; and Ngongo, *Histoire des Forces Religieuses*, 133–34.

55. Ngongo, *Histoire des Forces Religieuses*, 137.

56. Ngongo, *Histoire des Forces Religieuses*, 137–38; and Nyina, "L'enseignement dans la politique coloniale française," 210.

7

Information and Intelligence Collection among Imperial Subjects Abroad

The Case of Syrians and Lebanese in Latin America, 1915–1930

MARÍA DEL MAR LOGROÑO NARBONA

The establishment of French mandates throughout the former Ottoman provinces of Greater Syria and Mount Lebanon had certain unforeseen demographic consequences for France. One of these was the acquisition of administrative responsibility for multi-ethnic mandate populations of whom an estimated one-seventh of the total population of Syria and Lebanon lived abroad.[1] This far-flung diaspora of Greater Syria's indigenous peoples posed challenges that had previously afflicted the Ottoman Empire. The migrations that it represented were not consequences of the mandate regimes but, rather, originated in the larger population movements that had taken place throughout the Mediterranean in the last decades of the nineteenth century and the first decades of the twentieth. In a context of economic decline and worsening political difficulties at home, former Ottoman citizens migrated to Europe, West Africa, North America, and South America. Most of this migrant population settled in prominent urban centers of the United States, Argentina, and Brazil.[2] The result was that by 1920 the widespread geographical diffusion of those with familial connections, whether immediate or ancestral, to the newly partitioned territories of French-administered Syria and Lebanon made for something of a fragmented mandate, one in which the new imperial occupiers would have to keep a weather eye open for the views and actions of large Syrian and Lebanese expatriate communities.

What then did Greater Syria's demographic fragmentation mean for France's new colonial enterprise in the Levant? And how did this diffused population impact on French colonial minds in the interwar years? This chapter contends that the presence of substantial overseas communities of Syrians and Lebanese outside the French Middle Eastern mandate territories of Syria and Lebanon compelled the French authorities to look beyond the territorial boundaries assigned by the League of Nations in order to include these mandate populations living abroad. In other words the French mandate over Syria and Lebanon should be reconsidered as a subject-based mandate and not as a merely territorial-based one.

Syrians and Lebanese overseas could work either for or against French diplomatic aspirations to achieve political hegemony and legitimacy in the Levant. Some expatriate communities became valued pools of support for French political control; others were among its bitterest opponents. What is incontestable is that the voices of some Syrians and Lebanese around the world, including those in Argentina and Brazil, were influential. Once again, though, there was a duality to this process. While some were instrumental in formulating and supporting the propaganda that legitimized French colonial aspirations in the Levant, others challenged that same legitimacy. In this context the organization and systematization of intelligence gathering over French mandate citizens abroad highlights the extent of the political, cultural, and economic influence wielded by these communities within the larger French colonial project in the Levant.

As Martin Thomas explains, French intelligence gathering in the mandate territories has been analyzed by historians of mandate Syria and Lebanon predominantly in terms of the urban surveillance of notable elites.[3] Building on Jean-David Mizrahi's and Michael Provence's analyses of clan leaders in the Jabal Druze, in his work Thomas has broadened the subject of surveillance to the Bedouin tribes of the Jazeera region in Syria and, even more important, has advanced the notion of "colonial states as intelligence states."[4] Put simply, the survival of imperial rule rested both on the quality of information gathered about dependent populations and on the ability to exploit it quickly enough to provide potential sources of popular opposition from escalating into major existential threats to the colonial state.[5] While these scholars have identified state acquisition of political information about subjects' actions and intentions as constitutive of colonial state control, their focus has been largely restricted to the territorial confines of the mandate territories. As this chapter shows, another object of control—and a subject of constant surveillance—was the political activities of Syrians and Lebanese abroad. Given the breadth of Syrian and Lebanese emigration overseas, and the fact that so little attention has been paid to non-English-speaking destinations for these emigrants, this chapter concentrates on the particular case of Syrians and Lebanese in Brazil and Argentina.

The opening section provides some preliminary observations intended to help us understand the question of a territorial mandate versus a subject-based one. It is followed by analysis of the surveillance mechanisms set in place by the French government over its citizens in Latin America. Their chronological development is analyzed with reference to the particular cases of the Levantine emigrant communities in Brazil and Argentina.

Territorial-Based versus Subject-Based Mandate: "Filling in the Blanks?"

At first glance the existence in the French Foreign Ministry archives of extensive documentation regarding Syrian and Lebanese nationals abroad may seem difficult to explain. The legal basis and administrative structures of the French mandate system in Syria and Lebanon have traditionally been viewed in territorial terms as a mixture of colonial forms of governance, preexisting legal codes, and gradual development of proto-nation states. The result has been to diminish the value of these territories' emigrants in the sociopolitical and economic construction of the mandate territories. How, then, do we explain the existence of detailed intelligence material about these overseas populations in the French mandate archives held under Foreign Ministry auspices? Kohei Hashimoto, one of the first scholars to note the relevance of the French archives to the study of the Lebanese emigrant population, argued that in light of the vacuum caused by the legal lacunae of the Treaties of

Sèvres (August 1920) and Lausanne (July 1923), France "had to fill in the blanks between 1920 and 1926, protecting Syrian-Lebanese migrants by providing certificates identifying them as subjects under French custody."[6] By virtue of the Treaty of Sèvres, former Ottoman citizens automatically acquired the citizenship of their nation of residence. Article 123 of the treaty contained the following stipulation: "Turkish subjects habitually resident in territory which in accordance with the provisions of the present Treaty is detached from Turkey will become *ipso facto*, in the conditions laid down by the local law, nationals of the State to which such territory is transferred."[7] This territorially oriented clause placed those former Ottoman subjects abroad in a legal vacuum as it only provided nationality based on the principle of residence (jus soli). In an attempt to close the legal loophole that Sèvres had created for many new Syrians and Lebanese, the Treaty of Lausanne three years later introduced clauses that combined both jus soli and jus sanguinis principles, making it possible for Levantine residents overseas to opt for a different nationality under certain conditions within two years of the treaty's enactment.[8] Article 34 of the Lausanne Treaty was particularly forthright regarding differential rights of nationality:

> Subject to any agreements which it may be necessary to conclude between the Governments, exercising authority in the countries detached from Turkey and the Governments of the countries where the persons concerned are resident, Turkish nationals of over eighteen years of age who are natives of a territory detached from Turkey under the present Treaty, and who on its coming into force are habitually resident abroad, may opt for the nationality of the territory of which they are natives, if they belong by race to the majority of the population of that territory, and subject to the consent of the Government exercising authority therein.[9]

This legal protection did not expire after 1926 as Hashimoto suggests.[10] Instead it continued after the expiration of the treaty, reflecting the fact that not all Syrian and Lebanese migrants either had the opportunity or considered it appropriate to opt for their nationality of birth. For instance, those Syrians and Lebanese who had naturalized citizenship in Argentina could not opt for new nationality status as citizens of one of the mandate states without jeopardizing their existing legal status in their actual country of residence as per Argentine laws.[11] In the eyes of international law, however, any such migrants who did not opt for nationality were to become Turkish nationals by default after the expiration of the period established in Lausanne. Ultimately, however, this precarious legal situation was resolved thanks to bilateral agreements with Turkey that extended the period during which former Ottoman subjects overseas could opt for different nationality status, first to 1937 and then to 1952 (by which time, of course, both mandates had given away to independent Syrian and Lebanese nation-states).[12]

Important questions remain. Why, for instance, was France responsible for such bilateral agreements in the first place? And why does the archival documentation regarding these nationals abroad contain all sorts of minutiae with no connection to matters of nationality or citizenship status? Answers may be found by considering the nature of the French control over its mandate subjects abroad. This is best understood in legal terms as deriving from a series of articles agreed upon by the Council of the League of Nations in August 1922, the aim of which was to clarify further the "degree of authority, control, or administration to be exercised by the Mandatory."[13] For our purposes, the key instrument was Article 3 of the council's new instructions, which explained the limits on the authority of the mandate power as follows:

> The Mandatory shall be entrusted with the exclusive control of the foreign relations of Syria and Lebanon and with the right to issue exequaturs to the consuls appointed by foreign powers. Nationals of Syria and the Lebanon living outside the limit of the territory shall be under the diplomatic and consular protection of the Mandatory.[14]

This statement indicates that France was not merely "filling in the blanks" but rather was fulfilling its obligations toward its mandate subjects abroad. Even so, the zeal with which the French diplomatic authorities undertook these duties should not be regarded simply as adherence to the letter of the League of Nations edict, but in light of the political and economic importance that French diplomats and mandate officials ascribed to these emigrant communities. Their actions, in other words, rested on certain shared imperialist presumptions—on the workings of the colonial mind. France perceived Syrians and Lebanese in the Americas as economically thriving subjects of the Levant mandates whose great economic potential should be harnessed to French imperial benefit.[15] Yet this economic dimension was less significant than other political concerns of a more practical nature. These political questions reflected the overarching dynamics in the relationship between French authorities and their mandate territories. As mentioned above, segments of the population abroad became strong pillars upon which France could build valuable legitimacy that might help the consolidation of administrative control in the mandates while, at the same time, adding to the international respectability of the French presence in the Middle East. Yet this process did not go uncontested. Other sectors of the emigrant populations abroad became bitter opponents of the mandate system with damaging consequences for French imperial power and international prestige. Similar to the anticolonial, and often pan-Arab, opposition to the mandate regimes that developed in Cairo, Berlin, and Geneva, the Americas were important centers of an increasingly coordinated and global resistance to the mandate system. Opposition parties, for instance, established newspapers that were read beyond the Americas, and sometimes within the mandate territories themselves, in which they harshly criticized French policies. These external voices of dissent acquired greater importance by virtue of the fact that French censors and police severely punished any criticism of imperial rule made in the local press.

Those Syrians and Lebanese living outside the mandate territories and metropolitan France often operated in a more relaxed political environment, whether in raising funds, expressing dissentient opinions, or lending support to France's nationalist opponents in Damascus and Beirut. The fact that these Levantine subjects lived in territories outside French sovereign control necessarily limited France's ability to curtail or contain their activities. The emigrants' greater freedom of action leads us to the third and last preliminary consideration: in the less tightly regulated environments of Latin America, the mechanisms of surveillance adopted by the French offer a different perspective on the actual fragility of imperial power. In this particular context, as in rural locales far from the administrative hubs of colonial power, the development of a system of intelligence gathering highlights the inability of supposedly autocratic imperial masters to regulate or otherwise restrict the movement of knowledge within the civil society of a dependent territory or among the transnational communities affiliated to it.[16]

The establishment of an intelligence-gathering network covering Syrian and Lebanese overseas subjects in Brazil and Argentina occurred in three main phases. The first of these took root during the years prior to and during World War I. It marked a grudging acknowledgment of the political mobilization of Syrian and Lebanese communities in Brazil and Argentina that paralleled the myriad networks of comparable Syrian and Lebanese political movements in France, Europe, and the Middle East. The second phase occurred during the final years of the Great War as Franco-British rivalries in the Middle East intensified in the wake of British general Allenby's eviction of Ottoman forces from Palestine. During this period the French government decided to seek the endorsement of sympathizers among the Syrian and Lebanese in Brazil and Argentina as part of their broader search for cultural and material support against British imperialist aspirations in the Middle East. The third and final phase unfolded from July 1920 onward, immediately after the mandates were established. It was then that the French authorities moved to dismantle internal opposition and create new networks of indigenous support for the emergent mandate administrations in Syria and Lebanon. As part of this process, the French began mapping the different political affiliations and opinion trends among the Syrians and Lebanese abroad. Codifying and analyzing the information collected led to greater systematization of previous intelligence-gathering activities, a more or less covert process that nonetheless illustrated that the imposition of French mandate rule had far-reaching transnational dimensions.

Delineating Spheres of Interest: Committees and the French Colonial Party

The decision of Alexandre Millerand's French government in 1920 to set about this intelligence gathering overseas should be understood as a logical next step, as the formalization and bureaucratization of a previous, more informal system of information collection that had been in place since the early 1910s. Moreover, the need to acquire documentary material that might lend itself to strengthening France's claim on the Levant began in the twenty years prior to World War I when the French Colonial Party, in this instance represented first and foremost by the Comité de l'Asie Française, delineated their spheres of interest in the Middle East. That being the case, the dilemma for the historian remains to establish when and how exactly French diplomats started paying attention to the political potential of Ottoman emigrants abroad prior to the war.

At this early stage committees, or small associations and pressure groups formed around particular local political interests, were the main organizational unit of political activism among Syrians and Lebanese at home and overseas. As historian Eliezer Tauber explains, before 1914 the foremost association among these Syrian and Lebanese emigrants was the Amis de l'Orient. Founded in 1908 by two naturalized Syrian immigrants in Paris, Shukri Ghanem, a Maronite from Beirut, and Georges Samne, a Greek Melchite doctor from Damascus, this organization subsequently transformed itself into Comité de l'Orient in 1912. Its new title reflected the fact that it was, by this point, closely associated with the French Colonial Party. The erstwhile Amis de l'Orient rebranded itself in response to the intensification of European rivalries and the worsening internal problems of the Turkish Empire, all of which combined to change its political character as well.[17] Once relaunched under its new name, the Comité de l'Orient aligned itself more closely with the French government, which helps explain French official sensitivity to questions of emigration out of the Ottoman provinces of Greater Syria and Mount Lebanon as war loomed larger.

Organizing into committees that served as pressure groups and that subsequently developed into proto-nationalist parties was not something unique to the Ottoman emigrants (Syrians and Lebanese) in Paris. Indeed, as we have seen, its copycat aspect was evident in the fact that the Colonial Party, the main quasi-governmental actor in shaping French imperial policy in the Middle East, was structured along similar lines. Always an amalgam of imperial lobby groups, rather than a party political body, the Colonial Party's component societies and regional committees coalesced whenever their interests in a particular geographical area, an identifiable economic opportunity, or a key aspect of French expansion coincided.[18] One such committee was the aforementioned Comité de l'Asie Française, which became the association within the Colonial Party most closely identified with France's territorial ambitions in the Middle East.[19] Hampered by the internal competition and the regional rivalries among the Colonial Party's component groups, the Comité de l'Asie Française was restructured in 1912, with some of its supporters re-emerging under the name of the Comité de Défense des Intérêts Français en Orient. Like its forebear, this new committee also claimed to serve French interests in the Middle East. Revamped it may have been, but this committee had a short lifespan, not least because several of its leaders already belonged to the older Comité de l'Asie Française. Among them was Robert de Caix, who was directly responsible in 1920 for the formalization of intelligence gathering from the overseas communities. By 1913 the two committees had merged.[20]

We can only speculate about when and how these committees became aware of the political potential of the Levantine communities in the Americas in the years immediately preceding World War I. But it should be noted that emigration from the provinces of Greater Syria and Mount Lebanon had already aroused concern among members of the Comité de l'Asie. Their anxieties derived from several apparent triumphs of Anglo-Saxon cultural imperialism over the French civilizing mission in the region. French missionaries based in the Levant reported that "there is a great longing for America and the world of big business. Land and houses are mortgaged to pay for long and costly journeys thither in the hope of making fortunes. . . . This frantic emigration to America is a calamity for Lebanon."[21] The massive scale of emigration of Lebanese and Syrians to the Americas and Egypt was not new and had been identified as a critical factor a few years earlier by Bulus Nujaym in his text *La Question du Liban*. Written under the pseudonym of M. Jouplain, *La Question* is considered today to be one of the foundational texts of the Lebanese cultural revival.[22] Nujaym, along with his support for the creation of an independent Greater Lebanon, fixated upon what were probably exaggerated statistics to suggest that a veritable exodus of emigrants was under way at the time. Despite his inflated figures, Nujaym's emotive language still gives us a flavor of the disquiet that this large-scale demographic outflow caused among interested intellectuals and politicians living in France: "Every year around 12,000 emigrants leave Lebanon ... between 1870 and 1900 a third of the population was forced to migrate."[23] Nor was the matter simply one of quantity; it was also one of quality. Large numbers of highly educated professionals figured among Nujaym's statistics.[24] From a French colonial perspective, however, neither the alarm registered about the extensive emigration from Greater Syria nor the existence of a large well-educated emigrant community necessarily implied an immediate recognition of the political potential that lay behind harnessing the burgeoning communities of Levantine peoples overseas.

That said, what gave added intensity to this demographic alarm was the celebration in Paris of the First Arab Congress in 1913, an event that, it seems reasonable to conclude, increased the public visibility—and, hence, French awareness—of the interrelated political concerns felt by Syrians and Lebanese in the diaspora. The Congress was the idea of Al-Fatat, the Arab society founded in 1909 by Abd al-Hadi and Rustum Haydar in Paris.[25] More significant to us here, the event was jointly organized with Ghanem's Comité de l'Orient. Congressional sessions drew attention to the "Arab problem in Europe," an issue that bore directly on French concerns about the possible disintegration of the Ottoman Empire.[26] Beyond its avowed purpose, the composition of this Congress also highlighted the cosmopolitan makeup of these early Arabist movements. The delegates comprised a varied group in which Syrians made up the majority. Many of them lived in Paris, but they were joined by delegates from further afield: three from the United States, two from Ottoman Iraq, and one from Mexico.[27] In addition to its international membership the Congress received a series of telegrams of support sent from numerous destinations in Europe, the Middle East, and beyond, a fact that must have been noticed by the French Colonial Party members who attended Congress proceedings.[28]

Franco-British Wartime Propaganda Contest: The Committees at Work

Only in the final stages of World War I, however, did the French administration develop a sustained interest in the Syrian and Lebanese emigrant communities. Several factors contributed to this. First, the Sykes-Picot agreement concluded on 16 May 1916, far from reconciling the competing French and British colonial ambitions in the Middle East, actually exposed how deep the inter-Allied divisions were. Furthermore, Britain's military preeminence in the Middle East, secured by virtue of the dominance of its imperial forces in Egypt, Palestine, and Iraq, stood in sharp contrast to the structural and numerical weaknesses of the French military presence in the region.[29] Taking this strategic inferiority into account, alongside the potential that these communities abroad offered as some sort of counterweight, the French wartime coalition government moved to formalize its relationship with those émigré committees in Paris sympathetic to French claims on the Levant. This initiative crystallized in the creation of the Comité Central Syrien in May 1917, itself an offshoot of the previous Comité de l'Orient, the same committee that had previously enjoyed the backing of the French Colonial Party.[30]

The creation of the Comité Central Syrien represented a new departure in French efforts to manipulate Syrian and Lebanese elite opinion. Among the tasks assigned to the new committee's members, two of the most significant were, first, to coordinate the claims for self-determination made by those Syrians abroad who were amenable to French political protection and, second, to organize the recruitment of a military section, the Légion d'Orient, composed of loyal émigrés willing to fight alongside French forces in defeating the Ottoman Turks.[31] The Légion d'Orient, formally created by ministerial edict on 15 November 1916, was to consist of "Arab, Syrian, or Armenian volunteers" recruited mostly in the Americas and Europe. A volunteer force, it would serve under the orders of a French commander and would be paid for by the French government. Those coming forward for enlistment were first expected to formalize their recruitment in France, after which they would later be sent either to Cyprus or to Port Said in Egypt, where they were to receive their military apparel.[32] According to Meir Zamir, "the formation of the *Légion d'Orient* in Egypt and Cyprus in 1916 from Armenian, Syrian and Lebanese Christian volunteers was no more than an attempt to overcome France's inability to allocate its own forces to the campaign in Syria."[33] Zamir's judgment is militarily accurate perhaps but does not do justice to the symbolic importance attached to the Légion within the

Syrian and Lebanese communities in the Americas. Despite its predominantly military façade, both aspects of Comité Central Syrien's work — the coordination of self-determination interests abroad and the recruitment of mainly Syrian volunteers to the Légion — were actually two sides of the same political coin. Both were designed at French behest to garner support for France among the émigré populations. Each initiative, the Légion and the Comité, marked the culmination of years of overlapping interest, even symbiosis, between the French Colonial Party and the political activities of Syrian and Lebanese emigrants in Paris.[34]

In order to fulfill its new mandate, the Comité Central Syrien picked a team led by Jamil Mardam Bey and Dr. Lacah to travel to Brazil and Argentina. The delegation aimed to unite those sympathetic to France by canvassing for volunteers to the Legion d'Orient and putting in place local branches of the Comité Central Syrien. The delegates' arrival was widely publicized in emigrant community newspapers, thereby advancing its propaganda and organizational goals. Yet there was never any serious prospect that the Légion could become a military force of sufficient size to compete with the British military power already entrenched in the Middle East.[35] In light of this, the chief importance of the newly established local support committees was always political rather than military. These overseas branches of the Comité Central Syrien became the key intermediaries between the French diplomatic legations and the Syrian and Lebanese emigrant communities in South America.[36] While their central purpose was to foster public opinion favorable to French Middle Eastern interests, local committees also performed a surveillance function: the new groups provided French diplomats with valuable information about the political makeup of the emigrant community, its opinion makers, and their views.[37] In addition, from the beginning of the Allied military occupation of Syria and Lebanon in 1917 until the confirmation of the mandates in mid-1920, the local committees took charge of registering those Syrians to whom the French diplomatic legation had issued identification cards, as it was considered that these committees could best identify those individuals who remained loyal to France.

This registration process acquired greater significance after the British military takeover of Syria and Palestine. Britain's de facto occupation compounded French nervousness about the extent of British imperial ambitions in the Levant. In the twelve months from October 1918 (when British troops entered Damascus) until September 1919 (when the British formally agreed to cede control over Syria and Lebanon to a French occupation force under General Henri Gouraud), the issuing of travel documents to and the sending of remittances from Syrians and Lebanese abroad became a bone of contention between the French and British governments as each strove to demonstrate its military hegemony in the Levant. Despite this heightened tension, both registration and the release of travel documentation were left in the hands of the local committees, their ultimate supervision falling to the Comité Central Syrien in Paris.[38] As French colonial aspirations became clearer, the Paris government did intervene to regulate the flow of remittances, for the funds sent had been recognized as a valuable economic resource. As early as 27 October 1918 the Foreign Ministry advised its diplomatic mission in Buenos Aires of the increased sensitivity of sending money to Syria and Lebanon, territories that were now under Allied occupation.[39] This first telegram was further clarified in a memorandum sent to those missions most directly involved in monitoring overseas Levantine communities in February 1919. This second instruction insisted that letters to individuals in Syria had to be sent directly from the local post office with a note indicating "via Marseille." Any remittances were now to be sent by direct money transfer from a local bank to the Syrian Bank (the former Ottoman Bank) operating in Syria and Lebanon. This emphasis on centralizing the means of communication between overseas communities and the populations of the future mandates points to the precarious nature of French political control in the Levant at this point, particularly when compared with Britain's more firmly established Middle East position.

Formalization and Systematization of Intelligence Gathering Overseas

The conferral of the mandates over Syria and Lebanon at the San Remo conference rewarded long-held French imperial ambitions and opened a new phase in the handling of intelligence gathering over France's new Middle Eastern subjects. This new era of political control reverberated through French treatment of Syrians and Lebanese abroad and marked a transition characterized by the decay of the committee system that had been put in place during the war. Local branch committees were soon replaced by a more formalized surveillance system that sought to exert greater control over the collective behavior, social communication, and political contacts maintained by these overseas communities. Underlying fears of dissent drove the increasingly strident official efforts to regulate the transmission of knowledge between expatriate groups and their contacts within the mandate territories. The resulting struggle to contain the flow of political communication between Syrians and Lebanese at home and abroad became central features of French imperial policymaking and of French colonial presumptions regarding labyrinthine Levantine politics.[40]

French diplomats were clearly apprehensive of the negative effect that the rise of anti-French propaganda abroad could have upon the international legitimacy of their mandates. France's status as mandatory power in the two Levant states required formal confirmation by the League of Nations and was subject to annual League review of French governance, legal provision, and social policy thereafter. Hostile propaganda originating among overseas Levantine communities in the Americas both damaged France's image as a modernizing power and dispassionate lawgiver and threatened to have a destabilizing impact within the mandate territories.[41] In late August 1920, within weeks of assuming office as first French appointee as Levant high commissioner, General Gouraud acknowledged these problems in a letter to the French ambassador to Buenos Aires informing him of the fact that many Syrians coming from Argentina displayed strong "anti-French sentiments." The expression of such views, he continued, was having "detrimental" effects on the local population in the mandate territories. Although Gouraud's letter did not mention it explicitly, the high commissioner was clearly dissatisfied by the functioning of the committee system as a restraining influence on the overseas communities.[42]

The situation was no better six months later. On 28 December 1920 the high commissioner's right-hand man, his senior delegate, Robert De Caix, previously the driving force of the Comité de l'Asie Française, petitioned the Quai d'Orsay to press the French government into taking a firmer stand on the issue of hostile external propaganda.[43] De Caix noted that some twenty journals in the Americas regularly published inflammatory articles about specific problems faced by the French authorities in the Levant. These newspapers, although relatively small scale in terms of numbers produced, were nonetheless widely distributed overseas, as well as within Syria and Lebanon. As a result, De Caix requested a *mission de renseignement*, an intelligence-gathering exercise, in order to map the political affiliations and trends among Syrians in the Americas: their plans, their anti-French propaganda, their available resources, and the consequent prospects for a counterpropaganda offensive.[44] De Caix's petition was followed up a month later, on 19 January 1921, when a French parliamentary deputy who had just returned from a trip to the Americas addressed a letter to the Foreign Ministry outlining the likely political and economic benefits that the registration of Syrians (and Lebanese) in America might confer on France.[45]

In response, the Quai d'Orsay dispatched a circular to all its missions abroad on 19 February 1921, which stressed the imperative requirement to confer French diplomatic protection on the newly designated Syrian and Lebanese *protégés* in the Americas. Individual embassies were further requested to compile a report answering four questions regarding the Syrian and Lebanese subjects in their home country. The circular first requested details of the various committees and leagues organized by the local Syrian and Lebanese community, including information about the leaders of such groups. Second, the Foreign Ministry requested precise information about existing contacts between embassy staff and the local Syrian community, further enquiring whether an official Syrian representative should be designated to serve as mediator in all community dealings with France. Third, the circular demanded additional information regarding Syrian community contacts with the local authorities and other immigrant communities in their adopted state. Quai d'Orsay officials were particularly keen to know whether the local government would object if France assumed protecting powers over these Levantine communities. Finally, the circular enquired about the value of remittances sent by community members as well as the frequency of their return visits to the Middle East.

The Foreign Ministry justified this intelligence collection on the grounds that by conferring mandatory authority in Syria and Lebanon on France, the San Remo conference empowered the French government to collect detailed information about the political affiliations and socioeconomic background of the émigrés from the two states. On the question of remittances, however, the Quai d'Orsay was less high-handed, claiming that the information was only gathered in order to assess the feasibility of establishing Syrian bank branches in the host countries concerned. In addition to its requests for information about the Syrian and Lebanese communities, the Foreign Ministry also delineated new procedures for record keeping, the transmission of intelligence about Levantine emigrants, and the dissemination of pro-French propaganda among them. Clearly aware of Syrian and Lebanese sensitivity to the recent French takeover, the Foreign Ministry's Levant section compiled a separate letter explaining its official objectives as mandatory power and emphasizing the legitimacy conferred both by the San Remo decisions and by France's "traditional role" as a key cultural, economic, and strategic influence in the Levant.[46]

French Intelligence Gathering from Within: Dragomans and Intermediaries

The ministerial communication initiated by Robert De Caix's demands for tighter control over Syrians and Lebanese in the Americas spelled the end to the work of the committees among these communities. As previously indicated, diplomatic legations acted in their place as central repositories of Foreign Ministry and Beirut High Commission information about France's policies and plans in the Levant states. The objective was to disseminate this information to Levantine communities in such a way as to maximize the propaganda advantages accruing to France. The language barrier posed a major challenge, however. No provision had been made to employ the translators that this new structure demanded. The French authorities had organized translation teams within the Levant mandates but in the case of the diplomatic missions elsewhere,[47] embassy personnel lacked the linguistic skills necessary to monitor Syrian and Lebanese communities effectively, as few were proficient in Arabic, Spanish, or Portuguese, the languages most commonly used in the émigré press and in meetings. The solution to this language problem lay in the appointment of an official dragoman. With an administrative title evocative of the former intermediaries between European states and the

Ottoman Empire, dragomans played a pivotal role in the new French system of surveillance overseas.[48] In addition to demonstrating their linguistic aptitude, those appointed as dragomans had to fulfill two other conditions: serve as effective go-betweens for the French legations and the Syrian and Lebanese communities and demonstrate their sympathy for French imperial aspirations in the Levant. Selection of appropriate translators was not simply a matter of linguistic skills but of political loyalties and sound ideological pedigree as well.

The politicized nature of the dragoman's position inevitably gave rise to complications. Far from imposing their preferred views from on high, legation staff found themselves dragged into the internal conflicts among the Syrian and Lebanese factions. In Brazil, for instance, the need for a dragoman and for greater centralization of intelligence gathering and information dissemination among Syrian and Lebanese emigrants was apparent to the French ambassador in Rio de Janeiro before De Caix insisted on the adoption of the more sophisticated system of monitoring and propaganda. Like De Caix in Beirut, French embassy staff in Rio complained about the ineffectiveness of the existing committee networks in promoting French interests in the Middle Eastern community.[49] The consul in Sao Paulo, Lucciardi, demanded the appointment of an official dragoman who could report directly to French officials and, more importantly, in whom French diplomats could vest complete trust. Appointing a dragoman to serve the Brazilian mission proved to be a complex process, however. Lucciardi lamented that the two translators, whose appointment he had personally supervised to put an end to the shortcomings of the local branch committees, failed to deliver better results. Revealing his distinctly colonial, not to say racist, presumptions, Lucciardi complained about the feeblemindedness and lax morals of "oriental" types, traits supposedly exemplified by the two translators, Salim Akel and Nakkoul Hanna, both of whom were accused by community members of abusing their position.[50] It took the appointment of another consul and new negotiations with the emigrant communities to remove Salim Akel from his position, making way for the appointment of another dragoman. Community members accused the two ousted dragomans of corruption, but as Lucciardi noted, there was never any real proof of the charges. Considering the larger context of political factionalism at play within the communities, these accusations were probably a way for some community members to fill those positions with individuals more likely to work in their favor.[51] The apparent inability of French diplomats in Brazil to find a suitable figure to serve the embassy as dragoman points to a deeper truth: it was all but impossible to remain a step ahead of the shifting allegiances and internal factionalism within the Syrian and Lebanese communities in the Americas.[52]

In the case of Argentina the transition toward the dragoman system went more smoothly than in Brazil. Throughout World War I the French embassy in Buenos Aires relied on the services of its loyal and unofficial translator, Chekri Abi Saab.[53] Saab's appointment as dragoman fulfilled all the linguistic and ideological requirements, not just for a skilled translator but also for a proven loyalist. A prominent Lebanese Maronite from the area of Kisrwan, Saab was fluent in Spanish, French, and Arabic. He was also vice president of the pro-French Lebanese organization Tahaluf Lubnan/Alliance Libanaise, which actively supported the French mandate in Lebanon.[54] It is not clear when Saab began working as the embassy's unofficial translator, but in January 1920 he was referred to as one of the "Syrians" who had rendered, and could be expected to render, valuable service to the legation. Yet it was not until 1924 that Saab was formally granted the title of official dragoman, a position that he held throughout the mandate years.[55] His duties included the compilation of regular political intelligence reports detailing prevailing opinion and internal divisions within the emigrant community in Argentina and summarizing its press output, focusing in particular on any material critical of French policies in the Levant. Saab's reports are therefore highly revealing. They provide a window onto the evolution of Levantine emigrant politics in Argentina. But they are also heavily biased and overtly partisan. As an active participant in Lebanese politics abroad, Saab did not merely report about the deeds of his community but also tried to shape them. His commentaries frequently denounced his political rivals inside the community while promoting others. In this case the intelligence gatherer was clearly playing the role of opinion former—trying to manipulate the colonial minds of his nominal superiors in the Buenos Aires embassy.

French Intelligence Gathering Abroad: Preliminary Conclusions

This overview of the process that culminated in new methods of information collection, intelligence analysis, and propaganda dissemination among the Syrian and Lebanese communities in Brazil and Argentina represents a preliminary attempt to systematize a largely forgotten arena of relations between French mandate authorities and its subjects abroad. In this sense the chapter has sought to highlight the interactions between the mandate authorities in Syria and Lebanon, the wider French diplomatic establishment in the Americas, and the Syrian and Lebanese communities in Brazil and Argentina. The establishment of a comprehensive and subject-based system designed both to collect intelligence and to control social communication between emigrants and their former home country sheds a different light on the nature of French mandate rule in Syria and Lebanon, one that clearly extended beyond the territorial boundaries of the Levant territories. In this non–territorially bounded set of relations, it makes less sense to treat French imperialism in Syria and Lebanon within the narrow territorial confines of the two mandates assigned to France by the League of Nations in 1920.

The pivotal role of intermediaries in the surveillance of emigrant groups, whether working through committees or as dragomans, points to other important facets of French imperial power at large. For one thing, the process underlined the French requirement for a more efficient system of information collection, monitoring, and influence among emigrant communities with discrete interests and multiple connections to their homelands. For another, French efforts to regulate these communities' interactions with their compatriots in the Middle East were, in practice, entirely dependent on local intermediaries. Much as within the mandates, so within the emigrant communities, the promotion and preservation of French imperial power rested on reliable indigenous auxiliaries. Just as within Syria and Lebanon France was forced to rely on indigenous knowledge and local alliances to sustain political control over its newest imperial subjects, so in the case of Syrians and Lebanese in Brazil and Argentina, harnessing client groups and insider knowledge lay at the foundation of the intelligence apparatus set up by the French. All this points to one overarching conclusion: while the official minds that articulated the need for greater influence over Syrians and Lebanese abroad were decidedly colonial, the methods adopted rested far more on collaboration than coercion. In the context of French-emigrant relations, the balance of colonial power was in constant flux, often a product of compromise, and always subject to manipulation by those who were theoretically subject to French imperial control.

Notes

1. Edmond Rabbath in 1929 estimated 400,000 to 500,000 emigrants out of a total population of three million. See Edmond Rabbath, *L'evolution politique de la Syrie sous Mandat* (1929), 18. However, it is difficult to establish an accurate number from the available sources. For analysis of these statistical deficiencies, see Kemal H. Karpat, "The Ottoman Emigration to America, 1860–1914," *International Journal of Middle East Studies* 17:2 (1985), 175–209.

2. For a detailed study of Ottoman migration see the classic works of Albert Hourani and Nadim Shehadi, eds., *The Lebanese in the World: A Century of Emigration* (London: Centre for Lebanese Studies in association with I. B. Tauris, 1992); Karpat, "Ottoman Emigration to America"; Charles Issawi, "The Historical Background of Lebanese Emigration: 1800–1914," in Hourani and Shehadeh, *Lebanese in the World*, 13–33. More recent works include Akram Khater, *Inventing Home: Emigration, Gender, and the Middle Class in Lebanon, 1870–1920* (Berkeley: University of California Press, 2001).

3. For a detailed study of the politics and role of notables in the premandate and mandate eras in Syria, see Philip S. Khoury, *Urban Notables and Arab Nationalism: The Politics of Damascus, 1860–1920* (Cambridge: Cambridge University Press, 1983); and Khoury, *Syria and the French Mandate: The Politics of Arab Nationalism, 1920–1945* (Princeton NJ: Princeton University Press, 1987).

4. Jean-David Mizrahi, *Genèse de l'État mandataire: Service de renseignements et bandes armées en Syrie et au Liban dans les années 1920* (Paris: Publications de la Sorbonne, 2003); Michael Provence, *The Great Syrian Revolt and the Rise of Arab Nationalism* (Austin: University of Texas Press, 2005).

5. This idea has been fully developed in Martin Thomas, *Empires of Intelligence: Security Services and Colonial Disorder after 1914* (Berkeley: University of California Press, 2007). For a detailed analysis of the French mandate intelligence service see also Martin Thomas, "French Intelligence-

Gathering in the French Mandate, 1920–1940," *Middle Eastern Studies* 38:1 (2002), 1–32; and Thomas, "Bedouin Tribes and the Imperial Intelligence Services in Syria, Iraq, and Transjordan in the 1920s," *Journal of Contemporary History* 38:4 (2003), 539–61.

6. Kōhei Hashimoto, "Lebanese Population Movement, 1920–1939: Towards a Study," in Hourani and Shehadeh, *Lebanese in the World*, 74.

7. Article text for the Treaty of Sèvres is available at http://wwi.lib.byu.edu/index.php/Peace_Treaty_of_S%C3%A8vres.

8. Thibaut Jaulin, "Lebanese Politics of Nationality and Emigration," European University Institute Working Paper, RSCAS 2006/29, 2006, 3–4.

9. Article 34 went on to state: "This right of option must be exercised within two years from the coming into force of the present Treaty." This article was complemented with Article 36, which states, "For the purposes of the provisions of this Section, the status of a married woman will be governed by that of her husband, and the status of children under eighteen years of age by that of their parents." See http://wwi.lib.byu.edu/index.php/Treaty_of_Lausanne.

10. Kōhei Hashimoto, "Lebanese Population Movement," 74–76.

11. Ministère des Affaires Etrangères, Centre des Archives Diplomatiques Nantes, Buenos Aires (hereafter MAE/Nantes/BA), Carton 171. Report dated 1930 included as part of a letter from the French Consulate to the embassy in Buenos Aires on December 1937.

12. Jaulin, "Lebanese Politics of Nationality and Emigration," 4. Although Jaulin does not mention this difference, France concluded the 1937 agreement on behalf of its mandate subjects, whereas the 1952 extension was probably signed by the Lebanese government.

13. In the preamble of the Declaration of the Council of the League of Nations on "French Mandate for Syria and Lebanon," *American Journal of International Law* 17:3, Supplement Official Documents (July 1923), 177.

14. "French Mandate for Syria and Lebanon," 178.

15. The economic relevance of these communities was noted in French diplomatic sources. See, for example, MAE, Paris, Archives Diplomatiques, Série E-Levant, Carton 130, Letter from French Deputy Guernier to Foreign Minister, 19 January 1921. After visiting South America, Guernier contacted the Foreign Ministry highlighting the potential political and economic benefits for France of increased registration of Syrians in America. Kōhei Hashimoto, citing French sources, has noted that the estimated remittances from 1918 to 1920 were 30 to 40 million francs from Brazil, an amount that decreased to 4 million francs in 1926. See Hashimoto, "Lebanese Population Movement," 70.

16. Thomas, "Bedouin Tribes and the Imperial Intelligence Services," 5.

17. Christopher M. Andrew and A. S. Kanya-Forstner, *France Overseas: The Great War and the Climax of French Imperial Expansion* (London: Thames & Hudson, 1981), 47.

18. Andrew and Kanya-Forstner, *France Overseas*, 23; L. Abrams and D. J. Miller, "Who Were the French Colonialists? A Reassessment of the *Parti colonial*, 1890–1914," *Historical Journal* 19:3 (1976), 685–725.

19. Andrew and Kanya-Forstner, *France Overseas*, 40–55.

20. Andrew and Kanya-Forstner, *France Overseas*, 46–54.

21. Andrew and Kanya-Forstner, *France Overseas*, 45, quoting Flandin, *Rapport sur la Syrie et Palestine, 1915*.

22. For further information see Kais Firro, *Inventing Lebanon: Nationalism and the State under the Mandate* (London: I. B. Tauris, 2003); Asher Kaufman, *Reviving Phoenicia: In Search of Identity in Lebanon* (London: I. B. Tauris, 2004); and Eliezer Tauber, *The Emergence of the Arab Movements* (London: Frank Cass, 1993).

23. My translation from the original French contained in M. Jouplain, *La Question du Liban: Étude d'Histoire Diplomatique et de Droit Internationale* (Paris: Arthur Rosseau, 1908), 565.

24. Jouplain, *La Question du Liban*, 568.

25. Tauber, *Emergence of the Arab Movements*, 90–97.

26. Tauber, *Emergence of the Arab Movements*, 178.

27. Details of those attending the conference were recorded in the proceedings of the conference, Mu'tamar al-'Arabi, 1913, Paris (Proceedings of the First Arab Conference, in Arabic) (Beirut: Dar al-Hadathah, 1980). See also David S. Thomas, "The First Arab Congress and the Committee of Union and Progress, 1913–1914," in *Essays on Islamic Civilization: Presented to Nizayi Berkes*, ed. Donald P. Little (Leiden: Brill, 1976), 319.

28. On the telegrams see the appendix to the proceedings of the First Arab Congress (in Arabic).

29. Andrew and Kanya-Forstner, *France Overseas*, 64–81; for essential background see Matthew Hughes, *Allenby and British Strategy in the Middle East, 1917–1919* (London: Routledge, 1999).

30. In *Correspondance d'Orient*, May 1917.

31. The most detailed account on the Légion d'Orient to this date is Elizer Tauber, "La Légion d'Orient et la Légion Arabe," *Revue Française d'Histoire d'Outre-Mer* 81:303 (1994), 171–80.

32. Instruction no. 7966 9/11 dated 26 November 1916 in Georges Samné, *La Syrie* (Paris: Editions Bossard, 1920), 520–22.

33. Meir Zamir, *The Formation of Modern Lebanon* (Kent & Sydney: Croom Helm, 1985), 40.

34. MAE/NANTES/BA/: Carton 102, entry for 18 February 1918.

35. MAE/NANTES/BA/: Carton 102, entry for 18 February 1918. According to Andrew and Kanya-Forstner, *France Overseas*, French troops in the Middle East were insufficient when compared to the British deployment in the area.

36. MAE, Serie E-Levant/Carton 132.

37. MAE, Serie E-Levant/Carton 132, folio 25b.

38. MAE/NANTES/BA, carton 102. Memorandum sent to French embassy in Buenos Aires, 13 February 1919. On the scarcity of personnel and lack of resources that the French showed in their management of the newly acquired territories, see Elizabeth Thompson, *Colonial Citizens: Republican Rights, Paternal Privilege, and Gender in French Syria and Lebanon* (New York: Columbia University Press, 2000), 58–62.

39. MAE/NANTES/BA, carton 102, letter from Foreign Minister Pichon, 27 October 1918.

40. This argument follows Martin Thomas's argument as explained in his "Bedouin Tribes and the Imperial Intelligence Services," 5.

41. See General Henri Gouraud's correspondence with the French ambassador to Buenos Aires in MAE/Nantes/BA, Carton 102.

42. MAE/NANTES/BA, Carton 102, letter of 20 August 1920.

43. MAE/Paris/Série E-Levant, Carton 128, Robert De Caix letter to Foreign Ministry Levant Section, 28 December 1920.

44. MAE/Paris/Série E-Levant, Carton 128, De Caix to Foreign Ministry Levant Section, 28 December 1920.

45. MAE/Paris/Série E-Levant, Carton 130, entry for 19 January 1921. There is no further background to this specific event other than the name of Guernier.

46. MAE/Paris/Série E-Levant, Carton 130, Levant Section note, 19 February 1921.

47. Martin Thomas has defined the personnel working for the Service de Renseignements as a "close-knit elite (. . .) distinguished by their linguistic ability, their local knowledge and their unique role as information-providers." See Thomas, "French Intelligence-Gathering," 4–5.

48. As Bernard Lewis explains in *From Babel to Dragomans: Interpreting the Middle East* (Oxford: Oxford University Press, 2004), 18–32, dragomans were men of diverse social backgrounds who served as translators between Ottoman representatives and European powers until the emergence of professionally trained translators. Dragomans originally from the Greek patrician classes in Istanbul (Phanariots) were known for their loyalty to the Ottoman sultan.

49. MAE/Paris/Série E-Levant, Carton 132, folio 9b. One of the problems

observed was the fact that the community had complained about both the arbitrary treatment of the translators and their high charges.

50. MAE/Paris/Série E-Levant, Carton 132, folio 29a.

51. I discuss the political factionalism among emigrant communities in the case of Argentina in María del Mar Logroño Narbona, "La actividad política transnacional de las comunidades árabes en Argentina: El caso de Jorge Sawaya," in *La Contribución Árabe a las Identidades Iberoamericanas* (Madrid: Casa Arabe, 2009).

52. Regarding the Brazilian case of Salim Akel, see MAE/Paris/Série E-Levant, Carton 126, in which the dragoman was rejected by the local Lebanese community. When Ambassador Conty arrived in Rio, he therefore decided to select another dragoman; for details see MAE/Paris/Série E-Levant, Carton 408.

53. MAE/Nantes/BA, Carton 169.

54. *Revista Diplomática Argentina* (1921).

55. MAE/Nantes/BA, Carton 170.

8

Religious Rivalry and Cultural Policymaking in Lebanon under the French Mandate

JENNIFER M. DUECK

In 1929 the newly chosen Lebanese prime minister, Émile Eddé, initiated an ambitious agenda of reforms. This ill-fated program soon toppled his government and provoked demonstrations not only in Lebanon but also in Syria, Egypt, and Iraq. The spark that ignited the uproar pertained to schools: Eddé closed one hundred state schools allegedly in order to improve the quality of teaching. This move was seen throughout the region as an anti-Muslim offensive by a Christian prime minister, and after his government's demise seventy-five of the closed schools were subsequently reopened.[1] Crucially, although the popular demonstrations were primarily Muslim, the political opposition that ultimately led to Eddé's resignation over the issue was conducted by his Christian Maronite rival, Bishara al-Khuri, who capitalized on Muslim discontent. If demonstrators in the street were divided by religious affiliation, the political leaders were motivated by personal ambition and rivalry to find allies from across the sectarian spectrum.

As a colored block on the French mental map of empire, the Levant conjures up just such images of interconfessional power brokering, often heavily tinged by the influence of French Catholic missionaries. Although short-lived relative to French rule in other imperial territories, the French presence in Syria and Lebanon between 1920 and 1946 aptly illustrates the conflicted nature of imperial policymaking and of the colonial mind-sets behind it, which were shaped by an unstable constellation of metropolitan, Levantine, and international considerations. Lebanon's symbolic status in the French administrative mind owed much to its large proportion of Catholics, who historically benefited from French care and protection. This informal protectorate emerged through official arrangements, such as the Capitulations signed by the French government with the Ottoman Porte in 1569 and 1604, as well as through private enterprises carried out by French Catholic missionary societies. However, this privileged relationship with one demographic group hampered French relations with other communities, notably Muslim ones, whose members felt marginalized and disenfranchised under mandate rule.

In illuminating how these dynamics evolved over the course of the mandate, education serves as a useful lens. This is not only because the educational arena reveals how the close ties between French administrators and local Catholics operated in practice, but also because it demonstrates the tensions and inconsistencies that emerged in relations between French government officials and local communities. For example, did disputes over educational provision follow a similar pattern as negotiations over other issues, or can we see a divergence in the pattern of debates over education, as compared to debates on other political challenges? Whichever the case, what differentiated the French mandate administration's political and educational agendas from the agendas of the many nongovernmental bodies providing education for Lebanese students? In finding some answers to these questions, it is helpful to trace the relationships between the French government and the various French educators, as well as the relationships between these French parties and the Lebanese Catholic and Muslim educational bodies. Inevitably, this requires close observation of French official thinking—of colonial minds at work. Particular emphasis is placed on the interplay of relationships between the French Catholic missionaries, the Maronite Patriarchy, and the Muslim urban bourgeoisie. Finally, the picture is rounded out by looking at the interconfessional negotiations over Lebanese education that came in the early years of Lebanese independence.

The Colonial Mind: Officials and Educators

Before beginning, it is worth making a few preliminary comments on French rule in mandate Lebanon. The French colonial mind can be broken down into several broad categories. Although we certainly find divergent opinions within these groups and overlap between them, they can nevertheless serve as useful markers. On the government level, French policy was decided largely between the Ministry of Foreign Affairs in Paris and the High Commission in Beirut. Educational policy in particular fell under the jurisdiction of the Service des œuvres at the Quai d'Orsay in Paris and its branch office under Beirut's High Commission. In this milieu staunch secular republicans rubbed shoulders with fervent Catholics who saw the Levant as a haven for French Catholicism after the anticlerical laws of the early twentieth century.

On the nongovernmental level, there was a substantial French missionary contingent that must also be seen as part of France's colonial mind. Indeed, the main French contact with the Middle Eastern Catholics before the First World War had occurred through French missionary congregations, some of which dated as far back as the seventeenth century.[2] With the advent of the mandate, they became a pillar of French political authority partly thanks to their role in educating the Christian and, to some extent, Muslim elites. Overall, French policy in the Levant entailed creating a privileged relationship with the non-Sunni religious communities to diminish the wider regional weight of Sunni demographic strength. The resulting symbiosis between the French administration and the Catholic missionaries was fraught with difficulty, not least because of the fierce debates within France over the role of the clergy in French society.[3] Overall, however, French missionaries dodged the worst effects of the metropolitan anticlerical legislation and capitalized on the French government's need for locally established partners in entrenching mandate rule. The missions even grew in stature as French clerics sought outlets for their activities outside the metropolis, and the Levant soon became the "terre d'exil" for the Catholic congregations. Given this coexistence of republicanism and Catholicism among the French establishment in the Levant, fundamental tensions emerged and endured throughout the mandate period in the ensemble of parties making up France's colonial mind.[4]

Lebanon's Confessional Communities

In outlining the constituent elements of the "colonial mind" in Lebanon, it is also useful to consider the "colonized mind" since the territory's

Christians and Muslims were powerful actors who had their own role to play in shaping the character of French rule. The Christians, and especially the Catholic Maronites, were keen to profit from their long-standing attachment to France. Although disputes undeniably arose between the French High Commission and the Maronite Patriarchy, France certainly capitalized on the Maronites' support, especially in the early years of the mandate. According to French government census records of 1932, which likely inflated the Christian population for political reasons, Lebanon had a Christian population of 51.3 percent, just outnumbering the Muslims at 48.8 percent, who were broken down into 19.9 percent Shiite, 6.8 percent Druze, and 22.4 percent Sunni.[5] The Christian communities derived a special status from privileged relations with Europeans, which entailed an economic advantage as the main commercial interlocutors of the Europeans, along with the political protection and education provided by missionaries.[6]

While Lebanon's Muslims resented their sense of alienation from the ruling authorities and the consequent socioeconomic disadvantages, on a more fundamental level they objected to the very existence of their new state.[7] They saw the French-drawn borders of 1920 as an aberration and sought political reunification with Syria.[8] Lebanese nationalists, on the other hand, who were generally Christian and comprised an especially high number of Maronites, saw the Muslim Arab nationalists as the greatest threat to their vision of Lebanon as a national safe haven for Christians. Lebanese politics was, and still is, dominated by the difficulty of finding an equitable arrangement for dividing power among the different religious communities.[9]

In spite of Muslim opposition to Lebanon's very existence, during the interwar years the Lebanese Sunni commercial elite ultimately carved itself a niche and worked to further its interests within Lebanese national political structures. Moreover, Muslims were able to exploit rivalries within the Maronite political leadership. In the intraconfessional rivalry between the Maronites Emile Eddé and Bishara al-Khuri, both men formed alliances with Muslims to further their political careers, and similar rivalries played out within the Sunni elite. Although Eddé was supported by the French and occupied the presidency for much of the 1930s, Khuri eventually won out in 1943 when Lebanon became independent, and he reached an interconfessional political agreement with the Sunni prime minister Riad al-Sulh. This agreement allocated parliamentary seats to the myriad different religious communities, giving the presidency to the Maronites, the prime ministership to the Sunnis, the house speaker to the Shiites, and so on.[10]

French Schools Abroad: A Political Tool under the Mandate

Against this charged backdrop educators and their sponsors became significant political actors, and it is useful to examine French, Maronite, and Sunni educational efforts to illuminate the continuities and inconsistencies in French cultural policymaking. Although the close ties between Lebanese Catholics and French schools did not originate under the mandate, French authorities certainly benefited from them once they arrived. Indeed, the French administration saw education and language tuition as essential political tools and brought an injection of funding for private Christian schools, both foreign and local. This mostly benefited the Christian communities, since there were fewer private Muslim schools, and Muslim families relied more on state schools. When the Ottoman Porte established a state school system in the nineteenth century, Mount Lebanon, with its preponderance of Christians, was left largely to the foreign missionaries for their education. The network of Ottoman state schools inherited by the Lebanese government was less extensive than its Syrian counterpart, and teaching standards were lower than at foreign missionary establishments. Given that the state institutions were attended primarily by Muslims, education was an arena in which Muslims felt marginalized from the outset.[11]

The evolution of French educational policy under the mandate is inseparable from the figure of Gabriel Bounoure, an official singularly astute about the political implications of education. He lived in the Levant from 1923 to 1952, where he directed the High Commission's Service de l'instruction publique and the Service des œuvres françaises.[12] A literary critic and contributor to the *Nouvelle revue française*, he forged close relations with the great Lebanese Francophile thinkers and writers of the time, including Michel Chiha, the architect of Lebanon's first constitution, and the renowned poet Georges Shehadé.[13] Bounoure's significance to French policy arises from the way in which he combined a single-minded devotion to promoting French culture with flexibility in approaching Lebanese political struggles. In particular, he demonstrated a unique capacity to foster relationships with educators from many different political and religious environments. According to Gabriel Puaux, who arrived as high commissioner in 1939:

> He knew his educational chess board inside out, and maneuvered with cheerful diplomacy through a mosaic of teaching establishments: Syrian and Lebanese state high schools, Muslim schools, the Mission laïque, Jesuits, Lazarists, Marists, Orthodox, Protestant and Jewish schools. He seemed like the most circumspect and shrewd of orchestra conductors, demonstrating no preference for any one player as long as everyone was willing to make room for French culture in their teaching.[14]

Bounoure's initiatives achieved some success: from 1924 to 1936 the number of French schools in Syria and Lebanon increased from 315 to 450, and the number of pupils from 33,244 to 48,000.[15] Bounoure had a keen understanding of the role that education could serve in advancing France's political agenda and was quick to outline two potential paths for French education in the Levant. The first would favor Catholic missions and hence correspond to a political vision of the mandate as a protectorate for Catholics in Lebanon. The proponents of this vision were formidable, including not only various military and civil officers in the High Commission but also the powerful Jesuits.[16] However, unlike France's first two high commissioners, Generals Gouraud and Weygand, Bounoure did not identify French interests exclusively with those of Lebanon's French Catholic and Maronite communities. Rather, he held a second vision of French educational policy based on secular republicanism, which would promote Arab independence and play down the particularism of religious minorities in favor of a secular and tolerant Arab society. He generally supported Arab nationalists and, unlike many of his Catholic colleagues in the High Commission, was not categorically opposed to Syrian unity with Lebanon. Within the educational debates, he was a proponent of secular education as embodied by the Mission laïque française and was uneasy about the strong Christian orientation of most French educators in the Levant. Nevertheless, Bounoure enjoyed a relatively good working relationship with the Catholic missions. Above all, he wanted to save French education from being crushed between "a Muslim rock and a Vatican hard place."[17] Thus, although in principle he was anticlerical, in practice Bounoure wedded the two contradictory trends and supported French education in its religious and secular guises. Such an approach is representative of the Third Republic's strategies in Egypt and Palestine as well, which attempted to develop secular education and reach out to nontraditional clientele, all the while continuing to support the traditional Catholic schools.[18]

For Bounoure, as for much of the French officialdom, the commitment to French education derived not only from a general belief in its power to win political sympathy but also from a very specific conviction about language. For the French government, the educational goal was, first and foremost, to transmit the French language. The language was not simply a vehicle for expression; rather it was the key to unlocking a whole mind-set that would fundamentally shape the students' understanding of philosophy and history, mathematics and physics, and could impregnate the deepest recesses of their characters.[19] The French missionaries, like the government, were keen promoters of French, often to the detriment of Arabic. Consider, for example, the punishment technique used by the Jesuits, the Lazarists, and their colleagues against students who spoke Arabic on school grounds, a "game" that was similarly employed by French teachers in Brittany to stamp out the use of Breton. Any student caught speaking Arabic was forced to carry a "signal" that he could only pass on by catching another student speaking Arabic, who then had to repeat the procedure. The unfortunate transgressor holding the signal at the end of the day would be punished.[20] Such tactics clearly did little to foster positive relations with Arab nationalists, who similarly attached great significance to language as a force in shaping the identity and sympathies of an individual. Advocates of cultural Arabism and political Arab nationalism viewed the Arabic language as a central part of their identity and unity.[21]

Bounoure's most significant duty regarding schools was to dispense French government financial subsidies, which had, until 1923, been at the discretion of the High Commission. After that time the responsibility for subsidies fell to the Service des œuvres at the Ministry of Foreign Affairs in Paris.[22] The secular Mission laïque française was the only French educational association operating in Syria and Lebanon that had grown out of a colonial context and administered schools throughout the empire. French educators in the Levant shared some concerns with those in the rest of the empire. These fears included that of creating generations of *déclassés* or *déracinés* as a consequence of French education. However, other prominent debates about imperial education dealing, for example, with the relative merits of *association* and *assimilation* or with the comparative benefits of teaching the elite or the masses do not seem to have inspired extensive commentary among French officials with regard to Lebanon.[23]

More than any other educational association in the Levant, the Mission laïque might be considered an official agent of the French government.[24] Its patrons included high-ranking government officials such as Gaston Doumergue, Raymond Poincaré, and Édouard Herriot. In 1907 it was recognized as an "organization of public utility" and soon after became an informal branch of the Ministry of National Education. By 1936 the Mission laïque française boasted four schools in Beirut, Tartus, Aleppo, and Damascus, respectively.[25] Relations between the Mission laïque française and the Catholic missions were stormy, not least because the missionaries resented what they considered its excessive financial subsidies from the High Commission.[26] For all their disputes, however, the Catholics and the Mission laïque française shared their devotion to the French language and to French culture, which explains why Bounoure supported both.

The most significant Catholic missionary congregation in the Levant was undoubtedly the Society of Jesus, whose Province in Lyon took over the responsibility for Jesuit activities in the Levant in 1834. Their projects included numerous schools as well as an important printing press and the acclaimed Université St. Joseph in Beirut. Missionary superiors, including the Jesuit Father Louis Jalabert and the Lazarist Father Sarloutte, corresponded regularly with a range of politicians, military officers, and civil servants.[27] Most historians have discounted the role of the Jesuits and other Roman Catholics in the Levant, seeing their contribution as negligible or regrettable. This attitude is due in part to the republican Left in France, "'which drew on a long tradition of conspiracy theory to malign the Jesuits as power-hungry, autocratic, and secretive automatons seeking to subvert the Republic.'"[28] Based on her examination of the formidable Jesuit Father Jalabert, Elizabeth Thompson suggests an alternate interpretation of the Catholic missionaries' insular attachment to French culture. As she rightly argues, the Jesuits felt the constant threat of exile, and this sense of menace explains their rigid defense of their interests and personal political contacts.[29]

Maronites and Muslims: Lebanese Educators

Bounoure was not only content to deal with French institutions in promoting French culture and language in Lebanon. He also saw private schools run by local organizations, such as the Maronite Patriarchy and the Maqasid Islamic Charitable Association, as avenues to further French influence. The educational provision offered by both organizations is worth examining for what it reveals about French relations with the Muslim and Maronite communities. Turning first to the Maronite Patriarchy, it is important to note that in Lebanon there were two poles of Catholic power, each of which had important political networks in France and in the Levant. The French missionaries shared the limelight with the Maronite Patriarchy. Their respective claims to influence among the Lebanese population were quite different. The Jesuits' main power derived from their educational establishments, which trained generations of Lebanese leaders such as Emile Eddé and Bishara al-Khuri, who had retained close ties to many of them. The Maronite Patriarchy, unlike the Society of Jesus, was an indigenous institution with a strong allegiance both to the Catholic Church and to Lebanon. The patriarch and his personnel were Lebanese, and their claims to be community representatives went far beyond their status as educators.

In spite of the clear common interest between the French and the Maronites, a variety of political issues frustrated the relationship between the French High Commission and the Maronite Patriarchy. Patriarch Antoine Pierre 'Arida, elected in 1932, and Bishop Ignatius Mubarak of Beirut were both highly political characters at the forefront of lobbying to protect Lebanese independence and preserve the rights of Middle Eastern Catholics. Although 'Arida's rhetoric was peppered with expressions of Franco-Maronite interdependence and goodwill, his relationship with High Commissioner de Martel suffered in the early 1930s, especially after a dispute concerning the tobacco monopoly in 1934–35.[30] In 1936 the Maronites feared being sold out by the Popular Front French negotiators who might offer concessions to Syria that would diminish the integrity of Lebanon as an independent political entity. Maronite lobbyists mounted an extensive campaign to defend their interests, as did the French missionaries and other proponents of a Catholic Lebanon.[31] In spite of these difficulties, by and large the Maronites remained more politically supportive of France than other confessional communities.

Interestingly education was not at the forefront of the Maronite religious hierarchy's concerns in its relationship with the French administration, either as a point of friction or friendship. Although Maronite documents refer to all manner of economic, social, and political grievances, there is a general lack of communication with the High Commission over the issue of education.[32] Overall, educational collaboration between the Maronites and the French government diminished over the course of the mandate. In 1919 the French Ministry of Foreign Affairs had granted the Maronite schools a large educational subsidy.[33] With time, however, the French government came to see the Maronite schools as competitors to the French institutions. The generous funding granted to French schools was intended to shore up their edge over the Maronite institutions. The High Commission saw in the Maronite schools a greater menace precisely because their head teachers were increasingly adopting the French curriculum, thereby becoming a more attractive option for parents who would normally have sent their children to the French schools.[34]

In 1936 Bounoure cited the Maronite al-Hikma School as a special threat in this regard. In 1938 he refused a request for funding from Father Marun, the superior of al-Hikma, in spite of, or perhaps because of, Marun's proud boast that it was the most important school run by indigenous clergy and that it employed many French-educated teachers.[35] The French government also distanced itself from the funding structures that subsidized Maronite schools. Increasingly government subsidies were transmitted through the Lebanese government rather than through official French channels. By 1928 most subsidies destined for indigenous

Catholic schools were given lump sum to the Lebanese government, which had a special fund for private local schools.[36] Because distribution was controlled by Lebanon's government, negotiations over funding ultimately occurred with the local authority.

One symptom of the distance between the French government and the Maronite Patriarchy in educational matters was that this patriarchy demonstrated greater concern for religious instruction than for the transmission of French culture. Patriarchal officials focused primarily on the religious well-being of the community and the need to combat dissipation among young people. Patriarchy reports cast education as the only way to preserve the community's unity and called on teachers to instill religious devotion in their students, with a pronounced emphasis on religion over language or other aspects of the curriculum.[37] The national and cultural frame of reference in educational documents emanating from the patriarchy is Lebanese rather than French. The Patriarch 'Arida conflated the strength of religious schooling with the vitality of the Lebanese nation and its Christian character, not its Francophile culture. The French language, notably, was to be taught with books used in the government schools, and there is no mention of acquiring books from the French High Commission or metropolitan French publishers.[38]

The Maronite patriarch's concern extended beyond the private Maronite schools to include the Lebanese state institutions. While lobbying the French government to support his agenda, he dealt mainly with the Lebanese government in articulating his complaints. Here, too, his complaints pertained primarily to religious instruction and the weight of Muslim influence in the school system, rather than French cultural influence. A disproportionate number of Muslims, he claimed, were admitted to the normal school, and Muslims controlled the administration of Public Instruction. He particularly condemned the use of "books with Muslim and Syrian and anti-Lebanese characteristics and tendencies. Their authors avoid mentioning Lebanon. It is scandalous."[39]

An illustrative example of the greater focus on religion over culture can be found in the indictment by one Maronite commentator of Sati' Al-Husri, the prominent pedagogue and advocate of secular Arab nationalism who was responsible for Syrian educational reform in 1944–45. The Maronite's commentary, however, contains little reference to French culture and strikes out instead against Husri's reforms as an effort to Islamicize education at the expense of Christian catechism. Although such was not Husri's main purpose, the Maronite perceptions of and objections to the Syrian legislation were formulated on religious rather than cultural grounds and made scant reference to France.[40] The distance between the patriarchy and the French government over education was similarly reflected in the cool relations between 'Arida and the Jesuits, who frequently emerged on the opposite side of political debates.[41] The Jesuits colluded with the Vatican's apostolic delegate to diminish the patriarch's local standing and even participated in an attempt to have him removed from office in 1935.[42] Such rivalries continued throughout World War II and became acute in 1942 under Lebanese president Georges Naccache, who had been educated by the Jesuits and was intensely disliked by the patriarch.[43]

A common grievance among Middle Eastern Christian communities, Catholic and Orthodox alike, was that the Roman Catholics had a superiority complex and were excessively favored by the High Commission. Lebanese students and teachers felt this sharply in their schools. Adib Chkheiban remembers that some French Jesuit teachers thought of their pupils as "sales libanais," and that there were skirmishes between French expatriates and Lebanese students.[44] Father Marun at the flagship Maronite al-Hikma School believed that French missionaries sought to outshine local schools and that they were primarily interested in the well-being of their own institutions rather than the good of the nation.[45] The schools under the jurisdiction of the patriarch were not as academically rigorous or as well staffed as the missionary schools, a fact that clearly concerned 'Arida, who took measures to monitor yearly school reports as well as the attendance records of teachers and students.[46] Thus, although the patriarchy and the Jesuits fell on the same side of many binary divides—including the respective divides between Orthodox and Catholic Christians, Christians and Muslims, Lebanese and Arab nationalists, as well as French and Anglo-Saxon cultural influence—they often behaved like competitors in the sphere of education.

What then should the cool educational relations between the Maronites, on the one hand, and the Catholic congregations along with French officialdom, on the other, tell us about the French colonial mind? The lack of common purpose suggests that French missionaries and officials alike were sufficiently confident in the Maronites' cultural attachment to France and to the Catholic schools that they did not feel pressure to invest in the local Maronite schools as foci of French cultural *rayonnement*. Indeed, French missionary education in Lebanon has long outlasted the mandate, testifying largely to the strength of local Maronite loyalties. The missionary establishment capitalized on the French government's support while available, but it also cultivated a local constituency that ensured its survival after the mandate's demise. French officials, who during the 1930s began to understand the extent of Muslim opposition to French influence, relied on the missionaries to shore up Maronite support for the mandate, while turning ever more attention to French educational provision in Muslim milieus.

With hindsight it is plain to see that a colonial strategy based on courting Francophile Maronites could not simultaneously rally Muslim support. Lebanese Muslims felt marginalized on many fronts under the mandate, and most opposed the very existence of the new nation with what they perceived as its unnaturally drawn borders. One manifestation of their discontent played out in educational circles. In order to advance socio-economically the Muslim elites needed access to French education, and many Muslims resented the relative absence of non-Christian schools that could provide it. Those hostile to the regime saw missionary educators as part and parcel of their subjugation: one Lebanese commentator referred "not only [to] the ills and vices of the French Mandate, but also [to] the oppression of a Jesuit Mandate."[47] Doubtless Bounoure had this problem in mind when he noted in 1936, "Tomorrow's task will be to win the Muslim population over to French education."[48] As the French political position became more tenuous in Lebanon, French officials only intensified their efforts to expand French influence through cultural and educational enterprises.

On a symbolic level, for example, the French efforts to assuage Muslim opinion can be seen in the officials' discussions surrounding the names of the schools of the Mission laïque. The Mission laïque was significant to the French government not only because officials wanted a secular outlet for French cultural influence in Lebanon, but also because it was one of a few schools to offer Muslim children a high level of French education in a non-Catholic context. In 1940 High Commissioner Puaux objected to the name "Lycée franco-libanais" for the school in Beirut on the grounds that most Muslims subscribed to an Arab cultural identity and did not believe in a distinct Lebanese culture. He proposed instead the name "Lycée français de Beyrouth" in order to avoid offending Muslim sensibilities.[49] His decision flew in the face of the Catholic population's adamant insistence on Lebanon's Francophone identity and cultural distinctiveness in the Arab world.

On a more concrete level, French government funding allocated to Muslim institutions and to state schools increased in the late 1930s. In 1938 the High Commission provided funding for twenty-eight new government schools,[50] and the Service des œuvres, while not neglecting French Catholic institutions, turned greater attention toward private Muslim ones. In his 1940 budget for educational subsidies, Puaux requested a supplement, the majority of which was intended for schools among Muslims and minority populations little exposed to French instruction. Muslims, he noted, were unwilling to send their children to Christian schools yet desired a high level of French instruction. In a similar vein the Vichy high commissioner recommended funding Beirut's school for 'Ulama in 1941, noting with approval the reforms it instituted to include Western science and French in the curriculum.[51]

In keeping with this trend, private Muslim educational organizations, such as the Maqasid Islamic Charitable Association, took measures to incorporate French teaching into their programs. Established in 1878, this association provided primary education for poor Muslims and an elite Muslim alternative to Christian secondary education. In 1940 it ran two secondary and sixty-six primary schools. The Maqasid was set up by Beirut's Sunni mercantile elite for the express purpose of competing with French cultural penetration. The association combined pan-Arabism with an Islamic orientation, yet its members were also pragmatic and sought the benefits of French education. Although its schools could be found all over the country, the heart of the association rested in Beirut's great Sunni clans, among them the prominent Salam, Da'uq, and Bayhum families. 'Umar Da'uq, president of the association during the 1930s, was a key political figure during the 1920s and remained an extremely influential individual on Lebanon's political stage.⁵² These Muslims subscribed to the Islamic reformism of thinkers such as Muhammad ʾAbduh, who sought to revive the glory of Islam. One tenet of this program was to adopt Western learning in order to advance economically and to profit from relations with European entrepreneurs. Although strongly opposed, in principle, to the existence of Lebanon, most members of this milieu had accepted the Lebanese nation sufficiently by 1936 to work within its new political structures and were slowly coming to believe that they could thrive economically in an independent Lebanon.⁵³

In spite of the association's strong underlying political and economic objectives, the orientation of the schooling was religious, and school staff were instructed to keep their political opinions to themselves while at work. The mufti of Beirut was the association's president until 1931 and held the title of honorary president thereafter.⁵⁴ The Maqasid board established a special fund to reward pupils who learned the Qurʿan by heart.⁵⁵ As an educational organization, it fostered ties with Egypt through the Al-Azhar Mosque in Cairo, which was one of the most important centers of Islamic learning worldwide. Egyptian bursaries also paid for its students to study in Cairo, and Egyptian instructors taught religion and Arabic in Maqasid schools.⁵⁶ Political activism was actively discouraged among the teachers and students within the schools, and political reunification with Syria was not promoted in the curriculum or school programs.⁵⁷ The administrative council regularly reminded teachers that they were forbidden to participate in any political movements and ordered them to concentrate on their religious duties instead.⁵⁸

The Maqasid's approach to French culture was largely pragmatic, reflecting the ethos of many in the Islamic reform movement. Although the Sunni bourgeoisie opposed the mandate, its members nevertheless used Lebanese economic and political structures to further their interests. In their schools, the Maqasid sought to offer programs that were on par with those at French schools. Their curriculum had a strong French component, which included French literature. The schools preferred to employ Muslim school heads but had teachers of all religions on their staff.⁵⁹ The minutes of the Maqasid board meetings between 1936 and 1939 offer little insight into the association's formal relationship with the

High Commission; when references to the French administration occur, they usually pertain to settling litigation over land claims and building permits.⁶⁰ However, Hicham Nachabé, who was closely involved in all aspects of the Maqasid after 1950 and is well acquainted with its history, maintains that the High Commission assisted regularly with French teachers and books.⁶¹ In 1936 the Maqasid granted all students' requests for funding to go to the American University of Beirut but declined or attached strings to requests for students wanting to go to France or study at the Jesuit Université St. Joseph. From 1937 onward, however, they accorded bursaries without this sort of distinction.⁶² The Maqasid also requested subsidies for the salaries of French teachers, direct contact with French educational inspectors, as well as bursaries for their students to study in France.⁶³

Sources do not give evidence of any significant formal relationship between the Catholic missionaries and Muslim educational associations like the Maqasid. Instead the Maqasid's impact on the French colonial mind was felt through government channels and can be seen in the funding priorities and concerns of officials such as Bounoure and Puaux. Over the last ten years of the mandate, both French officials and missionaries kept their distance from the Maronite schools, while the French government fostered a nascent relationship with Muslim educators.

Education after Independence: Renegotiating Relationships

After Lebanese independence, clearly the French colonial mind began the slow transformation to a "postcolonial mind." This change can be seen in the patterns of political interaction concerning education, which reflected the changing political balance of power. The National Pact between the Maronite Bishara al-Khuri and the Sunni Riad al-Sulh in 1943 established a formula for interconfessional cooperation in Parliament. French power declined from that point on, paving the way for a new status quo not only in politics but also in education. Unlike Syria, Lebanon did not veer sharply away from French educational influence after independence, and French schools retained their pride of place as a valuable national asset.⁶⁴ With the end of French mandate rule, strong French cultural influence came to symbolize one vision of an independent Lebanon as a multicultural and multireligious Mediterranean nation, as opposed to the fervent cultural Arabism of those favoring pan-Arab or pan-Syrian nationalism.

This divide emerged especially prominently in 1944–46, when the Lebanese Ministry of National Education established a commission to draft a project to reform the Lebanese curriculum.[65] Two opposing lobby groups, one mainly Muslim and the other mainly Maronite, emerged to pressurize the commission. Underpinned by the Muslim youth associations, such as the Najjada and the Muslim Scouts, as well as staff at the American University of Beirut, the Arab nationalist camp was represented on the commission by, among others, the head of the Maqasid secondary school in Beirut, 'Abdallah Mashnuq.[66]

Although the minutes of the Maqasid board meetings contain few references to curriculum reform, its members were very involved in the government's education commission.[67] While most members of this lobby were Muslim, they did not base their arguments primarily on religion. Instead they formulated their objectives in nationalist terms: they sought to homogenize Lebanese education through greater government control over foreign and private schools and to instill a stronger sense of Arab identity in the state curriculum. This meant increasing the number of "nationalists" on textbook committees, imposing government programs and inspections on foreign schools, and insisting that all history and geography teachers be nationalists. The term "nationalist" here corresponded to a vision of Lebanon as a fundamentally Arab nation in opposition to the distinctive Lebanese identity favored by many Maronites. Underlying all these grievances was the conviction that French cultural preeminence in Lebanon was incompatible with independence.[68] While accepting the political existence of Lebanon—unlike some others who sought political reunification with Syria—this group nevertheless identified with a cultural pan-Arabism. Importantly, their arguments were formulated not on a religious foundation but rather on economic, cultural, and political grounds.

The most coherent collective opposition to Mashnuq's vision for the education system was led by Beirut's Bishop Mubarak and Father Marun, who in 1945 created a Ligue de l'enseignement libre. Their position, like that of the Najjada and Mashnuq, was secular in tone, laying out the need to collaborate with the national government, foster a love of

Lebanon, and promote Lebanese national identity. Beneath this layer of common rhetoric, however, there lay profound differences in objectives, particularly as concerned the political significance of education and language. The Muslims' repeated calls for nationalists to control the schools reflected a vision of Lebanese nationhood at odds with that of most participants in the Maronite-dominated league. This league sought to promote Lebanese cultural distinctiveness and foster Lebanese identity as discrete from the wider Arab world.

The league's platform centered on its refusal to see diminished the French cultural influence prevalent in most Catholic schools. Its members regarded such influence as consistent with an independent Lebanon and went further, arguing that it was integral to their national culture. They explicitly promoted the idea of Lebanese culture as a condensation of "oriental and occidental civilizations." Placing Lebanon in a Mediterranean rather than an Arab frame of reference, Mubarak elucidated Lebanese culture thus: "It is served by a rich and beautiful Arabic language. . . . But it can only grow and prosper by leaning on this rich French culture, heir to the Greco-Roman world. . . . It will then be embellished by the vast Anglo-Saxon culture."[69] In response the Najjada asked how Lebanon could develop as a politically independent nation if the mandate education system remained in place. The league countered with the argument that education should be separated from politics, that its "cultural orientation" should not be affected by any "political orientation."[70]

If the work of the commission ultimately brought little formal change to the Lebanese education system, it did signal a change in the position of the French government and the French missionaries.[71] The influence of the Catholic missionary congregations occurred indirectly but remained a powerful force in Lebanese education and politics. In 1946 France's documentation and counter-espionage bureau reported that the minister of national education and others took their orders from the Lazarist superior at Antoura, while the Lebanese president was under the Jesuits' thumb.[72] The French Catholics did adopt a more collaborative tone toward their local Maronite fellow-educators. This change came about as the missionary leaders came to realize that local figures, such as Bishop Mubarak and Father Marun, would be more effective advocates for the French educational influence in their schools than the ousted French government. Lebanese independence and the reform commission represented a sufficient threat to French Catholic and Maronite cultural interests to engender a more cooperative ethos toward educational provision than before.

The French government too increasingly saw the value of enlisting the Maronites as collaborators rather than treating them as competitors. French officials still expressed concern that the missionary schools should maintain their superiority and continued to support French education among Muslims, but because they were denied their previous political influence, they also adopted a more cooperative approach to the Maronites. General Beynet, the head of the French delegation in the Levant, wrote numerous times of his desire to discretely support Mubarak's league, as well as projects such as providing French books written specifically for a Lebanese audience.[73] On the whole, Beynet was pleased by the work of the educational reform commission and appreciated its focus on languages. Even though the disagreement over English and French was highly politicized, he saw the dispute as positive, believing that such debates would contribute to Lebanon's status as a turntable between East and West. Even better, according to Beynet, "the commission demonstrated its wish to find a solution to the teaching problem that is original and in no way borrowed from the other Arab countries."[74] Thus, although French funding efforts to Muslim schools continued unabated, by 1945 the French government also sought discretely to support the Maronite position on the commission.[75]

Conclusion

The goal here has been to explore how the provision of education in Lebanon shaped, and was in turn shaped by, the ensemble of French government officials and missionaries who made up the French colonial mind. As a bastion of French Roman Catholic influence with an unusual demographic concentration of Eastern Christians, Lebanon exemplifies the complexities of administering a land marked by interconfessional rivalries. Benefiting from the culturally and politically motivated Francophilia of the Maronite community, French influence in the education system was so secure in the pre-independence period that French Catholic congregations, such as the Jesuits, could afford not to cooperate and even actively to compete with the local Maronite school network. The French government, confident in French cultural influence among the Maronites, turned its attention to winning support for French education among Muslim communities hostile to the mandate regime. Bounoure's sponsorship of private Muslim educational institutions was a tiny step relative to the centuries-old relationship between France and Lebanese Catholics. There were certainly many Muslim Francophiles who personally admired or appreciated the value of French instruction. Even so, for most Muslims, French culture was a symbol of their marginalization in Lebanese politics and the Muslim-Christian political divide.

With Lebanese independence, the French government and the missionaries sought to maintain their influence while adapting to new political realities. The educational power concentrated in the hands of the French High Commission under the mandate did not simply pass to the Lebanese government after independence. Rather it was divided among an ideologically and religiously splintered conglomeration of community leaders with different educational priorities. In grappling with the change of political power, the French government continued to seek cultural "converts" among the Muslims and to support the French missionaries, but they also saw a greater need to support more actively Maronite educators fighting to retain French cultural influence in the schools.

Notes

This article draws on material presented in chapters 1 and 3 of the author's book *The Claims of Culture at Empire's End* (Oxford: Oxford University Press, 2010).

    1. Nasri Salhab, *La France et les Maronites* (Beyrouth: Dar el-Machreq, 1997), 206–7; Elizabeth Thompson, *Colonial Citizens: Republican Rights, Paternal Privilege, and Gender in French Syria and Lebanon* (New York: Columbia University Press, 2000), 166; Meir Zamir, *Lebanon's Quest: The Road to Statehood, 1926–1939* (London: I. B. Tauris, 1997), 76–83.

    2. Jean-Pierre Valognes, *Vie et mort des Chrétiens d'Orient: Des origines à nos jours* (Paris: Fayard, 1994), 502–19; Chantal Verdeil, "Travailler à la renaissance de l'Orient chrétien: Les missions latines en Syrie (1830–1945)," *Proche-orient chrétien* 51 (2001), 267–316.

3. Robert Aldrich, *Greater France: A History of Overseas Expansion* (London: Macmillan, 1996), 128–31; J. P. Daughton, *An Empire Divided: Religion, Republicanism, and the Making of French Colonialism, 1880–1914* (Oxford: Oxford University Press, 2006), chaps. 2–4, 262–64.

4. Pierre Fournié, "Le Mandat à l'épreuve des passions françaises: L'affaire Sarrail (1925)," in *France, Syrie et Liban, 1918–1946: Les ambiguïtés et les dynamiques de la relation mandataire*, ed. Nadine Méouchy (Damascus: Institut français d'études arabes de Damas, 2002), 125–68.

5. Helena Cobban, *The Making of Modern Lebanon* (London: Hutchinson, 1985), 16; Albert Hourani, *Syria and Lebanon: A Political Essay* (London: Oxford University Press, 1946), 385–86; Rania Maktabi, "The Lebanese Census of 1932 Revisited: Who are the Lebanese?" *British Journal of Middle Eastern Studies* 26:2 (November 1999), 219–41.

6. Dominique Chevallier, "Lyon et la Syrie en 1919," *Revue historique* 224 (1960), 276–97.

7. Sofia Saadeh, "Greater Lebanon: The Formation of a Caste System?" in *State and Society in Syria and Lebanon*, ed. Youssef M. Choueiri (Exeter: University of Exeter Press, 1993), 67–69. For more nuanced perspectives see Raghid El-Solh, *Lebanon and Arabism: National Identity and State Formation* (London: I. B. Tauris, 2004); Meir Zamir, *The Formation of Modern Lebanon* (London: Croom Helm, 1985); Zamir, *Lebanon's Quest*.

8. Philip S. Khoury, *Syria and the French Mandate: The Politics of Arab Nationalism, 1920–1945* (London: I. B. Tauris, 1987), 464–68; Yossi Olmert, "A False Dilemma? Syria and Lebanon's Independence during the Mandatory Period," *Middle Eastern Studies* 32:3 (July 1996), 41–73; El-Solh, *Lebanon and Arabism*, chap. 1; Zamir, *Lebanon's Quest*, 187–92.

9. David Mizrahi, "La France et sa politique de mandate en Syrie et au Liban (1920–1939)," in Méouchy, *France, Syrie et Liban*; Peter A. Shambrook, *French Imperialism in Syria, 1927–1936* (Reading UK: Ithaca Press, 1998).

10. Albert Hourani, "Ideologies of the Mountain and the City," in *Essays on the Crisis in Lebanon*, ed. Roger Owen (London: Ithaca Press, 1976), 33–41. See also El-Solh, *Lebanon and Arabism*; Zamir, *Lebanon's Quest*. Habib Letayf, nephew of Bishara al-Khuri, places great emphasis on his uncle's personal desire to bring about fruitful Muslim-Christian cooperation. Interview with author, September 2003, Beirut.

11. Roderic D. Matthews and Matta Akrawi, *Education in Arab Countries of the Near East* (Washington DC: American Council on Education, 1949), 407–8; Thompson, *Colonial Citizens* 4–9.

12. Général Catroux, *Dans la bataille de la Méditerranée* (Paris: Julliard, 1949), 204.

13. Pierre Fournié, "La carrière de Gabriel Bounoure à Beyrouth, 1923–1952," in *Vergers d'exil*, ed. Gérard D. Khoury (Paris: Geuthner, 2004), 63–64.

14. Gabriel Puaux, *Deux années au Levant: Souvenirs de Syrie et du Liban, 1939–1940* (Paris: Hachette, 1952), 70. All translations are by the author unless otherwise noted.

15. Ministère des Affaires Etrangères (henceforth MAE, CPC, E Levant, 543, Bounoure, "Note au sujet des œuvres françaises," sent from Meyrier to MAE (Af-Lev), 1 April 1936. These figures roughly correspond to those provided in the *Bulletin de l'instruction publique* for 1936.

16. Fournié, "La carrière de Gabriel Bounoure," 58.

17. Jérôme Bocquet, "Gabriel Bounoure et les congrégations enseignantes," in Khoury, *Vergers d'exil*, 205–8, quote on 208; Fournié, "La Carrière de Gabriel Bounoure," 58.

18. Frédéric Abécassis, "Les lycées de la Mission laïque française en Égypte (1909–1961): L'exportation d'un 'modèle français' en Orient et ses contradictions," *Actes du colloque: Lycées et lycéens en France (1802–2002)*, La Sorbonne, 9–10 July 2002; Mathew Burrows, "'Mission civilisatrice': French Cultural Policy in the Middle East, 1860–1914," *Historical Journal* 29:1 (1986), 131; Dominique Trimbur, "L'action culturelle française en Palestine dans l'entre-deux-guerres," in *Entre rayonnement et réciprocité: Contributions à l'histoire de la diplomatie culturelle*, ed. Alain Dubosclard et al. (Paris: Publications de la Sorbonne, 2002), 41–72.

19. Burrows, "'Mission Civilisatrice,'" 127; Alice L. Conklin, *A Mission to Civilize: The Republican Idea of Empire in France and West Africa, 1895–1930* (Stanford: Stanford University Press, 1997), 84–85, 94, 131–32; Antoine Léon, *Colonisation, enseignement et éducation: Étude historique et comparative* (Paris: L'Harmattan, 1991), 55–61.

20. Adib Chkheiban, interview with author, September 2003, Beirut; Ile de Fonse (Frère des écoles chrétiennes), interview with author, September 2003, Beirut. Pierre-Jakez Hélias describes a similar practice used in Brittany in order to prevent children from speaking Breton. Pierre-Jakez Hélias, *Le cheval d'orgueil* (Paris: Plon, 1975), 211–12. See also Jérôme Bocquet, "Le Collège Saint-Vincent, un agent de la présence française?" in Méouchy, *France, Syrie et Liban*, 112.

21. Albert Hourani, *Arabic Thought in the Liberal Age, 1798–1939* (London: Oxford University Press, 1962), 260; William L. Cleveland, *The Making of an Arab Nationalist: Ottomanism and Arabism in the Life and Thought of Sati' Al-Husri* (Princeton NJ: Princeton University Press, 1971), 140–41.

22. See, for example, the correspondence about funding between the

Mission laïque française (MLF) and the Service des œuvres (MAE) in Paris in MLF, Fonds Moscou (temporary classification), 125221 and Fonds Moscou, 125227.

23. Studies of French colonial education include Léon, *Colonisation, enseignement et éducation*; Denise Bouche, *L'enseignement dans les territoires français de l'Afrique occidentale de 1817 à 1920: Mission civilisatrice ou formation d'une élite?* (Lille: Atelier reproduction des thèses, 1975); Fanny Colonna, *Les instituteurs algériens, 1883–1939* (Algiers: OPU, 1975); Gail Paradise Kelly, *French Colonial Education: Essays on Vietnam and West Africa*, ed. David H. Kelly (New York: AMS Press, 2000); Van Thao Trinh, *L'école française en Indochine* (Paris: Karthala, 1995).

24. Matthew Burrows, "Les origines de la Mission laïque," in *Éléments pour une histoire de la Mission laïque française, 1902–1982*, ed. Alain Gourdon, Jean-Pierre Maillard, and Marc Scotto d'Abusco (Paris: Mission laïque française, 1982), 41–52.

25. Randi Deguilhem, "Impérialisme, colonisation intellectuelle et politique culturelle de la Mission Laïque Française en Syrie sous mandat," in *The British and French Mandates in Comparative Perspectives/Les Mandats français et anglais dans une Perspective comparative*, ed. Nadine Méouchy and Peter Sluglett (Leiden: Brill, 2004), 328–32; MLF, Fonds Moscou, 125221, Note sur l'état actuel au Lycée d'Alep, 18 May 1927.

26. See, for example, MAE.N, SO, 1920–40, 376, Jesuit representative of the missions in the Middle East to Marx, 13 July 1936; Deguilhem, "Impérialisme, colonisation intellectuelle," 321–41.

27. See, for example, the correspondence between Puaux and Jalabert in JES.V, FLJ, 5-Q; or between Sarloutte and De Martel, Jean Marx, Robert de Caix, and Gabriel Bounoure in the Lazarist Archives (Antoura, Lebanon), Père Sarloutte: Lettres; Elizabeth Thompson, "Neither Conspiracy nor Hypocrisy: The Jesuits and the French Mandate in Syria and Lebanon," in *Altruism and Imperialism: Western Cultural and Religious Missions in the Middle East*, ed. Eleanor H. Tejirian and Reeva Spector Simon (New York: Middle East Institute/Columbia University, 2002), 66–87; Jérôme Bocquet, "Le collège Saint-Vincent des pères lazaristes de Damas: L'enseignement français en Syrie (1864–1967)," 2 vols., Thèse Doctorat (Université de Panthéon-Sorbonne, 2002).

28. Thompson, "Neither Conspiracy," 67.

29. Thompson, "Neither Conspiracy," 68–69.

30. Salhab, *La France*, 201–3; Thompson, *Colonial Citizens*, 150; Zamir, *Lebanon's Quest*, 163–71.

31. El-Solh, *Lebanon and Arabism*, chap. 1.

32. See, for example, Maronite Patriachy (Bkerke, Lebanon) (hereafter MAR), Al-Batriyark ʾArida, dossier: Al-Mufawwad al-Sami, Khalil M . . . [?] to ʾArida, 20 March 1937; Achille Mestre, "Le protectorat de la France sur les Chrétiens orientaux," undated report.

33. Thompson, *Colonial Citizens*, 60.

34. Puaux's and Dentz's respective budgets for 1940 and 1941 both recognize the need for French schools to compete with Maronite ones. MAE.N, SO, 1920–40, 373, Puaux to MAE, 3 May 1940. MAE, Guerre, 1939–45, E Vichy-Levant, 31, Dentz to MAE, 29 April 1941.

35. MAE.N, SO, 1920–40, 376, Jean Marun to Haut Commissaire, 25 April, 1938; Haut Commissaire to Marun, 7 July 1938; MAE, CPC, E Levant, 543, Bounoure, "Note au sujet des œuvres françaises," sent from Meyrier to MAE (Af-Lev), 1 April 1936.

36. MAE.N, Beyrouth, Instruction publique, 130, délégué du Haut Commissaire auprès du gouv. libainais to Meyrier, 9 September 1936.

37. MAR, Al-Batriyark ʾArida, dossier: Al-Madaris, note by ʾArida, 29 December 1942.

38. MAR, Al-Batriyark ʾArida, dossier: Al-Madaris, Taʾlimat ilà muʾalimi al-madaris al-maftuha bi-amrina (Announcement to the teachers of the schools that are open at our behest), 8 June 1943.

39. MAR, Al-Batriyark, ʾArida, dossier: Al-Mufawwad al-Sami, ʾArida to HC, 26 April 1940; ʾArida to Catroux, Memorandum, undated.

40. MAR, Al-Batriyark ʾArida, dossier: Al-Madaris, unsigned report "Taqrir thanin al-barnamaj al-jadid . . ." (The second decree: The new program . . .), undated.

41. For a contemporary account of Lebanese-Jesuit relations see National Archives and Research Administration (Washington DC) (hereafter NARA), PF84, Lebanon (Confidential), 7, report by an anonymous Lebanese informer, "Ins and Outs of Jesuit Policy in Lebanon," sent by C. Van H. Engert to State Department, 25 May 1942.

42. Zamir, *Lebanon's Quest*, 120–22, 171–72.

43. NARA, PF84, Lebanon (Confidential), 7, Spears to Engert, 28 April 1942.

44. Adib Chkheiban, interview with author, September 2003 Beirut. Similar views were expressed to me by the Greek-Catholic Father Ignace Dick, interview with author, August 2003, Aleppo.

45. MAE, RC, Enseignement, 1945–61, 109, Ignace Marun to MAE, 18 August 1946.

46. MAR, Al-Batriyark ʾArida, dossier: Al-Madaris, Taʾlimat ilà muʾalimi al-madaris al-maftuhha bi-amrina (Announcement to the teachers of the schools that are open at our behest), 8 June 1943.

47. NARA, PF84, Lebanon (Confidential), 7, report by an anonymous Lebanese informer, "Ins and Outs of Jesuit Policy in Lebanon," sent by C. Van H. Engert to State Department, 25 May 1942.

48. Bounoure, "Note au sujet des œuvres françaises," sent from Meyrier to MAE (Af-Lev), 1 April 1936.

49. MAE, Guerre, 1939–1945, E Vichy-Levant, 31, Puaux to MAE Vichy, 12 September 1940.

50. Thompson, *Colonial Citizens*, 166.

51. MAE.N, SO, 1920–40, 373, Puaux to MAE, 3 May 1940. MAE, Guerre, 1939–45, E Vichy-Levant, 31, Dentz to MAE, 29 April 1941.

52. Amin Daouk (grandson of ʾUmar Daʾuq), interview with author, June 2004, Beirut. See also ʾIsam Muhammad Shbaro, *Jamʾiyat al-Maqasid al-Khayriya fi Bayrut* (Maqasid Islamic Charitable Association in Beirut) (Dar Misbah al-fikr li-l-tibaʾa wa-l-nashr, 2000), 65–66, 99–109.

53. NARA, PF84, Lebanon (Confidential), 1, Theodore Marriner to State Department, 9 July 1936; Michael Johnson, *Class and Client in Beirut: The Sunni Muslim Community and the Lebanese State, 1840–1985* (London: Ithaca Press, 1986), 16–17, 60–67.

54. Johnson, *Class and Client*, 46.

55. Maqasid, Majlis al-Idara (hereafter MI), sessions: 23 April 1937, 24 February 1939, 7 April 1939.

56. Maqasid, MI, sessions: 10 April 1936, 16 August 1936, 24 December 1937, 21 January 1938, 24 February 1938, 8 April 1938, 25 July 1938, 2 December 1938, 29 March 1940, 3 May 1940, 14 March 1941.

57. This is reflected in the minutes, which contain almost no mention of Syria whatsoever and was confirmed by Hicham Nachabé, interview with author, Beirut, June 2004. They participated in the occasional event in Damascus but turned down a request for funding from the one student who wished to pursue his secondary studies in Damascus. Maqasid, MI, session: 14 October 1938. Documents about curriculum were provided to me by the vice president of the Maqasid, Mohammad Farchoukh.

58. Maqasid, MI, sessions: 6 October 1939, 15 April 1936, 8 January 1937, 3 January 1936.

59. Maqasid, MI, sessions: 3 July 1936, 15 July 1940.

60. Maqasid, MI, sessions: 28 February 1936, 1 March 1940, 2 August 1940, 11 October 1940.

61. Hicham Nachabé, interview with author, Beirut, June 2004.

62. Maqasid, MI, sessions: 3 January 1936, 16 August 1936, 2 November 1937, 24 February 1938, 6 October 1939, 18 April 1941, 7 November 1941, 14 October 1938, 10 March 1939, 11 June 1937, 25 October 1939, 28 October 1939, 8 November 1940.

63. MAE.N, SO, 1920–40, 373, Puaux to MAE, 3 May 1940; HC to MAE (Écoles), budget of the *œuvres francaises*, 12 April 1938. Maqasid, MI, sessions: 2 November 1937, 8 January 1937, 22 January 1937.

64. NARA, PF84, Lebanon (Confidential), 10, Monthly political review—Lebanon, George Wadsworth to SD, 14 October 1944; NARA, PF84, Lebanon (Confidential), 11, Wadsworth to State Department, 7 November 1944; MAE, RC, Enseignement, 1945–61, 109, Ignace Marun to MAE, 18 August 1946.

65. MAE.N, Beyrouth, Sûreté Générale, 46, SG (Beirut), report, "Unification de l'enseignement au Liban," 29 September 1944.

66. MAE.N, Beyrouth, Sûreté Générale, 46, SG (Beirut), Info., 26 July 1945 (including translation of the Najjada petition to the prime minister and the minister of national education); Info., 18 December 1944 (including a translation of a presentation by Mashnuq), Info. 31 January 1945.

67. One such reference can be found in Maqasid, MI, session: 18 July 1941.

68. MAE.N, Beyrouth, Sûreté Générale, 46, SG (Beirut), Info., 18 December 1944, 31 January 1945, 26 July 1945; NARA, PF84, Lebanon (Confidential), 11, Wadsworth to State Department, 7 November 1944.

69. MAE, RC, Enseignement, 1945–61, 108, Beynet to Bidault, 13 August 1945.

70. MAE, RC, Enseignement, 1945–61, 108, Beynet to Bidault, 6 August 1945, 13 August 1945, 3 September 1945.

71. MAE, RC, Enseignement, 1945–61, 108, Beynet to Bidault, 3 September 1945; Beynet to RC, 10 September 1945; Beynet to Bidault, 4 February 1946.

72. MAE, RC, Enseignement, 1945–61, 109, Documentation extérieure et contre-espionnage, report, "Etudes Sociales et Culturelles: Activité culturelle en Syrie Liban," 10 October 1946.

73. MAE, RC, Enseignement, 1945–61, 108, Beynet to Bidault, 1 October 1945, 6 August 1945.

74. MAE, RC, Enseignement, 1945–61, 108, Beynet to MAE, 20 August 1945.

75. MAE, RC, Enseignement, 1945–61, 109, Documentation extérieure et contre-espionnage, report "Etudes Sociales et Culturelles: Activité culturelle en Syrie Liban," 10 October 1946.

9

France's Arabic Educational Reforms in Algeria during the Colonial Era

Language Instruction in Colonial and Anticolonial Minds before and after Algerian Independence

JAMES D. LE SUEUR

After the European empires retreated from the colonial world, postcolonial politicians initiated vigorous language policies that played out in many national arenas. As a result, from Asia to the Middle East, from South to North Africa, and within North and South America, debates over language came to form a key element of the domestic discourse of identity politics within the postcolonial nation state. Algeria is no exception. And as in other nations emerging from the grip of colonial rule, the continued use of the colonizer's French language in Algeria carried for many policymakers the stigma of colonial inauthenticity, similar to the way in which Afrikaans did for many indigenous South Africans after apartheid, or that English and Cantonese do today for mainland Chinese politicians who wish to curtail English and Cantonese language instruction in Hong Kong and replace both with Mandarin in primary and secondary schools. Algeria's politicians called their unique solution Arabization and pushed to Arabize educational institutions through a gradual, grade-by-grade process. Despite its evolving nature, Arabization was to be a totalizing effort to reclaim identity at its core, at the level of communication, by controlling national language and language instruction at all levels of education. This process was intended to be both a physical and symbolic reclaiming of the postcolonial self, following national liberation.[1] Pragmatically, Arabization was led by Arabophone Front de Libération National (FLN) political leaders such as Ahmed Taleb-Ibrahimi—appointed minister of education in 1965—who insisted that Arabization should be interpreted as an understandable political outcome of decolonization and as the by-product of a brutal eight-year war of national liberation. With this in mind, Arabization reflected the broader cultural aspirations and anxieties resting on the very nature of Algerian cultural life after the termination in 1962 of over 130 years of violent colonial occupation by France.

While there has been considerable attention paid to the government's projects for Arabization in the postcolonial era, relatively little has been written about the longer history of Arabization and the politics of teaching Arabic in Algeria in the colonial period. This hitherto untold story about colonial Algeria now needs to be told because, in fact, French reformers and scholars in the period preceding decolonization attempted to jumpstart Arabic instruction in an effort to transcend traditional political and cultural debates and to work toward a more profound understanding of the territory and its indigenous inhabitants. Moreover, for reformers such as Louis Massignon (chair of Muslim Sociology at the Collège de France) and Germaine Tillion (a professor at the École des hautes études in Paris) a vibrant Arabic curriculum was capable of transforming education in Algeria and North Africa in meaningful ways that celebrated the profundity of literary Arabic and Arab civilization. Yet, as in all things colonial in Algeria, benevolent metropolitan reformers encountered stiff resistance from *colon* professors, educators, and administrators who wanted to keep Arabic instruction, if it was taught at all, on the level of a more practical and commerce-based orientation. These conservative colonial forces tended to see Arabic more as a means of communicating with laborers and less as a language on a par with French. To be sure these same conservative forces also feared the potential for a creeping Islamization from within Arabic instruction and thus sought to limit its influence in the still French-controlled primary and secondary schools. This chapter therefore seeks to highlight the tensions between those engaged in the debates over Arabic instruction and to situate the debates over postcolonial Arabization within a broader history of Arabic instruction in the colonial period.

Postcolonial Arabization

For many reasons and consistent with the goals of revolutionaries across the globe during the era of decolonization, the Algerian political elite believed that securing a cultural revolution necessitated consolidating and empowering a truly national and nationalizing language. Taleb-Ibrahimi is especially important because after being released from a several-month detention for his opposition to Algeria's first president, Ahmed Ben Bella (who was overthrown in a bloodless military coup in June 1965 by Houari Boumediene), Taleb-Ibrahimi helped President Boumediene (an Arabophone himself) construct a new government and is largely seen as the principal architect of Arabization. Under Boumediene, Arabization and state Socialism remained vital transformative projects deemed necessary to help solidify an entirely new non-aligned polity. With a ministerial portfolio in hand, Taleb-Ibrahimi insisted that the state had the responsibility to oversee and administer a cultural and linguistic revolution commensurate with its political revolution. Within this logic, replacing the colonizer's language remained as symbolic as it was important for regenerating an authentic identity founded an Arabo-Islamic civilization. Rapid, ground-up Arabic instruction was used by the FLN as a tool (and as a weapon against opposition groups) in the effort to re-imagine Algeria's national identity based on a shared linguistic community and practices. Consequently, these language games met important opposition from ethnic and linguistic minorities—especially the Tamazight-speaking Berbers, who represented some 20 to 25 percent of the population and whose language and culture were viewed by the government as a threat to the notion of a unified Arabic-speaking population.

The FLN's desire to create state-centered political and cultural life complete with a national language is something that even the French could understand. Indeed, a common revolutionary logic connects mid-twentieth-century Algerian language goals to late eighteenth-century France. During the French Revolution, for example, the national revolutionary government attempted to overcome the various fragmented regional languages of the Old Regime and replace them with a unified national language. Just like Algeria, France generated its own revolutionary debates about linguistic reform even before the monarchy was put to an indigent rest in 1793. In post-1962 Algeria, revolutionaries attempted to downplay or suppress local languages, as well as the foreigner's tongue, French. In this sense the FLN's move to fashion Arabic into the primary national language mirrored French revolutionary goals. It was, after all, Abbé Grégoire who had once insisted that there could be no national culture in France without a single national language.²

The key difference between what the French did and what the Algerians hoped to do was that pro-Arabization politicians presented the case for Arabic in Algeria as an issue of cultural return. Within this context, Arabic did not merely represent a rupture with the colonial status quo because Algeria would not be born anew but reborn, and for Taleb-Ibrahimi, the emerging nation could not come into its own until Algerians returned to their cultural roots in an Arabo-Islamic–based civilization. This linguistic process would thus reintegrate Algeria into the broader pan-Arab world and could cleanse Algerians of negative Western influences. As Taleb-Ibrahimi put it in *De la Décolonisation à la révolution culturelle*: "In borrowing the language of the colonizer, we also borrowed, in an inconsistent way, its intellectual evolution, especially its scale of values. Only by returning to the national culture can we make the sequels disappear. Hence, our culture, which is to say above all else, our education, should be Algerian, founded on the Arabic language (profoundly enrooted in the country) and which remains largely open to foreign cultures."³ Arguing that, in Algeria, Arabic was a true means for Algerians to restore the universal values of Arabo-Islamic culture, Taleb-Ibrahimi insisted that the move to reclaim identity through Arabic would lead to a "rediscovery of the self." "Today," he wrote as early as autumn 1962, "this revalorization should be not only verbal, but scientific and structured, and it is the knowledge of Arabic that will notably make it possible to bring out all the riches of our country."⁴

For a nation focused on the reconstitution of national identity in the aftermath of one of the twentieth century's bloodiest wars of national liberation, the move to replace the language of the colonizer with the language that predated France is easily understood. It was certainly seen by many as a natural impulse that accompanied anticolonial war, a common impulse whose echoes would reverberate even more strongly in the postcolonial context. In explaining this impulse, Kateb Yacine, an advocate of Arabization and indigenous languages and one of Algeria's most important writers, considered French in 1962 as a "spoil of war [*butin de guerre*]."⁵ And since an anticolonial war had brought new spoils, the liberation won by the Algerians brought with it the power to liberate themselves from French itself. Yacine and some other writers therefore began to write in Arabic as a measure of this liberation.

Today, in truth, the battle against the linguistic residues of colonialism is far from settled in Algeria, and the government of President Abelazziz Bouteflika continues to demonstrate its resolve to curtail the actions of those schools where the colonizer's language is still taught. For example, in March 2006 *Le Monde* reported that forty-two private Algerian schools were closed (from Algiers to Kabylia) for refusing to properly Arabicize and thereby conform to the regulations of the Ministry of National Education.⁶ Bouteflika's actions occurred in the context of an official link between Arabic and contemporary nationalism, and the link in the official Algerian mind was evident even before Ahmed Ben Bella started the Arabization programs in 1964. These links grew increasingly stronger throughout the Boumediene era during which time Arabization was the official code word for "de-Frenchification."⁷ All of these debates appear consistent with the anxieties of the postcolonial era, and since independence language has been seen as the government's attempt to undo the intentional "deculturation" (to use Pierre Bourdieu's well-known term for the process) made a reality during the French colonial period. Recall, for example, that the French Popular Front government labeled Arabic a foreign language in 1938, a move that greatly restricted the use of Arabic in official documents and administrative offices.

Underlying much of the debate, both in the past and today, regarding the Arabization programs that the Algerian state embraced after independence, is the specter of Islam. There has indeed been constant connection made in the official discourse of the Algerian state between the state's linguistic reforms and the reinvention of a national "Arabo-Islamic" identity. Many of the first political tracts issued by the FLN, for instance, repeatedly made connections between Islam as the religion of the state and Arabic as an official language. No scholar disputes these connections, although there are a variety of disagreements over how much Boumediene's government bears responsibility for the creeping Islamization of the state via the Arabic language reforms it pioneered.

Nevertheless, there were consequences for merging Arabic and Islam-oriented discourses. For example, toward the end of the Boumediene era in 1976, as Algerian scholar Hafid Gafaiti notes, the constitution reiterated the state's commitment to linguistic reforms and to protecting Islam as the state's official religion, and as a result, by "the late 1970s and early 1980s, the 'Islamization' that followed a policy of systematic and authoritarian 'Arabization' further separated even progressive and secular Arabophones from other Algerians."[8] To be sure, this was an unintended by-product because, as Robert Malley points out, the Algerian state after independence attempted to "appropriate Islamic discourse to enhance its own legitimacy."[9] The deliberate appropriation of Islamic discourse to shore up support for a decidedly secular regime ironically triggered a number of important cultural changes that could be seen in everyday life. For example, under this rubric overt markers of religious identity became more visible in society, such as Friday becoming the official day off, prohibition of the breeding of pigs, and other obvious markers of Islamic observance. Arabization was part of this effort to return to the imaginary Arabo-Islamic past, but far from unifying the nation, the Arabic served to further divide the Arab majority from the other ethnic minorities, especially the Berbers. Moreover, as the noted scholar of Algeria Hugh Roberts has argued, the government's Arabization programs initiated in the 1970s led to other divisions and complications (especially in the disconnect between French-speaking elites who had greater access to jobs and the newly educated Arabophones, who had less success securing employment), and the reliance on foreign Arabic instructors (coming from throughout the Middle East) whose influence was probably a contributing factor in the radicalization of Islam in Algeria.[10]

Arabic Instruction during the Colonial Era

While much is known about the state's linguistic plans for postcolonial deculturation, relatively little is known of French and Algerian educators' plans to teach Arabic during decolonization, during those final years of French colonial rule. In fact, to date, very little is known of what

French officials had in mind for Arabic reforms and how the Algerians reacted to them, though the story of Algeria's postcolonial relationship to Arabic cannot be fully explained without knowing more about the French efforts to teach Arabic during the last years of empire. Investigating this hitherto untold part the French story in Algeria helps to contextualize the language policies adopted in Algeria after independence and illustrates the depths of the longer history to the Arabization programs of the postcolonial era. This is an especially important matter because much of the recent scholarship on the Arabization programs after independence tends to focus on the question of Arabization as a problem of the postcolonial era, a problem the independent government first addressed with a totalizing approach. This view, while making sense and while holding true, does not account for the full picture, because key French educators began discussing plans for the Arabization of Algeria even before the beginning of the French-Algerian War in 1954. Moreover, as becomes clear, the French plans suffered from that curious combination of goodwill and frustration. And while some language reformers tended to see the debate over the teaching of Arabic as a positive step toward the recognition of Algerian culture, others tended to see in Arabic a chance to democratize the Muslim population before Algeria achieved independence.

When the French National Assembly passed the law declaring Arabic a foreign language in 1938 in a move to accommodate the French colonial lobby, neither the debate nor the reforms ended. Just five years later, among the many actions that Ferhat Abbas called for in his March 1943 Manifesto of the Algerian People, a document given to Governor-General Marcel Peyrouton, was a call to make Arabic, along with French, an official language in Algeria. Once de Gaulle's Free French movement moved to Algiers in September 1943, General Georges Catroux, as Peyrouton's replacement, initiated new policies. Catroux's reforms did offer some concessions to the nationalists, such as granting 65,000 Algerians immediate French citizenship, but nothing significant happened regarding Arabic. The Organic Statute of Algeria, passed by the French National Assembly in September 1947, called for an extension of Arabic instruction in Algeria. But, as John Ruedy notes, the application of these laws was left to the discretion of the governor-general, so very little real progress was made because the French in Algeria had no real incentive to carry out the reforms.[11]

Louis Massignon: Educational Reformer in a Time of Change

The lack of real progress frustrated one key participant in this debate, Louis Massignon. As a scholar of Islam at the Collège de France and one of France's foremost scholars of North Africa and Islam, Massignon was one, if not the most, important French advocate for Arabization during the colonial era. Massignon applied a simple and pragmatic logic in advancing his claims. According to him, with proper Arabic instruction the French government could create a shared community through linguistic practices. This would consequently strengthen bonds between the Europeans and North Africans and generate enormous goodwill among the skeptical Algerian population. He therefore consistently addressed the failure of the French to require Arabic instruction for all students (French and Algerian) in Algeria. Putting first things first, Massignon insisted that proper instruction meant that the French would have to create a cadre of competent educators. This would in turn mean that metropolitan France must not be held captive to the anti-Muslim, anti-Islam hysteria of French colonists in North Africa. In an internal memorandum called "Agrégation d'Arab 1953," Massignon complained about the "absurd 'anti-Arab pressure'" that was equivalent to the "Mac-Carthy obscurantism of the United States, as if the Arabic language were organically 'communist.'"[12]

The same document contained an official justification for Arabic instruction that pointed to pragmatic concerns linking language instruction to colonial policies. For example, in a section entitled "ADDITIONAL NOTE ON THE IMPORTANCE OF *AGRÉGATIONS* AND ESPECIALLY THE *AGRÉGATIONS* IN ARABIC TO MAINTAIN THE METROPOLE'S CULTURAL COMMAND OVER NORTH AFRICA," which was written for the attention of the French minister of national education, Massignon stated clearly five main policy concerns for France about teaching Arabic. First, France could not remain in Algeria unless its "superior culture" respected the majority born into "another culture, Arab." Moreover, the Arabic language *agrégation*, as a formal component of the French higher educational apparatus, was educationally speaking the best way to "dispose the métropole" to form an "elite generation of teachers and disciples from the French-Muslims capable of guiding, in their mutual respect, the French minority and the Muslim majority, toward a common future, and in common confidence." Second, since the *agrégation* examination was a critical feature within the French model of education and led directly to the teaching of Arabic in the public school system, *agrégations* were as important as doctorates (the terminal degree) because they would have more complete teaching syndicates and corporations to support instruction and diffusion. Third, Arabic as a major language with different dialectics had to be normalized and standardized and also taught throughout more institutions in France. Four, "we have confronted a reaction" because the "French colonists in North Africa have studied Arabic as a military necessity, an offensive reconnaissance of the enemy's positions; meaning, Arabic was a liturgical language of Islam, at which French colonialism threw itself as in a crusade." Learning Arabic was, hence, primarily a pragmatic necessity that accompanied conquest. As he put it, "Against the dangers of seduction by the language of Arabic thought, the defensive reaction of the colonists was to limit the study of Arabic to the immediate necessity of a conquering caste: local dialect." In effect, teaching primarily dialectal Arabic ensured that Arabic instruction would be confined to banal expressions "without any intellectual value" because it consisted only of "slang." According to Massignon, the effect of this approach, as it has been applied to a country like Morocco, is to "disgust the two clients: the French by the stupidity of the texts and the indigenous with the sacrilegious disfiguring of the language of prayer and hope."[13]

Massignon's fifth point is perhaps most startling today, given that this administrative report was written in 1953. Concerned that teaching Arabic in North Africa was not enough, he pointed out that he had been insisting on the need to teach Arabic to the proletariat immigrants in metropolitan French *banlieus* since 1929. Massignon's favoring of Arabic was especially bold. For example, in reminding educational officials of his long-standing request that Arabic be taught throughout France, he not only insisted that Arabic instruction be required in France but also that classical Arabic should replace Latin and Greek in what he referred to as the official "Eurafrican" secondary schools overseas. Moreover, in the southern French city of Marseilles, where there was—and is—a large North African population, Arabic should also be a required secondary language in the public schools. With regard to Algeria, more specifically, Massignon reminded the government that an "immense majority of French citizens" already spoke "Arabic at birth" and pointed out that Arabic was already the official "second national language of French Eurafrique of tomorrow."[14] As a result Massignon recommended that Arabic should be *"required"* for all the children of the French colonists in North Africa and for all North Africans more generally.

Massignon's concern did not remain confined to interior educational reports. Believing that Arabic would be an important ingredient of any recipe for a French presence in Algeria and North Africa, he wrote directly to those in power or close to it. For example, on 22 March 1955, just two days after he penned a private letter to Guy Mollet pleading for the prime minister to grant a stay of execution for fifty-eight Algerians sentenced to death, Massignon wrote to his trusted friend, Germain Tillion.[15] Before Tillion was captured by the Nazis for her actions in the French Resistance and sent to Ravensbrück concentration camp during World War II, Massignon had been Tillion's doctoral thesis supervisor for her ethnographic research in Algeria during the 1930s. Now, in the spring of 1955, Tillion, a professor in Paris, was on special assignment in Algeria at the request of the French government. (She would subsequently become one of the most important French intellectuals during decolonization, working within the French government, leading educational reforms in Algeria, and writing several important books on Algeria and France.) In his letter to Tillion, Massignon explained that he had only just written to ask Governor-General Jacques Soustelle to endorse his proposal to make Arabic a second national language in French Algeria. "This public homage to a very beautiful and a noble language ... is a matter of public health." Knowing that Tillion had Soustelle's ear (arguably the most important in Algeria) at the time and that Tillion was then involved with very important educational projects in Algeria, Massignon asked her to convey the rightful place of Arabic, because, as he put it, it was the only way to "ensure the future."[16]

Not content with this indirect lobbying of Soustelle, three days later, on 25 March 1956, Massignon wrote to French president René Coty, again reiterating the importance of Arabic instruction. To make his case he pointed to the linguistic and historical connections between French and Arabic. As he put it, "There is between Islam and France something we take for granted. There are affinities between Arabic, an instrument of scientific diffusion during the middle ages and French that do not exist between Arabic and English."[17] In this same letter Massignon asked President Coty to take action against the French colonial educators who were taking strident colonial stances within the faculty at the University of Algiers. As Massignon well knew, within the university system in Algeria, conservative, pro-colonial educators, who represented a powerful block within the faculty in Algiers, objected vehemently to the progressive reforms advanced by their Parisian counterparts and were often publically protesting against concessions to Algerian Muslims. During the colonial period the Algerian indigenous population had come to be generally referred to as Muslim in lieu of Algerian, which meant that these "anti-Muslim" demonstrations in Algeria were generally anti-nationalistic in orientation. At the University of Algiers, conservative pro-colonial faculty had for years publically advocated for the colonial status quo and were thus frequently seen at anti-Muslim (but read anti-Algerian nationalist) protest rallies. To counter these conservative voices Massignon suggested to Coty that he should forbid all those involved in public education in the university from "participating in the scandalous and fanatical anti-Muslim demonstrations that have dishonored the University of Algiers for over twenty years." For Massignon the connection between the pieds-noirs' anti-Muslim position and the efforts to keep Arabic out of the classroom clearly originated in the colonists' desire to suppress indigenous culture at all costs. Arabic was often on the front lines of this cultural war. Logically it was, as Massignon continued, this same fanatical group that voted infamously on 5 March 1954 for the "suppression of Arabic in primary schools." This colonial attitude needed to be confronted with the full authority of the state, which was not being directly challenged by Algerian nationalists. Arabic instruction was, in this sense, no longer just a question of language instruction.

Massignon's concerns for updating France's relationship to the indigenous population in Algeria also touched on the issue of modernizing the existing Muslim courts. In his letter to President Coty, Massignon suggested that the French government had the opportunity to enhance the status of the Muslim legal system by working directly with Islamic jurists to create a center where Muslims from North Africa would come as they prepared for their diploma of Qur'anic law. This step would be important because, as he put it, Maghrebian Qur'anic law was the most obscurantist of the Muslim legal systems. Through this interaction, therefore, these Muslim professors of law would develop more professional practices and the legal system would become more transparent and rational.

It is telling that Massignon knew that in order to sell his plans for educational reform he needed to appeal to an underlying sense of vulnerability among Europeans. Against the nationalist revolutionary movement already underway in Algeria, Massignon framed his push for Arabic education as a matter of self-preservation for the French settlers. How could the pieds-noirs not see the connection? For example, in January 1955 he argued in an article in the Parisian journal *Esprit* (the liberal Catholic journal) that if Gandhi were alive, he would have urged the French to make "Arabic the second national language in Algeria because we want to rest '*chez nous*' with those who speak it and to construct a common future with them."[18] This position was entirely consistent with Massignon's advocacy of Arabic. A few months earlier Massignon also pushed for Arabic instruction in a July 1954 issue of *Esprit*. As he put it, the "maintenance of colonists [in Algeria] is only possible" with "common social hope." For this to happen French girls and boys must decide to study Arabic without the fear of "*bicotisation*" [*bicot* being a pejorative term for Algerians].[19] Furthermore, the need to teach Arabic was almost an ontological necessity for France because, as he went on, classical Arabic had had a decisive influence on the French language and European sciences. In other words, Arabic was as much a part of France's own civilization as Latin and Greek.

Language in Context

As the French government calculated the odds of considered possible reforms in teaching Arabic, it also assessed other complex language questions that the French state had recently addressed. For example, in its efforts to reintegrate the lost provinces of Alsace and Lorraine after

1919, French educators had also gauged how much German had been taught in Alsatian primary schools in the years after the end of German rule. German was taught in primary schools in Alsace in the following way: from 1919 to 1939, three hours per week from the third year on; from 1945 to 1951, German was not taught at all; and since 1951, seventh and eighth years had two hours per week.[20] Though the question of German language instruction in Alsace and Lorraine generated its own issues that were separate from the French experience in Algeria, French educational policymakers did understand that there were still useful lines of comparison between the German case and Arabic instruction in North Africa.

Yet it was the urgency of decolonization that most mattered when assessing Arabic. Consequently, as France began to escalate the military conflict with Algerian nationalists, French officials in Algeria began to think more seriously about Arabic instruction. And when Governor-General Soustelle left office in 1955, the newly appointed resident minister Robert Lacoste took up the question of Arabic directly in August 1956, when he met with the rector of the University of Algiers, Laurent Capdecomme.[21] Contrary to Massignon's optimistic image of Arabic as a transformative interaction between Algerians and Europeans, Capdecomme (known to many as a fair-minded administrator) argued that while making Arabic instruction mandatory was an excellent idea, the truth was that French colonial educators were ill-prepared to take on such an enormous undertaking. Furthermore, to make even more unfulfilled promises to Algerians in the middle of a revolution would only make matters worse.[22] Moreover, the rector pointed out that while it was already complicated enough to propose to teach Arabic to European children, the question of what to do with Berber children was even more vexing. Would the Berbers be taught Algerian dialectical Arabic or Modern Standard Arabic, for example?

At the same time, both Lacoste (as minister resident) and Capdecomme (rector of the University) understood that the French had to begin the process of setting up the educational apparatus for comprehensive Arabic instruction. This would require both a plan for primary and secondary education and would involve creating an institutional structure capable of delivering Arabic language classes to students at all levels.²³ Lacoste's government considered more educational blueprints, drawn up in Algiers by R. Le Tourneau and Mohammed Hadj-Sad, under the title of "Schema d'organisation de l'enseignment de la langue arabe en Algérie."²⁴ But the schema also posed the same question that Massignon had asked and to which Algerians after independence would return: which kind of Arabic should be taught, dialectal or classical? If Europeans were going to learn Arabic, the plan acknowledged, these would be children who probably already spoke a dialect of Algerian Arabic, so it would be preferable to teach them local, spoken Arabic, and in Berber-speaking areas Algerian Arabic could be substituted for the dialectic of local Berber, Tamizight. In order to accomplish any large-scale educational reform in Arabic, it would also be necessary to create and sustain the personnel to carry out the instruction. Then a secondary system of evaluators would also have to be put in place to monitor the progress and the quality of instruction. All of this, the report concluded, would necessarily depend on the net budgetary funds available.

While many were beginning to see the logic of teaching Arabic and the links between Arabic and French colonial rule, not all Frenchmen agreed with the campaign to broaden Arabic instruction in Algeria and France. Some even feared that Arabic instructors could not always be trusted because of their nationalist tendencies. In a private letter dated 8 November 1958 to Régis Blachère (another leading French scholar of Islam and one of the French professors responsible for supervising Arabic instruction in France), J. Grandsimon wrote from inside the Ministry of National Education that one of the Arabic instructors in Strasbourg, a Mr. Arkoum, had been suspected by the French police of having pro-FLN sympathies. Régis Blachère was advised to replace him.²⁵ This French suspicion of Algerian educators was, of course, nothing new.²⁶ Jim House and Neil MacMaster have, for example, carefully detailed the French surveillance of suspected Algerian FLN sympathizers, and it is clear from their study that the French police were well aware of the use of metropolitan France as a second front in the battle for Algeria.²⁷ Yet suspicions of even educators aside, the French Ministry of National Education issued decree no. 59.194 on 30 January 1959. This decree created a "Corps des Maîtres d'arabe de l'Académie d'Alger" (a corps of Arabic instructors in Algiers).²⁸ On 3 February 1959 *Le*

Monde confirmed the government's decision to invest in Arabic education by creating qualified language instructors. According to the plan, this group would be trained in the pedagogy of Arabic instruction and would eventually, in about five years, be in a position to give proper qualifying exams and thereby prepare a new generation of educators.

Four years into the Algerian Revolution, the French government finally devised a plan to teach Arabic in Algeria, but coming as late in the colonial gambit as it did, this resolve did not translate into a coherent strategy. In fact, French officials still confronted pragmatic and more political issues. These issues did not escape the French military. For example, a note made after a conversation with Colonel Schoen in Germaine Tillion's archives states clearly that one of the frustrations that the French government was attempting to address concerned the separation between "enseignement libre" and "enseignement officiel." Because a good deal of Arabic instruction was unmonitored in the "enseignement libre" settings, Muslim thought was "exiled in the interior." By "integrating it back into an honorable" educational setting, Arabic would be given an "elevated status," which, in turn, would be "a just and wise" political act. This integration was necessary, the note continued, because while these Arabic instructors were generally of good will and genuinely concerned about the loss of tradition, they did pose political difficulties. Because they allegedly operated within the confines of a Qur'anic worldview and were not from the university-educated system, their "ignorance of contemporary realities was very bad. . . . In a word, there is no space for the risk that their vision of the world (very Fourth Century) could influence our teachers; on the contrary, it is more difficult for the opposite to become true . . . [that the] second generation would affect the first."[29]

At the same time, the French Ministry of National Education encouraged resistance from the colonial lobby in Algeria. Bowing to political pressures, the government in Algiers made it known that it planned to pursue a program that would teach "Magrebian Arabic dialect" as part of the baccalaureate program at the University of Algiers. Both Henri Laoust (a professor of Muslim sociology at the Collège de France) and Régis Blachère (director of Institut d'études islamique de Paris) objected to teaching dialectical Arabic. In a letter written to the minister of national education on 24 April 1959, they declared that this plan to teach a dialect of Arabic was ill-conceived and would have "nefarious" effects from both pedagogical and political points of view. To begin making their case, they argued against teaching a dialect of Arabic for several reasons. First, according to them, was the pragmatic issue that a single "Maghrebian dialectical Arabic did not exist."[30] In fact, there were many dialectics across North Africa, and to assume that one such monolithic form existed would be to force an arbitrary, blundering choice on students. Second, Maghrebian dialectical Arabic, insofar as it did exist, was not a written language. Because there was no extant, recognized from of the dialect, any attempt to formalize it in print was likely to result in too imprecise a phonetic transcription to render the exercise of any value. Since the Arabic speakers had not formalized such a written language, doing so would only "denature the language and lower its level in the Arab world." Moreover, this would provoke indignation, they warned, thereby putting at risk "the prestige of our country." Third, the attempt to eliminate the regional and national dialects in North Africa in order to create a unified dialect had been tried several times and had always yielded mediocre results at best. Fourth was the matter of audience and reception: interest among secondary education students in "oral literature" "*est nul.*" And the demands on students were bound to be challenging. The study of Arabic dialects required a serious appreciation and profound knowledge of classical Arabic, which had "humanistic value." Fifth, because a Maghrebian dialectical required an arbitrary choice, this would have different cultural and educational effects because it would mean that one particular regional dialectic would carry more weight than others. Finally, and as a result of their preceding observations, neither Laoust nor Blachère could discern any advantages in this approach, only the "dangers" involved.[31]

In a separate note entitled "Enseignement de l'arabe" written by Blachère it becomes clear what those dangers were perceived to be. Even Algerian Arabic, which was broken by Blachère into six major and different dialects, would be difficult to reduce into one dialect.[32] This fixing of the Algerian dialect would erase regional variations, the existence of which was part and parcel of local culture. It would be the equivalent of telling the "people of Auvergne that they would hereafter replace Italian or Spanish [phrases] under the pretext that the Spanish were Franks and the Italians Catholics." Moreover, the argument made for substituting Arabic dialects for modern standard Arabic was inherently political and was bound to be viewed as such. Modern Arabic was, after all, the language spoken in Egypt and Tunisia, thus in the countries suspected of pan-Arabism. To make such a clumsy mistake would produce the opposite effect of that intended. Blachère did, however, concede the advantages of having young Europeans learn "basic Algerian."[33]

As the French-Algerian War continued into the era of the early Fifth Republic with Charles de Gaulle unable to put an end to the revolution, in mid-1959 Régis Blachère and Germaine Tillion exchanged several letters regarding the standardization of Arabic in Algeria. On 6 May 1959 Blachère reiterated his view that there were dangers in the attempt to privilege a dialect of Arabic, writing to Tillion directly so they could join forces in influencing the actions of the cabinet of the minister of national education.[34] On 2 June 1959 Tillion replied, saying that she had been contacted by Massignon about the same topic. As a result she had already contacted the minister and made the two important points. First, in contrast to Blachère's views, she noted that there were practical advantages in creating and rationalizing "basic Algerian," especially for use by nurses, social assistance personnel, monitors, and so on. Second, to mix "basic Algerian, which has not been selected yet, with a real language which is Modern Arabic, would be a big mistake." "Modern Arabic exists," Tillion continued, "in novels, newspapers, music, and on the radio." By this, Tillion suggested that the decision to teach Algerian dialectical Arabic (in lieu of modern standard or classical Arabic) in no way facilitated Egyptian-style pan-Arab politics.[35]

Despite the more purist protests of Massignon and Blachère, the government in Algeria won the approval of the faculty at the University of Algiers to teach what it called North African Arabic at the baccalaureate level and confirmed this in a letter to Tillion on 3 June 1959.[36] From the government's point of view this decision conferred two primary advantages: it would make access to the baccalaureate easier for Arabophone Muslims to attain, as long as they did not neglect their French or their sciences, and it would serve as an incentive for Europeans going to Algeria to learn Arabic. In addition, it would "constitute a means [to] bring together the Muslims with the most advanced from the European communities." This amounted to an important advantage for the French government. "These advantages, in the political and practical interests, do not escape us; [they] coincide with the governmental directives in view of the promotion of the Algerian youth." The letter stated that some could object that this substitution of literary Arabic with a dialect could be seen as something intended to devalue the baccalaureate. "But in Algeria," the truth was, "the arguments of a political and psychological order can never be ignored." And, finally, should students wish to move from basic Algerian to "high classical culture," this was something they could do at the most advanced levels of their education.[37]

On 10 June 1959 Régis Blachère wrote to Germaine Tillion, who was at the time in the cabinet of the minister of national education in Paris, pointing out that he had for many years attempted to teach Algerian Arabic in various cities in France and had even recorded a record to be used by beginners. Despite this, Blachère warned Tillion not to allow short-term preoccupation with the politics of the day to win out and urged her not to allow the "monstrous political mistake" of turning Arabophones away from the study of their own more complex and literary language, by which he meant Modern Standard Arabic (and not Algerian dialectical Arabic). If the French government made this mistake of turning to a dialect that did not really exist, the inevitable result would be the exact reverse of what the government intended. As he concluded: "if this Modern Arabic is not taught by us, it will be taught without us in Tunisia, in Morocco, in Cairo, and therefore against us."[38] Hence, controlling Arabic instruction during decolonization and giving it the appropriate status would help the French case in a time of crisis, whereas the failure to do this would allow political rivals into a critical cultural space.

A year later, toward the end of the French-Algerian War, the conversation about Arabic reforms continued. A meeting was held in Paris in May 1961 with leading experts and a group of North African students. The young Pierre Bourdieu was there, along with Blachère and others. While Blachère celebrated the bilingualism of the Tunsians and the Moroccans, as well as their Arabization programs, and continued to argue for a gradualist approach to Arabization in Algeria, Bourdieu offered a new perspective. The elites in Algeria, he pointed out, would not come from the schools; they would come from the ranks of the FLN. Because they would not come from the universities, the future of the Algerian republic would be "secular, democratic, and social."[39] This would mean, Bourdieu predicted, that an independent Algeria would be "disengaged from the Qur'anic grip that continues to be seen in the two neighbors." He continued in this vein, concluding that after seven years of war and "regrouping," new experiences had created the conditions necessary for "saturation in the future Algerian Republic [of] a true permanent education and an acceleration of polyvalent frameworks."

By the time the Arabization programs began in the mid-1960s, the Algerian political elite had decided that Arabic would remain the primary cultural means of unifying the nation. Hence, the successive efforts to rebuild the nation gradually through a newly constructed national language that would be grafted onto a newly minted national youth would acquire new significance as Algerian politicians, like the French before them, wrestled with the pragmatic aspects of linguistic reform. That these very reforms would also give rise to serious debates within Algeria over the hegemonic notion of the nation (based on the flawed presumptions of *la pensée unique*) would catch the FLN off guard, as would the constant pressure from pro-Islamist Arabophone political activists to move the nation toward a religious agenda that would ultimately challenge the state's cultural architects of the postcolonial *pensée unique*. In addition to concerns over Islamization via Arabization, the nation's transition to Arabic would, ironically, have the unintended consequence of underscoring ethnic and class differences that would come out into the open during the 1980s.

In the end, whether the youth would ever became more "authentically Algerian" vis-à-vis this linguistic reform, as its advocates hoped in the aftermath of decolonization, remains open to interpretation. What is less open to question, ironically, is that many secular Algerian officials would, like pro-colonial French politicians and educators in Algeria during the 1940s, suffer from the same fears about teaching Arabic. As a result many would increasingly argue that some of the Arabic instructors brought in to fill the language gap were bringing with them an Islamist project that sought to undermine the secular state. Moreover, as Gafaiti has demonstrated, the effects of linguistic reforms eventually came full circle to work against even Arabophone writers whose independence, criticism, and art were challenged by radical Islamists who imposed censorship through violence during the 1990s.[40] At the same time, postcolonial Arabic reforms highlighted a growing divide between Arab and Berbers, which continued to undermine the notion of a unified postcolonial state.

Conclusion

As crucial as contemporary conflicts over language instruction are for understanding the dynamics of identity politics today, it is also important not to lose sight of how the debates over the teaching of Arabic during the last decades of the colonial era transformed the ways in which the Algerian state after 1962 attempted to implement a progressive Arabization program. In many ways the linguistic reformers of the postcolonial era were seeking to finish something that the French, however confused, had in fact begun. The French reformers started this debate primarily out of a desire to come to terms with the realities of a changing colonial world and to valorize Muslim identity and history. As well-intentioned specialists of the colonial era like Massignon tried in vain to convince a skeptical *colon* population that something would have to give in order for France to have any hope of remaining in Algeria, the growing cracks in the official colonial mind came into full focus. And as pro-colonialist educators dug in their heels and refused to listen to the counsel of linguistic reformers who wished to bring Arabic instruction into a more celebratory curriculum in Algeria, the forces of the day gave way to increasing paranoia and fear about decolonization. The result was a connection made by the *colons* between the teaching of Arabic, the specter of Islamism, and a rebellion that connected Algerians to the wider spirit of pan-Arab revolt in North Africa. Hence, when the Algerian politicians finally assumed control over their own curriculum after liberation, it is understandable, given the schizophrenic nature of the French colonial mind in regard to language policy, that Algerians would quickly engage in the effort to refashion civil society through language reforms. That they inherited the same debates about which form of Arabic to teach, an Algerian dialect or a more standardized Arabic, mattered no less to the

Algerians than the French. But unlike the French, Algerians were undeterred and plunged forward into a massive program of comprehensive reforms. Yet viewed without an appreciation of the complex history of linguist reforms at the end of the colonial era, the lingering effects of Arabic reforms make far less sense. What this chapter has attempted to demonstrate is that the transfer of power in Algeria also opened the door to a fundamental shift in attitudes about the relationship between language and national identity.

Notes

1. For a good overview of Arabization in North Africa, see Gilbe Grandquillaume, *Arabisation et politique linguistique au Maghreb* (Paris: Maisonneuve et Larose, 1995).

2. See Alyssa Goldstein Sepinwall, *The Abbé Grégoire and the French Revolution* (Berkeley: University of California Press, 2005); and Graham Robb, *The Discovery of France: A Historical Geography* (New York: W. W. Norton, 2008).

3. Ahmed Taleb-Ibrahimi, *De la Décolonisation à la révolution culturelle*, (Algiers: N.E.D., 1973), 16. All translations are by the author unless otherwise noted. The original French reads as follows: "En empruntant la langue du colonisateur, nous empruntons aussi, et de façon inconsciente, sa démarche intellectuelle, vois son échelle de valeurs. Et seul en retour à la culture nationale peut faire disparaître ces séquelles. . . . Donc, notre culture, qui veut dire avant tout notre enseignement, doit être algérienne, fondée sure la langue arabe (profondément enracinée dans le pays) tout en demeurant largement ouverte sur les cultures étrangères."

4. Taleb-Ibrahimi, *De la Decolonisation*, 17.

5. Kateb Yacine, *Lettres françaises*, 7 February 1963.

6. "Alger ferme 42 écoles pour refus d'arabisation," *Le Monde*, 2 March 2006.

7. "Schizophonie," José Garçon, *Libération*, 16 March 2006.

8. Hafid Gafaïti, "The Monothesism of the Other: Language and De/Construction of National Identity in Postcolonial Algeria," in *Algeria in Others' Languages*, ed. Anne-Emmanuelle Berger (Ithaca NY: Cornell University Press, 2002), 27.

9. Robert Malley, *The Call from Algeria: Third Worldism, Revolution, and the Turn to Islam* (Berkeley: University of California Press, 1996).

10. Hugh Roberts, *The Battlefield: Algeria, 1988–2002: Studies in a Broken Polity* (London: Verso, 2003), 12.

11. See John Ruedy, *Modern Algeria. The Origins and Development of a Nation* (Bloomington: Indiana University Press, 1992).

12. Private papers of Louis Massignon, Paris, "Agrégation d'Arab, 1953."

13. Massignon private papers, "Agrégation d'Arab," 3.

14. Massignon private papers, "Agrégation d'Arab," 4.

15. Massignon private papers, Louis Massignon to Guy Mollet, 20 March 1956.

16. Massignon private papers, Massignon to Germaine Tillion, Paris, 22 March 1956.

17. Massignon private papers, Massignon to René Coty, 25 March 1956.

18. Louis Massignon, "L'exemplarité singulière de la vie de Gandhi," *Esprit* 222 (January 1955), 42.

19. Louis Massignon, "La Renaissance arabe," *Esprit* 216 (July 1954), 58.

20. Germaine Tillion papers, Paris, "Enseignement de l'Allemand dans les Ecoles Primaires en Alsace."

21. After Soustelle resigned in 1955, the office of governor-general was changed to that of resident minister. This change gave the resident minister more autonomy and authority.

22. Centre d'Archives d'Outre-Mer (hereafter CAOM), Aix-en-Provence, Papiers Lacoste, Cabinet Lacoste 219, Entretien avec M. Capdecomme, "Question de la langue arabe," 7 August 1956.

23. CAOM, "Question de la langue arabe."

24. CAOM, Cabinet Lacoste 219, "Schema d'originisation de l'enseignement de la langue arabe en Algérie," no date.

25. Fonds Ministère de l'Education Nationale, Paris, file 770508139, J. Grandsimon to Monsieur Blachère, 12 November 1958.

26. I have written about this suspicion affecting Algerians working within the French educational institution known as Centres Sociaux d'Algérie. See James D. Le Sueur, *Uncivil War: Intellectuals and Identity Politics during the Decolonization of Algeria* (Lincoln: University of Nebraska Press, 2005).

27. For a super history of surveillance of Algerians in France during decolonization see Jim House and Neil MacMaster, *Paris 1961: Algeria, State Terror, and Memory* (New York: Oxford University Press, 2006).

28. Tillion papers, "Rémunération des agents du Corps de Maîtres d'arabe de l'Académie d'Alger," no date.

29. Tillion papers, "Les Professeurs arabes de l'enseignment libre," no date.

30. Tillion papers, Régis Blachère and Henri Laoust to Ministre de l'Education Nationale, Paris, 24 April 1959.

31. Tillion papers, Blachère and Laoust to Ministre de l'Education Nationale.

32. Tillion papers, "Enseignement de l'arabe."

33. Tillion papers, "Enseignement de l'arabe."

34. Tillion papers, Blachère to Tillion, 6 May 1959.

35. Tillion papers, Tillion to Massigon, 2 June 1959.

36. Tillion papers, Paul Delouvrier to Mr. Rousselier, Director du Cabinet, Minister of National Education, 3 June 1959.

37. Tillion papers, Paul Delouvrier to Monsieur le Ministre de l'Education Nationale, à l'attention de Monsieur Rousselier, Directeur du Cabinet, 3 June, 1959.

38. Tillion papers, Blachère to Tillion, 10 June 1959.

39. "Comment peuvent être résolues des problèmes de l'enseignement au Maghreb," *France observateur* (18 May 1961), 16.

40. Hafid Gafaiti, "Between God and the President: Literature and Censorship in North Africa," *Diacritics* 27:2 (Summer 1997), 65.

PART 3

*Administrators and the Colonial Mind
after World War II*

10

Thinking Like an Empire

*Governor Henri Laurentie and
Postwar Plans for the Late Colonial
French "Empire-State"*

MARTIN SHIPWAY

Sometime in late 2004, an e-mail dropped into my inbox that caused me a momentary *frisson*, as it appeared to originate from a man whom I had never met, though I felt I had come to know him quite well; I also knew him to have died in ripe old age in October 1984 (as it happens, less than a year before I first encountered him in the archives). In broad daylight, a second glance revealed that the communication was not in fact from the late Governor Henri Laurentie, director of political affairs in the French Ministry of Colonies at the Liberation of France, and hence, in effect, France's senior official colonial policymaker in the key period from early 1944 to March 1947. Rather my correspondent was Laurentie's elder son, who was writing to express his family's appreciation of the portrait I had given of their father in the published version of my doctoral dissertation.[1] Laurentie was not the intended focus of that research, but he seemed at times to have taken it over, his voice speaking clearly to me from the dusty boxes of his personal papers, through his official memoranda and telegrams, many annotated with sarcastic and impatient marginal scribbling in a surprisingly clear hand (signed with an unmistakable lowercase "hl," which I transcribed countless times into my notes), and through a voluminous correspondence that revealed him to be both a warm and loyal ally to a select band of like-minded colleagues and an acerbic and pitiless critic of those—apparently far more numerous—officials and politicians with whom he fell out. I have since corresponded and dined with the two Laurentie brothers, though I have not met their younger sister, born after the family was reunited in 1945, and their reminiscences have greatly added to my understanding of their father. This encounter inspired me to return to Laurentie's private papers,[2] and to return anew to a question that I had never addressed to my entire satisfaction: why write about Henri Laurentie?

This chapter advances several answers to this question. First, aside from his central policymaking role at a pivotal moment in France's political, constitutional, and colonial history, there is a self-justifying biographical interest in an engaging character as he emerges from the archives. Henri Laurentie was in many ways a contradictory figure: following de Gaulle almost from the outset, his career was boosted by his courage in 1940, but he was never a Gaullist by conviction and distanced himself from party affiliations; he was a career colonial administrator who had eschewed the normal training at the National Academy for Overseas France (École nationale de la France d'Outre-Mer, ENFOM). He despised the conformism of the "bureaucratic spirit" (*esprit administrateur*); he was a published poet; an establishment figure who encouraged Senghor to launch his political career; he corresponded amicably with future "rebels" (e.g., the Malagasy nationalist leaders) and invited Ho Chi Minh home to dinner; he was a senior policymaker who found himself at odds with the drift of colonial policy and at loggerheads with de Gaulle, a series of colonial ministers, and a range of senior officials and newspaper editors.[3] The problem for the historian is that Laurentie's was all too often a lone voice, urgent, irascible, and, as it seemed to a novice researcher, so obviously *right* that it was difficult to place him objectively in the context of French colonial policymaking. Like Cassandra, it seemed as if Laurentie might be cursed to be always right but never heeded;[4] but curiously, that potentially relegated what he had to say to a valueless, counterfactual parallel history of "what might have been." That, it may be suspected, was how he saw himself at times, particularly after he left the colonial administration under something of a cloud in March 1947, and this is also how his family has come to remember him, as France's heroic decolonizer *avant la lettre*.

A further biographical contradiction lies in the fact that all of the above arises from Laurentie's private voice, as expressed in marginalia and in his correspondence, whereas the public, official voice of "M. le Directeur des Aff.Pol." was necessarily more measured, constrained within the bland contours of French colonial rhetoric, of which he was a prolific and eloquent practitioner. Sometimes, conversely, he did not cleave closely enough to official *langue de bois*, and his career was irreparably blighted by his injudicious semi-public championing of what appeared to be an offer of "independence" to Indochina in September 1945.[5] Worse, he was increasingly persuaded, or obliged, to take on the uncomfortable role of "enforcer" of policy decisions that by late 1946 were steering France toward war in Indochina and violent counterinsurgency in Madagascar, in the origins of both of which Laurentie was implicated.[6] Moreover, in representing the Ministry for Overseas France (as it became in January 1946) in the bitter imbroglio over the revision of the French Union articles in the second draft of the new Constitution, Laurentie has come to be portrayed as advocate-in-chief of a policy of paternalist "conservative reform," charged with having destroyed the "liberal" hopes for a "gradual decolonization" that had allegedly been raised by the first constitutional draft rejected by referendum in May 1946.[7] Clearly, both his overt ideological position and his policymaking role lend themselves to this superficial interpretation, but the difficulty inherent in judging the man behind the official mask should already be clear enough.

Two further broad and interlinked reasons for writing about Henri Laurentie suggest far more than simple biographical interest. The first is for what he may tell us of the French "official mind" at this crucial period. In British historiography the concept of an "official mind" has a lineage stretching back to Robinson and Gallagher's seminal work, *Africa and the Victorians*, and even in recent accounts of British decolonization can still dominate the landscape, at times to the exclusion of other perspectives.[8] For an understanding of the French "official mind," by contrast, there was little scholarly follow-up to the pioneering work of William B. Cohen, focusing chiefly on the ENFOM, although more recently Véronique Dimier's work has started to fill this significant gap.[9] It may already be clear that Laurentie was far from being a "typical"

French colonial official; but given the centrality of his role (while it lasted), he was hardly a peripheral figure either. Rather his significance to the historian is akin to that of a double agent or even *agent provocateur*: that is to say, he was a key decision maker who was simultaneously a critical outsider, reporting back (or rather, forward) to an eventual reader of his papers.

The second reason why Laurentie's short-lived career at the heart of French colonial policymaking is of interest is for his efforts to create a sustainable constitutional framework for a postwar French "empire-state." The problem here is not simply to determine or evaluate Laurentie's role in policymaking, as to interpret what he achieved and what he failed to achieve. At the heart of this problem of interpretation, as so often in the history of decolonization, is the misleading supposition that, as Frederick Cooper has put it, "we know the end of the story," and so we tend to read backward from the end of empire to its origins in the immediate postwar period (at the latest).[10] Thus, to present the paradigm of "inevitable" decolonization in somewhat caricatured form, the fate of the British Empire, in particular, may readily be seen to have been settled by 1945, when Churchill's "Pyrrhic victory" left the empire so weakened that graceful withdrawal was the only sensible option;[11] a view in which, it follows, the British "official mind" sensibly acquiesced by managing Britain's subsequent "peaceful" decolonization. French officials and politicians were, by this view, considerably less sensible, failing to realize that the writing was on the wall until it had been spelled out to them by the Vietnamese at Dien Bien Phu, the Egyptians at Suez, the Algerian FLN (increasingly at the UN more than in the Algerian *djebel*), and, finally, by their own great decolonizer, President Charles de Gaulle.

In the British case, these views do not bear close scholarly examination, and the historiographical trend has been to place the decisive moment for decolonization ever later.[12] In the French case, however, the view still holds some currency that, as James Lewis puts it:

> The fundamental deficiency of [the Fourth Republic] and its leaders was an inability to recognize and adapt to the fact that the age of colonial empires was coming to a close. The endless parliamentary and party disputes over overseas policy that accompanied succes-

sive colonial crises were in reality struggles over the details of a single, fundamentally unsound policy of preserving colonial-style hegemony over the dependencies.[13]

By contrast, it is axiomatic to what follows in this chapter that, whatever else we may conclude, the history of French (or British, or Dutch, etc.) decolonization after 1945 amounts to considerably more than "struggles" over "details"; or at the least, that understanding these "struggles," however futile, and these "details," however trivial, is essential to an understanding of what follows.

The corollary to Lewis's view is that all those officials, ministers, and parliamentarians who did not "recognize and adapt" in the required fashion were "conservatives," enthralled with a colonial "myth" that sustained France's relationship with its colonial dependencies. By implication, as one of the propagators of this "myth," as well as being the principal originator of the postwar idea of a French Union, an idea that may be traced back to the 1944 Brazzaville Conference that he planned and masterminded, Laurentie is indelibly marked as a colonial "conservative"—if, that is, the term has by this stage retained any meaning. There was, of course, a "liberal"/"conservative" debate in the constitution-making period of 1945–47, within both the colonial administration and the Constituent Assemblies, but this was not it. Indeed, it might be argued that Lewis's "conservative" label might be applied to *all* officials and ministers and almost all members of Parliament and party leaders, including, arguably (though not for Lewis), those of the French Communist Party (PCF), since there was no sustained argument in this period in favor of an as yet largely unthinkable decolonization (the term itself had no currency until much later), and even Maurice Thorez, general secretary of the PCF, argued casuistically that "the right to divorce does not signify the necessity to divorce." Laurentie's problem was that as a would-be liberal reformer of empire, as we will see, he was repeatedly defeated, or at best undermined, by the weight of *truly* conservative opinion coming from within the colonial administration, whether on the question of Indochina (which I have considered in depth elsewhere) or over the constitutional status of the French Union. His blueprint for empire was therefore substantially compromised even before he moved to head off what he saw as the administrative and legal chaos that he believed would arise from implementation of the first constitutional draft, the so-called Senghor Constitution.

This is where the question of historiographical interpretation becomes crucial. For, if, as Lewis argues, the Senghor Constitution really represented a chance for gradual decolonization, or "at a minimum" the transformation of the French empire into "something akin to the self-governing dominions of the British Commonwealth," then Laurentie and his colleagues were all equally guilty as charged.[14] If, on the other hand, the stakes were not as superficial as they might appear if viewed within an anachronistic framework of "inevitable" decolonization, then Laurentie may offer us an insight into a somewhat different phenomenon, which Cooper has called "thinking like an empire," which embraces not only thinking, but also planning and policymaking for the French empire (or French Union—the terminology of the time did not of course change reality), on the not unreasonable assumption that there was something to plan for.[15] In short, given that there was no general recognition that independence from France was just around the corner, the political battles of 1945–46 were conceivably about something else, namely the forms within which *future* political relations between the French metropolitan center and its imperial periphery would be conducted—and this supposed that the French Union *had* a future. According to this view, the relatively "conservative" form taken by the French Union in the constitutional draft finally accepted in October 1946 represented a regrettable turn of events for liberal officials such as Laurentie, though as discussed below, he had his reasons; they were also a setback, but arguably no more than that, for an emerging generation of African politicians who would have to conduct their politics on somewhat more restrictive terms than they had supposed and would have to wait until, say, the Framework Law of 1956 to achieve goals that might have seemed to be achievable already in 1946—and beyond 1956, decolonization was certainly imaginable in a way that was not the case ten years earlier.

Before coming back to the debates and defeats that marked Laurentie's career in Paris, some further biographical background may help to elucidate his personality, which readily transcends the bureaucratic cipher we find in much of the official record. Born in 1901, in Saint-Symphorien (Indre-et-Loire), the son of a lawyer at the Paris Court of Appeal, Laurentie studied law and, somewhat unusually, took a diploma in Arabic and Armenian at the School of Oriental Languages. Having joined the colonial administration following his military service in 1922, he served in the then newly created League of Nations B-class Mandate in Cameroon for much of the 1920s, reaching the grade of *administrateur des Colonies* in 1927, and then was posted to the French A-class Mandate administration in Syria from 1930 to 1934, including a spell as adviser to the municipality of Damascus (again, an unusual line in his curriculum vitae). Following a posting in Guinea and a period in Paris, he was a *commandant de cercle* (district officer) at Kanem in Chad beginning in September 1938.[16] After the outbreak of war he pleaded with his governor, Félix Éboué, and appealed to the governor-general at Brazzaville, Pierre Boisson, to be allowed to return to France to take up arms, but his requests were refused.[17] Éboué recognized Laurentie's talents and moved him to the capital, Fort-Lamy (N'Djamena today), as his secretary-general, and it was here that Laurentie was instrumental in persuading Éboué to declare for de Gaulle in August 1940. From Chad, Laurentie followed Éboué on the latter's nomination as governor-general of French Equatorial Africa (FEA), and figurehead of "Free French Africa" (i.e., FEA and Cameroon). Then, when de Gaulle established his French Committee for National Liberation (FCNL) at Algiers in 1943, Laurentie was appointed director of political affairs in the Commissariat for the Colonies, directed by René Pleven. It was in this capacity that he organized and masterminded the Brazzaville Conference of January–February 1944.[18] He retained his director's title in the Ministry of Colonies when the provisional government was established in Paris following the Liberation.

The account of Laurentie given by Brian Weinstein, biographer of Félix Éboué, may be worth quoting in full here:

> A sharp-featured man with a shock of hair over his right forehead, his religion, cutting wit and a disarming modesty were as well-known as his emotional patriotism. Mr and Mrs Laurentie's house had the largest library in Tchad, and many said the young

administrator wrote poetry. . . . Éboué and he were practically the only Frenchmen to address [African dignitaries and civil servants] with the respectful *vous* form in French.[19]

To this portrait of an almost impossibly liberal, French colonial Atticus Finch should perhaps be added Éboué's more double-edged estimation of his subordinate's "strong personality and brutal frankness."[20] Laurentie's sense of wartime isolation from the center of the action was no doubt accentuated by the circumstances of his family. When his wife came to join him in Chad in 1940, she left the Laurentie boys in the care of their grandmother in the Loire valley, where they participated in the mass exodus before the German advance in May–June 1940, fleeing on a farm cart before returning to their home some days later.[21] Mme. Laurentie subsequently returned to occupied France, working in Paris until 1942, when she was denounced as the wife of a "dissident," quite possibly by a Ministry official; she was deported, as Laurentie wrote to his colleague Léon Pignon, to "a camp somewhere in Mecklenburg [Ravensbrück?] where she must be suffering greatly," returning only in the summer of 1945.[22]

Having thus rapidly traced the prehistory of Laurentie's policymaking career in Paris, I also add a comment on its aftermath. Though his career in the Ministry for Overseas France culminated in failure—failure to recover from the ostracism that followed his "gaffe" on Indochina, failure to impose his vision of a French Union or to head off conflict in Indochina or Madagascar—there is little sense in his subsequent correspondence of a "tragic," wasted talent or thwarted career. Indeed, Laurentie's letters from "exile" in a sunny, snowbound, prosperous New York suburb radiate the sense of a lucky escape as he contemplated a still devastated, demoralized France apparently on the verge of civil war.[23] Moreover, his subsequent diplomatic career as an international administrator ostensibly fulfilled the promise toward which his family background, education, and personal ambition had earlier directed him, as he served first on the Trusteeship Council of the United Nations in New York and then as a resident representative for the United Nations Relief and Rehabilitation Administration (UNRRA) in Rio de Janeiro and in the Belgian Trusteeship Territory of Ruanda-Urundi (subsequently

Rwanda and Burundi), before retiring in 1957. He even returned very briefly to French government, acting as technical counselor (*conseiller technique*) to the second, short-lived government of his former boss, René Pleven (August 1951–January 1952).[24]

If "failure" thus seems an unduly harsh final judgment on Laurentie's short but in some ways brilliant career in Paris, then perhaps I might suggest more generously, but no less comprehensively, that he was defeated in his core objectives. In the rest of this chapter, I identify four key battles that Laurentie lost, the first of which to be considered was his unequal fight with the colonial "official mind." Next I turn to two battles—or, it might be suggested, lost causes—that Laurentie may be seen to have fought in his efforts to engage those around him in the process of "thinking like an empire" à la Cooper: his struggle to impose a new vision of how the French Union might develop as a rationalized, unified French "empire-state," and his campaign to "sell" his idea of empire to the wider audience of French public opinion. Finally, I examine Laurentie's motivation in the key battleground of French constitutional debates in mid- to late 1946, a battle that Laurentie won, but arguably at the expense of his own liberal principles. It should be understood at the outset that the extended metaphor of "battle" embraces the fact that, like Stendhal's famous vision of Waterloo in *The Charterhouse of Parma*, the lines of Laurentie's battles were often blurred and the battle fronts overlapping and difficult to distinguish.

Laurentie and the Official Mind

The first of Laurentie's battles was thus a straightforward struggle for power and influence within the colonial administration, as the maverick outsider and "ideas man" came up against more orthodox manifestations of the French "official mind," whether in the form of rooted bureaucracy within the "dark corridors of the Rue Oudinot," or in the limited vision of senior field officers, the "proconsuls" of empire.[25] As we have seen, Laurentie failed to fit the profile of a "typical" colonial administrator in significant ways. For one thing, he was a relative youngster and outsider who had risen to prominence for reasons that had little to do with steady promotion through the ranks, and more to do with his bravery and patriotism in 1940, particularly his role in the African proconsuls' *ralliements* (declarations of loyalty) to de Gaulle of August 1940. He was just short of his forty-second birthday when he was appointed director of political affairs in Algiers in 1943; when the time came in March 1947 he duly passed on the job to an older man, Robert Delavignette, already a *chef de cabinet* in Marius Moutet's tenure at the Ministry of Colonies in Léon Blum's 1936 Popular Front government and, more recently, director of ENFOM.[26] Most strikingly, of the twenty governors and governors-general present at the Brazzaville Conference, Laurentie was one of only three who was not a graduate of ENFOM—the other two, Félix Éboué and Pierre de Saint-Mart (governor-general of Madagascar), having started their careers before the First World War, when ENFOM was not yet central to the formation of the colonial administration.[27]

Laurentie would thus seem to have been largely immune to the *esprit de corps* that ENFOM engendered, and in particular he resisted the prevailing orthodoxy of Republican assimilationism, against which he argued vehemently but fruitlessly in his preparations for the Brazzaville Conference and at the conference itself.[28] Esprit de corps could determine not only loyalty to imperial orthodoxies and institutions but also the framework of an administrator's entire career. Thus on graduation from ENFOM, in the ruthlessly meritocratic manner of the French elite *grandes écoles*, cadets were allowed to choose, according to their ranking within the year class, which branch of the service they would enter; better placed cadets tended to choose Indochina over Africa, although, for example, Pierre Messmer opted for Africa in preference to what he saw as the grubbily commercial aspects of Indochinese administration.[29] Laurentie, by contrast, maintained a resolutely generalist perspective, resisting the pull of regionalist expertise that could skew a more global perspective.

If Laurentie appeared to thrive in the chaos of the FCNL's improvised quarters in Algiers, in Paris he found himself parachuted into the Rue Oudinot, at the head of a ministry that had largely stayed intact since before the occupation, and that would be only minimally purged in the official purges to follow.[30] He was ostensibly sympathetic to the plight of those who had sat out the occupation; as he wrote to his deputy at the time, Léon Pignon (initially left behind at Algiers): "You cannot imagine what it is like for an administration to have lived under this crushing regime for four long years and to have had nothing useful to do for two years."[31] The problem was not so much a question of political loyalties as of administrative temperament. Already at the Brazzaville Conference, as has been argued elsewhere, the more ambitious aspects of Laurentie's agenda were largely sidestepped by the cautious approach of his proconsular colleagues, the corps of African governors and governors-general, whom he characterized in a diatribe to de Gaulle written at the end of 1944 as, "with a few exceptions, conscientious administrators, very sensitive to the problems of a sub-district, but with no understanding of general political questions."[32] Now, back in Paris, Laurentie found himself additionally confronting ministerial officials: "a soulless bunch, who believe only in their own capacity for survival; what might have happened in their absence doesn't interest them; they know nothing of Washington, and pay attention only to precedents."[33]

Laurentie identified a further problem in this note to de Gaulle, which was that a palpable shift in focus away from colonial policy had been reflected in the recent reshuffle in the provisional government, which saw René Pleven replaced by Paul Giacobbi, a Corsican Radical and former senator who had voted against Pétain on 10 July 1940. Whereas Pleven had acted energetically as the champion of a "Brazzaville" policy (i.e., the policy that he and Laurentie might have liked to have seen emerge from the Brazzaville Conference), Giacobbi had little to recommend him to the impatient Laurentie, who complained: "After only a month of his tenure, it seems we have sunk back into a rut, which suits the majority but is unbearable for everyone else."[34] Giacobbi was to remain at the Rue Oudinot for most of 1945, until he was replaced in November by Jacques Soustelle. Soustelle barely had time to make an impression as minister—his time was yet to come—before he was in turn replaced, following de Gaulle's resignation in January 1946, by the veteran Socialist colonial expert and minister of colonies in Léon Blum's Popular Front government, Marius Moutet, who is discussed below. The best that can be said of Giacobbi is that he allowed his director of political affairs to take the initiative in the crucial year 1945; however, this did little to ease Laurentie's difficulties in dealing with the proconsuls.

Laurentie's decisive, but probably ill-chosen, skirmish with the proconsuls in 1945 was over the establishment of a voting system in the colonies for the Constituent Assembly elections of October 1945. This was supposed to have been drawn up by a commission chaired by the Guyanese member of de Gaulle's Consultative Assembly (and future president of the Fifth Republic Senate), Gaston Monnerville. Indeed, the agenda of the Monnerville Commission was originally intended to cover the whole constitutional status of the French Union, as it was just starting to be called, but for reasons explored below a more restrictive agenda had to be adopted. Nonetheless, it had a broad-based membership including officials, semi-official and academic colonial "experts" (representatives of what once would have been called the "Parti Colonial"), and an unrepresentative (because they were unelected) but nonetheless impressive group of African, Malagasy, and Indochinese intellectuals residing in Paris. Thus, it constituted a forum—which in many ways the closed, official conference at Brazzaville had failed to be—for wide-ranging and sometimes acrimonious debate on the future of the empire. Laurentie, for one, had to mind his tongue and almost caused the commission to fall at the first hurdle, when he referred, with strict juridical accuracy but a want of political tact, to the African territories' "dominated status" (*statut de domination*).[35] Much can be made of the disagreements in the commission's meetings, and of the minority reports that accompanied the commission's final report, originating both from the dissenting colonial "experts" and from the Indochinese contingent who rejected the Commission Report outright.[36] The fact was, however, that the majority, including the ministerial representatives headed by Laurentie, supported the report that went forward to the ministry for consultation. The report recommended a system of effective universal suffrage, with a single electoral college, albeit with a dual voting system that distinguished between citizens and noncitizens, with direct voting for Europeans and those Africans who had acquired French citizenship, and an indirect vote (*à deux degrés*) for "non-citizens"; and with a relatively generous division into constituencies on a territorial basis, which thus defined, in effect, the boundaries of the future states of Francophone Africa.[37]

It was here that Laurentie found himself outflanked, when in July 1945 Giacobbi convened a meeting in Paris of the three governors-general of French West Africa (FWA), FEA and Madagascar and the governor of Cameroon, in order to discuss their objections to the Monnerville Report—objections that were largely couched in practical terms but with unavoidable ideological overtones.[38] Giacobbi acceded to the proconsuls' demands, and the Ordonnance passed on 22 August 1945 represented a substantial step back from the Monnerville recommendations, most notably with the perpetuation of a two-college system that effectively ensured the representation of the tiny settler communities across the African federations, with a second noncitizens college restricted to various categories of entitlement (*capacitaires*, such as war veterans, village chiefs, those literate in French); the Ordonnance also set out a far more limited number of constituencies, each based on two adjacent territories (for example, Senegal with Mauritania), which effectively nullified the political character of either.[39] Laurentie had objected strenuously to the African proconsuls' arguments, but to no avail; in consequence, he feared that an electoral system guided by "prudence" would achieve the opposite of the intended result.[40] As he argued, not only did the two-college system exclude African citizens from being elected (except in Senegal, where they were in the majority), but by pulling back from universal suffrage France had lost the moral high ground in the face of the African citizens, the so-called *évolués*, who were doing most of the running; or, as he put it more cynically, it effectively called the citizens' bluff, as they could hardly raise any complaint against universal suffrage.[41]

Quite apart from arguments of principle, however, Laurentie feared that citizens would respond by abstaining, especially as news of the Monnerville recommendations had spread rapidly across Africa and Madagascar. As Laurentie wrote to Aimé Bayardelle, Éboué's successor as governor-general at Brazzaville, who had not attended the July meeting, the system that emerged went against everything toward which he had worked since the Liberation. The odds against him had been high, though Bayardelle also cast doubts on Laurentie's tactics; though he had clearly been overruled, it had been a possibly foolhardy gambit to have summoned to Paris all the most reactionary governors and governors-general.[42] In the event it is difficult to suppose that Laurentie could have performed better in what amounted to a shouting match with the authentic voice of the colonial "official mind."

"Thinking like an Empire"

By the time of the Monnerville Commission, Laurentie had already lost ground in what might be considered his major battle, which was for a conception of empire that was at once flexible enough to encompass the variety of constitutional forms contained within the French empire and yet also unified within an overarching structure. This structure was initially conceived, at the time of the Brazzaville Conference, as a French federation, but this transmuted into the French Union, a term first used in the Declaration on Indochina made on 24 March 1945. As Laurentie's federal conception of empire has been extensively discussed elsewhere,[43] I focus here briefly on the institutional implications of Laurentie's assaults on the high ground of the imperial hierarchy.

Laurentie showed remarkable consistency in his vision of empire, which can be traced back to the improvisatory ethos of the FCNL at Algiers. In the run-up to the Brazzaville Conference, Laurentie wrote revealingly to de Gaulle's *directeur de cabinet*, Gaston Palewski, setting out what he saw as the wider project directing the forthcoming conference:

1. Africans should be raised to complete responsibility within the framework of, and through the advance of, their own customs and institutions.
2. The personality of French Overseas countries (*pays*) must be assured within a federation in which Metropole and dependencies (*possessions*) will be associated on an equal footing, while maintaining the originality and the developing character of their political institutions.[44]

The key to this approach, as Laurentie further explained, was to devise means to involve North Africa in this scheme, or rather, to "inoculate" North Africa with the new policies. As he put it:

Although the first of these propositions theoretically applies only to Black Africa, it cannot fail to have an effect by contagion on the rest of Empire, and particularly on North Africa. The second proposition, if I may say so, directly implicates North Africa in the federal policy of the Ministry of Colonies.

The key to this was institutional reform: Laurentie called for the creation, in the forthcoming governmental structure of liberated France, of a Ministry for North Africa combining responsibility *both* for the protectorates of Morocco and Tunisia, *and* for Algeria, as a prior condition for all subsequent developments. What Laurentie was in effect proposing was a direct assault on the closely guarded bastions of North African administration—in other words, the system of so-called sealed partitions (*cloisons étanches*) that separated the Ministry of Colonies from the protectorate and mandate administrations of Morocco, Tunisia, and the Levant (under the aegis of the Ministry of Foreign Affairs), and the Algerian administration (directed from the Ministry of the Interior). Even at Algiers, there was little appetite for such a profound institutional makeover, and at Brazzaville official observers from all three North African administrations maintained a frosty distance from the deliberations of their interministerial rivals.[45]

Laurentie made one further attempt to draw the North African protectorates into his federal scheme, although even for Laurentie, Algeria seems to have constituted a step too far. As already mentioned, it was hoped at the Rue Oudinot, following on from the work of a study group that had taken further the federal idea for empire, that what became the Monnerville Commission would draw on similarly ambitious terms of reference. In February 1945 Giacobbi approached Foreign Minister Georges Bidault with a request for two participants from the Quai d'Orsay in the forthcoming commission; Bidault's reply merely reminded Giacobbi of the "particular conventional ties" existing between France and the North African territories and of their protected status in international law; for this reason the Foreign Ministry could send only observers to the commission.[46] Giacobbi's further reply, in early April, then sought to argue that the Declaration on Indochina of 24 March 1945, constituted a model for future imperial relations along the lines of the "Brazzaville policy." As Giacobbi put it, the Declaration

> marked a step forward in this direction and has established the principle of a revision of the relations between the Metropole and each of the member countries of the French community.
>
> The Constitution of the French Federal Union [*sic*] cannot help

but have an impact on Morocco and Tunisia; and they will certainly be affected by any decisions made about the composition of the Constituent Assembly that will be called upon to draw up the Constitution.[47]

At the commission's first session the observers from the Africa-Levant Directorate at the Quai d'Orsay insisted that while they had no deep-seated objections to the idea, the eventual inclusion of Tunisia and Morocco in the French Union should first be "the object of a preparatory, wide-ranging study." No answer was given or needed to Laurentie's exasperated question as to whether the Quai d'Orsay believed that it could make "its own little constitution for itself."[48]

The fact that the North African protectorates thus remained apart from deliberations over the future of the French Union—and indeed, in the longer term, were never accepted as "associated states" within the structure of the Union—thus placed a greater emphasis on Indochina's role as an implied model for imperial development. It is to Laurentie's credit that, as I have shown elsewhere, he distanced himself from the March 1945 Declaration, over the terms of which he had negotiated long and hard, as it became clear over the summer of 1945 just how unlikely it was to be accepted on the ground. It is in this context that we must place Laurentie's near disgrace in September 1945. In the wake of the Japanese surrender in the Far East, and with confused intelligence coming out of Indochina as to the extent of the Vietminh's August Revolution or the interpretation to be placed on Ho Chi Minh's Declaration of Independence of 2 September 1945, Laurentie spoke to a confidential conference of newspaper editors in terms that seemed to imply that official policy was moving toward an acceptance of Indochinese independence.[49] In the present context two observations may be made. First, at this point Laurentie seems to have drifted away from his commitment to a federal French Union, in his pragmatic and not unrealistic response to the force of circumstance in the Far East; however, it is worth noting that six months later we find him again promoting the concept of Indochina as a (by now somewhat different) model for the French Union.[50] The second observation concerns less the substance than the mode of Laurentie's pronouncement: arguably, not only was he "thinking like an empire," but he was doing so *out loud*, blurring the line—or indeed, crossing that line—between internal debate and external presentation. This brings us to our next point.

Thinking Out Loud—Imperial Propaganda

The third of Laurentie's battles was of a different nature, though it also reflected a dimension of his job as he conceived it: this was for public awareness of empire, or as we might more bluntly call it, propaganda. Laurentie's papers reveal a tireless publicist and polemicist, stretching the conventions of his role as a *directeur de ministère* in order to take his message to print, to the lecture hall, and even to the airwaves. The papers contain more than 350 pages of typescript of lectures and articles, which include the following:

:: The opening speech given at the reopening of ENFOM in November 1944, and a series of lectures given to cadets at ENFOM in late 1944 and early 1945; also an "Information session on Indochina," given to an unspecified audience in May 1945.
:: Lectures to an international audience, including a lecture, on "Recent Developments in French colonial policy," given at King's College, London, on 28 November 1946 (which he started by apologizing for the "kind of torture" he was about to inflict on his audience by speaking in English); and one delivered soon after his transfer to New York, also in English, on "The new institutions of the French Union," at the School of International Affairs, Columbia University, 23 April 1947.
:: Papers given to official and semi-official bodies such as the Academy of Colonial Sciences and the Centre for Foreign Policy.
:: Public lectures, for example, on the stirring theme of "The Empire comes to the aid of the Metropole," given at the Palais de Chaillot in January 1945.
:: A series of articles, of which seven are listed as having been published, mostly in the periodical *Renaissances*, from January 1944 (when the journal was presumably based at Algiers) to October 1945, with one further article listed as "to appear in 1946," and another as unpublished. The topics of these articles range from

the celebratory, for example "Éboué, the great Frenchman" or "The anniversary of Brazzaville," to the expository, for example, "Notes on a philosophy of French colonial policy" or "The French Union before a new world," although these two categories overlap very broadly.[51]

How is this body of work to be interpreted? First, it no doubt tells us something significant about Laurentie's conception of his job, and perhaps also about his shifting priorities as time passed. In particular the dating of this material shows a preponderance in the first year after the Liberation, and thus before the end of the Second World War, before the stepping up of policy developments both in Indochina and in the constitution-making process. It was in this early period, it might be suggested, that Laurentie was most keen to promote the "big idea" of the Brazzaville policy, and to do so to as wide an audience as he could reach; later he was either too busy, or too disillusioned, or both.[52] Second, how are we to interpret its contents? Subjecting these publications to a close discourse analysis—which space precludes in the present context—might raise a range of issues concerning the public presentation of policy, the interface between official colonial doctrine and the implementation of policy, or that between Gaullist propaganda ("The Empire comes to the aid of the Metropole," indeed) and practical colonial policy initiatives—and on this latter point in particular, the ambiguities of Laurentie's public role may be seen as following on directly from the propagandistic or "mythic" dimension of the Brazzaville Conference.[53] However, it would surely be stretching credibility to take this public output as a reliable guide to Laurentie's outlook, his view of the "philosophy" of colonial policy, or indeed his own place on an ideological spectrum between relative "liberalism" or "conservatism."[54]

The question of timing is also paramount for the other aspect of Laurentie's public output, a series of weekly or sometimes fortnightly radio broadcasts, entitled *Chronique*, which he gave over the best part of a year, each of between two and five pages (that is, between about four hundred and a thousand words). The first, a general piece on the empire since 1939, was given on 16 July 1945, the last, on 17 June 1946, celebrated—what else?—the sixth anniversary of de Gaulle's *appel* of

18 June 1940.⁵⁵ The context for the broadcasts was a more general daily current affairs program entitled *Ce Soir en France* (France This Evening). The tone of the scripts is avuncular and high-minded, with an occasional passage of self-conscious interior dialogue, perhaps also evoking de Gaulle's public style in its rhetorical tics and the personification of "la France," as in the following extract (from an early piece on the forthcoming colonial elections):

> Oh! I am aware of what sceptics are preparing to whisper: that the prestige of the colonial system has taken a pounding, that the colonial powers are nonetheless seeking to hang on, that various means, or dare I say tricks, are being cooked up to help them to hang on for longer. *Eh bien*! Let me say without hesitation: France has no tricks up her sleeve, France does not seek to adapt to the force of events, France creates her own events.⁵⁶

As their title suggests, the *Chronique* broadcasts offer an alternative chronology to the events of 1945–46, tracking closely the course of France's "return" to Indochina and the course of negotiations leading to the Accords of 6 March 1946, the deliberations on the French Union articles in the first constitutional draft and the aftermath of its rejection (to which I turn in a moment), as well as proposing more general topics that suggested the events of the week were either lacking or too confidential to be broadcast. The series petered out in July, when the director of information, M. Noguères, wrote to Laurentie declining further broadcasts with the feeble excuse, which to Laurentie's suspicious mind immediately suggested a conspiracy, that there was too much material available for broadcast on "France This Evening." Failing to avoid sounding miffed, Laurentie argued to Moutet that the "general mediocrity and occasional vulgarity" of the program's content militated against the excuse given and assumed that he, Laurentie, must have displeased someone ("Whom? And for what reason? I do not exactly know, and am reduced to hypotheses").⁵⁷ The truth was probably more banal, which was that even as the debates in the Second Constituent Assembly concerning the French Union articles reached their climax, the topic was not considered of burning enough public interest to warrant a weekly slot. Laurentie's *Chronique* pieces never aspired to the status of de Gaulle's wartime broadcasts or Roosevelt's "fireside chats," nor yet that of the *Voice of Algeria* broadcast clandestinely during the Algerian War, but arguably they demonstrate by their very lack of impact just how far the project of a French "empire-state" fell short of the crucial dimension of public recognition.

From One French Union to Another— Laurentie and the Constituent Assembly

Laurentie's fourth and final battle did not, in fact, result in defeat at all, since at one level he was entirely successful in leading his ministry's intervention over the summer of 1946 to revise the French Union articles presented in the first, failed, constitutional draft. At another level, however, this result may be seen to have been achieved at the expense of his own liberal principles, or perhaps simply of his own reputation. Here I explore the reasons for this apparent volte-face and in particular consider the evidence for suggesting that Laurentie was impelled by his analysis of forthcoming ideological battles in France and the wider world—in short, the impending Cold War—to accept a "conservative" solution to the constitutional problem of the French Union. But this investigation of Laurentie's motivation may also help us to address the interpretative conundrum already invoked—that is, the problem that arises from "knowing the end of the story"—to evaluate more fully the significance of the French Union debacle of 1946.

Before turning to the background to the debates of 1946, I return briefly to the relative calm of the previous summer for an intriguing piece of evidence that throws into relief the battles to come. Following the publication of Giacobbi's Ordonnance of 22 August 1945 on the colonial electoral system, Laurentie received a letter from his fellow commission member Léopold Sédar Senghor, which, not least, helps to confirm Laurentie's position, acknowledging that "no-one listened to you"; in reply, Laurentie affirmed: "I did everything I could, and indeed rather more than my own position suggested I should, in a failed attempt to achieve something quite different."[58] The exchange between the two men, only a few years apart in age (Senghor was thirty-eight, Laurentie, forty-three), must no doubt to an extent be read as wary ideological positioning between the African intellectual and the colonial functionary as they sought to establish rhetorical common ground: on the legacy of Vichy, the racism of reactionary "colonials"; or the conspiracy of the "trusts," the "money men and the colonialist spirit" (Senghor), and the "Anglo-Saxon" untrustworthiness (Laurentie). However, there was no mistaking the sincerity of Senghor's appeal for advice and support as the elections approached, and as Senghor considered whether to launch his political career. Laurentie's response sheds light not only on the degree of trust that he assumed to exist between his office and the African elite (the "*évolués*"), of whom Senghor was the foremost representative, but also his own view of the significance of the forthcoming Constituent Assembly's work. Thus, he advised Senghor to stand, while denying that this necessarily entailed a political career to which Senghor might not be destined ("I do not believe that this is the goal you are meant to achieve"). Rather, as he argued, "being a member of a Constituent Assembly is in a political category of its very own," and Senghor was more qualified than any to undertake it.[59] On a different note, he also reassured Senghor that the governor-general at Dakar, Pierre Cournarie (a particular antagonist of Laurentie's going back to Brazzaville), would receive orders not to stand in the way of Senghor's candidature—reassurance that was particularly valuable given the notoriously interventionist approach of French colonial officials to "their" elections.[60]

Notwithstanding the setback in trust occasioned by the failure to honor the Monnerville recommendations (and even the more restrictive system imposed, as Senghor acknowledged, represented "a significant advance over the system under the Third Republic"), the patent goodwill between Senghor and Laurentie seems to have prevailed more generally, and there is little sense, in the period that followed the elections of 21 October 1945, of the crisis to come. Indeed, for the whole period of the first Constituent Assembly's deliberations, there is a marked paucity of correspondence between the African and Caribbean *députés*, on the one hand, and the Rue Oudinot on the other, almost as if Laurentie and his colleagues simply left the Assembly to get on with its work. (This was also a key period in Indochina, which may be a further factor in this loss of focus on Africa.) Laurentie's radio broadcasts, on the other hand, returned frequently to the linked themes of the elections (1, 22, and 29

October), the opening of the Assembly (5, 12, and 26 November), to the Assembly's work on the French Union articles and the ensuing debate (4, 11, and 26 February; 11 and 26 March; 1 April), the failure of the first draft (6 May), and the forthcoming work of the second Assembly (3 and 10 June).[61]

Laurentie's concerns start to emerge in February 1946, when in a memo to Moutet Laurentie explicated the formula that famously headed the French Union articles in this first draft, and that spoke of a "freely consented Union." Although he described this text as "dangerous enough," this was not because of any implicit promise of decolonization, but because it implied that Morocco and Indochina had *already* acquired the status of associated states; Laurentie thought the question was best passed over in silence, especially in the context of ongoing negotiations in Indochina, and he therefore put forward an alternative, suitably vague text that had been drawn up in the ministry.[62] The following day, however, he accepted that the previous day's resolutions in the Assembly all seemed to correspond to ministerial policy, commenting only (perhaps with tongue in cheek) that the language in which they were written was "dreadful," whereas they should aspire to a "style approaching that of 1789"![63] Finally, in a letter to Bayardelle on 3 April, Laurentie came close to the core of his later campaign, complaining that the proposals for local government structures (*l'organisation intérieure des colonies*) were incoherent in that the Constituent Assembly was seeking to draw up a single law to govern local assemblies in each and every territory, and that the results would be "truly daft." He was trying to "bring some order" into the discussion but was unsure whether he would succeed.[64] The problem for Laurentie would seem therefore to have been one of constitutional and administrative illiteracy (as well as any remaining stylistic infelicities), rather than of political principle. In the same letter, Laurentie reported that "[there] is a good atmosphere in the Ministry, and for the first time in ages there is a feeling that we are marching in step with events"—this would seem to have been a somewhat short-lived state of affairs, associated with the short honeymoon period that followed the signature of the March Accords in Hanoi.

What then changed in Laurentie's attitude between his relative equanimity in April, as the referendum approached, and the apparent ferocity of his assault on the French Union articles over the summer? Clearly the failure of the constitutional text in the referendum of 5 May 1946 was in itself a paradigm-shifting event, the possibility of which Laurentie seems to have overlooked: to Bayardelle, he predicted a slight rise in the Communist vote at the expense of the Socialists and a slight rise in the Right, benefiting the MRP, but he thought that "this will not make very much difference, particularly from a colonial point of view."[65] Even in the immediate wake of the results, Laurentie's broadcast for 6 May 1946 affirmed the official line: "that the French Union system, as it has been defined by the Constituent Assembly, is not up for renegotiation."[66]

By the beginning of June, however, Laurentie had not only radically changed his position, but he was also apparently reinterpreting the work of the first Assembly and in particular what he now saw as the spoiling role of the Communists. As he put it:

> In April 1946, when it was apparent that world peace was not around the corner, the Communist Party barged in to the French Union which had barely begun to take shape at that point, and immediately skewed the whole picture. [. . .] Lozeray pitched in and got his way on the electoral law; [. . .] he didn't manage quite as well with the law on local assemblies, but did enough all the same to throw Africa and Madagascar into chaos.[67]

It is difficult in this memorandum to distinguish between the elements of genuine analysis, an effort to galvanize Moutet into action, and a kind of creeping paranoia concerning Communist strategy concerning the French Union and perhaps more generally. However, in the shadow of Churchill's very recent "iron curtain" speech at Fulton, Missouri (April 1946), we should perhaps not judge too harshly Laurentie's somewhat extreme, but not outlandish, view that "at the present moment, the policy of the great powers is one that is dominated by the prospect of war"; that while some territorial takeovers—for example, in North Africa—would constitute a casus belli, some more peripheral territories (Madagascar was foremost on Laurentie's list) might be swallowed up by rival powers in order to improve battle lines before the conflict; and that it was a similar jockeying for position that had led the "recently colonialist" Communist Party to take up the autonomist cause in the Constituent Assembly. Moreover, while the vehemence of Laurentie's anti-Communist sentiments comes as a surprise, this should be placed in the context of his parallel policy on Indochina in this period, which was similarly starting to shift on the interpretation to be placed on the March 1946 Accords;[68] moreover, the result of the May 1946 referendum reflected growing unease at the extent to which the constitutional draft reflected Communist designs for a single-chamber "People's Republic."

At this point the scene was set for the drama that played out over the summer of 1946, although it must surely be concluded that Laurentie's role was relatively minor in *determining* the course of the colonial debate or of the resulting Title VIII of the constitutional draft eventually approved in the October 1946 repeat referendum. Far more momentous were the heavyweight interventions of politicians such as de Gaulle (returning to the political fray after six months of self-imposed internal exile), Georges Bidault, Édouard Herriot, or even Laurentie's minister, Marius Moutet, who seems an unlikely contender for the role of "tragically" misled colonial liberal.[69] Anti-Communism aside, the question of Laurentie's motivation arises again here. The theme of institutional incoherence, chaos, and potential disorder recurs with sufficient frequency to bear significant interpretative weight. It may be worth quoting in full a statement of Laurentie's position, which shows a remarkable consistency with his views before the referendum. This was written to Senghor's senior Senegalese colleague, Lamine Guèye, but he asked for it to be passed on to Senghor and others, just as Laurentie was poised to intervene on his minister's behalf in the redrafting process:

1. The overseas territories are part of the French Republic and benefit from all liberties written in to its Constitution;
2. Political representation of the overseas territories in the National Assembly must not be at a lesser level than that prescribed by the first Constituent Assembly;
3. There is no reason why overseas territories should not have equal representation, at an equivalent proportion, in the Council of the Republic [i.e., the second chamber];
4. The system of local representation is not up for discussion; the

only principle to be observed is that the organization of local assemblies should be decided separately for each territory or group of territories (with an organic law fixing the statute of each territory or group of territories), and not by a general law for all overseas territories; this is a question of method only; I repeat, the system of local representation is untouchable;

5. The Constitution of the French Union, which will address the case of the Associated States must coexist with, and must therefore be compatible with, the Constitution of the French Republic in the overseas territories.[70]

As Laurentie further added, a properly constituted French Union was all the more timely given the nature of the discussions currently taking place at Fontainebleau (where French negotiators were comprehensively failing to make headway against their Vietnamese counterparts).

Certainly, it would be implausible to conclude on the basis of the available evidence that Laurentie was seeking to head off an opportunity for gradual decolonization allegedly created by the first constitutional draft, even if the scenario concocted by Laurentie over the summer of 1946—a Communist-inspired disaggregation of French colonial structures, imperial takeover by the "Anglo-Saxon" powers, a third world war—was hardly less far-fetched. A more charitable reading of what happened in the redrafting of the Constitution over the summer of 1946 is that Laurentie's concerns for the imperial system coincided with the more properly "conservative" political agenda of a de Gaulle or a Bidault. However, the net impact of these political and official interventions was to impose a breathing space, slowing, but not preventing, a process of political development in sub-Saharan Africa, such that over a period of some ten years—that is, the lives of two parliaments—the French Union territories acquired a robust system of autonomous local assemblies elected by universal suffrage, which, to place it in comparative perspective, was more politically advanced than anything the British had so far devised, even in the Gold Coast; moreover, this system had been achieved not by imperial *fiat*, but by a dynamic and conflictual political process engaging African political elites.[71] In the end, of course, the prospect of independence trumped even the most advanced colonial political developments, and beyond Defferre's Framework Law of 1956, decolonization certainly beckoned—but this was almost literally unimaginable ten years earlier.

Conclusion

In all of Laurentie's battles, the aim here has not been to outline a counterfactual "what might have happened" had Laurentie been more effective or encountered fewer obstacles, or not fitted, however uncomfortably, into the institutional role allotted him as director of political affairs. In the early years that took him from Brazzaville to Algiers and thence to liberated Paris, to be sure, Laurentie's policymaking career had an alluring dimension of heroic individual agency that emulated, and was no doubt inspired by, the example of de Gaulle, to whom he wrote in December 1944: "We have a magnificent colonial policy, but there are only a dozen of 'us' in France and the colonies."[72] Laurentie's "thinking like an empire" was akin to "rethinking France," the febrile, protean, and ultimately fruitless activity of those many intellectuals and Résistants who imagined and idealized the forms that a renewed France might (but ultimately never did) take after the Liberation.[73] Rather, the evidence powerfully suggests the limits of individual agency in the face of entrenched institutional norms and ideological positions. Laurentie was in effect beaten, or at best co-opted, by "the system," but mostly because "thinking like an empire" had necessarily to be a corporate activity, and while Laurentie could bear witness—and did so eloquently and perceptively in his capacity as historical "double agent"—the changes he brought about were at best incremental, and either obscured or were frustrated by setbacks in the short term. As it turned out in any case, "thinking like an empire" was for France an unexpectedly short-term enterprise.

Notes

1. Martin Shipway, *A Road to War: France and Vietnam, 1944–1947* (Oxford: Berghahn Books, 1996; reprint, 2003).

2. Archives Nationales, Paris (hereafter AN), 72AJ 535-540, papiers Henri Laurentie.

3. The Laurentie family memorabilia include a volume of poetry, Henri Laurentie, *Choix de poèmes* (Paris: Seghers, 1957), and a children's book,

Marie Colmont, *Histoire du tigre en bois* (Paris: Flammarion, 1945), the latter inscribed "with affectionate kisses" (*Baisers affectueux*) from one "Uncle Ho," a gift to the younger son ("To my little nephew, Jean Laurentie") from the then-president of the Democratic Republic of Vietnam, on the occasion of a private dinner at the Laurentie's apartment in the XVIe *arrondissement* in August 1946. All translations are by the author unless otherwise noted.

4. "As for the Rue Oudinot [i.e., the Ministry of Colonies], the role I play there is the piteous Cassandra," AN, 72AJ 538, Laurentie to Aimé Bayardelle, Governor-General of French Equatorial Africa, 9 February 1945.

5. Shipway, *Road to War*, 142–45. The blight to Laurentie's career was confirmed by the junior colonial administrator (at the time) and long-lived Gaullist insider Pierre Messmer; Messmer, interview with the author and Philippe Oulmont, 12 March 2007.

6. See Shipway, *Road to War*; and Martin Shipway, "Madagascar on the Eve of Insurrection, 1944–1947: The Impasse of a Liberal Colonial Policy," *Journal of Imperial and Commonwealth History* 24:1 (1996), 72–100, reprinted in *A Decolonization Reader*, ed. James Le Sueur (London: Routledge, 2003), 80–102.

7. See especially James I. Lewis, "The French Colonial Service and the Issues of Reform, 1944–48," *Contemporary European History* 4:2 (1995), 153–88.

8. Ronald Robinson and John Gallagher, *Africa and the Victorians: The Official Mind of Imperialism* (Oxford: Oxford University Press, 1961); and see, e.g., Ronald Hyam, *Britain's Declining Empire: The Road to Decolonization, 1918–1968* (Cambridge: Cambridge University Press, 2006), and review by Robert Holland, *Journal of Imperial and Commonwealth Studies* 36:1 (2008), 135–37.

9. William B. Cohen, *Rulers of Empire: The French Colonial Service in Africa* (Stanford CA: Hoover Institute Press, 1971); see also Véronique Dimier's chapter in this volume.

10. Frederick Cooper, *Decolonization and African Society: The Labor Question in French and British Africa* (Cambridge: Cambridge University Press, 1996), 6.

11. Niall Ferguson, *Empire: How Britain Changed the Modern World* (London: Penguin, 2003), 363.

12. See Martin Lynn, ed., *The British Empire in the 1950s: Retreat or Revival?* (New York: Palgrave Macmillan, 2005).

13. James I. Lewis, "The MRP and the Genesis of the French Union, 1944–1948," *French History* 12:3 (1998), 276–314, quote at 276.

14. Lewis, "MRP and the Genesis," 283. It might be suggested that no

French colonial possession even potentially resembled the British Dominions—Canada, Australia, New Zealand, and South Africa—nor did any other British dependency, with the possible, dubious exception of settler-dominated Southern Rhodesia.

15. As Frederick Cooper comments: "both the way the leaders of empire-states thought and the forms in which political contestation took place reflect 'thinking like an empire'. [. . .] Far from being an anachronistic political form in the 'modern era', this imperial perspective applies to France, Britain, and other important states of the nineteenth and twentieth centuries"; Cooper, *Colonialism in Question: Theory, Knowledge, History* (Berkeley: University of California Press, 2005), 154.

16. Biographical details from Centre des Archives d'Outre-mer, Aix-en-Provence (hereafter CAOM), 39APOM3, *Fichier des anciens élèves de l'Ecole nationale de la France d'Outre-Mer*, (but note he was *not* a graduate of EN-FOM); and see his page as a Compagnon de l'Ordre de la Libération, including a striking photograph, http://www.ordredelaliberation.fr/fr_compagnon/562.html.

17. Following Eboué's refusal, Laurentie wrote to Boisson (who had lost a leg in the Great War), on 13 February 1940: "You had the honour of fighting in the War. As I was too young to fight in 1918, you cannot refuse me permission to take part this time, nor humiliate me by forcing me to escape the common danger yet again, this time for no good reason." AN, 72AJ 538, quoted by Philippe Oulmont, in an unpublished contribution to the September 2004 colloquium on Félix Eboué, "'L'équipe Eboué-Laurentie' et le général de Gaulle, 1939–1943," 3n. Laurentie's elder brother was killed on the Western Front at age eighteen.

18. For a recent account see Martin Shipway, "Brazzaville, entre mythe et non-dit," in *De Gaulle, Chef de Guerre: De l'appel de Londres à la libération de Paris, 1940–1944* (Paris: Plon 2008), 392–404.

19. Brian Weinstein, *Eboué* (New York: Oxford University Press, 1972), 310–11; and see Shipway, *Road to War*, 22.

20. CAOM, *Fichier des anciens élèves*. Oulmont, "'L'équipe Eboué-Laurentie,'" quotes Eboué's advice to Laurentie: "Do not write or speak under the influence of that caustic spirit of yours which so discomfits others. Keep your pointed remarks for private company." This advice seems to have been comprehensively ignored.

21. Communication to the author by Sébastien (who was age ten in 1940) and Jean Laurentie, April 2006.

22. AN, 72AJ 538, Laurentie to Pignon, 25 September 1944; AN, 72AJ 535, "Note pour Monsieur le Ministre," 6 April 1945, which identifies the likely culprit, still working in the Direction du Personnel.

23. AN, 72AJ 538, Laurentie letter to Pierre Launois, 8 January 1948.
24. See "Henri Laurentie," http://www.ordredelaliberation.fr/fr_compagnon/562.html.
25. AN, 72AJ 538, Laurentie letter to Pignon, 22 September 1944. See also Laurentie's gloss on the "official mind," which he refers to as "the bureaucratic spirit . . . honest, hard-working and ultimately impermeable to any kind of general thinking," AN, 72AJ 538, Laurentie letter to Bayardelle, 4 August 1944.
26. CAOM, *Fichier des anciens élèves*, 39APOM2.
27. See Cohen, *Rulers of Empire*. On Éboué and Saint-Mart, see CAOM, *Fichier des anciens élèves*, 39APOM3.
28. See Shipway, "Brazzaville, entre mythe et non-dit."
29. Interview with the author and Philippe Oulmont, 12 March 2007. Although Indochina was not represented at Brazzaville given the circumstances of Japanese occupation, this absence did not ostensibly trouble the Africanists who were present.
30. See Shipway, *Road to War*, 97.
31. AN, 72AJ 539, Laurentie letter to Pignon, 25 September 1944.
32. AN, 72AJ 535, NOTE PERSONNELLE pour M. le Général de Gaulle, 28 December 1944.
33. AN, 72AJ 535, NOTE PERSONNELLE pour M. le Général de Gaulle. The note to de Gaulle was written as a response to de Gaulle's recent signature of a Treaty of Friendship with Moscow, in the wake of which Laurentie expressed the hope that the focus of policy would return to the empire; the allusion to Washington is presumably to de Gaulle's visit to the American capital in July 1944, where he had set out his clearest statement on a post-Brazzaville "federal" empire; see Shipway, *Road to War*, 39. Note the characteristically Gaullist perspective on the Vichy administration's "absence."
34. AN, 72AJ 535, NOTE PERSONNELLE pour M. le Général de Gaulle. Laurentie's later assessment of Pleven is no more flattering: "I realized a long time ago that he never remained true to anything, not even to his own ideas, but only, at any given moment, to himself; in his way, he is a practitioner of existentialism." AN, 72AJ 540, Laurentie letter to Pacha, 4 August 1949.
35. CAOM, Affaires politiques (AP), 215d.II, Commission chargée de l'étude de la représentation des territoires d'Outre-Mer à la future Assemblée Constituante, P.v., séance du 11 avril 1945 (Ière séance). Objections to Laurentie's terminology were raised by Sourou-Migan Apithy, future *député* of Dahomey; see his Memoirs, quoted by Tony Chafer, *The End of Empire in French West Africa: France's Successful Decolonization?* (Oxford: Berg, 2002).
36. See Lewis, "French Colonial Service," 159–60. Indochinese representa-

tion was in any case a purely theoretical proposition in advance of any French "liberation" or reoccupation of Indochina.

37. CAOM, AP, 214d.III, Rapport de la Commission chargée de l'étude de la représentation des territoires d'Outre-Mer à la future Assemblée Constituante (Report of the Commission established to study overseas representation in the forthcoming Constituent Assembly).

38. Cameroon was accorded special status as a League of Nations Mandate and future UN Trusteeship Territory. The governor-general of FEA, Aimé Bayardelle, did not attend; see below.

39. Ordonnance no. 45-1874 du 22 Août 1945.

40. CAOM, Cab. 10, NOTE au MINISTRE au sujet des élections coloniales, 4 August 1945.

41. CAOM, Cab. 10, NOTE au MINISTRE au sujet des élections coloniales. Léopold Sédar Senghor, a member of the Monnerville Commission, made the reciprocal argument in a letter to a European colleague (intercepted by the French postal censor in Dakar): "If we defend the principle of equality between citizens and non-citizens, it is first of all a question of justice. But above all, we avoid being divided amongst ourselves. Moreover, taking this position makes us stronger when it comes to demanding equality between Europeans and Africans. Or rather, if we insist on equality between Europeans and Africans, we have no choice but to claim the same equality between Africans." CAOM, AOM, AP/2230d.1, Senghor à M. A. de Saint Jean, 11 May 1945.

42. AN, 72AJ 538, Laurentie to Bayardelle, 30 August 1945; Bayardelle to Laurentie, 1 September 1945.

43. See Shipway, *Road to War*, esp. 43–62; for a recent summary see Martin Shipway, *Decolonization and Its Impact: A Comparative Approach to the End of the Colonial Empires* (Oxford: Blackwell, 2008), 88–90.

44. AN, 3 AG 1/279 (Papiers de Gaulle), Laurentie note to Gaston Palewski, directeur de cabinet du général de Gaulle, 8 December 1943.

45. Shipway, *Road to War*, 30.

46. CAOM, AP/215, Giacobbi to Bidault, no. 2421, 28 February 1945; Bidault to Giacobbi, no. 381, 17 March 1945.

47. CAOM, AP/215, Giacobbi to Bidault, no10RC 6, 3 April 1945.

48. CAOM, AP, 214d.III, Rapport de la Commission chargée de l'étude de la représentation des territoires d'Outre-Mer à la future Assemblée Constituante (Report of the Commission established to study overseas representation in the forthcoming Constituent Assembly). Minister of the Interior Adrien Tixier (SFIO), was blandly sympathetic to the general principle and relayed to the Monnerville Commission, via the Algerian observer, his hope that the commission would "extend its scope to include the study of every overseas

country's institutions." It is an open question whether Algeria constituted an overseas country (*pays d'outre-mer*) in this sense; in any case the Monnerville Commission did not discuss Algeria.

49. Shipway, *Road to War*, 142–44. The transcript of Laurentie's two press conferences, on 13 and 14 September 1945 (the latter given to *directeurs de journaux*), is in AN, 72AJ 535. Ironically, Laurentie was accused by the correspondent for *Combat*, one Colonel Bernard, of not having replied to a certain number of questions, an accusation that Laurentie denied vigorously, pointing out also that Bernard was chairman of seven company boards with Indochinese interests and a member of four others, and it therefore ill behooved Bernard to "spontaneously seek to outdo the French government in liberalism and generosity": Laurentie to M. le Directeur, *Combat*, 15 September 1945, AN, 72AJ 535.

50. Shipway, *Road to War*, 174–75.

51. All in AN, 72AJ 535.

52. Falling outside the main period of the publications, the date of the lecture in London, 28 November 1946, is also highly suggestive: at the height of the Haiphong incident, Laurentie had been in Paris the day before, 27 November, for a briefing meeting drawing up a set of instructions for the high commissioner, to be discussed at the interministerial committee on Indochina, Cominindo, on the 29th, for which he was also presumably back in Paris; see Shipway, *Road to War*, 244–45, 250.

53. See Shipway, "Brazzaville, entre mythe et non-dit."

54. Cf. Lewis's account of the "limits of Laurentie's reformism," based on the October 1944 article "Notes sur une philosophie de la politique coloniale française," in "French Colonial Service," 166.

55. Forty scripts are contained in AN, 72AJ 535.

56. AN, 72AJ 535, *Chronique*, 30 July 1945.

57. AN, 72AJ 535, Note pour Monsieur le Ministre, 3 August 1946.

58. Senghor to Laurentie, "Monsieur le Gouverneur Général [sic]," 29 August 1945; Laurentie to Senghor, "Cher Monsieur et Ami," 13 September 1945, AN, 72AJ 538.

59. Senghor to Laurentie, "Monsieur le Gouverneur Général [sic]"; Laurentie to Senghor, "Cher Monsieur et Ami."

60. On Cournarie, see Chafer, *End of Empire in French West Africa*, 42–43, 45, 59–60.

61. AN, 72AJ 535, *Chronique*, various dates. By contrast, Indochina is the theme of only one broadcast, on 11 March 1946, immediately following the Franco-Vietnamese accords.

62. AN, 72AJ 535, Note pour Monsieur le Ministre, 7 February 1946.

63. AN, 72AJ 535, Note pour Monsieur le Ministre, 8 February 1946.
64. AN, 72AJ 538, Laurentie letter to Bayardelle, 3 April 1946.
65. AN, 72AJ 538, Laurentie letter to Bayardelle.
66. AN, 72AJ 535, *Chronique*, 6 May 1946.
67. AN, 72AJ 535, Note personnelle pour Monsieur le Ministre, 4 June 1946.
68. See Shipway, *Road to War*.
69. James I. Lewis, "The Tragic Career of Marius Moutet," *European History Quarterly* 38:1 (2008), 66–92.
70. AN, 72AJ 538, Laurentie letter to Lamine Guèye, 22 July 1946.
71. This argument is developed in Shipway, *Decolonization and Its Impact*, chaps. 5 and 7.
72. AN, 72AJ 535, Note personnelle pour M. le Général de Gaulle, 28 December 1944.
73. Andrew Shennan, *Rethinking France: Plans for Renewal, 1940–1946* (Oxford: Oxford University Press, 1989).

11

Recycling Empire

*French Colonial Administrators at the
Heart of European Development Policy*

VÉRONIQUE DIMIER

When I arrived at the European Commission (DG VIII, development), the style was very colonial indeed. If French colonial officers had not implemented indirect rule during colonial times, they certainly did so while at the DG VIII.

    C. CHEYSSON, commissioner for development, 1973–81,
        interview with author, 21 December 2001

It is hard to find more fitting words than Monsieur Cheysson's to describe the influence and role of ex-colonial officers on the newly minted development policy of the European Economic Community (EEC) from its inception in the early 1960s through the mid-1970s. So far this role, and the centrality of colonial minds to it, have been largely neglected. The circumstances are now well known in which, during the 1957 negotiations leading to the Treaty of Rome, France, then still a colonial power, imposed on its European partners what was then called the Association with Overseas Territories.[1] The history of that association, which was subsequently transformed, first into the Yaoundé Convention and then the Lomé Convention with African, Caribbean, and Pacific countries, has also been related in depth.[2] However, scholars have yet to examine the manner in which this development policy—its procedures and principles—were shaped. Nor has much attention been given to the means by which the European Commission's Directorate General VIII

(DG VIII)—the administration responsible for implementing development—came to be institutionalized. More generally, we have yet to see much systematic analysis of the second career of ex-colonial officers, focusing on the ways in which they transferred their colonial experience back to Europe.[3]

As far as French colonial administrators were concerned, since 1887 they had been part of a unified colonial administrative service run by the Colonial Ministry, whose personnel were trained at a dedicated colonial school in Paris. Faced with decolonization, these specialist bureaucrats were offered several solutions.[4] They could request reassignment to one of the branches of the French civil service, which, for many, would prove a long and difficult process. Or they could ask for a period of "special leave," paid for five years by the government, which would either tide them over prior to retirement or provide the wherewithal to find employment elsewhere in the private sector. Anticipating these alternatives, as early as 1958 some colonial officials sought transfers to Brussels, hoping to work within the framework of the future European Economic Community and, more specifically, within that new French governmental initiative: the association with the overseas territories.

Before proceeding further, it is worth recalling the context in which this association was first approved. While negotiating the Treaty of Rome, French representatives made clear to their future European partners that France would not "sacrifice her African vocation for a European one."[5] Colonial territories were an integral part of the Republic, so leaving them outside the European common market would simply be unconstitutional and would surely lead them to what was still dubbed "secession," code for independence.[6] Moreover, in economic terms, France had already created a form of "common market" with her overseas territories, an economic system that was more highly integrated than the future European one, based as it was on commercial preferences and a Fonds d'Investissement pour le Développement Économique et Social (FIDES), created in 1946 and intended to underpin the development of these dependencies. (See Tony Chafer's contribution to this volume for further details.) Forcefully defended by the French delegation, the adaptation of these existing mechanisms to the EEC was eventually accepted by fellow negotiators albeit with considerable reluctance on the part of

Germany and the Netherlands. Certain arrangements were agreed upon and were soon to be dubbed "association" with overseas territories, a term with decidedly French colonial connotations. These arrangements, as inscribed in the Treaty of Rome, included trade agreements (which effectively preserved commercial preferences) and a foreign grant in aid named European Development Fund for Overseas Territories and devised in accordance with French colonial principles. Initially, at least, these provisions were largely confined to Francophone territories in sub-Saharan Africa, those that had longstanding "special," not to say "colonial," attachments with France and Belgium.[7]

Ironically, although French overseas territories in sub-Saharan Africa were granted substantial political autonomy under the terms of Gaston Defferre's eponymously named Framework Law of 1956, they were not asked whether they wanted to be associated with the impending European Economic Community or not.[8] As one French commentator noted, this form of colonialism was "not the least contestable."[9] This may explain why African elites remained skeptical toward an association that many judged to be merely the continuation of the old colonial pact by which colonies served the economic requirements of the imperial power.[10] Even those leaders who had fought for the establishment of a Euro-African economic bloc such as Léopold Senghor, Senegal's representative to the French National Assembly in the 1950s, had warned that "we may agree in this marriage of convenience [i.e., the European Community] to be the attendants who carry the bride's veil, but we do not want to be the wedding gift."[11] Once these states opted for independence, however, their explicit consent became necessary. Negotiations therefore began with the newly independent states, the outcome of which was the 1963 Yaoundé Convention (later superseded by the Lomé Convention), with the former African and Malagasy associated states. Convincing them that the association marked a fundamental departure from the colonial past was an essential task that fell to the EEC's European Commission. In a further ironic twist, the job was, in practice, delegated to former French colonial officers.

As we shall see, these erstwhile colonial bureaucrats played the pivotal role in creating the European Commission's new development administration, known as Directorate General VIII, whose main function was to run the European Development Fund for Overseas Territories.[12] Whether they represented and defended French interests in Brussels is still a matter of debate, but there is little doubt that the key to their success, as architects of DG VIII, was their knowledge of—and adaptation to—the requirements of their client constituency, namely the Francophone African elites at the apex of newly sovereign states. Indeed, drawing upon both their formal training and their erstwhile practices as field officers, those ex-colonial officials brought to DG VIII a distinctive esprit de corps, some decidedly colonial ethos and methods that resemble, or at least were well adapted to deal with, the quasi-patriarchal style of their African political clients. Most were pragmatic, uneasy with the constraints of formal bureaucratic procedure, and opposed to any kind of rationalization. Accustomed to the practices of indirect rule, they relied, above all, on the discretionary powers of some leaders, exploiting their personal relationships and opaque bonds of trust with the African elites. Face-to-face compromises and bending of the rules were commonplace.[13] Such informal methods soon marked out the DG VIII's identity, a DG whose unique skill, as viewed by outside observers, was to deal with "negro kings." These deal-making skills also constituted the main source of its legitimacy. Indeed, the same colonial practices, especially that of touring territories, were crucial in persuading the African elite of the benefits of the association, transforming what some dismissed as "a mere survival of a historical situation" into something altogether unique: a "great work of solidarity."[14] Last but not least, these networks of African contacts gave European development policy a decidedly French flavor, a postcolonial aftertaste that would soon stick in the throats of other European Community (EC) members and their bureaucrats in Brussels.

Colonizing DG VIII

The association afforded France an opportune means to continue its colonial mission, pursuing its African interests while defraying the costs among its European partners. The deal that French negotiators proposed during the Treaty of Rome talks was clear: France would open its protected colonial market to the goods and firms of its partners; in return, it expected them to participate in the financing of the European Development Fund for Overseas Territories (Fonds Européen de Développement pour l'Outre-Mer). Despite German and Dutch resistance, the French proposal was eventually accepted with relatively few modifications, albeit less in the interests of the African peoples affected than for the sake of the European Economic Community. The monies concerned, soon to be renamed the European Development Fund (EDF) to avoid any confusion with the colonial past, was financed by direct contributions from the member states, Germany contributing on equal terms with France.[15]

To retain a tight hold over aid projects and avoid any outside interference in those territories still under French sovereign control, France insisted on the following mechanisms: it was the responsibility of the associated territories' authorities (meaning, at the time, their colonial administration) to put forward economic and social projects for EEC funding, in agreement with local representatives. The same authorities would then implement the resultant schemes and launch the call for tenders. For its part, the European Commission was to assess the development projects proposed by the associated territories, make funding proposals to the Council of Minister (representing the member states), and then supervise technically and financially the execution of the projects. The EEC Council of Ministers' role was, for the main economic projects at least, confined to approving the projects selected by the European Commission. These procedures were eventually accepted by member states, albeit grudgingly by Germany in particular. Based on public investment and the principle of state action, the EDF's operating assumptions derived entirely from France's FIDES. In a further bid to foster its interests at the community level, France took responsibility for filling the post of commissioner for development, the first appointee being Robert Lemaignen, formerly a renowned businessman in Africa. According to historian Catherine Hodeir, Félix Houphouët-Boigny endorsed Lemaignen's selection.[16] The new commissioner had an entire administration to help him, the DG VIII, whose director-general was, by convention, German. The precise distribution of authority between the commissioner and the director-general was not predetermined and could vary according to circumstances. Ironically in the case of the DG VIII the man who soon came to be the "boss" was neither of them, but a French—or, more precisely, Corsican—ex-colonial officer, Jacques Ferrandi.

By early 1958 Lemaignen had invited Ferrandi to become his key *chef de cabinet*. Prior to this Ferrandi had worked for the French Colonial Ministry and the colonial government in Dakar, where he rose to take charge of economic affairs, a post he held from 1953 to 1958. The role enabled him to oversee the implementation of FIDES-related development projects in French West Africa.[17] He thus wielded substantial power already and was accustomed to working hand-in-glove with local politicians soon to become the leaders of their newly independent states, who, it seems, held him in high regard. Ferrandi also was acknowledged as an outstanding specialist in overseas development within French colonial circles.[18] Thanks to his personal relationships, his intimate knowledge of Africa, and his expertise in development policy, he was ideally placed to assist the new commissioner in interpreting and implementing the European Development Fund. Ferrandi was quick to exploit his new position and the changed institutional setting in which he found himself. He imposed his ideas within DG VIII and ousted those officials liable to challenge his approach, beginning with the first director-general, Helmuth Allardt, a former German ambassador to Indonesia who had made the mistake of publicly criticizing Franco-African predominance within the association.[19] Following French governmental pressure on West German authorities in Bonn, Allardt was hastily replaced by someone "who by his culture and his character was much closer to the French character," an individual better "acquainted with French preoccupations in Africa."[20] The new nominee selected was Heinrich Hendus, former West German ambassador to Algeria.

Hendus promptly undertook a major reorganization of DG VIII. He delegated most of his responsibilities as chief authorizing officer to Ferrandi, who in 1962 was appointed head of one of the divisions responsible for the EDF (Direction Études et Programmes de Développement). A year later, following a reorganization of the DG, Ferrandi was promoted further, becoming the EDF's sole director. Ultimate power over fund management was thereby concentrated in his hands. It fell to him to assess development projects submitted by associated countries before their referral to EEC member states on the EDF committee (which represented the EEC Council of Ministers). It also fell to him to supervise the call for tenders launched by the administration of the associated countries and control financially and technically the implementation of the projects. In so doing Ferrandi was equally well placed to guide European businesses interested in the execution of these projects through the tendering process. When combined with his mastery of his African dossiers and his connections with African elites, it is easy to see why he enjoyed decisive influence in the preliminary negotiations with the member states on one side and African countries on the other—the former anxious for their businesses to reap contracts, and the latter anxious to reap the manna from Europe. As Ferrandi put it, "I have never had so much power to dispose of public money. DG VIII was the EDF, and I was the EDF."[21] An exaggeration perhaps, but it was a sentiment that none of the African heads of state would have contested. Indeed, it seems that with relatively little discussion the EDF committee approved the bulk of those projects proposed by African states and supported by Ferrandi's team.[22] As a British expert later concluded:

> The general impression is that the commission is dominating the meetings of the EDF committee. Thanks to their position as technocrats they are able to present suitable proposals and they are very skilful in foreseeing suitable questions. They often resort to experts in order to deal with specific details. On their side, the representatives of the member states in the Committee are often sent by finance ministries ... and their experience in development issues is rather limited.[23]

Ferrandi's discretionary powers were all the more decisive because the criteria for assessing projects were only slowly formalized and even then remained very general.[24] The same British expert commentator observed that the distribution of aid among the associated states largely rested on the "secret decisions" of a handful DG VIII officials.[25] Asked by the Development Aid Committee of the Organisation for Economic Co-operation and Development (OECD) to provide details about how this system worked in practice, "Ferrandi said that the Commission had serious difficulties in finding objective criteria on which funds distribution should be based. They did not think that it was a good policy to distribute aid on an agreed key and they had moved away from this notion towards a policy of distribution based on individual appraisal of the projects."[26] As far as the appraisal of the projects was concerned, Ferrandi consistently maintained that it was not "possible to determine uniform criteria valid in all countries." He went on to insist that it was quite right that this broad framework "left great freedom of action to the services responsible for establishing the dossiers, and to the EDF officials charged with evaluating them"—in other words, to his own staff.[27]

As this comment suggests, Ferrandi's "clan" or "mafia" of ex-colonial officers, whom he managed to place in strategic posts at DG VIII, helped cement his growing authority. (Ferrandi remarked in an interview, "when I say mafia, I don't mean an Italian mafia, [but] rather a big family."[28]) Use of these sympathetic placemen was facilitated by the fact that before 1962 there were no EEC regulations governing the recruitment of top European civil servants, except those unwritten conventions concerning the retention of balance between nationalities. As one such appointee later remarked, "Nominations were decided behind closed doors. Each negotiator came with his own team."[29] The highest positions within the commission were later exempted from the *concours* system established for other commission officials and were reserved for political nominees, a practice known in French official parlance as *parachutage*. As early as 1958 Émile Fay, one of Ferrandi's contemporaries at the École Coloniale, had joined him as head of the unit responsible for trade liberalization (*libération des échanges*) in the DG VIII trade division (Direction Échanges Commerciaux).[30] Michel Cellerier soon followed and was put in charge of the West Africa development program of the EDF in the division later headed by Ferrandi, the Direction Études et Programmes de Développement.[31] Another appointee to arrive in 1958 was Pierre Cros. Initially recruited to the European Commission's Press and Information Office, he was seconded to DG VIII to organize what was soon called "propaganda."[32] Other former colonial officers followed somewhat later.[33]

Last but not least, Ferrandi placed a pair of his closest erstwhile collaborators in Africa in two strategic positions. André Auclert came directly to the DG VIII in Brussels with his former "patron" at the Direction Générale des Affaires Économiques et du Plan in French West Africa.[34] In 1958 he took up his post in the Direction des Études et Programmes de Développement, where he later worked in close cooperation with Ferrandi. After the reorganization of the DG in 1963, he remained as assistant to Ferrandi in the division responsible for EDF spending, where he was promoted to head of financial operations in 1967. In this role he oversaw the implementation of projects, ensuring that funds were correctly disbursed. "I was always on tour . . . in a way, this new position did not really change my [old] job. I was a remote colonial administrator. I would not say that in front of the European officials, even though many thought the same."[35] Ferrandi also successfully nominated his own successor as *chef de cabinet* to the Commissioners for Development, first Henri Rochereau (1962–67), and later Jean François Deniau (1967–73). His chosen successor was Jean Chapperon, another former colleague from his days in the French Colonial Ministry and in Dakar.[36] Preoccupied with the advancement of their French political careers, both Rochereau and Deniau delegated much of their workload to Chapperon. Interviews with the men concerned indicate that Ferrandi and Chapperon pursued a consistent goal: exploiting the negotiating skills they had learned as colonial officials to make the most of their new roles.

All the French ex-colonial officers recruited were former École Coloniale graduates with several years of service in West Africa behind them. Some of these appointees—André Auclert, Pierre Cros, and Jean Chapperon—combined extensive experience in the bush, where they typically served as assistant district officers, with posts as senior officials, either in the Dakar federal administration or in the Paris Colonial Ministry.[37] It does, of course, bear emphasis that the overall number of French colonial administrators at DG VIII was constrained by the necessity to retain some numerical balance between the nationalities of all serving European Community officials. This restriction on French dominance notwithstanding, as Chapperon commented, "we were all at key positions." He further observed that thanks to his colleagues' former links and the esprit de corps acquired at the École Coloniale, "we made up a *sacrée équipe*."[38] At the heart of Brussels this elite team met once every three months for a special dinner of former *colo*. Chapperon had no doubt that "our effectiveness in policymaking over fifteen years in Brussels was linked to our *colo* spirit, our comradeship. In my view, we were the *levain dans la pâte* [literally, 'the yeast in the dough']."[39]

Le Levain dans la Pâte

There is no doubt that the colonial expertise and diverse personal contacts with the governing elites of Francophone Africa that Ferrandi and his team brought to the DG VIII consolidated their power within it, while at the same time acculturating other officials to their neocolonial objectives and methods of work. Whether they were the sole African development specialists in the early years of DG VIII remains unproven. The clear inference to be drawn from interviews with those involved, borne out by Lemaignen's comments in his biography, is that many DG VIII personnel had comparatively limited practical knowledge in that field.[40] The French appointees certainly cast themselves in the role of uniquely qualified experts and evidently enjoyed considerable success in convincing other DG VIII's officials that such was the case. Take, for instance, the comments of one of their Italian colleagues: "The French in DG VIII . . . were the only ones who could get things done. They were determined. They had a methodology derived from their experience. They were our mentors. We considered them our masters."[41]

So what, exactly, was the intellectual baggage—the colonial mindsets—that these former French colonial officials carried into DG VIII? First was the distinctive imperial training of the French colonial school, an institution whose raison d'être gradually changed in the critical years from 1930 to 1945 into an embrace of developmentalism and imperial federation, ideas that underpinned the French Union, the constitutional framework devised for the postwar empire and launched in October 1946.[42] Yet this accent on development was necessarily ambiguous: it claimed to favor development of the economic infrastructure of African dependencies for the welfare of their inhabitants while simultaneously respecting the integrity of their civilizations. It was devised in the 1930s, at a time when the very idea of French racial superiority and French civilizing mission were increasingly challenged by colonial specialists like Robert Delavignette, director of the colonial school between 1937 and 1946. A new but no less paternalistic view of African societies was by then developed: forcibly brought into contact with the world market and facing the requirements of adaptation to new forms of economic, social, and political organization, all of which brought with them new demands, African peoples, it was thought, were not able to find by themselves the necessary balance between the social and political organization of their cultures and the new ways. Drawing from these paternalistic assumptions, Delavignette and other French officials favored a characteristically paternalist solution: it fell to the colonial state to implement a pragmatic native policy designed to protect these societies from the worst effects of economic exploitation and acculturation, helping them to adjust to Western societal norms while retaining their own specificity. Social and economic development might then proceed, but in sympathy with indigenous cultures and traditions.[43] The contradictions inherent to this approach were never squarely addressed. Instead, policy guidelines remained sufficiently vague to allow for different interpretations over time. However, their core elements—a certain pragmatism and support for the gradual adaptation of native societies to economic modernization—were central to the official doctrine of the colonial school and the esprit de corps of colonial officials.[44] Thanks to Ferrandi and his team, these ideas also survived under the aegis of DG VIII.

The Treaty of Rome stipulated that the association with overseas territories "shall serve primarily to further the interests and prosperity of the inhabitants of these countries and territories in order to lead them to the economic, social and cultural development to which they aspire" (article 131, part IV). DG VIII officials depicted this as a "moral responsibility towards Africa" in terms that echoed the paternalistic colonial discourse of the 1930s.[45] The precise meaning of development was never strictly defined, except in the vaguest terms of socioeconomic infrastructures intended to promote economic growth and social welfare. In contrast to the experience of the World Bank, neither economists nor technical experts were mobilized to codify DG VIII's understanding of economic modernization. Indeed, Ferrandi's methods remained determinedly pragmatic, eschewing rationalization and technocratic "doctrine." DG VIII officials took pride in their more practical outlook, seeing in it a means to distance themselves from the World Bank's "technocratic approach." Ferrandi's one golden rule was that projects and the techniques adopted to implement them "should be adapted, should yield to the human and social constraints of the society being developed." He went on to add that "in the same way there is no sickness but only sick patients, there is no under-development but only under-developed countries, each with their own characteristics, their particular needs, their own possibilities and their specific solutions."[46] Consequently, he concluded: "Fighting against underdevelopment is not a technique, which consists in applying to a predetermined situation, a solution prefabricated in a laboratory. The battle against underdevelopment applies to men and women. It can only be won in collaboration with them, in the country where they live."[47] According to Ferrandi, this was where the DG VIII came into its own: "In Brussels, we prefer the school of reality. It is difficult and demands constant attention. . . . It means also that we have to consider those associates as equal partners."[48] This idealization of practical adaptation was repeated time after time in DG VIII's official documents and discourse and, ironic as it was in light of Ferrandi's defense of pragmatism, became something of a doctrine in itself.[49] Whether it was really applied is an issue beyond the scope of this analysis. Suffice to say that its rhetoric masked the absence of clearly identified policy criteria to be fulfilled. Once the overseas territories achieved independence, Ferrandi's ideas also informed a core principle of both the Yaoundé and Lomé Conventions: namely, the absence of any economic or political conditionality from what was depicted as "cooperation between equal partners."[50]

Such ideas were mirrored in the pragmatic, antibureaucratic methods that guided aid distribution, what DG VIII officials would call "Ferrandi's style." Those methods were antibureaucratic insofar as they were opposed to any rationalization of procedures. They were predicated on personal relationships, bonds of trust, loyalty, and compromise, traits central to effective indirect rule and entirely consistent with colonial school training.[51] According to one German observer, "Jacques Ferrandi's system was based on his experience and intuition. He did not like theories and a rational approach. . . . He did not see the interest in program [planning], I mean of establishing priorities, for example. He used to say 'in Africa everything is a priority.'"[52] In accordance with this approach, individual projects were presented and adopted ad hoc, according to vague criteria. Insofar as they existed, these criteria were tied less to the projects' anticipated social impact or economic benefits than to Ferrandi's personal relationships with the African heads of states and the consideration of French and European political interest that underlay them. According to Chapperon, no African representative, from Presidents Jean-Bédel Bokassa of the Central African Republic to Léopold Senghor of Senegal, ever came to Brussels without receiving a personal dinner invitation from Ferrandi. This is confirmed by the itineraries of dignitaries' visits available in the commission archives.[53] It is also evidenced by the array of photographs of African heads of state on the walls of Ferrandi's villa, all signed "to my dear friend J. Ferrandi," by the elephant's tusk given him by Bokassa, apparently "as long as the one he had given to de Gaulle," or by the knighthood eventually conferred on Ferrandi by the president of the Cote d'Ivoire.[54]

As British representatives remarked pointedly after joining the EC, Ferrandi's methods had resulted in giving money to those countries that needed it least, as well as public works contracts to French enterprises.[55] According to Marjorie Lister, "the EDF had the reputation of being a soft donor, of accepting projects which were not economically justifiable. The EDF's philosophy (based on the French one) was that a project could be worthwhile for its social or other quantifiable benefits, even if its economic return were low. These intangible of unquantifiable benefits in practice included keeping or courting the favor of the ACP government involved."[56] In the context of the Cold War, community aid encouraged African, Caribbean, and Pacific governments to maintain friendly relations with Europe, supporting the latter in international forums like the UN. Besides, prestigious projects helped African heads of state to increase their own prestige and legitimacy, as well as maintaining their own political clientele.

Ferrandi never denied this bias. He was, after all, cutting deals, primarily with members of a Franco-African elite whose demands largely coincided with French political and economic interests. Their authority and legitimacy still depended to a considerable extent on France's financial and political backing.[57] Their personal interests were often tied to those of French companies, many of which had been fixtures in Africa for a long time and thus enjoyed huge advantage next to their German or other EEC rivals when bidding for tenders. Put simply, in trying to adapt DG VIII's mission to its environment and constituency, Ferrandi could hardly ignore French political priorities in Africa and the political needs of its African "protégé." However, as discussed later, to accuse him of systematic favoritism toward French interests in Africa is misleading. As one British observer, otherwise highly critical of Ferrandi's methods and networks, acknowledged in the 1970s, many African heads of state still praised the EDF both for its political neutrality and ready accessibility: "the most convincing argument was that those associated territories, formerly French territories, which have bad relationships with France, seem to value the EDF Committee as a guarantee."[58]

While its methods may have been questionable, the "Ferrandi style" at DG VIII secured widespread acceptance among DG VIII officials. There was one reason for this above all: Ferrandi's approach was highly successful in legitimizing the new style of European development policy. As one official recalled, "Without him, half of our initiatives in Africa would not have taken place."[59] Seen in this light, the socialization process led by Ferrandi and his team was quite successful, albeit incomplete. Even those who later spurned the "Ferrandi style" recognized its utility in a 1960s context, when the association still had to be sold to Africa's governing elites.[60] Indeed, these personal methods not only were a way to run the EDF but also became a means to convince African heads of state that the association served their interests.[61] Herein lies yet another irony intrinsic to these hangovers of the colonial mind: colonial administrative "arts" like touring and personal dialogue, or *palabre*, were instrumental in dispelling residual suspicion of the colonial aspects of EEC development policy. In the late colonial period touring not only provided an essential link between colonial authorities and local elites, providing a veneer of legitimacy to the cooperation between the two, but it also enabled colonial administration to display its power.[62] The pomp and ceremony of parades and visits made colonial authority more visible and imposing. In much the same way, in a postcolonial setting where a central DG VIII priority was to establish its material presence, inspections and the inauguration of prestigious EDF-funded projects were highlights of any visits by the commissioner or director-general to recipient countries in Africa, a way for DG VIII to celebrate its work to the acclamation of an invited African audience. The fact that both the EDF and the African elite whom Ferrandi wanted to please favored large-scale projects made it easier still to increase DG VIII's already high profile and visibility. These ceremonial occasions, much like the regular visits of African leaders, journalists, and civil servants to Brussels, were orchestrated by the head of the DG VIII information service, Pierre Cros, who brought with him a network of African contacts developed earlier in his career. This strategy of highly visible partnership proved very successful in the short term. With the sole exception of Guinea, all the newly independent African states signed up to the Yaoundé Convention and, over the years, reasserted their "unquestionable attachment to the Association, their political willingness to maintain it by all means."[63] These states also sought direct representation in Brussels, which became a means to escape France's tutelage.[64]

Here was the rub. Not surprisingly, these demands, the consequent direct links established between Brussels and many African capitals, and the "growing autonomy of DG VIII" caused irritation in Paris. French governments strove hard to convince the newly independent African states to accept representation in Brussels through the existing structure of French permanent representatives.[65] French officials even felt obliged to remind their former "pupils" in Africa that the European Economic Community not only included the commission but also the member states, foremost among which was France, the main initiator of the association.[66] The Paris bureaucracy, it seems, grew increasingly fearful of being bypassed by Ferrandi, and these fears were, to some extent, well founded. In the process of institutionalizing DG VIII, Ferrandi had built up his own fiefdom, with networks that required defending, sometimes against competing French demands. He could play on the rivalry between the member states to reinforce his own position. This is best exemplified by an episode relating to the technical assistance and control.[67]

Even though the commission was entrusted with control over the technical and financial implementation of EDF projects, France always sought to restrict that control insofar as it applied to its former dependencies. This explains French insistence during the negotiation of the Treaty of Rome in 1957 that the authorities within the associated territories—in other words, its own colonial administration—should both put forward project schemes and take charge of their implementation. When these territories became independent, French negotiators suggested that the commission should delegate its powers of control to French companies in situ, a more or less analogous proposal designed to safeguard French control over project planning and execution. The French government was in no doubt that whenever newly independent Francophone states required assistance in formulating development projects, French companies were uniquely well placed to furnish the necessary technical assistance. For Ferrandi, who knew only too well the bribes and tricks needed to grease the wheels of cooperation in former colonies, these French proposals were wholly unacceptable: the French proposal meant that the same company would help the African local administrations devising the project (or even worse would pay them to propose some projects where the company would have a crucial role to play), would implement the project, and would control this implementation financially and technically. Anxious to preserve his own influence, Ferrandi tried to thwart French scheming by proposing to mandate his own *contrôleur-technique* to supervise the project support process. Although this brought him into conflict with the French government, the issue was resolved with typical pragmatism. From 1960 DG VIII used consultancy firms to hire project supervisors on private contracts. The system, however, remained unsatisfactory. As recognized by a later report, there was a clear contradiction between the supervisor's role—namely, controlling public money, which was normally the prerogative of a public authority—and the private commercial interests of these consultancy firms often linked to companies, whose aim was to maximize profits.[68] As Chapperon, himself a former colonial district officer, noted, "a territorial mission of control had to be set up" both to ensure the independence of project control and to render it more difficult for local inspectors to "indulge in compromising themselves" with the local elite.[69]

Eventually in March 1965 the commission established the post of EDF *contrôleur-délégué*. Ferrandi retained the decisive role, having set up a nonprofit association under Belgian law, the Association Européenne de Coopération (AEC), which served as an annex to DG VIII and took charge of recruiting and monitoring these inspectors. The new *délégués* served as Ferrandi's "men on the spot." In addition to controlling existing projects, the inspectors advised African governments on the formulation of new project proposals in conformity with Ferrandi's wishes. Hired under Belgian law on individual private contracts, the inspectors were typically seconded to the same country for several years. Many of them were recruited from the ranks of former colonial officers, their competency subsequently recognized by the European parliament.⁷⁰ Working in situ, they had to deal with diverse interests, including the consultancy bureaus, competing private enterprises generally backed by a member state (France in particular), African heads of state who typically shared the investment priorities of their former colonial power, and the interests of the commission. Compromises were essential. African administrations knew that project work could not proceed without the inspectors' assent, but the inspectors were, in turn, reliant on the local administration, which was ultimately responsible for proposing and implementing project work. Faithful to the traditions of indirect rule, the *délégués* therefore worked as colonial-style men "of influence."⁷¹ As one such inspector, a former French colonial district officer, conceded, "this new job did not change anything in my function. As *contrôleur technique* I did exactly what I had always done as a colonial administrator: persuading the population, their chiefs that such projects could be beneficial to them . . . , negotiating with the Minister of Planning to initiate or work out a rural modernization project, for example . . . and I spent hours talking with the authorities. . . . In some cases, we did a great job, I considered X, Minister of Planning, my brother. Having a reliable intermediary and getting on well with him was absolutely essential." True to the precepts of associationist thinking, according to this inspector, the key element was "proximity" and understanding, achieved through regular tours and the famous "*palabre.*"⁷² This image is probably no less idealized than that of the ideal district officer as taught at the École Coloniale. In practical terms, the actual influence of those inspectors is difficult to gauge, but it is revealing that some were dubbed "viceroys" by DG VIII headquarters staff. Much depended on their personal relationships with Ferrandi as far as their degree of autonomy was concerned. The flexibility inherent in his selection system enabled Ferrandi both to appoint and to move personnel as he wished, promoting those who shared his outlook, whom he could trust, and to whom he could easily delegate decision-making powers.

Consequently, DG VIII field inspectors became the cornerstone of Ferrandi's powerful network: a system of authority based on personal relationships, bonds of loyalty and patronage, and what Ferrandi labeled his "clan" or "mafia," a system that was extended to the African associates through a form of "collective clientelism."[73] Within that system the guiding principle of adaptation to African realities became a useful means to guarantee policy flexibility, ensuring that association goals were, at best, vaguely defined and that project selection criteria remained vague. Unbound by strict rules, Ferrandi's DG VIII system both resembled the quasi-patriarchal character of the postcolonial state in Africa, itself a product of colonial rule and blended well with it. Whether this latter-day "pope," this new Corsican "despot," really built his own empire, as the British later claimed, is bound to remain a matter of controversy. His system certainly came under closer and more hostile scrutiny when Britain joined the EEC. The British request under the terms of the 1975 Lomé Convention to admit the poorest Commonwealth countries to the association signified a new Waterloo heralding Ferrandi's departure.[74] Yet the influence of his "colonial mind" and that of the like minds in his circle lived on; indeed, according to some, it lives on to the present day.[75]

Notes

This article is drawn from a project started in 1999 and soon to be published as "Recycling Empire: The Invention of a EEC Aid Bureaucracy."

1. Gérard Bossuat, ed., "Europe et Afrique au tournant des indépendances," special issue of *Journal Matérieux pour l'Histoire de notre Temps*, 7 (January–March 2005); Véronique Dimier, "Legitimizing the DG VIII: A Small Family Business (1958-1975)," European Consortium for Political Research paper, Grenoble, 6–10 April 2001; R. Schreurs, "Un leg historique: L'eurafrique dans les négociations du Traité de Rome," *Politique Africaine* 49 (1993), 82–92; Pierre Guillen, "L'avenir de l'Union Française dans les négociations du traité de Rome," *Relations Internationales* 57:1 (1989), 103–12.

2. E. Grilli, *The European Community and the Developing Countries* (Cambridge: Cambridge University Press, 1993), 55; M. Lister, *The European Community and the Developing World* (Aldershot UK: Avebury, 1988); C. Twitchett, *Europe and Africa: From Association to Partnership* (Farnborough UK: Saxon House, 1978); C. Twitchett, *A Framework for Development: The EEC and ACP* (London: Allen and Unwin, 1981); J. Ravenshill, *Collective Clientelism: The Lomé Conventions and North-South Relations* (New York: Columbia University Press, 1985).

3. Véronique Dimier, "For a New Start? Resettling Colonial Administrators in the French Prefectoral Corps (1960–1980s)," *Itinerario, The European Journal of Overseas History* 28:1 (2004), 49–66; Anthony Kirk-Greene, "Decolonization: The Ultimate Diaspora," *Journal of Contemporary History* 36:1 (2001), 133–51.

4. Dimier, "For a New Start?" 49–66.

5. Ministère des Affaires Étrangères (hereafter MAE) Archives, Paris, série Affaires économiques et financières, sous-série Service de la coopération économique, box 719, letter from the French Minister of Overseas Territories to the French Minister of Foreign Affairs, 17 May 1956 (written during French preparations for the Venice Conference). All translations are by the author unless otherwise noted.

6. MAE, French Minister of Overseas Territories to the French Minister of Foreign Affairs.

7. The word "special" is used in the Treaty of Rome. The treaty also included the Trust Territory of Somaliland under Italian Administration and Netherland New Guinea.

8. On this evolution see Tony Chafer, *The End of Empire in French West Africa: France's Successful Decolonization?* (Oxford: Berg, 2002).

9. Réné Moreux, "La République française doit entrer avec ses TOM dans une Europe instituée, mais la France seule pourra négocier et décider dans nos pays d'outre-mer," *Marchés Coloniaux du Monde*, 24 October 1953, p. 2882.

10. Véronique Dimier, "The Invention of the DG VIII," in *Politics and the European Commission: Actors, Interdependence, Legitimacy*, ed. A. Smith (London: Routledge, ECPR series, 2004), 83–95.

11. Léopold Senghor, "Nous sommes pour la Communauté Européenne, et par delà elle, pour la Communauté Eurafricaine," *Marchés Coloniaux du Monde*, 17 January 1953, p. 124. See also Léopold Senghor speech, *Journal Officiel*, Assemblée Nationale, Débats, 18 January 1957, pp. 166–67, and 4 July 1957, pp. 3262–64.

12. The commercial side remained essentially in the hands of the member states during that period.

13. Indirect rule connotes the practice of governing through chiefly elites, ideally by persuading them to apply policies determined by the colonial state.

14. Archives of the European Commission (hereafter AEC), Bac 25/1980/1894, speech by Commissioner for Development J. F. Deniau, no date, 1972.

15. The first fund totaled 581 million European Currency Units (ECUs, to which France and Germany each contributed 200 million.

16. Lemaignen was formerly president of the Société commerciale des

ports africains (1941–1958). He had also been a member of the governing board of the Compagnie de l'Afrique Orientale as well as the Banque d'Afrique Occidentale. From 1942 to 1958 he served as vice president of the Chambre de Commerce Internationale. After 1945 he also emerged as a leading figure within the French employers' organization, the Conseil National du Patronat Français; see Catherine Hodeir, *Stratégies d'Empire: Le grand patronat colonial face à la decolonisation* (Paris: Belin, 2003), 72–73, 270.

17. A former École Coloniale student (entry 1935), Ferrandi served as assistant to the district officer in Casamance, Senegal, from 1941 to 1943. In 1945 he moved to the Ministry for Overseas Territories in Paris working in the division responsible for disbursing FIDES development funding (the Direction Générale des Services Économiques et du Plan). In 1947 he became head of the ministry's International Affairs Division and in 1949 was appointed as French delegate to the Overseas Territories Committee at the OECD. In 1951 he became technical adviser to the minister for overseas territories. Two years later, in 1953, he was assigned to the federal government in Dakar and was promoted to head to division responsible for implementing the FIDES in French West Africa (Directeur général des services économiques de l'Afrique Occidentale Française), where he remained until 1958.

18. Article published in *Marchés Tropicaux du Monde* when J. Ferrandi was promoted to Directeur du Fonds Européen de Développement, 25 May 1963, no signature.

19. MAE, série Affaires économiques et financières, sous-série Service de la coopération économique, box 722, letter from Secretary-General Foyer (in charge of relations with French African Community States) to the Service des relations avec la Communauté Française, 21 March 1960.

20. J. Chapperon, interview with author, 23 June 2000; see his biography in note 36. MAE, série Affaires économiques et financières, sous-série Service de la coopération économique, box 722, letter from the French Ambassador (Bonn) to the Minister of Foreign Affairs, 15 June 1960.

21. J. Ferrandi, interview with author, 26 August 1999.

22. Archives of the EDF Committee, Minutes for 1971 (Council, 74880–1).

23. D. Jones, *Les élus d'Europe* (London: ODI, 1974), 52.

24. On this aspect see also Grilli, *European Community and the Developing Countries*, 124; Lister, *European Community and the Developing World*, 49.

25. Jones, *Les élus d'Europe*, 66.

26. Foreign and Commonwealth Office Archives, London, box 30/653, 1970 DAC Aid Review of EEC report, comments by Ferrandi.

27. AEC, 25/1980, box 1035, criteria for appraisal of projects submitted to the EDF, study collection, Overseas Development Series, no. 3, Brussels, 1965:

introduction by J. Ferrandi. Some of these criteria were copied from those of FIDES: see the annex to this report.

28. J. Ferrandi, interview with author, 26 August 1999.

29. A. Auclert, interview with author, 16 May 1999.

30. Pierre Émile Fay, former École Coloniale student (1935), worked alongside Ferrandi in the Ministry for Overseas Territories' Direction Générale des services Économiques et du Plan from 1946 to 1948. He headed the "imports" service in that division beginning in 1953, after which he followed Ferrandi to Dakar, where he served in the "Plan équipement" division, becoming assistant director of economic services from 1954 to 1957. Between 1957 and 1958 he worked in the World Bank.

31. Michel Cellerier, another graduate of the École Coloniale (1943), served from 1956 to 1958 in the Ministry for Overseas Territories' Direction Générale des Services Économiques et du Plan au Ministère de la France d'Outre-Mer.

32. P. Cros, another École Coloniale graduate (1949), worked first as an assistant district officer before returning in 1956 to the Ministry for Overseas Territories, from which he was seconded to the French National Assembly.

33. Jean Petit Laurent arrived in 1967, and Guy Salmon in 1970. Petit Laurent graduated from the École Coloniale in 1939. He headed a section of the Ministry for Overseas Territories' Direction des Affaires Économiques et du Plan from 1953 to 1958. Salmon, another École Coloniale graduate (1946) served as assistant district officer in Cameroon from 1948 to 1962.

34. A. Auclert, interview with author, 16 May 1999. André Auclert, yet another former student at the École Coloniale (1945), worked alongside Ferrandi in the Dakar Direction Générale des Affaires Économiques et du Plan from 1953 to 1957.

35. A. Auclert, interview with author, 16 May 1999.

36. Jean Chapperon, École Coloniale graduate (1940), worked in the Ministry for Overseas Territories in 1945–46 and 1950–53 and then as *chef de cabinet* to the secretary-general of the Afrique Occidentale Française federal government between 1953 and 1958.

37. P. Cros, interview with author, 2 March 2002; Auclert, interview with author, 16 May 1999; Chapperon, interview with author, 23 June 2000.

38. J. Chapperon, interview with author, 23 June 2000.

39. J. Chapperon, interview with author, 23 June 2000.

40. R. Lemaignen, *L'Europe au berceau: Souvenirs d'un technocrate* (Paris: Plon, 1964), 117.

41. U. Stefani, interview with author, 22 February 2001. (Stefani was an Italian official at DG VIII from 1958 to 1961.)

42. Véronique Dimier, *Le Gouvernement des colonies: Regards croisés*

franco-britanniques (Brussels: Editions de l'Université de Bruxelles: 2004); Frederick Cooper, *Decolonization and African Society: The Labour Question in French and British Africa* (Cambridge: Cambridge University Press, 1996).

43. Robert Delavignette, *Service Africain* (Paris: Gallimard, 1946), 231.

44. Dimier, "For a New Start."

45. Speech by Hendus to the meeting of ambassadors of the Congo Republic at Leopoldville, 25 January 1963: Archives of the EC delegation in the USA, 448/3.

46. Statement by J. Ferrandi to le Comité européen d'ingénieurs-conseils (Brussels), reproduced in *Marchés Tropicaux* (1974), 1055–56.

47. J. Ferrandi, "La communauté Européenne et l'assistance technique," *International Development Review* 8 (September 1964), 9.

48. J. Ferrandi, article in *La Revue Nouvelle*, 7–8 (July–August 1967), 29.

49. See, for instance, Hendus's speech cited in note 45: Archives of the EC delegation in the USA, 448/3; see also the commission's annual reports to the council.

50. Statement by Rocherau, conférence parlementaire de l'Association, 8–11 December 1964, Dakar: Archives of the EC delegation in the USA, 448/3.

51. Dimier, *Le Gouvernement des colonies*.

52. D. Frisch, interview with author, 21 February 2001. A trained economist, Frisch was a German official who served as assistant to Director-General Hendus from 1964 to 1970.

53. AEC, Bac 25/1980, box 1503: includes the program of those visits.

54. Ferrandi, interview with author, 26 August 1999; AEC, Bac 25/1980, box 1076, Note from the Ivory Coast Permanent Representative to the EEC to Director-General Hendus, 21 December 1962. The note asked Hendus to assist at the ceremony.

55. This awarding of money to countries with less need is confirmed by the EC figures, which indicate that richer states like Gabon, whose wealth was measured in terms of per capita GNP, received more than poorer states such as Burundi; see Lister, *European Community and the Developing World*, 50. The first EDF percentage disbursement of the "marché des travaux" (in monetary terms): France (46.35%); Italy (13.88%); Germany (3.28%); Belgium (2.37%); Netherlands (4.48%); Luxembourg (0.25%); AAMS (29.39%). The second EDF round (31 December 1967): France (58.11%); Germany (18.28%); Italy (4.87%); Belgium (2.72%), AAMS (16.02%). These figures are available in "Answer from the Commission to the written question no. 308, by M. Pedini (Italy), European Assembly, concerning the distribution of EDF funds by nationality of the firms concerned," 26 January 1968: Archives of the EC delegation in the USA, 448/3. Regarding British criticisms see Jones,

Les élus d'Europe; Véronique Dimier, "Constructing Conditionality: The Bureaucratization of EC Development Aid," *Journal of European Foreign Affairs* 11:2 (2006), 263–80.

56. Lister, *European Community and the Developing World*, 135.
57. On this interdependence see Chafer, *End of Empire*.
58. Jones, *Les élus d'Europe*, 53.
59. Stefani, interview with author, 22 February 2001.
60. J. Durieux, interview with author, 21 February 2001. Another trained economist, Durieux was a Belgian official who headed the Direction B, Études de Développement from 1964 to 1977. A supporter of greater rationalization, he became one of the sharpest critics of Ferrandi's more pragmatic methods.
61. Dimier, "Invention of the DG VIII."
62. See Anne Raffin's contribution to this volume.
63. AEC, Bac 25/1980, box 1035, record of speech by H. Rochereau, Commissionner for Development, 8 February 1968.
64. MAE, série Affaires économiques et financières, sous-série Service de la coopération économique, box 723, Report from Gorse, French Permanent Representative to the EC, to Minister for Foreign Affairs, 22 September 1960. The report details his trip to Africa between 18 August and 3 September 1960. See also Véronique Dimier, "Construire l'Association: Regards croisés euro-africains," *Matériaux pour l'histoire de notre temps présent* 77 (January–March 2005), 32–38.
65. MAE, série Affaires économiques et financières, sous-série Service de la coopération économique, box 721, letter from Carbonnel, French Permanent Representative to the EC to Minister for Foreign Affairs, 16 March 1959.
66. MAE, série Affaires économiques et financières, sous-série Service de la coopération économique, Carton 723, Compte rendu de la réunion euro-africaine, Paris, conférence du 8 novembre 1960.
67. Véronique Dimier, "L'institutionnalisation de la Commission Européenne (DG Développement): Du rôle des leaders dans la construction d'une administration multinationale, 1958–1975," *Etudes Internationales* (Canada) 34:3 (September 2003), 401–28.
68. AEC, bac 26/1969, box 665, report: "Réforme du contrôle technique," no date, probably 1964.
69. AEC, box 26/1969, box 665, Chapperon comments in minutes of a meeting of heads of cabinet chaired by Hendus, director-general of DG VIII, 5 March 1964.
70. See Véronique Dimier and M. McGeever, "Diplomats without a Flag: The Institutionalization of the Delegations of the European Commission in ACP Countries," *Journal of Common Market Studies* 44:3 (2006), 483–505.

Interviews were conducted with the following delegates, all of whom were ex-colonial officers: R. Teissonnière, (26 June 2000); R. Calais (answer to questionnaire, 27 November 1999); P. Hugot (26 September 2002); C. Blanchard (22 January 2000); former colonial magistrate Aubenas (18 December 2003); ex-Belgian colonial administrator, A. Van Haeverbeke (4 May 2002).

71. Van Haeverbeke, interview with author, 4 May 2002.
72. Teissonière, interview with author, 26 June 2000.
73. Ravenshill, *Collective clientelism*.
74. Dimier, "Constructing Conditionality"; and Véronique Dimier, *Recycling Empire: The Invention of a European Aid Bureaucracy, 1998–2008*, forthcoming.
75. D. Bocquet and S. Viallon, *La budgétisation du* FED, *une étape dans la modernisation de l'aide*, Ministère de l'Economie, des Finances et de l'Industrie, 2003, quoted by J. J. Gabas, *L'aide publique française au développement* (Paris: La documentation Française, 2005), 69.

12

Friend or Foe?

Competing Visions of Empire in French West Africa in the Run-up to Independence

TONY CHAFER

It is generally accepted that French decolonization in Africa south of the Sahara was, from the French point of view at least, largely successful. Unlike in Madagascar, Indochina, and Algeria, there was no war of decolonization or widespread loss of life. The transition to independence was relatively smooth and peaceful. I have argued elsewhere that this "successful decolonization" was not the product of any grand plan and that the narrative of France's "successful decolonization" in French West Africa is essentially a post hoc construction, promoted among others by those French and African political leaders involved in the process.[1] In 1994, for example, at his last Franco-African summit in Biarritz, François Mitterrand claimed that "France and its African partners succeeded in organizing a peaceful decolonisation," and he then went on to explain: "if we have been able to overcome the obstacles, it is because we have never lacked the will."[2] It is a view that has also, implicitly if not explicitly, underpinned the approach of many analysts of French decolonization.[3]

In recent years a number of historians have challenged this orthodoxy. For example, Martin Thomas has usefully reminded us that "the French colonial system was broken apart by external pressure, by internal dissent among rulers and ruled, and uniquely in the French case, *by the rivalries of competing colonial elites.*"[4] Thus, if we accept that the process of decolonization was indeed largely "successful" from the French point of view, in the sense that the transition was for the most part relatively smooth and peaceful, and if we also accept that it was not the product of some "grand plan," this then begs the question: how did the successful transition come about? If we are not to dismiss it as simply a "happy accident," how are we to explain it? Who were the political actors and what was the specific set of historical conditions that brought about this outcome?

It is not possible to offer a comprehensive explanation of this "success" in a short chapter such as this. I therefore focus on one specific factor which, I would like to suggest, can add an extra dimension to our understanding of the specificity of the decolonization process in French West Africa. Essentially, I argue here that the competing visions and policy agendas of different colonial elites played a significant role in both shaping the pattern of decolonization in French West Africa and laying the foundation for France's continuing "special relationship" with Africa after independence.[5] I also argue that the French Communist Party (PCF) played a significant role in strengthening the ties between France and French-educated African elites during the politically important period 1944–47. This diversity of visions and policy agendas among France's governing elites inevitably led to a degree of policy confusion, yet I think it can be argued that this very confusion in some sense actually served French interests in the run-up to independence and may provide part of the explanation for France's "successful decolonization" in French West Africa. However in arguing this it is important to understand that this diversity was underpinned after the Second World War by shared assumptions about the importance of retaining empire as a means of restoring French global power status after the debacle of 1940.[6] Thus, even as we study the different imperial visions of competing colonial elites, we need to bear in mind that the visions—or mental maps—of those responsible for colonial policymaking were built on, and rooted in, an imperial mind-set that traversed the political spectrum from left to right and that, at least until the late 1950s, attached overriding importance to the maintenance of empire.

New Policymaking Context at the End of the War

The transformation of the colonial political landscape resulting from the experience of war hardly needs underlining. The French imperial position had been dramatically weakened by defeat and occupation. The African empire was for part of the war divided against itself, with French Equatorial Africa declaring for De Gaulle in 1940, while French West Africa and North Africa declared for Vichy. Following the Allied landings in North Africa in late 1942, all of the African empire swung behind the Gaullist cause and was immediately called upon to make a major contribution to the French war effort.[7] At the 1944 Brazzaville Conference Africans were promised colonial reform after the war in return for their sacrifices and loyalty.[8] At the same time, the government feared no longer being master in its own house: there was an urgent need to restore French authority in the colonial empire after the destabilization and divisions provoked by the war. Yet this could not be achieved simply by a return to the colonial authoritarianism of the prewar Third Republic or the Vichy empire.[9] The colonial government needed to establish a firm distinction between the racist thinking and stark racial discrimination that characterized Vichy colonial policy (and indeed, apart from during the brief interlude of the Popular Front, the colonial policy of the Third Republic) and restore the credentials of republican colonial policy as modernizing and progressive. For this to happen, fine words were no longer sufficient, as African politicians made clear in speeches to the Constituent Assembly in March 1946.[10] They now expected positive action by the government to deliver on the promises of economic, social, and political reform made at Brazzaville, and they used the political platform offered to them by their presence in the Constituent, and subsequently National, Assembly to bring their demands to the attention of policymakers and the wider public.

The consequence of these developments was to provoke an interest in colonial policy across government and among a far wider range of groups in French society than had previously been the case. Under the Third Republic oversight of colonial affairs was weak, as they were rarely discussed by Parliament, and the Colonial Ministry was traditionally the Cinderella ministry, the least prestigious of the offices of state and thus the preserve for much of the period of colonial enthusiasts who were often the only ones prepared to accept the post.[11] After the war this situation changed. No longer would colonial policy be the preserve of an activist minority. The increased political prominence of colonial issues meant that new political actors were drawn into the policymaking process. As a result the Ministry for Overseas France (as the Colonial Ministry was renamed in 1946) and the Government-General in Dakar no longer enjoyed more or less exclusive authority over the development and implementation of colonial policy. As Governor-General Delavignette put it: "France's overseas mission will no longer reside in the hands of an activist minority isolated from the mass of French people."[12] I examine who these new metropolitan actors were and their impact on policymaking below. First however, in order to understand the "mind maps" of these various political actors, I need briefly to sketch the intellectual underpinning for the different visions of empire that emerged after the war.

Two competing notions underlie French colonial policy: assimilation and association. Applied fully, they imply two quite distinct approaches to ruling over colonial populations. The concept of assimilation is rooted in cultural universalism. Its origins lie in the Enlightenment view of man's perfectibility and of human progress coming about through the adoption of universal reason. It entails the acculturation, through education and contact with the culture of the colonizer, of colonial populations so that they leave behind their own, inferior culture and espouse the superior culture of the colonizer. In policy terms it means giving priority to promoting and collaborating with the French-educated African elite of so-called *assimilés* and *évolués*, and it holds out the promise of full citizenship rights and an end to discrimination based on race for those who achieve full acculturation. Association, on the other hand, emphasizes the value of "tradition" and implies respect for indigenous hierarchies as a stabilizing force in colonial society. Rather than cultural universalism, it emphasizes and seeks to retain the cultural particularism and distinctiveness, indeed separateness, of different peoples. In policy terms it implies promoting and collaborating with indigenous authorities, such as traditional chiefs and religious leaders, in order to preserve "traditional" society and ethnographic differences as far as possible. These differences also provide the justification for not extending universal political and civil rights to Africans, other than the small minority who have assimilated to French culture.

Of course, the situation in practice was not so clear-cut. Assimilation and association were not mutually exclusive. Neither was applied integrally, and both continued to underpin aspects of policymaking during the colonial period. Moreover some policies, as Alice Conklin has pointed out, cannot easily be labeled either assimilationist or associationist. For example, *mise en valeur*—the rational development of the colonies' natural and human resources—was developed as a policy response to the economic poverty of colonial populations, as it was deemed impossible to civilize them without improving their standard of living.[13] As a policy it can be justified in terms of either assimilation or association.

This intellectual landscape became more complex with the emergence in the 1930s of the notion of "colonial humanism" (*colonisation altruiste*) as the ideological underpinning of the colonial policy of the Popular Front.[14] While much of the Left remained instinctively committed to assimilation because of its implicit universalism and its roots in the revolutionary ideals of 1789, the Left's political leaders were only too aware of the impracticality, if only in terms of the cost involved and the political consequences that would ensue, of implementing a policy of assimilation throughout such a vast and diverse empire. "Colonial humanism" thus emerged as the ideological underpinning for the Popular Front's colonial policy, partly in order to distinguish it from that of previous right-wing governments and partly to provide an alternative, middle way between the cultural universalism of assimilation, that was seen as destabilizing of colonial societies, and the cultural particularism of a policy of "pure" association, that was seen as insufficiently progressive and republican. Carefully targeted economic and social development—the aforementioned *mise en valeur*—was integral to colonial humanism.

These were the key notions that framed the debates about the aims and nature of French colonial rule in the interwar period. The disputes within France's colonial elites revolved around the importance that should be attached to assimilation versus association, universalism versus particularism, and of a rational, scientific approach versus an ethnographic approach to empire. Those politicians and officials who were charged with responsibility for making and implementing colonial policy after the war would have been influenced by—and many actually participated in—these debates, which continued to influence the mental maps of policymakers after the war. Indeed, many of those who were centrally involved in the renewal of colonial policy after the war, such as Marius Moutet, who was colonial minister under the Popular Front, and Robert Delavignette, had been major participants in these debates and played a key role in the development of the Popular Front's colonial policy.[15] These debates had more than purely intellectual significance insofar as one's stance on these issues inevitably shaped one's views on the nature of the alliances that should be concluded with African society. For example, were French interests advanced more effectively by promoting and supporting a "modern" French-educated elite of *assimilés* and *évolués*, or by bolstering "traditional" elites such as village chiefs and religious leaders? And were French influence and control threatened more by the increasingly pressing demands of the former, particularly in the main colonial towns, for equality and an end to discrimination, or by the more diffuse threat of "traditional" authorities, particularly in the rural areas, who were seen as resistant to French projects of modernization and progress? Such questions took on increased urgency in the context of the postwar commitment to colonial renewal and development. Indeed, beyond the shared assumptions of the imperial mind-set to which I refer above, these debates became increasingly ideologically charged and politically divisive as an array of new political actors emerged to stake their claim to play a role in colonial policymaking. However, it is important to emphasize that the political tensions to which they gave rise cut across traditional party lines as often as they followed such lines.

New Political Actors

The Brazzaville African Conference marked a turning point in the history of France's African empire. The latter was central to General de Gaulle's claim to be the leader of "free" France, since metropolitan France was at the time still under German occupation. It was also only thanks to the African empire that France was able to contribute to the Allied war effort, thereby providing some justification for de Gaulle's claim to be an equal partner with the Allies. In recognition of this importance, de Gaulle, who was shortly to become the head of the provisional government, became the first leader of the incipient new French regime to its African empire. He flew to Brazzaville to open the conference and in so doing marked the emergence of France's African empire from the periphery to the center of government policymaking. Never again would African policy be the quasi-monopoly of the Colonial Ministry and the Governments-General in Dakar and Brazzaville.

After the war the constitutional commitment to a "one and indivisible" French Union, comprising metropolitan France and its overseas territories, established the framework for the introduction of new metropolitan actors into the colonial policymaking process by potentially extending the area of competence of each government ministry and its agencies to the overseas territories. Once this framework was in place the new political actors were keen to establish their "sphere of influence" over colonial policy, with the result that the Ministry for Overseas France now had to share responsibility for policymaking in the colonies. Specialist technical ministries henceforth expected to be consulted about decisions relating to their policy area. Moreover the Ministry for Overseas France increasingly needed their expertise as the areas of government intervention into the economic and social life of the colony expanded and colonial administration became more complex. Thus, the Finance Ministry expected to be involved in decisions about economic development projects; the Ministry of Agriculture expected to be consulted on matters pertaining to agricultural development, the Education Ministry on education matters, and so on. Sometimes consultation was formalized through the establishment of joint committees, such as the Comité Supérieur Consultatif de l'Instruction Publique in the education field. The result was that the "colonial state" became a far more complex entity after the war.

This sharing of responsibility would not necessarily have been problematic but for the fact that relations between the Ministry for Overseas France and the different specialist ministries were sometimes tense, even conflictual. The experience of Jean Capelle is illustrative in this respect. René Barthes, who had been a member of Marius Moutet's cabinet during the Popular Front and had a reputation as a colonial reformer, appointed Capelle as head of the education service in Dakar shortly after his arrival in French West Africa in April 1946.[16] Capelle was a career educationist with no experience of the colonial service. Seconded from the Education Ministry, his brief was to initiate a root and branch reform of the education system in the colony and bring the quality of education up to metropolitan standards. However his appointment was seen by some in Paris and Dakar as a threat to their position, and his term of office, from January 1947 to September 1949, was marked by a running battle with officials from the Ministry for Overseas France.

The primary function of the education system in French West Africa until 1946 had been to train Africans to be loyal and efficient auxiliaries of the colonial power. In practice this meant providing the majority of Africans with an essentially utilitarian education in so-called rural schools.[17] Here they received training in basic skills, including hygiene, numeracy, and a rudimentary knowledge of French, together with some basic vocational training, usually in agricultural techniques, as the assumption was that most of them would remain on the land as farmers. From this group, a carefully selected minority would be chosen to attend the École William Ponty or one of the other two federal schools in Senegal to train as colonial auxiliaries such as clerks, interpreters, primary school teachers, medical assistants (*médecins africains*) or technicians.[18] When the empire was renamed the French Union, the colonized ceased to be "subjects" and became citizens of the Union. For Capelle this meant transforming the education system. Its primary aim could no longer be simply to train loyal colonial auxiliaries; instead, it now needed to produce an indigenous elite "and involve it in our efforts to make all the sons of these territories into fellow citizens within the greater fatherland that is the French Union."[19] This aim, to train Africans to be "fellow citizens"—and thus equal partners—within the French Union, meant introducing curricula and examinations in Africa that were equivalent in prestige and status to those in the metropole and that opened up the same employment opportunities: "the most important, if not the most immediate, effect of the [new education] law would be the assimilation—not necessarily in the sense of making them identical—of school curricula [and also] of the structure of education overseas. This reform is consistent with the very spirit of the Constitution, which makes the autochthonous residents of overseas territories citizens of the French Republic."[20] This also meant allowing Africans to compete on an equal footing with Europeans for posts in the colonial service.

Capelle's reform plan, which was supported by the Education Ministry, also had the support of African *députés* in the National Assembly, who rightly perceived the Ministry for Overseas France as the main bastion of resistance to colonial reform. The maintenance and promotion of cultural difference between Europeans and Africans, in keeping with the policy of association, had been a central tenet of Colonial Ministry policy before the war. Such views continued to inform how senior officials in the Ministry for Overseas France conceived of the colonial partnership between France and Africa after the war. As a result they were highly ambivalent about allowing Africans equal access with Europeans not only to jobs but also to "universal" French culture and saw Capelle's plans as a threat to their own conservative reform agenda for Africa. Not surprisingly then, Senghor's introduction of a bill into Parliament in June 1947 to transfer responsibility for colonial education from the Ministry for Overseas France to the Education Ministry provoked a bitter battle between the two ministries over who should control education in Africa.[21] In presenting his bill Senghor attached central importance to the cultural issue: 'The problem is not precisely to remove political control of overseas education from the Ministry for Overseas France. It is to transfer cultural control. . . . In this way French education will not be turned against France. . . . On the contrary, it will have served as a stimulus for sleepy civilizations isolated from the march of time. . . . It is the University that will create the French Union."[22]

There was a concerted response from the Ministry for Overseas France. The inspector-general for education and youth overseas complained that the bill would put overseas education on a different footing from the ministry's other services; that it would reduce the powers of the overseas territories; that it implied assimilation and would remove from the Ministry for Overseas France the possibility of undertaking initiatives independently; and that it went against the spirit of the French Union, which was to give greater autonomy to the territories. Moreover, he complained, the Education Ministry had no experience in overseas education, and the bill would not increase the money available for education overseas, which in his view was the root of the problem facing colonial education.[23] The director of political affairs in Dakar weighed in with an equally strongly worded memo to his minister in Paris. He pointed out that the reform would be too expensive to implement, as it would lead to demands from the overseas territories for colonial education to be funded at the same level as in the metropole; that it did not address the (real) problem facing education in Africa, which was lack of money; and—most importantly—that it threatened the very existence of the Ministry for Overseas France, which would in effect be reduced to an advisory function: "The issue is nothing less than the continued existence of the Ministry for Overseas France or its disappearance."[24] Political turmoil in Paris and the resignation of the Ramadier government in November led to the abandonment of Senghor's bill. The wider issues it had thrown up would not, however, go away so easily. The bill raised key questions about the ultimate aims of colonial policy and about who should be responsible for policymaking after the war that revealed tensions and divisions at the very heart of the postwar "colonial state."

Following the change of government Moutet was replaced by the more conservative Coste-Floret, and Barthes was recalled to Paris in January 1948, to be replaced by the right-wing Socialist Paul Béchard. The latter's brief was to slow the pace of reform and "restore stability" in the colony in the face of intensifying campaigns by political parties and trade unions for reform. As a result Capelle no longer enjoyed the political cover of his superiors, and the Ministry for Overseas France effectively forced him out in September 1949. However in 1954, after five years as rector of the Académie (local education authority) of Nancy in eastern France, he was called back to Dakar by the newly appointed governor-general, Cornut-Gentile, to take up the post of rector of the new Académie of Dakar and head of the education service in French West Africa. His specific brief on this occasion was to bring to fruition the plan to create a full French university in Dakar. Although he had the support of the governor-general and the minister of education, his three-year term of office was again marked by a series of running battles with officials in the Ministry for Overseas France, notably over his plan to place the new university under the responsibility of the Education Ministry so as to guarantee it the same status and prestige as universities in France.[25]

At the center of these conflicts were Capelle's efforts to introduce metropolitan-style education into Africa, including diplomas recognized in the metropole, fully qualified staff recruited to the same standards as in France, and a metropolitan-style inspection system to guarantee comparable quality with the metropole. Responding to the demands of African *députés*, he also sought to introduce higher education into French West Africa. This plan fell into abeyance after his departure from Dakar in 1949 but was revived following his return in 1954, and the University of Dakar finally came into being in 1957. Capelle's essentially "assimilationist" vision of education was consistent with the ideals of the French Union, which was rooted in the notion of an indivisible union between France and its overseas territories. However, it ran counter to the far more "associationist" vision of the Ministry for Overseas France of a distinct education system, geared to what it perceived as the specific nature and needs of African society.

Capelle was well aware of the risks of his policy of training an elite group of Africans to be equal partners in, and citizens of, the French Union. However, he felt the alternative—denying Africans access to French education and culture—would inevitably exacerbate anticolonial sentiment and demands for secession from France. If the French Union was to become a genuine partnership between France and Africa, then Africans needed to be educated and trained to enable them to take over responsibility for their own affairs. Moreover, French civilization was the cement that would hold this Union together. Capelle was a great admirer of Houphouët-Boigny and Senghor and shared the latter's vision of a Francophone community bound together by French language and culture: "for us, Francophonie is our culture . . . it is a spiritual community. . . . In short, over and above the language, Francophonie is French civilization; or more precisely, the spirit of this civilization."[26]

The creation in 1946 of the Fonds d'Investissement pour le Développement Economique et Social (Economic and Social Development Fund: FIDES), which established the principle of metropolitan finance for colonial development, introduced yet another actor into the colonial decision-making process. The fund, which spent substantial sums in French West Africa up to independence, was administered by a special Commission de Modernisation et d'Équipement aux Territoires d'Outre-Mer. Its decision-making structures were entirely separate from the Government-General in Dakar and outside the control of the Ministry for Overseas France, since it was based in the Commissariat Général du Plan.

Representatives from the Ministry for Overseas France, the Ministry of Finance, the Commissariat du Plan, the National Assembly, and the Assemblée de l'Union Française sat on the commission, together with a number of other interested parties, such as a delegate from France's main trade union confederation, the Confédération Générale du Travail (CGT). The commission thus comprised politicians and officials with knowledge and experience of the colonies, together with technical specialists—economists, planners, and so forth—with no specific expertise in or knowledge of the colonial empire. One indication of its policy significance is the size of its budget, which in the local currency rose from 200 million CFA francs in 1947 to 9,300 million CFA francs in 1950. Most of this was spent on capital investment in infrastructure projects, but there was also major investment in health and education.[27] Alongside the FIDES there was also the less well-known Fonds d'Equipement Rural pour le Développement Économique et Social (Rural Economic and Social Development Fund: FERDES), which was created in 1949 and invested 2500m CFA in mainly rural development projects in French West Africa between 1949 and 1954. Taken together, they were the central planks of the government's plan for the development—*mise en valeur*—of Africa. From a policymaking perspective the existence of these bodies further complicated the process of policy coordination and implementation in French West Africa.[28]

Finally, specialist government agencies such as the Inspection du travail (Work Inspectorate) also became significant players in the implementation of colonial policy. In his excellent study of the labor question in French and British Africa, Fred Cooper has shown how the Work Inspectorate played a major role in defining the terms within which the labor question was addressed in French West Africa after the war, which in turn had a profound impact on labor politics in the period leading up to independence. Official colonial discourse up to the end of the Second World War had traditionally conceived of African societies as divided, essentially, into two broad categories: the "traditional" rural population of *paysans* (peasant farmers) and the French-educated elite of *évolués* and *assimilés*. The "labor question" did not therefore arise in Africa. Of course, the existence of a working class could not entirely be denied, but the African worker was regarded as an essentially transient phenomenon, a peasant farmer or villager only temporarily in an industrial situation. This conceptualization of the African worker came under partial challenge during the Popular Front when "officials briefly contemplated using European social legislation to mould an urban working population whose numbers they insisted must be kept to a minimum."[29] The fall of the Popular Front put a temporary end to such debates. But they surfaced again with renewed urgency at the end of the war, following the legalization of trade unions and the resumption of strike activity in French West Africa. The general strike of January 1946, which saw French-educated Africans ally with manual workers in a number of different sectors to press their demands for wage increases, was a turning point. As Cooper has observed: "The strikes put a very rapid end to the fantasy of reconstructing French Africa through a *politique du paysannat* (policy to promote peasant farming), and French officials—in the course of the first major challenge of this sort—embraced modernizing solutions, based on the French industrial relations model, with startling rapidity."[30] The main reason for this abrupt change of heart was that official conceptualizations of African society that had hitherto dominated colonial thinking had no place for the labor question and therefore could not provide a basis for understanding, let alone dealing with, labor unrest. It fell to the Work Inspectorate to propose such a strategy.

Essentially, the Work Inspectorate's view was that if such strike movements were to be managed in the future, African workers would have to be recognized as workers, and contracts based on the French collective bargaining model would have to be negotiated separately, sector by sector, with each group of workers. This represented a profound change of approach, because it effectively assimilated African workers into European workers and treated them in the same way as the latter. It meant acknowledging that African workers were "normal" workers with whom one negotiated over pay and conditions, and that when labor disputes arose, they could be dealt with via the normal machinery of labor negotiation. In this way they did not have to be dealt with as colonial opposition movements with a wider political significance but could be managed as "technical" issues, to be resolved through the normal processes of negotiation and collective bargaining. Following the 1946 general strike, the responsibilities and role of the Inspectorate expanded, its organizational capacity was strengthened, and an inspector-general was appointed with responsibility for the whole federation.[31]

These new metropolitan political actors often espoused an idealistic republicanism unsullied by the complex realities of the colonial situation. This orthodox republicanism laid stress on universalist and egalitarian assimilationism, with the result that those who held such views had, for the most part, a broadly "assimilationist" approach to African policy, insofar as they sought to transpose metropolitan structures and practices to Africa or, in the case of FIDES, to promote economic and social "modernization." They came into conflict with officials in the Ministry for Overseas France whose approach to colonial modernization continued to be informed, as it had been during the interwar period, by notions of cultural particularism and the preservation of ethnographic difference.[32] In this perspective development was to be promoted as far as possible within the context of "traditional" society by working with indigenous authorities, such as traditional chiefs and religious leaders. This approach did not appeal to the majority of African *assimilés* and *évolués*, who saw it as part of a strategy to "keep Africans in their place" by impeding the process of modernization. In short, most of the "modern" elite of French-educated Africans saw it as an attempt by colonial conservatives to perpetuate colonial structures of domination, albeit now justified on "cultural" rather than racial grounds, and prevent Africans from gaining equality with Europeans.

The Communist Party and the "Colonial Question" after the Second World War

Dating back to its creation in 1920, the French Communist Party had established itself as a strongly anti-imperialist party. It did not, however, support colonial nationalist movements, deeming the colonies not yet ready for self-government. Nor did it espouse a straightforward assimilationist position, believing that precisely because of the backwardness of African societies, they needed to evolve gradually so as to avoid being destabilized. In this respect its position was not dissimilar from that of the colonial humanists of the interwar period, who sought to promote the modernization of African societies while respecting and preserving their cultural difference, albeit with the important distinction that its critique of the colonial regime was integrated within a Marxist discourse of international revolution. Although the party attracted and gave political support to Africans in France between the wars, it was not until after the war that the party became active in sub-Saharan Africa.[33] From 1943 it encouraged its members in Africa to set up associations, such as France combattante and the Groupes d'actions républicaines, in the major urban centers to work for the restoration of the republic.[34] These groups drew in Europeans and French-educated Africans, as did the Groupes d'études communistes, that the party began establishing from 1946. The party also actively supported the creation of the first interterritorial political party, the Rassemblement Démocratique Africain (RDA), which held its inaugural congress in Bamako in 1946, and supported Africans to organize strikes, such as the Dakar general strike of 1946, and create local branches of the CGT to press their demands for better pay and working conditions. At the same time, the party's stance on the colonial question remained somewhat ambivalent. On the one hand it was part of the government that established the French Union, believing that if French imperialism was in many respects reprehensible, it was nonetheless ultimately more progressive, less flawed, and less dangerous than British and U.S. imperialism. On the other hand, but also as a logical consequence of this since the colonies were part of the French Union and thus an integral part of the republic, the party allied itself with the "forces of progress" in Africa to campaign for the implementation of the social and economic reforms promised at Brazzaville. The PCF was not therefore anticolonial but was anti-imperialist, and it spoke the language of political revolution.

Following the victory over fascism, in which French African soldiers had played a key part, the PCF's stance chimed with that of many French-educated Africans.[35] The party's role in the Resistance and the prestige and political prominence it gained as a result, its electoral successes in 1945–46, its emergence as a party of government in Paris and its increased activity in Africa after the war led many Africans, including the deeply conservative Félix Houphouët-Boigny, to see the PCF as a natural ally in their campaign for new political freedoms and for colonial economic and social reform.[36] The role played by the party in supporting African political leaders to hold the inaugural conference of the RDA cemented these ties. Moreover, for a brief period at the end of the war Communists such as Christian Lambert, Governor Latrille's right-hand man in Côte d'Ivoire, and Marcel Faure, the acting secretary-general of Niger, occupied prominent positions in the colonial administration in French West Africa.

The increased prominence of the PCF in postwar French West African politics was significant for three reasons. First, the party's active support for RDA activists and African trade unionists in their campaigns for colonial reform was an important counterweight to the Ministry for Overseas France as it sought to pursue its agenda of conservative reform in Africa. Even if the party did not support assimilation, it effectively contributed to a process that led in that direction and that undermined the colonial regime by holding out the promise, sometime in the future, of equal rights for Africans.[37] Second, by increasing pressure on the colonial government to speed up the process of reform, it reinforced the view among many French-educated Africans that radical reform of the colonial regime within the context of the French Union was possible. Finally, among a radical minority of Africans, its language of international revolution and links with the Soviet bloc also encouraged the belief that by working with the PCF and its allies in the CGT, the colonial state could be overthrown.

Following the PCF's departure from government and the outbreak of the Cold War in 1947, a major concern of the colonial government was to counter Communist influence. Governor-General Béchard in Dakar and Governor Pechoux in Côte d'Ivoire were appointed in 1948 to "restore order," which meant repressing the RDA, defusing strike movements, and suppressing any other potential vectors of Communist influence in the colony. Since these vectors of influence were mostly to be found among the French-educated African elite, this was one of the factors that led to a renewed focus on "traditional," rural Africa and the promotion of rural elites, in an effort to counter the growing political importance of the French-educated elites. This was accompanied by vigorous repression of the RDA, notably in Côte d'Ivoire in 1949–50, and coordinated efforts on the part of the colonial administration to prevent RDA candidates from getting elected.[38] Even after the party leadership decided to disaffiliate from the PCF in 1950, many colonial officials refused to believe this represented a genuine change of strategy on the part of the RDA. As a result anticolonial movements continued to be interpreted through a Cold War prism, as being inspired by the forces of international Communism.[39] These efforts to reduce the RDA's support base and marginalize it politically were accompanied by a policy of accelerated Africanization of the civil service in an attempt to provide more French-educated Africans with jobs and thereby discourage them from becoming politically disaffected and thus more susceptible to Communist influence.[40]

The increased prominence of Communists in French West Africa after the Second World War and the outbreak of the Cold War impacted on colonial policy in two ways. At one level, as the struggle against international Communism now extended to the colonies, it justified a policy of increased repression against all those, including notably RDA and CGT activists, who were perceived as sympathetic to the forces of international Communism. In this respect it played into the hands of colonial conservatives whose approach to colonial government continued to be informed by notions of ethnographic difference and the gradual evolution of African societies within their own, distinct cultural frameworks. In political terms this translated into a policy of cementing alliances between the colonial government and rural elites that were seen as largely impervious to the clarion calls of international Communism. At another level the increased prominence of Communists in French West Africa provided grist to the mill of those in government, on both the right and non-Communist left, whose political priority was to cement alliances with the French-educated African elite. In this view the best way of consolidating the links between France and Africa was to accelerate the process of colonial economic and social modernization, for example, through the expansion of education and training and the investment of funds from the FIDES, in an effort to deter French-educated Africans from becoming involved in radical anticolonial politics.

Conclusion

Behind the imperial mind-set of shared assumptions about the vital importance of retaining the empire, to which I referred at the beginning of this chapter, the "mental maps" of republican colonialists were exceptionally diverse, often ideologically charged, and also politically divisive (although their differences as often cut across party lines as they followed them: Barthes and Capelle, for example, were Gaullists and colonial liberals, while Béchard was a Socialist but an authoritarian). Against this background, the emergence of new political actors with their own colonial policy agendas and their divergent views about the alliances that should be concluded with African society so as to maintain French influence and control inevitably meant that policymaking became less coherent. This lack of coherence was exacerbated by the absence of a strong political lead from politicians that was a product of the frequent changes of government under the Fourth Republic.[41] The emergence of these new actors also drew attention once again to the deep ambivalence underlying French African policy. At one level top officials in the Ministry for Overseas France and the Government-General sought to pursue their agenda of conservative reform by reasserting French authority and containing colonial opposition movements, while creating the conditions that would allow Africans to continue to evolve gradually within their own societies. The discourse this produced, and the policy that emerged from it, were essentially an updated version of the policy of association. It was an approach that, between the wars, aimed at producing a new Africanized elite that would serve as an antidote to the French-educated elite that embodied both the threat of Communist revolution and the racial Other that too closely resembled the metropolitan Self. However, in other government departments, such as the Education Ministry and the Work Inspectorate, the discourse was "universalist" and the colonial policy that emerged from it "assimilationist," in the sense that officials in the Education Ministry advocated the extension of metropolitan-style French education to Africa, and the Work Inspectorate favored treating African workers like European workers, which entailed establishing labor relations machinery on the metropolitan model in Africa.

The differences between these actors and their respective policy agendas were not necessarily so stark when it came to policy implementation. Top officials in the Education Ministry and the Work Inspectorate did not believe that all Africans could be assimilated into French metropolitan social structures and institutions, any more than did officials in the Ministry for Overseas France. Assimilationist ideas had in any case traditionally coexisted with associationist ideas in French colonial doctrine. Moreover, many of these officials, from whatever ministry, would have been influenced by the "colonial humanist" ideas that had been circulating in the interwar period. In this sense "colonial humanism" can be seen as representing an ideological point of convergence between assimilation and association, insofar as its very ambiguity meant that it could underpin and justify policies of "modernization" that could be presented as either assimilationist or associationist, depending on who was promoting them and the context in which they were being presented.

A significant change had taken place nonetheless. Official French discourse in Paris and in French West Africa had accorded pride of place to association over assimilation in the interwar period.[42] After the war the renewed prominence of a discourse of assimilation among parts of France's governing elites was therefore a significant change. While these competing visions and policy agendas suggest at one level a degree of confusion at the centre of government over colonial policy, their crucial importance lies elsewhere. On the one hand "assimilationist" discourses and practices supported the notion that there were French people of goodwill at the center of policymaking who were committed to the idea of a "one and indivisible" French Union. In doing this they helped sustain the notion among French-educated Africans of a Franco-African relationship rooted in the ideal of equality. Even if this was far from being realized in practice, the promise of future benefits did provide some Africans, especially among the French-educated elite, with a stake in the maintenance of the Franco-African link. At the same time, the rearguard action of the Ministry for Overseas France to promote strategies to bolster "traditional" African society found new allies in those African political leaders, such as Senghor and Houphouët-Boigny, who depended politically on a strong rural support base following the expansion of the suffrage.[43] Senghorian *négritude* and Houphouët-Boigny's defense of *la personnalité africaine* provided a vision of African society continuing to evolve, but on its own terms and without Africans assimilating to French culture.[44] This was not dissimilar from the colonial humanist vision of the gradual modernization of African society while preserving its ethnographic and cultural distinctiveness. The key difference was that it was no longer the colonial government that claimed to speak for this "traditional" rural society but African political leaders supported by the French government. The result was a de facto political arrangement from which both parties gained. For the colonial government and Africa's political leaders this support provided a counterweight to the increasingly radical anticolonialism of largely urban, French-educated African elites. For the French government it also meant that there were sufficient rural Africans with a stake in the Franco-African link to support its continuance up to and beyond independence.

In this respect the multiplicity of actors in colonial policymaking after the war, with their different visions of African society and its future evolution, may actually have served French interests in the run-up to independence. While their immediate obvious consequence was divergent policy priorities resulting in an apparent confusion at the heart of policymaking, the effect of this diversity was to offer, if not "something for everyone," then at least some stake in the maintenance of close links with France to a large number of different sectors of African society. In short, this diversity of policy agendas and actors made France plenty of "friends" and isolated its "foes." This was especially important as it provided the foundation for French success in maintaining a dense network of links that were the basis for its special relationship with Africa after independence.

Notes

1. Tony Chafer, *The End of Empire in French West Africa: France's Successful Decolonization?* (Oxford: Berg, 2002), 223–24.

2. François Mitterrand, quoted in *Jeune Afrique Economie*, December 1994, 29. All translations are by the author unless otherwise noted.

3. See, for example, Henri Grimal, *La Décolonisation de 1919 à nos jours* (Brussels: Editions Complexe), 282; Raymond F. Betts, *France and Decolonisation, 1900–1960* (Basingstoke UK: Macmillan, 1991), 115–16.

4. Martin Thomas, *The French Empire between the Wars: Imperialism, Politics and Society* (Manchester: Manchester University Press, 2005), 355 (emphasis mine). Of course, "colonial elites" refers here to *French*, not African, colonial elites.

5. Tony Chafer, "Franco-African Relations: No Longer So Exceptional?" *African Affairs* 101 (2002), 343–63.

6. Andrew Shennan, *Rethinking France: Plans for Renewal* (Oxford: Clarendon Press, 1989), 141–68.

7. Afrique Occidentale Française (hereafter AOF), *Conseil de Gouvernement*, procès-verbal de la session de décembre 1943 (Rufisque: Imprimerie du Gouvernement-Général, 1943), 3–15; Martin Thomas, *The French Empire at War, 1940–45* (Manchester: Manchester University Press, 1998), 225–32.

8. Chafer, *End of Empire*, 50.

9. Ruth Ginio, *French Colonialism Unmasked: The Vichy Years in French West Africa* (Lincoln: University of Nebraska Press, 2006), 183–84.

10. Yves Benot, *Les Députés africains au Palais Bourbon de 1914 à 1958* (Paris: Chaka, 1989), 47–49.

11. Robert Aldrich, *Greater France: A History of French Overseas Expansion* (Basingstoke UK: Macmillan, 1996), 100, 109.

12. Jean Capelle, *L'Education en Afrique noire à la veille des indépendances* (Paris: Kathala/ACCT, 1990), 32.

13. Alice C. Conklin, *A Mission to Civilize: The Republican Idea of Empire in France and West Africa, 1895–1930* (Stanford CA: Stanford University Press, 1997), 6.

14. Tony Chafer and Amanda Sackur, eds., *French Colonial Empire and the Popular Front* (Basingstoke UK: Macmillan, 1999).

15. Marius Moutet, who was the Popular Front's colonial minister in 1936–37, returned as minister for overseas France in 1946, and Robert Delavignette, who was a member of his cabinet in 1936–37, returned as director of political affairs at the Ministry for Overseas France after the war.

16. Barthes belonged to the colonial humanist *mouvance* and was Marius Moutet's *directeur du cabinet* in the Popular Front government. He was seen as a "Communist" by French settlers in Dakar, according to Jean Suret-Canale, personal communication, 9 July 1983.

17. Denise Bouche, "L'école rurale en Afrique Occidentale Française," in *Etudes africaines offertes à Henri Brunschwig*, by Jan Vansina et al. (Paris: Publications de l'Ecole des Hautes Etudes en Sciences Sociales, 1982), 271–96.

18. I should note here that by the Second World War those who had been to a French school of some sort represented no more than 5 percent of the total population. And of these many would have spent no more than one or two years in a French school, receiving a rudimentary skills-based education: Tony Chafer, "Decolonisation and the Politics of Education in French West Africa, 1944–58," PhD thesis, University of London, 1993, 375. See also AOF, *Conseil de Gouvernement*, session de décembre 1943, 237.

19. Capelle, *L'Education en Afrique*, 35.

20. Capelle, *L'Education en Afrique*, 44.

21. Proposition de loi Senghor, dated 26 June 1947. The dispute over the

proposed transfer of responsibility for education from the Ministry for Overseas France to the Education Ministry is documented in the Education Ministry Education archives, MinEd F17bis 3298. See also Capelle, *L'Education en Afrique*, 42–43.

22. Quoted in Capelle, *L'Education en Afrique*, 44–45.

23. Inspecteur Général de l'Enseignement et de la Jeunesse, Ministère de la France d'Outre-mer, note dated 11 August 1947, in MinEd F17bis 3298.

24. Note de la Direction des Affaires Politiques, Dakar, to the Minister for Overseas France, dated 19 September 1947, in MinEd F17bis 3298.

25. Capelle, *L'Education en Afrique*, 161–70.

26. Quotation from a speech made by Senghor in Quebec in 1966, cited in Capelle, *L'Education en Afrique*, 312. "La civilisation française, ciment d'union" (French civilization, cement of the union) is the title of the chapter in which this quotation appears.

27. By 1954 the FIDES had spent 1400m CFA on capital investment in education, 31 percent of this on primary, 38 percent on secondary, 23 percent on technical, and 7 percent on higher education, according to the Rapport Général de la Commission d'Etude et de Coordination des Plans de Modernisation et d'Equipement des Territoires d'Outre-Mer, April 1954, p. 126.

28. See, for example, the report by a 1952 government-appointed mission to French West Africa in Archives Nationales Section Outre-Mer, Aff. Pol. 2111/1.

29. Frederick Cooper, *Decolonization and African Society* (Cambridge: Cambridge University Press, 1996), 17.

30. Cooper, *Decolonization and African Society*, 226.

31. For an analysis of the central importance attached by the Inspectorate to organizing work on a rational basis and to job classification and differentiation, see Cooper, *Decolonization and African Society*, 232–33.

32. See James Genova, *Colonial Ambivalence, Cultural Authenticity, and the Limitations of Mimicry in French-Ruled West Africa, 1914–1956* (New York: Peter Lang, 2004); Gary Wilder, *The French Imperial Nation-State: Negritude and Colonial Humanism between the Two World Wars* (Chicago: University of Chicago Press, 2005).

33. J.-P. Dozon, *Frères et sujets: La France et l'Afrique en perspective* (Paris: Flammarion, 2003), 322–31.

34. Dozon, *Frères et sujets*, 329.

35. See Gregory Mann, *Native Sons: West African Veterans and France in the Twentieth Century* (Durham NC: Duke University Press, 2006); Tony Chafer and Martin Evans, "The Second World War and the Colonial imagination," in *The Lasting War: Society and Identity in Britain, France and*

Germany after 1945, ed. M. Riera and G. Schaffer (Basingstoke UK: Palgrave Macmillan, 2008).

36. Tony Chafer, "Education and Political Socialisation of a National-Colonial Political Elite in French West Africa, 1936–47," *Journal of Imperial and Commonwealth History* 35:3 (2007), 449–51.

37. Dozon, *Frères et sujets*, 333–34.

38. J.-R. de Benoist, *L'Afrique Occidentale Française de 1944 à 1960* (Dakar: Nouvelles Editions Africaines, 1982), 188–89.

39. Alexander Keese, *Living with Ambiguity: Integrating an African Elite in French and Portuguese Africa, 1930–61* (Stuttgart: Franz Steiner Verlag, 2007), 140–44.

40. In this respect Capelle's efforts to educate and train more Africans to a higher level was fully consistent with the policy of accelerated Africanization of the civil service.

41. This is not intended to suggest that I agree with the "Gaullist" explanation for the failings of the Fourth Republic in the field of colonial policy, which essentially attributed France's problems during this period to the instability of parties and parliamentary coalitions. On the contrary, I am inclined to agree with those historians, such as D. Bruce Marshall, who suggest that the problem lay with political and bureaucratic elites who were unable to accept and adapt to decolonization. See Marshall, *The French Colonial Myth and Constitution-Making in the Fourth Republic* (New Haven CT: Yale University Press, 1973).

42. Conklin, *Mission to Civilize*, 187–202.

43. The suffrage expanded with every election after the war, and universal suffrage was introduced in 1956.

44. Benoist, *L'Afrique Occidentale Française*, 69.

13

Thinking between Metropole and Colony

The French Republic, "Exceptional Promotion," and the "Integration" of Algerians, 1955–1962

TODD SHEPARD

The Algerian Revolution (1954–62) was one of the signal events of the modern history of Western imperialism, particularly its mid-twentieth-century crisis. From the first months of this fight for national independence, however, many French commentators who sought to avoid what they saw as Algeria's "secession" did so by arguing that what was at stake there was not the worldwide problem termed "colonialism," but a set of overlapping domestic problems. Algerians, they proposed, were not colonial subjects yearning for statehood, but French citizens whose exclusion from the nation resulted from racial, ethnic, and religious discrimination (with the latter notably less important). To give Algerians the types of economic and social possibilities available to other French citizens, these people argued—as well as make Algerians feel they were French—it was necessary to take into account what currently defined them as different. In early 1955 a number of key politicians and bureaucrats took up this understanding, using it to anchor a new policy approach to making Algeria French (which also was supposed to renovate the republic). This strategy developed under the name of "integration."[1]

From February 1955, when the "liberal Gaullist" politician Jacques Soustelle was named as the governor-general of Algeria, until February 1956, when he was replaced, his cabinet elaborated a series of "integrationist" policies. These aimed to identify the foundations and remedy the symptoms of the exclusion of "Muslim Algerians" from the nation. Their marginalization resulted not only from their unwillingness to abandon their "traditional" ways or their religious irrationality, as previous explanations had argued; moreover, French policies claiming universalist inspiration had pushed them away from France. After establishing a legal definition of "Muslim French citizens from Algeria" (FMAs), defined by shared "origins" (and explicitly not by religion), they put in place "exceptional promotion" policies meant to increase quickly the number of FMAs in government posts—a necessary precursor, they argued, for refounding a new "Franco-Muslim nation." In 1958 the "events of May" brought General Charles de Gaulle to power in France and announced the establishment of a new Fifth French Republic. Over the next several years, more sweeping and ambitious versions of the reforms developed in 1955 were implemented across all of France, the metropole, and Algeria. The most emblematic was the transformation of exceptional promotion from measures that encouraged the hiring of FMAs to a quota system, which reserved a fixed percentage of open posts for FMA candidates.

Scholars of post-independence Algeria have paid significant attention to the after-effects of integration, with many drawing inspiration from Pierre Bourdieu and Abdelmalek Sayad's *Le déracinement: La crise de l'agriculture traditionnelle en Algérie*. Historians of French imperialism, to the contrary, present integrationism as simply a new name for modern French colonial ideology, with the doyen of French historians of Algeria, Charles-Robert Ageron, tagging it as "assimilation, now renamed," and American historian James Le Sueur dismissing a "linguistic legerdemain." More interestingly, diplomatic historian Matthew Connelly describes French depictions of their policies to American and international audiences as an attempt to repackage the "mission to civilize" as a "mission to modernize."[2]

Beyond public relations propaganda, I argue, such representations were symptomatic of wide-ranging efforts among French politicians and bureaucrats to rethink and redefine French state institutions and the relations between those institutions and the people they governed. These changes were central to post-1945 French plans to be at the forefront of modernity, influencing government schemes to modernize (as

James Miller shows for the Moselle). Even in its final years, overseas colonialism continued to be crucial for the governance of France. While some recent work has begun to inform us about the shift of numerous functionnaires and policy approaches from imperial tasks to dealing with immigration or cooperation, and my previous work has focused on how decolonization reshaped French political institutions, there is also much to learn about how social policies aimed at "French people" emerged directly from efforts to keep Algeria French. Modern French thinking about empire, even as French rule in Algeria was collapsing, was always also part of a discussion about how to govern France and French people. Integrationism was formative for late-twentieth-century France, although its raison d'être was to keep Algeria French.[3]

One way of interpreting integrationist plans is to parallel them with what the new generation of historians of empire is trying to do: "treat metropole and colony in the same analytic field." Integrationists did so, however, by denying that "colonialism" was at stake and pretending that only discrimination, shaped by racism, needed to be addressed. As part of an effort to ignore Algerian nationalist arguments they tried to domesticate them: to reject the need for distinct political *institutions* by offering Algerians innovative and aggressive social and economic measures as well as newly meaningful political *participation* in the nation. During this moment scholars, bureaucrats, and politicians sought to think metropole and colony together, treating Algerian symptoms through holistic remedies for France. As they worked to erase certain internal boundaries, however, they recognized others. They created new categories meant to provide tools to overcome exclusion within the French Republic. Their definition relied on "origins." The workings of integrationism, that is, challenge current understandings of French history by revealing the existence of what sociologists term a "color-conscious" quota policy, which undoes the current consensus that such policies are "unimaginable" in republican France.

Assimilationism: French Universalism in the Colonies

The premises and methods of integrationism broke with the post-1789 beliefs of French politicians that laws, reforms, and institutions defined in "universal" terms would suffice to overcome inequalities. In Algeria, as elsewhere in the French empire (and France itself), the theory of assimilationism mediated between such thinking and actual practices. Republican assimilationism asserted that French control of overseas territories was designed to give the people of those territories, eventually, the same access to citizenship as other French people. In Algeria, for example, after first declaring the territory "French soil" in 1834, French authorities began to reduce the purview of the "local" legal systems (the laws, courts, and jurists that preexisted their 1830 conquest of Algiers, which the victors had agreed to leave in place). With each step, officials argued that greater contact with French laws and procedures would reveal to local people the attractiveness of French institutions, their superior logic, and their fairer outcomes. By 1865, when a law declared all Algerians French nationals, assimilationist measures had reduced the dominion of what were termed "local laws" to questions of civil status (rules of paternity, marriage, divorce, and inheritance).[4]

Local civil status served a key role in categorizing noncitizens. The vast majority of people in Algeria had what was named "Qur'anic Civil Status," while minorities had "Mosaic Civil Status" or "Berber Customary Civil Status." In 1870, with the return of republican rule, a final instance of proactive assimilationism forced Algerian Jews to abandon "Mosaic Civil Status," although they had overwhelmingly rejected the opportunity to do so voluntarily; in return, the state recognized them as French citizens. The Third Republic (1870s–1940), however, made only negligible efforts to draw Algerians with Qur'anic Civil Status into the nation. The continued existence of different statuses before the law became the most frequently cited excuse in official explanations—far more frequent than racial, ethnic, or even explicitly religious reasons—of why "Muslims," although possessing French nationality, had very few rights and burdensome obligations, similar to those of colonial subjects. From the assimilationist perspective, what prevented these French nationals living on French soil from becoming citizens was their attachment to what French theorists termed "particularisms," "communities," to their backward, feudal, or religious traditions. From the assimilationist viewpoint, attachment to group "difference," which backward social structures—like Qur'anic Law—encouraged, prevented Algerians from becoming individuals who could become citizens and abetted inequalities. Criticizing group differences, then, was the clearest sign that France wanted to free people born into under-"civilized" societies to be French.[5]

"Victims of the Most Basic and Odious Form of Racism"

Between the 1 November 1954 attacks and late February 1955 the ongoing influence of this understanding was manifest, as were some of its limits. When in December, Interior Minister François Mitterrand sketched out how France planned to respond to the challenges in Algeria, he announced that "the unity of the nation and the equality of all citizens is our motto." It is noteworthy that this affirmation anchored his rejection of "what some are calling for: first, establish order." Faced with calls from the Right and from representatives of Algeria's European elites to focus only on repression, he remarked: "What an odd idea! We should abandon our efforts to reform because a small minority of rebels attacks us?"[6] Officials continued to frame proposed reforms in general ("universalist") terms: what worked to make France a better place should be applied fully in Algeria. Typical was the 1 January 1955 exchange between a Parisian journalist and the highest-ranked French official in Algeria, Governor-General Roger Léonard, in which both agreed that the same type of economic growth that "last year, in 1954, had such positive effects in the metropole" would solve Algeria's problems. While Algeria had not yet felt the benefits of metropolitan growth, "the solidarity of the whole nation" would make sure that what had worked in the metropole would lift up Algerians.[7]

Another element of Mitterrand's mid-December 1954 statement, however, suggested that a new way of thinking about Algeria's problems might be at hand: "The seven million Algerian Muslims," he remarked, "make France the world's second biggest Muslim nation (after Pakistan) [sic]. We need to understand this."[8] Retrospectively, what needed to be understood was probably the international situation, in which Pakistan had obtained independence from the British Empire, with self-declaredly Arab and Muslim voices increasingly heard in the United Nations (in the first week of January, Saudi Arabia called on the UN General Assembly to debate the Algerian situation) and in the international public sphere (Nasserite Egypt's "Voice of the Arabs," for example). What, in fact, soon accompanied the idea of France as a "Muslim nation" was a shift in French policies, from fighting against "Muslim Algerian" difference and condemning "Muslim" reticence to abandon their "particularisms," to combating the discrimination suffered by Algerian "Muslims"—to identifying, in order to overcome, impediments to their participation in the nation.

From 1 November 1954 through February 1955 there were endless French public discussions about how to get Algerians to recognize that they wanted to remain part of the French Republic. In this debate, claims that the racist discrimination endured by "Muslims" had helped create, and continued to aggravate, their exclusion from the French nation gained new footing. Sparked by the Front de Libération National (FLN) call to arms, a debate raged in the French press about the situation of Algerian "Muslims." One position sought balance between reassuring the French that they had done well by Algerians and recognizing that certain problems existed, as in an editorial in the center-left newspaper *Combat*, which, while claiming that "the metropole, with a political will that only the Roman Empire has matched, actively erased [in Algeria] all legal forms of discrimination based on race or religion," still warned readers that the "exasperation" of many Algerians "is growing" due to their realization that "most of them are excluded from the advantages [of being French], whether economic or cultural." Mitterrand, speaking before the Assembly of the French Union in early December, similarly cautioned that the "temptation too many Algerians have felt, the temptation to separate and to fight" resulted, at least in part, from "not having the feeling that their hopes as citizens would coincide with the hopes France has for them."[9]

The language and arguments of writers and politicians who were wholly opposed to any policy of reforms, however, quickly overshadowed such poetic reminders that France had to do more. Speaking in the name of "European" Algerians, politicians and self-identified "ordinary" people, who wrote to metropolitan periodicals to share their local knowledge, rejected government proposals for political reform and insisted that immediate and harsh repression would end violence and upheaval in Algeria. They did so with explicit racism, leading a pro-government newspaper to qualify statements in the Algerian Assembly as "sickening." In the words of one late-December letter-writer to the left-wing weekly *France-Observateur*: "do you really think the Arabs have the intellectual level, the morality, and understanding of politics . . . that would allow them to manage Algeria by themselves?" Several weeks later, however, a "wave" of responses to the first letter attacked what the editors soft-peddled as "a certain racism" on M. Berthet's part. Most of the published letters described Algerian Muslims as, in the words of Mme. Duchet, a teacher in Algeria, the "victims of the most basic and odious form of racism." (Although the editors indicated they had received many missives from "Muslims," they printed none.) In a guest editorial that appeared in a Francophone-Swiss newspaper, the author argued that what had led to recent violence was "racial segregation," along with "miserable conditions" and "illiteracy." In this situation "eight million natives" had "no legal means to make themselves heard and are pushed to the limit by the feeling that their demands, which in any democracy would be judged legitimate" were silenced.[10]

The intensification of debates where questions of race and racism were at stake undercut more radical voices in the French debate. They rejected claims that "Algeria is France" and pointed to the need in Algeria — as across the world — to overcome colonialism. This was the message, most notably, of Messali Hadj, the self-educated militant who in 1926, along with other Algerians working in Paris-area factories, had founded the first Algerian nationalist group, the North African Star (many French politicians wrongly blamed him for the events of 1 November). In an article entitled "If Algeria Were France," published by *France-Observateur*, he laid out a critical history of French exploitation of Algeria and mocked French media coverage following 1 November, which revealed, he stated, "a press wholly devoted" to "colonialist interests." French Communist Party (PCF) proclamations, similarly, associated Algerian "misery" with one overriding political problem: "the denial of the national fact." During the first National Assembly debate after 1 November, one PCF deputy stated that Algerian violence "essentially resulted from the French government's out-of-hand rejection of nationalist demands." Robert Bellanger taunted: "if Algeria is a French province, why aren't unemployment insurance or family allowances (*la sécurité sociale ou l'allocation familiale*) the same as in France?" Another Communist speaker informed the chamber that "a few crumbs for economic and social concerns" would not suffice; only "meeting the desire for liberty shared by the vast majority" could stop the violence, and only ending "the colonial regime will bring prosperity."[11]

By changing the subject—away from colonialism and onto a discussion of racism—the early 1955 public debate about racism opened up arguments and elaborated terms on which French authorities would rely to take action to keep Algeria French, to define "integrationism." These voices were indicative of a novel effort among some in France to think more incisively about racism in the post-Holocaust era. As Gérard Noiriel has shown, the first use of the term "discrimination" in any official French document appeared in 1954, in a government-commissioned study concerning Algerian workers in the metropole. What is most noteworthy in this debut was that it marked a shift away from the left-wing French strategy of using the term "racism" exclusively to evoke situations such as fascism, Nazism, or, in the 1950s, American segregationism. The use of the term "discrimination" explicitly indicated the need to recognize that even policies that rejected biological or scientific understandings of "race"—as French (republican) policies did—could still have racist effects.[12]

Admitting that racism was a serious issue both undercut radical arguments that the only solution was political and allowed a reconfiguration of the center-left certainty that "the Algerian problem is, above all, a social problem," as the Socialist deputy Jean Capdeville was still arguing in December. From this new perspective Algeria's problems, while mainly economic, were directly tied to the real limits on most Algerians' formal citizenship. What marked these limits was the role that discrimination and racist exclusion played, historically and in the present, in producing dramatic inequalities.[13] For Algerians, policy responses that offered education and training to "Muslim" children and adults, massive investment and development schemes, and increased entry to government jobs and positions of political decision making would reveal that France recognized and sought to overcome the discrimination that had denied them opportunities. Rather than repeating that "Muslims" had "legal equality," integration began, as a 1959 report summarized, with the "recognition that equality of rights had had little effect in reality."[14]

Integration and Federation

In a cabinet meeting on 5 January 1955 Mitterrand announced that a new doctrine termed "integration" would guide efforts to refound French relations with "Muslims" from Algeria. The reforms Mitterrand sketched out were not particularly novel. In fact, most of the propositions in early 1955 could be summarized, as they were in a headline from the newspaper *Le Monde*, as seeking "A More Complete Application of the Statute of Algeria Law," which had been on the books since 1947. The first measure was a reorganization of the territorial government of Algeria in order to bring local administrations into greater contact with their constituents. Another proposed measure would liberalize "Muslim" access to the First College of Electors. In effect, since 1919 all eligible voters in Algeria voted in either the "First" or "Second" College. After various reforms in the 1944–47 period, the First College included all eligible French citizens with French civil status (in 1947 there were 464,000; this included all adult "Europeans" and the roughly 5,000 adult "assimilated" Algerians) and also included a small number of "distinguished" Algerians with Qurʾanic Civil Status (French officials identified 64,000 men as distinguished; over half rejected participation on nationalist grounds); the Second College was composed of some 1,300,000 "Muslims." In voting for the French Parliament and the Algerian Assembly, each college voted for half of those elected. Following the logic of the 1947 law, the Mitterrand reforms would increase "Muslim" political representation, yet still without approaching "one person, one vote." Mitterrand's third proposal brings the limitations on "Muslim" political representation into clearer perspective: it would extend the right to vote to adult "Muslim" women, who were excluded from the Second as well as the First College (women with French civil status in Algeria, as in the metropole, had won the right to vote in 1944).[15]

What was most novel in the 5 January 1955 announcement was the term "integration," introducing into the official lexicon a word that scholars and insiders already employed. References to integration had appeared in early twentieth-century analyses and proposals concerning other colonial empires; the term was used somewhat regularly, for example, in discussions of U.S. policy in the Philippines and Hawaii.[16]

It also was quite widely invoked in Latin America, from Brazil in the mid-nineteenth century to Mexico in the 1930s, where it was deployed in policies and debates about how governments should manage and pursue the relation between their "indigenous" populations and the nation-states they were building. (In these discussions proponents sometimes contrasted integration with "assimilation.") In 1946 an article by the jurist Clotaire Bée introduced the idea of a "doctrine of integration" into the French imperial(ist) discussion.[17]

Although Bée's call for integration appears to have played no role in French post-1945 plans, the fixation in his article on building a new supranational state structure, clearly distinct from a republic, was symptomatic of a congeries of official concerns and proposals that guided action within the colonial space until the Algerian War.[18] The French experience of World War II, Bée argued, "was a unique event in universal history, when a metropole was saved from servitude by its empire." In Bée's reading, this undeniable proof that France could flourish only within an empire—the recognition that France did not "have" but "was" an empire—should lead to "a new, and definitive, doctrine: integration," which would move beyond the limits of assimilationism and more recent theories like associationism (which, though based on fine sentiments, had failed to think the diverse peoples and territories together). His definition of integration resonated with the 1943 exhortation of the French poet, theorist of *negritude*, and Senegalese politician, Leopold Sédar Senghor, who had argued that France "need[ed] to transcend the false antinomy assimilation *or* association, and speak of assimilation *and* association." Both insisted that the division between "metropole" and "colonies" must be rethought in reference to a new whole, which Bée named *la France mondiale*, or "Global France." Within Global France, "European France" would be one unit "integrated, which is why we term our doctrine integration," alongside the units of "Overseas France" into a novel state form, a "French Union, which might be inspired by a federal formula . . . like the U.S.A. or the U.S.S.R.," although he also admired the "difference within unity" he saw in the British Commonwealth. The structure of the state, he argued, could be whatever "our statesmen decide."[19]

Post-1945 efforts to reform the French empire resulted, in part, from a serious crisis in the hegemony of the nation-state model. The Nazi and fascist embrace of highly centralized ultranationalism had sapped its legitimacy; the emergence of new international institutions—from the United Nations to the Bretton Woods economic structures—further undermined belief in the utility of nation-states. Many postwar French reformers thus claimed to recognize and sought to redefine the "expanded and disjointed political formation," which historian Gary Wilder describes as the "French imperial nation-state," by looking to political systems beyond the nation-state. Between 1944 and 1956, federalist solutions were particularly popular, in France as elsewhere. As the British political scientist Max Beloff proclaimed in 1953, "in the post-war years the federal idea itself enjoys a widespread popularity such as it had never known before." Federalism, proponents proclaimed, could respond to the newly obvious failures of centralized states and alone was capable of confronting the challenges of the postwar world. French federalists proposed that France and the territories and peoples that France had conquered should seek, together, to move beyond the nation-state.[20]

Beyond doubts about the nation-state, the embrace by the Nazis and their allies of racial categories and racist definitions had made rethinking empire imperative. The types of racially charged (or simply racist) explanations that all modern empires had relied on to explain their control of other peoples now seemed untenable, at least in public. W. E. B. Du Bois's claim, in the midst of World War II, that for Americans "this war in essence is a war for racial equality" took on a new reality when social movements, militants, and intellectuals across the world struggled to force the war's victors to recognize that government policies based on racist presumptions needed to be changed, and changed immediately. In his stirring yet incisive *Discourse on Colonialism*, the poet and politician Aimé Césaire gave voice to this global imperative, arguing that what troubled Europe's ruling classes about the rise of Nazism, what they "cannot forgive Hitler is not the crime in itself, it is not the humiliation of man as such . . . [but] the fact that he applied to Europe colonialist procedures which until then had been reserved exclusively for the Arabs of Algeria, the coolies of India, and the blacks of Africa." These demands for racial justice—expressed in terms, not of revenge for the uncountable crimes, but of equality, of a "new humanism," of "we shall overcome," or "freedom, now"—provoked activism around the world and, in Western capitals, compelled governments to respond, which they struggled to do on their own terms. Frederick Cooper identifies such efforts as post-Nazi "deracialized imperialism."[21]

Integrating the French Republic

Jacques Soustelle, whom the left-reformist prime minister Pierre Mendès-France asked to take over the position of governor-general of Algeria in January 1955, had been a visible supporter of federalism since his brief tenure as minister of the colonies in 1945. Right-wing critics of the government's response to the rebellion took what one European deputy from Algeria, François Quilici, termed Soustelle's "declarations of federalist faith" as another sign that "Arab terrorism" would be coddled, rather than crushed. Their suspicions played a key role in the 5 February 1955 no-confidence vote that turned the Mendès France government out of office. During the preceding debate the prime minister repeatedly took the podium (over twenty times) to insist that the only option in Algeria was either the reform program he and Mitterrand had entrusted to Soustelle or violent repression, which would fail. Yet during the same debate, and just after Quilici's complaint, a "Second College" deputy from Algeria, Abdelmajid Ourabah, referred to a different aspect of Soustelle's public reputation to call for further reforms. He quoted from one of Soustelle's first books, *Mexico, An Indian Land*: "'It's together, as the history of their peoples and their lands have shaped them . . . that those at the bottom will leave their humiliation behind and win their place in the sun,'" which he interpreted as "the role that Mr. Soustelle claimed for the Indian people in the Mexican nation. How, today," he asked, as Soustelle looked on, "could you refuse to admit the Algerian people to the same place in the French nation?"[22]

The criticisms from Quilici and Ourabah announced an important aspect of the approach that Soustelle, whose nomination was confirmed by the new prime minister, Edgar Faure, defined as "integrationism." They also reveal how different this definition of "integration" was than what Bée and others proposed. As soon as Soustelle took up his functions in Algeria, he publicly abandoned his previous support for moving toward a federation. He emphasized that what was at stake were exclusively the connections between France and Algeria, and more particularly between Algerians and the French nation. Integrationism would propose policies for Algeria not in terms of more general concerns about the French Union but in terms of the interest of France, which included Algeria. In his first public speech after he arrived in Algeria, Soustelle began by emphasizing that from now on all the French policy choices should be understood as "integrationist," for they would all have a "clearly identified goal: that every day Algeria will become more fully a province that, despite its uniqueness, is wholly French." Emphasizing the word "integration," he later stated, was meant to convey his conversion to a republican, rather than federalist, solution and to give it content. Soustelle presented integration as allowing the establishment of a renewed French nation-state—a revitalized republic that would, as one effect of this revitalization, be able to keep Algeria French. This rejection of federalism was explicitly circumstantial: as he explained one year later to *Le Monde*, there were "no guidelines for how to pursue federalism," whereas the Law of 1947 offered a "clear starting point" for integration. Indeed, Soustelle later claimed that he hoped that eventually a renewed French Republic, anchored in a jointly French and Algerian nation, would be able to establish the type of federation with other parts of the French Union that it had failed to build since 1945. To keep Algeria French, however, the focus now had to be on creating a republic in which Algerian "Muslims" felt included.[23]

To do this, and here Soustelle's initial public declaration was extremely clear, Algeria's differences needed to be taken into account: "it is no longer possible to simply apply to this African land that which was designed and tested elsewhere. Rather, it is necessary to fully take into account the geography, the history, and the ethnology of this region." With this statement, Soustelle announced the method he would always claim to rely on, the production of anthropological and sociological "scientific expertise" in order to devise remedies appropriate to the Algerian situation. Soustelle and the members of his cabinet (Germaine Tillion, Vincent-Mansûr Monteil, and Jean Servier) were all trained ethnologists, and their schemas relied on models and evidence drawn from anthropological fieldwork; they also came out of a French anthropological tradition that believed in possibilities for revolutionary change.[24] Speaking as an ethnologist, Soustelle argued strongly (using claims similar to those of other defenders of colonial rule, whether the French in Algeria or the British in India) that Algeria was not a nation, highlighting the many differences in language, custom, habits, as well as religious practice that divided the numerous groups that made up Algeria's "Muslim" population. The more intriguing aspect of his argument was that since other important distinctions fractured the "European" population of Algeria, French efforts could work to create unity among all Algerians and, in doing so, establish the conditions for all "Algerians" and French people to join together as a newly "Franco-Algerian" nation. It was necessary, as he stated, to "resolve *at the same time* the question of how Algeria connects with the metropole and how Europeans and Muslims can live together within Algeria."[25]

During the twelve months that he was governor-general, Soustelle oversaw the establishment of several integrationist programs, failed to implement others, and laid the foundations for the policy's keystone, exceptional promotion. New educational policies were quickly established. The ethnologist Germaine Tillion oversaw the extension of an adult educational and vocational program in Algeria's cities. Under the leadership of the young ethnologist and "Arabist," Vincent-Mansûr Monteil (who resigned in June 1955 to protest the French Army's widespread use of torture on interned Algerians), the most well-known program, the Specialized Administrative Services (SAS), oversaw, supplemented, or simply replaced local administrators in rural "Muslim" areas who were widely seen as either absent, corrupt, or incompetent. The SAS, which was composed of army officers, took its model for administrative responsibilities and military staffing from the *Bureaux arabes* that, after disappearing in Algeria under the Third Republic, had reappeared in the Moroccan protectorate in the early twentieth century.[26]

Soustelle's efforts as governor-general to apply the political reforms that Mitterrand had called for in early 1955 went nowhere. Whether in terms of the administrative reorganization of departmental and municipal government, or increasing the percentage of "Second College" officeholders in most municipal and departmental assemblies, opposition from "European" politicians blocked his attempts to apply the 1947 Statute of Algeria Law. The aspect of this law that Soustelle considered the most important because of the role it would play in creating a bilingual "Algerian people," namely, the establishment of Arabic as an official language of France in Algeria, also failed to overcome the opposition of local politicians. Soustelle made no attempt to impose the other element of the 1947 law that Mitterrand had emphasized, the extension of the vote to "Muslim" women. According to him "the urgency that Muslims expressed for this reform was so lukewarm, to say the least, that I decided that it would be inopportune to push too quickly beyond what was presumed normal." Soustelle did receive some support for a reform that went beyond the limits of the 1947 Mitterrand proposals: he proposed the abolition of the Second College and the extension of equal political rights to all French citizens with Qurʾanic Civil Status; the extension of political rights would be uncoupled from legal rights, with Qurʾanic civil law left in place. But nothing came of it in 1955.[27]

Alongside the failed political reforms, there were the failed economic and social reforms. Soustelle proposed that the foundational programs of the Fourth Republic's social welfare policies—the minimum wage (the SMIG, established in 1950; antecedent to the post-1970 SMIC), national unemployment insurance (known as social security, established in 1947), and stipends for large families ("*allocation familiale*," mandated in 1932)—be extended to Algeria at the same levels as in the metropole. (Albert Camus, writing in support of Soustelle's project, informed readers that "a father of three children receives 7,200 ff in Algeria versus 19,000 ff in France.") Soustelle further proposed reversing the 1947 statute, stipulating that all separate Algerian government functions be taken over by their metropolitan equivalents, from the post of governor-general and the Algerian Assembly to all state administrations and state-owned utilities. The political economist Ya'akov Firestone argues that, with these proposals, Soustelle directly attacked the interests of the small and powerful European economic elite who also controlled Algerian politics (and patronage), the so-called *gros colons*. The only one of these reforms that received local support from European politicians was a proposal to have the metropole assume full responsibility for the Algerian budget.[28]

Exceptional Promotion, 1955–1958

In 1958, with the establishment of the Fifth Republic, most of these political, economic, and social proposals became law. They appeared as subclauses of sweeping measures that claimed, on the one hand, to efface any legal, administrative, or political distinctions between the metropole and Algeria and, on the other hand, in all of France, the establishment of distinct social, religious, and cultural rights for "Muslim French citizens from Algeria" along with the same political rights as other citizens. The transformation of the most emblematic reform, exceptional promotion, reveals how the 1958 integrationist "revolution" emerged from the understanding of integrationism that Soustelle proposed in 1955. Exceptional promotion began, in 1956, as a targeted hiring program. In 1958 it became a binding quota (the term used was *"réserve"*) for any and every public sector job filled via exam, a quota that guaranteed a fixed percentage of openings exclusively for members of a new legal category: Muslim French citizens from Algeria (FMAs).

Soustelle and his associates did not give much explanation of how they developed the exceptional promotion approach, yet their idea of using ethnic-based hiring targets to fight discrimination and advance public policy clearly drew from multiple sources. One, although never cited in official discussion, was Algerian nationalists. The 1943 Manifesto of the Algerian People, perhaps the most well-known pre-revolutionary nationalist proclamation, demanded that 50 percent of all civil service posts in Algeria should be held by "Muslims." This was the exact goal that, according to Soustelle, his proposals were meant to achieve. What was necessary, he argued, were "exceptional measures that allow us quickly to bring the proportion of Muslims up to 50 percent in the public and semi-public services and administrations, nationalized industries, etc."[29]

For Soustelle, exceptional promotion embodied the integrationist synthesis of social and economic concerns with the recognition of Algerian difference. As he argued:

> It is not enough to forbid all the forms of discrimination that they have had to confront; we must not hesitate, when necessary, to make use of such forms in their favor. True equity demands that

when one side of the scale is too light, we must add to it in order to create equilibrium.

Responding to unnamed critics, he affirmed that "French sovereignty will not be threatened, indeed the opposite is the case, if we make sure that the *fellah* [Algerian peasant] lives better and the prefect is named Belkacem." By "exceptional" he meant "the authority to hire on the basis of qualifications, putting aside the rules, whether or not statutory requirements were met or the required sheepskins were in hand." Exceptional promotion, that is, crystallized integrationist claims to recognize "Algerian Muslim" differences in order to remedy the discrimination that alone supposedly kept them from uniting with other French people.[30]

Applying proposals that the Soustelle cabinet left them, the government of Guy Mollet promulgated the first exceptional promotion measures in March 1956.[31] The beneficiaries were members of a newly recognized group, "Muslim French citizens from Algeria." As the original memorandum defining this category put it:

> the expression Muslim French citizens from Algeria (*citoyens français musulmans d'Algérie*) includes not only all citizens originally from Algeria who have conserved their local civil status, but also those citizens, and their descendants, who have renounced this status.[32]

"Having an ancestor who had Muslim status" in 1830 was the "foundation" underlying membership in the FMA category, as a Justice Ministry senior official later explained. He used the word *"originaires."*[33] The premises of the FMA status broke with the logic underpinning the other legal categories that, since the mid-nineteenth century, had been central to official justifications for claiming that all Algerians were French—while still denying the vast majority legal (as well as real) equality with other French nationals. In addition to the over eight million Algerians who, in 1956, still had Qur'anic Civil Status, the FMA category also included the fewer than ten thousand people of "Algerian" origin with full French citizenship who, whether by individual choice or that of an ancestor, were legally "assimilated" (who had "French Civil Status," not Qur'anic). This recognition of an ethnic-group identity authorized the state to fight against the racist discrimination that people in this group suffered. All "Muslim French citizens from Algeria," legally "assimilated" or not, were eligible to benefit from exceptional promotion measures.

The 1956 ordinances created optional exams reserved for FMAS in subjects such as Arabic, Berber Customary Law, or Economic Development in Algeria that could replace other subjects for the entrance examinations to public sector jobs.[34] A 17 March 1956 decree exempted FMA candidates for any civil service position from existing age requirements. Most importantly, it decreed that 50 percent of all openings in "public administrations, municipalities, and state-owned companies" *could* be filled by FMA applicants. If such applicants "met the general standards for physical and moral aptitude required of all candidates for a civil service position," a "committee made up of Muslims and non-Muslims" would assess their candidacy on the basis of "diplomas and qualifications," rather than through a competitive civil service test. These positions, however, would not be permanent civil service positions, but temporary "contracts." The plan was that applicants would receive training and instruction that would later allow them to take the regular civil service exam successfully.[35]

In 1958 exceptional promotion was transformed from a series of measures facilitating the recruitment of FMAS into French public service in Algeria into a quota policy that worked to bring "Muslim French citizens from Algeria" into the mainstream of French life. With the Ordinances of 28–29 October 1958, all public service positions filled by exam were required to reserve 10 percent (in the metropole) or between 10 and 70 percent (in Algeria, depending on the level) of available posts for FMAS.[36] The government named a special commission that could nominate qualified FMAS to the highest positions in the French public service (categories "A" and "B," so-called *hauts fonctionnaires*), to jobs such as prefect (fourteen prefects and twenty deputy prefects were named in the first six months), state counselor (two *conseillers d'état* were named within days of the ordinance), or counselor of the *cour des comptes* (two named in the first six months), bypassing exams or required credentials.

It also directed that the École normale d'administration (ENA) and the various Institut d'etudes politiques (Sciences Po Paris; Grenoble) recruit and train special cohorts of FMA students to meet future Category "A" quotas. In 1960 a ruling of the new Constitutional Council concerning the application of exceptional promotion to the training and naming of judges proclaimed that such measures did not violate the republican principle of equality.[37]

The Republican Quota Principle

Supporters of integration presented exceptional promotion and its attendant quotas as emblematic of how France now proposed to make Algerians a constitutive part of the nation. With the "Two Colleges" system abolished, a legally defined quota (each electoral list in Algerian districts included a fixed number of candidates of each "origin") guaranteed that the national elections of November 1958 produced forty-seven FMA seats and twenty-three seats for "Europeans" (in previous elections, each college had elected fifteen deputies).[38] On 8 December 1958 a gathering of all but three of Algeria's newly elected deputies endorsed a four-point plan "under the sign of a concerted drive for the speedy implementation of integration," in Firestone's terms. Point four called for the extension of "French promotion for Muslims" to facilitate "their natural evolution within the framework of full citizenship." Even many government officials who saw the embrace of integrationism by "European" leaders in Algeria as wholly hypocritical argued that it could be used to immediately "appoint several Muslim prefects," which "would have a significant impact on domestic and international opinion."[39]

Between 1958 and mid-1961 all agencies reported great difficulty in filling their quotas. Yet the French executive emphatically maintained the obligation (*impératif*) to retain them.[40] Instead of abandoning the policy due to difficulties, French officials in fact worked to extend application of the new republican principle of quotas. The government discussed how to secure private sector participation, although in the end such efforts were limited to active encouragement by government officials. In November 1959 Senator Abdallan Tebib opened parliamentary debate about extending exceptional promotion to the armed forces by narrating a history of Algerians' contribution to the defense of France. His speech ended with a reminder to his listeners that with such measures France was showing the world that it was "one of the great Muslim nations." In early 1961 the minister of culture submitted a series of plans that would have extended exceptional promotion to government artistic, intellectual, and cultural policies. In addition to hiring FMAs for jobs in the Ministry of Culture, the proposals sought both to encourage existing "Muslim" cultural activities and to support Algerian artists. The ministry proposed creating chairs at universities throughout France in order to promote appreciation of "specifically Algerian cultural forms (literature, music, singing, for example) whether of Arab, Berber, Jewish, French, or more generally Mediterranean inspiration." In its conclusion the report made clear that its most important goals were the following: "1. To give the existing Muslim elite in the specified areas the possibility to be noticed. 2. To allow the training of a new elite within a French cultural framework, but in complete respect of their uniquely Algerian inspirations." All French universities—indeed, all of France—would benefit.[41]

Conclusion: Affirmative Action Republics

All of this has been forgotten. Indeed, an increasing number of French, North American, and British scholars write on the history and practice of what they often call French "color-blind" policies, contrasting them with American or British "color-conscious" policies. All affirm that France has never had such policies in order to analyze why they are "unimaginable" in France. Most argue that current French reluctance to take questions of race or ethnicity into account to address the effects of discrimination at once reveals and results from the history of what a number of scholars have termed "republican racism." Recently, from a very different perspective, French public commentators, intellectuals, and politicians have taken up such contrasts in order to discredit a wide variety of efforts to redress the effects of historical and present-day discrimination based in ethnicity or race as well as in terms of gender and sexuality. They laud what they describe as a still-vigorous French history of universalism, which supposedly refuses to accept race-thinking whatever its form.[42]

The existence and workings of exceptional promotion unsettles this discussion. The archival record shows that the French Republic could imagine ethnic- and race-based policies aimed at redressing the effects of historical and actual discrimination. The Fifth Republic did so in terms very similar to (and before) American affirmative action. Indeed, French officials put into place the types of policies—in terms of strict quotas, scope, timetable, and support mechanisms for those involved—that, one decade later, as historian Nancy MacLean shows, American proponents of affirmative action sought but failed to achieve. Both countries took action in the name of recognizing that a history of state-authorized racism and discrimination had produced damaging effects on specified groups of people, which required state action to redress. It is telling that while trying to keep Algeria French, French officials would constantly point to exceptional promotion and other integrationist measures as proof that it was France, and not its hypocritical American and Soviet critics, that had the imagination and the will to actually address "domestic" racism. To maintain its empire in Algeria, that is, French officials proved willing to think about what needed to change in France—as well as celebrating what France had already proven: its capacity to achieve. Overseas empire was good to think with, to act on, and directly shaped the government of all French people.[43]

Notes

1. On the Algerian Revolution and decolonization, see Todd Shepard, *The Invention of Decolonization: The Algerian War and the Remaking of France*, 2nd. ed. (Ithaca NY: Cornell University Press, 2008); and Robert Malley, *The Call from Algeria: Third Worldism, Revolution, and the Turn to Islam* (Berkeley: University of California Press, 1996).

2. Pierre Bourdieu and Abdelmalek Sayad, *Le déracinement: La crise de l'agriculture traditionnelle en Algérie* (Paris: Editions de Minuit, 1964); Charles-Robert Ageron, *Modern Algeria: A History from 1830 to the Present* (London: C. Hurst, 1991), 111; James D. Le Sueur, *Uncivil War: Intellectuals and Identity Politics during the Decolonization of Algeria* (Lincoln: University of Nebraska Press, 2001), 25; Matthew Connelly, *A Diplomatic Revolution: Algeria's Fight for Independence and the Origins of the Cold War World* (New York: Oxford University Press, 2002), 216.

3. James I. Miller, "Reconstructing the Nation in the Regions: State Planners, Immigration and the Crucible of National Modernization in the Moselle, 1947–1962," PhD diss., University of Chicago, 2005. On

shifts of policies and personnel see, e.g., Alexis Spire, *Étrangers à la carte: L'administration de l'immigration en France, 1945–1975* (Paris: Grasset, 2005); Veronique Dimier, "For a New Start? Resettling Colonial Administrators in the French Prefectoral Corps (1960–1980s)," *Itinerario: The European Journal of Overseas History* 28:1 (2004), 49–66.

4. See Shepard, *Invention of Decolonization*, 19–31.

5. Shepard, *Invention of Decolonization*, 31–39.

6. François Mitterrand, "Une petite minorité revoltée ne nous fera pas renoncer aux reformes," *Paris-Presse*, 12 November 1954. All translations are by the author unless otherwise noted.

7. "Dans une interview exclusive, M. Roger Léonard, Gouverneur général de l'Algérie, nous déclare," *Information*, 1 January 1955, 1.

8. Mitterrand, "Une petite minorité revoltée."

9. Marc Benoit, "Tribune Libre: Nationalisme ou contre-colonisation," *Combat*, 16 November 1954; "Les algériens doivent pouvoir identifier leur espérance...,' *Le Monde*, 9 December 1954.

10. "L'Algérie c'est la France? Oui, mais avec tous les droits qui s'attachent à la démocratie," *Le Populaire*, 7 January 1955; M. Berthet, "Ce que veulent les Algériens non musulmans," *France-Observateur*, 30 December 1954); Mme. Duchet, "Ce que veulent les Algériens non musulmans (suite)," *France-Observateur*, 20 January 1955; Daniel V. Kaeser, "La lettre du jour: La responsabilité des Européens en Algérie," *La Gazette*, 11 November 1954.

11. Messali Hadj, "Si l'Algérie était la France," *France-Observateur*, 23 December 1954; Robert Bellanger, "Arrêter immédiatement les répressions...," *L'Humanité*, 15 November 1954; Alice Sportisee, "Tenir compte des aspirations à la liberté...," *L'Humanité*, 15 November 1954.

12. Gérard Noiriel, *Immigration, antisémitisme et racisme en France: Discours publics, humiliations privées* (Paris: Fayard, 2007), 468, 552–53; Léo Bogart, "Les Algériens en France: Adaptation réussie et non réussie," in *Français et immigrés*, ed. Alain Girard and Jean Stoetzel (Paris: PUF, 1954).

13. "Jean Capdeville: Le problème algérien est avant tout social," *Le Populaire*, 15 December 1954.

14. Centre des archives contemporaines des Archives nationales, Fontainebleau, France (hereafter CAC), 19770391/3, Mission d'etudes RE, "La Participation des Français Musulmans a la Fonction Publique," (6 July 1959), 1–16, and annex 4.

15. R. A. Martel, "Les réformes proposées par M. Mitterrand tendent d'abord a l'application plus complète du Statut de l'Algérie," *Le Monde*, 9 January 1955, 1 and 8; for number of electors see Benjamin Stora, *Histoire de l'Algérie Coloniale, 1830–1962* (Paris: La Découverte, 1991), 109.

16. See, for example, Frank W. Blackmar, "Spanish Colonial Policy," *Publications of the American Economic Association*, 3rd ser., 1:3 (August 1900), 112–43; Serafin Egmidio Macaraig and Luther B. Bewley, *The Social Integration of the Philippines* (Manila: Philippines Information Pamphlets, 1924).

17. Clotaire Bée, 'La doctrine d'intégration,' *Recueil Penant* 2 (1946), 27–48; on Mexican discussions contrasting integration with assimilation (and incorporation) see Guillermo Palacios, "Postrevolutionary Intellectuals, Rural Readings and the Shaping of the 'Peasant Problem' in Mexico: *El Maestro Rural*, 1932–34," *Journal of Latin American Studies* 30:2 (May 1998), 309–39; 318 n. 28.

18. This was the meaning the term "integration" had in late 1954 statements by the "European" deputy François Quilici, who referred to the "presence of overseas deputies in our assemblies" as "what I would term integration." See "Le terrorisme en Afrique du nord," *L'Information*, 3 November 1954, 10.

19. Bée, "La doctrine d'intégration," 33–34; Robert Lemaignen, Léopold Sédar Senghor, and Prince Sisowath Youtévong, *La communauté impériale française* (Paris: Editions Alsatia, 1945), 64.

20. For a more extensive discussion of these questions see Todd Shepard, "'History Is Past Politics'? Archives, 'Tainted Evidence,' and the Return of the State," *American Historical Review*, 115:2 (April 2010), 474–83; Gary Wilder, *The French Imperial Nation-State: Negritude and Colonial Humanism between the Two World Wars* (Chicago: University of Chicago Press, 2005), 3; Max Beloff, "The Federal Solution in Its Application to Europe, Asia, and Africa," *Political Studies* 1:2 (1953), 114–31.

21. W. E. B. Du Bois, "A Chronicle of Race Relations," *Phylon* 3:3 (1942), 320–34; Aimé Césaire, *Discours sur le colonialisme* (Paris: éd. Réclame, 1950); citation from *Discourse on Colonialism*, trans. Joan Pinkham (New York: Monthly Review Press, 1972), 14; Frederick Cooper, "A Parting of the Ways: Colonial Africa and South Africa, 1946–48," *African Studies* 65:1 (Summer 2006), 27–44; esp. 28–30.

22. On the Mexican inspiration for French integrationism, see Todd Shepard, "Algeria, France, Mexico UNESCO: A Transnational History of Anti-Racism and Empire, 1932–1962," *Journal of Global History* 6:2 (forthcoming Spring 2011). For quotes, see Bernard Ulmann, *Jacques Soustelle, le mal aimé* (Paris: Plon, 1995), 188; Jacques Soustelle, *Mexique, terre indienne*, preface by Paul Rivet (Paris: Bernard Grasset, 1936).

23. Jacques Soustelle, *L'Algérie, aimée et souffrante* (Paris: Plon, 1956), 36; "Entretien: Jacques Soustelle," *Le Monde*, 15 January 1956, 1; "L'Algérie c'est la France? Oui, mais avec tous les droits qui s'attachent a la démocra-

tie," *Le Populaire*, 7 January 1955). On territorialization see Frederick Cooper, *Africa since 1940: The Past of the Present* (Cambridge: Cambridge University Press, 2002), 78–80.

24. On the particular readiness of many French anthropologists to envision "revolution," see Susan Bayly, "French Anthropology and the Durkheimians in Colonial Indochina," *Modern Asian Studies* 34:3 (July 2000), 581–622; esp. 582 and 585. Soustelle and Tillion were protégés of Paul Rivet, students of Marcel Mauss, and trained at the Institut d'ethnologie and the Musée de l'homme; he did his fieldwork in Mexico, she among the Chaouia peoples of Algeria. Vincent-Mansûr Monteil, an Arabist and expert on Islam, was trained by Louis Massignon. Jean Servier received his doctorate in ethnology in 1955 for his work on Algerian Berbers, under the direction of the prominent Durkheimian ethnologist Marcel Griaule. Note that the distinctions between "anthropologists," "ethnographers," and "ethnologists" owe more to national traditions and often to how they distinguish between "physical" and "cultural" approaches. I employ the terms privileged by my French sources.

25. Soustelle, *L'Algérie, aimée et souffrante*, 92–94; italics added. For a more elaborate example of how Soustelle presented his arguments against a "nationalist" depiction of Algeria as based in "science," see Soustelle, "Lettre d'un intellectuel à quelques autres à propos de l'Algérie," *Combat*, 26 Novembre 26, 1955.

26. On Tillion, see Le Sueur, *Uncivil War*, 62–97.

27. Soustelle, *L'Algérie, aimée et souffrante*, 88.

28. Albert Camus, "Actuelles: La bonne conscience," *Express*, 21 October 1955, 1; Ya'akov Firestone, "The Doctrine of Integration with France among the Europeans of Algeria, 1955–1960," *Comparative Political Studies* 4:2 (July 1971), 177–203, 185.

29. "Manifeste du Peuple Algérien" (1943), as printed in Paul-Emile Sarrasin, *La crise algérienne* (Paris: Du Cerf, 1949), 174–92; Soustelle, *L'Algérie, aimée et souffrante*, 81–82; Benjamin Stora and Zakya Daoud, *Ferhat Abbas, une utopie algérienne* (Paris: Denoël, 1995). The term *"réserve,"* for example, was most probably directly drawn from the Reservations Policy that the 1950 Constitution of the Indian Republic established for so-called Scheduled Castes, but I have seen no reference to this.

30. Soustelle, *L'Algérie, aimée et souffrante*, 74, 81–82. In legal terms, "exceptional" meant for a defined length of time. The measures were to expire, variously, after five or ten years.

31. Law 56–258 of 16 March 1956; Decree n. 56–273 of 17 March 1956.

32. P. Metayer, Secrétaire d'Etat à la Présidence du Conseil chargé de la Fonction Publique, "Définition et justification de la qualité de citoyen français

musulman d'Algérie" (Paris, 27 November 1956), 1, in CAC 950236/7. The term "Français musulman d'Algérie," according to Guy Pervillé, began to be used as of 1945; see Pervillé, "Comment appeler les habitants de l'Algérie avant la définition légale d'une nationalité algérienne?" *Cahiers de la Méditerranée* 54 (June 1997), 55–60, esp. 59.

33. This use transformed the term "originaires," which was typically associated with inhabitants of the Four Communes of Senegal, who had citizenship rights, by adding history to the usually geographic signifier. See CAC/AN, 950236/7 [C/3612], Chef du contentieux de la nationalité, Ministère de la Justice, "Note pour M. le Directeur du Centre National d'Études Judiciaires," Paris, 28 April 1959, p. 2.

34. CAC, 19980514/1–2, HC/YR Sous-direction de la Fonction Publique, "n. 1147 DPAA/FP," Algiers, 18 July 1959.

35. See CAC, 19960393/1, Decree of 17 March 1956, and "Servez dans la fonction publique en Algérie," Algiers, June 1961; italics added.

36. For the metropole in 1958, see, in particular, CAC, 19980514/1, 1, Ordinance no. 58-1016 of 29 October 1958, and the Decree no. 58-1454 of 31 December 1958; for Algeria, see no. 58-1017 of 29 October 1958; "no. 1147 DPAA/FP," Algiers, 18 July 1959.

37. CAC, 19770346/7, Bureau du Corps prefectoral et des Tribunaux administratifs Ministère de l'Intérieur, "Effectif des fonctionnaires nommés en application des dipos de l'ord du 29 octobre 1958," 12 March 1961, 1; CAC, 19830739/3, "Métropole—Accès des Français musulmans d'Algérie a la fonction publique," 15 November 1960, 1; see Loi organique portant promotion exceptionnelle des Français musulmans dans la magistrature; for the decision see http://www.conseil-constitutionnel.fr/decision/1960/606dc.htm.

38. Ordinance no. 58-964 of 16 October 1958 prescribed a list system; on each list, "the number and place on the list of candidates of Common Civil Status and of Local Civil Status will be fixed for each district." Yet when the Constitutional Council validated the candidacies, it reaffirmed the FMA category, based on origin, rather than the distinction between "civil statuses." It did so by rereading the text's reference to "civil status" in reference to the ordinance's preamble, which called for "a fair representation of the diverse *communities*" and affirmed that "citizens who, *by origin*, would be under the governance of local law but have opted for common Civil Status, and their descendants, can choose to appear under either category." See Conseil Constitutionnel, "Décision no. 58-42/191 du 5 mai 1959," Paris, 5 May 1959; italics added; accessible via the search engine at http://www.conseil-constitu tionnel.fr/.

39. Firestone, "Doctrine of Integration," 190; see also Marc Lauriol and

Philippe Marçais, *Au service de l'Algérie française* (Algiers: Imprimerie Baconnier Frères, 1960); and CAC, 19770346/8, M. Jean Bozzi, Secretaire Général de la Préfecture d'Alger, "La situation locale peut être analysée," 18 octobre 1958, 3.

40. CAC, 19960393/1, Joseph Gand (signed), the Prime Minister, "FP/3 n. 2067," Paris, 9 June 1959.

41. Presentation and debate in Senate concerning "Loi n. 59-1480 du 28 décembre 1959 . . . assurant, par des mesures exceptionnelles, la promotion des Français musulmans, *Journal Officiel du Sénat*" (26 November 1959 session), 1205–20; CAC, 19830229/3, "Note au sujet de la Promotion exceptionnelle des Français musulmans d'Algérie," n.d. (early 1961), 1–2.

42. See, for example, Erik Bleich, *Race Politics in Britain and France: Ideas and Policymaking since the 1960s* (Cambridge: Cambridge University Press, 2003); Adrian Favell, *Philosophies of Integration: Immigration and the Idea of Citizenship in France and Britain* (Basingstoke UK: Palgrave, 2001); Peter Fysh and Jim Wolfreys, *The Politics of Racism in France* (London: Macmillan, 1998); Robert C. Lieberman, *Shaping Race Policy: The United States in Comparative Perspective* (Princeton NJ: Princeton University Press, 2005); see also Anne-Marie Le Pourhiet, "Pour une analyse critique de la discrimination positive," *Débat* 114 (March–April 2001); Julien Landfried, *Contre le Communautarisme* (Paris: Armand Colin, 2007).

43. See Nancy MacLean, *Freedom Is Not Enough: The Opening of the American Workplace* (Cambridge MA: Harvard University Press, 2006), 95–107.

14

Rigged Elections?

Democracy and Manipulation in the Late Colonial State in French West Africa and Togo, 1944–1958

ALEXANDER KEESE

The enactment of voting rights for African populations was a watershed in colonial rule throughout sub-Saharan Africa after the Second World War.[1] No one devised or enacted electoral reforms with quite the complexity or with such dogged persistence as the French. Nearly every year from the end of World War II in 1945 until the final, formal decolonization of Francophone black Africa in 1960, Africans under French rule were called upon to elect deputies. At the outset of this process voter numbers were severely restricted by criteria requiring evidence of literacy and individual service to the French state. But matters soon changed. For one thing, the second of these criteria applied, in particular, to colonial army war veterans, a vocal and increasingly influential constituency in numerous territories. Moreover, the group of persons enjoying the right to vote grew steadily until the territorial elections of 31 March 1957, the first that could be genuinely labeled "general" and "national."[2] The elections for the Territorial Assemblies in French West Africa and French Equatorial Africa held on 31 March 1957 were the first to elect representatives who would thereby wield genuine power of decision in some, though not all, areas of administration. These elections were also the first in which the electoral franchise was freed from any principles of exclusion such as literacy, fulfillment of military service, and so on, which had previously been the general rule. More important still, the former practice of organizing voters on the basis of two electoral colleges was abolished. The first electoral college was typically reserved for French citizens, mainly Europeans, while the huge majority of the inhabitants of the colonies were confined to voting for the second electoral college—a form of de facto racial segregation. While the institution of voting rights for nonwhite populations of the French colonial empire had antecedents dating back to the eighteenth century, in sub-Saharan Africa the practice was, for many decades, restricted to the inhabitants of Senegal's Four Communes.[3] Mass democracy in the bulk of France's West African territories remained unimaginable during the first fifty years after the establishment of the administrative "federation" of French West Africa in 1895.[4] The 1957 polls therefore marked a fundamental break with the past.

To be sure, some old habits died hard, even after World War II. It is not surprising that senior colonial officials faced with a loss of authoritarian prerogative as a result of new electoral rules were reluctant to endorse the full-blooded application of democratic principles. Furthermore, continued manipulation of local electoral processes at the lower levels of administration, in the *cercles* and *subdivisions*, often remained feasible. This being said, we should bear in mind that French administrators ran increasing risks—to political stability and to personal career—in persisting with such methods. The voting bureaus were controlled by representatives of those on participant lists, and while it was theoretically possible to inscribe adherents of a favored party twice or to destroy some of the ballot papers during their transportation from the voting bureau to the headquarters of the administration, this was nevertheless complicated, and officials ran a high risk of causing scandal by doing so. At the end of the period in question, in 1958, so well apprised of their voting rights were local electors that administrative manipulation of the ballot was effectively out of the question.[5] A final point to note here is that any presumption of continuing and widespread electoral manipulation in the final years of colonial rule in French West Africa necessarily implicates the emerging elites of African politicians. In fact, as is discussed below, in most cases it was neither practicable nor attractive for the French to intervene in the electoral processes newly instituted in their African territories.

The reform decrees announced by General de Gaulle's provisional government on 31 August 1945 dramatically altered one of the pillars of French rule in sub-Saharan Africa: differential voting rights for French citizens and colonial subjects. A major impetus for this reform was the fact that French politicians wanted to respond to the ideas and imaginings of liberation dominating French colonial minds following the end of Nazi occupation in France during 1944–45.[6] Numerous measures were discussed before and during the Brazzaville Conference in early 1944 and in the Monnerville Commission (named after its leading figure, the French Guyanese deputy Gaston Monnerville) the following year. Diverse proposals sought to give new form to the political and administrative structure of Overseas France after the end of the war. Yet most of these plans were little elaborated and reflected the newfound optimism of victory more than an unambiguous commitment to the improvement of African rights.[7] Nevertheless, democratic rights for the African inhabitants of French territories became an indispensable element of the civil status planned for "citizens of the French Union." Following the centralist logic of the French republics, African voters were to elect deputies to the National Assembly in Paris and councilors of the Territorial Assemblies, the latter being modeled on the *conseils généraux* of the *départements* of metropolitan France. The one crucial difference was that the territorial African assemblies had budgetary responsibilities.[8] In spite of the initial restrictions placed upon the number of Africans who obtained the right to vote, the reform nevertheless signified a revolutionary departure from the practice of the 1920s and 1930s. Interwar principles had posited that African institutions should conform to "autochthonous" ways of life. This, in turn, corresponded to the rather vague principle of *association* and meant that "traditional rulers," more or less under French administrative control, had dominated the rural politics of individual territories, to the detriment of wider participation by the local population.[9]

With the notable exception of Frederick Cooper's pioneering work, this postwar revolution in the electoral rights accorded to African populations has elicited little comment in the historiography of sub-Saharan Africa.[10] The huge extension of colonial franchises has not gone unnoticed, but few scholars, Wolfgang Reinhard excepted, acknowledge the major implications involved.[11] Many commentators have even misunderstood the nature of colonial elections as a phenomenon. It is, for instance, entirely wrong to claim that elections under French colonial rule were *local* events—quite the contrary: such elections had ramifications at both the territorial level and at the level of French metropolitan politics.[12] By contrast, democratically elected local institutions were only to be created from 1956, thus at the very end of colonial rule, and few had time to develop any life of their own. Yet, despite this, for an African politician, participation as an electoral candidate meant entering a politics, at once colonial and transnational, that concerned millions of local people.

As described below, the establishment of territorial electoral competition created serious difficulties for French colonial administrations and triggered considerable soul-searching among senior colonial officials. The institution of national elections was unproblematic so long as African elites behaved according to certain French criteria. As soon as "radical" leaders appeared who challenged the conceptions of paternalist colonial rule as exercised by the late colonial state, those leaders stood to profit from the elections both as a means to diffuse nationalist programs and, in the process, to mobilize mass support for their cause. The French administration soon found itself under pressure from the institutions it had created, and unsurprisingly French officials felt compelled to react to the challenge. How far, then, would colonial minds and "traditional" forms of administrative practice change?

Colonial Officials and Electoral Manipulation

While elections as a central phenomenon of the late colonial state are largely ignored, it is more or less taken for granted by commentators and historians alike that individual French administrators manipulated the results of many elections after 1944. This presumption applies to elections at all levels. Kenneth Robinson, an erstwhile British colonial official who spent time on exchange in French West Africa, exemplified this opinion in an article contrasting the differing practices of French and British colonial rule.[13] The assumption that elections were routinely and systematically rigged has been taken at face value and has even found its way into Francophone African literature. Archetypically, the Ivorian author Ahmadou Kourouma characterizes the electoral system in a fictive country modeled on Dahomey-Benin and Togo as being thoroughly manipulated by the French authorities. Commenting on Tima, one of the contenders for the presidency of the fictitious country that, in this account, was recently decolonized, Kourouma wrote the following:

> He jumped into politics, creating the Northern League. This party was defeated by the local authorities and by the French colonial administration because it presented itself as Socialist and demanded the collectivization of the means of production.

Kourouma then moves on to describe another contender, this time a *métis* politician who was portrayed as a dominant figure during the late years of the colonial regime:

> Systematically, for fifteen years and during all the electoral contests, by manipulating elections the colonial administration managed to guarantee the victory of J.-L. Crunet's party. The *métis* Crunet remained the deputy of his country in the French National Assembly for ten years and became Prime Minister of the territory when the colony's autonomy was proclaimed.[14]

Two now-classic studies of French decolonization in sub-Saharan Africa and of the French late colonial state by Edward Mortimer and Ruth Schachter-Morgenthau follow those assumptions almost uncritically. In their conclusions, we find French interference in all electoral events between 1945 and 1958 taken as given, part of an interpretative picture that paints an extensive array of administrators wishing to protect their own clients in the territories through a repertoire of electoral chicanery. By contrast, the constraints under which representatives of the late colonial state operated in respect of intervention in electoral processes are frequently omitted from such studies.[15]

African Parties, French Officials, and New Democratic Structures

In principle, the response of French administrators to mass democratization in sub-Saharan Africa was comparable to their reaction to the abolition of forced labor and of discriminatory legal statutes (the *indigénat*).[16]

While most French administrators in the field were initially opposed to democratization measures, their negative reaction was typically expressed in notes of protest and critical remarks in their regular reports.[17] Covert spoiling tactics were rare indeed. After gradual democratization had been approved in Paris, the same administrators adapted quite rapidly to the conferral of voting rights. In this context there was little long-lasting debate about the capacity of Africans to vote.

In exceptional cases some officials, including most notably Côte d'Ivoire governor André Latrille's administrative team led by the ultraliberal director of cabinet Christian Lambert, were even so enthusiastic about the impending extension of voting rights that they became fervent protagonists of the electoral reforms proposed. At the other end of the official spectrum even the unremittingly paternalistic and most racist of senior administrators rapidly learned to cope with the measures. By 1947 official complaints about the rights of Africans to elect their own representatives were already a thing of the past. That said, it was nonetheless crucial from the perspective of officials in the Ministry for Overseas France to ensure that the "right persons" were elected.[18] In the first phase of postwar colonial administrative reform, this was not yet a chronic problem. Seen from the standpoint of these colonial minds, there remained a sufficient number of eligible candidates—moderate French-educated *évolués*—deemed suitable to occupy the post of parliamentary deputy. But this situation would change as French administrators became increasingly concerned, indeed nearly hysterical or paranoid, that African parties might serve the interests of the most dangerous enemy, namely, the Soviet Union and its French Communist supporters in France. This was still not the case in 1945, but from 1946 onward French administrative debate increasingly revealed such anxieties.[19]

In 1946 French officials looked on the foundation of the Rassemblement Démocratique Africain (RDA), at once a federal party and an umbrella organization for nationalist parties that spanned the French black African territories, as a clear step in this direction. It should be pointed out that the first elections in sub-Saharan Africa had already taken place by then, and that in those October 1945 ballots even hardliners among the territorial governors, such as Edmond Louveau in Soudan and Jean Toby in Niger, had not dared to interfere with the election of candidates from the constituent parties soon to form territorial affiliate sections of the RDA. In 1945 and 1946, Hamani Diori of the Parti Progressiste du Niger (PPN) was elected deputy for this territory, and Mamadou Konaté was selected as deputy for Soudan on the ticket of the Union soudanaise. Each of these groups would subsequently become RDA sections.[20] Even the RDA's founding father, Félix Houphouët-Boigny, was accepted as a suitable candidate, and in Côte d'Ivoire his Union Démocratique, predecessor of the Parti Démocratique de la Côte d'Ivoire (PDCI), was openly endorsed by the administration.[21] Once the struggles over the emancipation of local African planters had ended, this official support included most administrators in the territory and not merely the enthusiasts for reform grouped around Latrille. The notable exception was French administrators in Upper Côte d'Ivoire who preferred to work with the Mossi headmen of what was to become Upper Volta. They backed a candidate from the ruling family of the Mossi region as a result.[22]

The advent of the RDA changed matters. The fact that African parties and deputies could now federate in a single movement capable of mobilizing support across West Africa changed the entire constellation of reform and administrative reaction to it. From the point of view of French officials, this single movement institutionalized the preexisting and well-known sympathies of many African deputies for the French Communist Party (PCF), making their alleged ideological preferences seem dangerous as never before.[23] Functionaries of the Ministry for Overseas France thus became increasingly worried. The key role played by the minister responsible, the Socialist veteran Marius Moutet, in convincing prominent African politicians not to participate in the RDA's founding congress at Bamako is now well known. Moutet's intervention is seen as the catalyst to their decision not to sign up to a common front of "leftist" African political leaders, thus sabotaging the idea of African political unity in French West African party politics. Moutet's alleged intrigue hinged on the Senegalese deputies Lamine Guèye and Léopold Sédar Senghor, although one could probably say a lot about the ulterior motives of the two Senegalese leaders.[24] But what is most noteworthy here is that from late 1946 the negative official characterization of RDA militants as Communist fellow travelers drove the French authorities to react. And this reaction extended to elections as well.

The trust territory of Togo has to be mentioned as a special case among France's West African territories, but here, too, the Comité d'Union Togolaise (CUT) fell victim to a similar hostility from French administrators toward the territory's new electoral politics. The Togolese party had formerly lobbied the United Nations for regional autonomy based on the territory's distinct ethnocultural identity and was, as a result, increasingly suspected by senior French colonial officials as being receptive to Communist subversion.[25] The Togo administration drew upon supposedly proven facts indicating the CUT's treacherous and subversive intent. Patently absurd, these accusations were of a piece with growing official paranoia about the Communist menace in West Africa. In reality, the CUT was at best pro-British in a very circumscribed sense and never showed any interest in Communist sloganizing.[26] Moreover, in their enthusiasm for liberalization in sub-Saharan Africa as evident since at least 1944, French officials found themselves trapped by their own rhetoric: they had committed themselves to a sort of "fair play" when it came to coping with political adversaries. With both a domestic audience and a wider international public to whom successive French governments of the early Fourth Republic wanted to demonstrate the generosity of the late colonial state, gross interference in the electoral process was not an option. By complying with the rules of the democratic game since 1945, French colonial administrations across West Africa had already limited their opportunities to manipulate the free operation of African party politics. Locally, the political initiative consequently passed to other political forces.

Rules of the Game: Chiefs, Administrators, and Deputies

French reactions—and French colonial minds—were, however, far from uniform. Isolated officials in the rural interior of the West African colonies adopted different administrative styles, varying from attempts at modernization to old-style, pro-chief conservatism. Yet whatever their methods or motives, it did not serve administrators' interests to interfere in the electoral process. For one thing, low-level administrators were in principle less directly engaged by the outcome of elections, whose results affected large electoral districts and deputyships of territories. These were not, then, local elections in the truly "local" sense of district administration. For another, new procedures for the election of rural councilors, introduced under the auspices of municipal and communal reform, only came into effect on the brink of independence and, as multiparty democracy would in some places give way to new African one-party regimes, rarely had much effect.[27]

Whatever the case, in the early 1950s local officials saw no immediate reason to interfere in the electoral process.[28] There was, of course, always the risk that an elected deputy or councilor might provide a focal point for popular antagonism to colonial authority and accuse the local administrator of being a "tyrant." The Senegalese *cercle* of Nioro du Rip is one example where such agitation took place in the late 1940s.[29] However, this was the exception rather than the rule. Whether or not local councilors were affiliated with the RDA, few among them directly challenged the local authority of the *administrateur de cercle*. In rural areas it was rather the so-called traditional chiefs who were most active in influencing the local populations to vote for or against a party.[30] There were several instances in Côte d'Ivoire in which chiefs broke with the PDCI-RDA and subsequently attempted to coerce party members and voters among "their" populations to cut their links with the party. Correspondence with senior RDA organizers clearly indicates that leading Ivorian chiefs remained insistent that they had a right to decide whether "their subjects" should join a political party.[31] Chiefly opposition such as this to RDA encroachment on their traditional political prerogatives was widespread. Anxious not to jeopardize their working relationship with the French administration on the one hand, and resentful of mounting RDA influence over "their" populations on the other, numerous chiefs tried to block party activity within their customary areas of regional authority. Aware that conflict between the RDA leadership and the French colonial regime was reaching its climax in the late 1940s, undisguised interference in electoral battles by local chiefs also seemed less risky than it had been before. Cases of such interference were, for example, registered in Côte d'Ivoire, Upper Volta, and Guinea-Conakry in 1950–51.[32] While French officials were understandably content to see popular support for the "radicals" of the RDA challenged from within, there are no indications that the chiefs acted under direct orders.

Similar grassroots conflicts over the new electoral politics were apparent in territories where the RDA threat did not play a role, notably in Senegal. There, local "traditional" chiefs pressed "their" populations to vote either for the Section Française de l'Internationale Ouvrière (SFIO) of Lamine Guèye or for the Bloc Démocratique Sénégalais (BDS) of Léopold Sédar Senghar and Mamadou Dia. Yet, in doing so, most Senegalese paramount chiefs did not meet with success. In some cases they significantly undermined their standing in the community, an outcome that did not apparently diminish their readiness to intervene. As in Côte d'Ivoire and in adjacent French-ruled territories, chiefs in Senegal had reason enough for such behavior. Most important was that here, as elsewhere, elected councilors threatened to become dangerous rivals within the networks of influence in their region. Thus, most chiefs sought to ensure that the elected councilor was a person who belonged to the chief's patronage network (either as a patron or in some cases as a client). Commenting on such an occurrence of internal conflict over the maintenance of patronage networks, in 1952 one *cercle* administrator cited the case of Omar Bayo Fall, chief of the canton of M'Bayar, who "found himself in a difficult position owing to the hostility of certain BDS supporters in his region, which had become intractable after he opposed [their candidacy] in earlier electoral campaigns."[33]

In some local elections, the clash between traditional support for the local chief and new party political alignments could produce a stalemate that resembled more a ceasefire in a civil war than normal democratic practices. In the Senegalese city of Kaolack, for instance, both the BDS and SFIO tried to guarantee members of their own party the post of chief of town quarter, while the chiefs thus installed did their best to force voters in their quarter to elect the "right" list. As this example suggests, chiefly activity remained an important component in the voting behavior of local electors until the end of the colonial period.[34] There was no difference in this respect between "calm territories" such as Senegal and "hot territories" such as Côte d'Ivoire. Yet French administrators in AOF remained remarkably passive in most such cases of local electoral manipulation. Those practices increasingly persisted *despite* their presence rather than as a result of their influence.

The Limits of Manipulation

Where historians discuss those elections under French colonial rule that they claim were rigged, they normally focus on the experience in territories where a clear favorite was confronted with unexpected difficulties. In many such cases French interference did indeed explain the surprising success of rank outsiders. However, the scope for French manipulation of this kind was not as great as might be assumed. Perhaps unsurprisingly the perspective of the *territorial administration* differed from the rather passive approach of local officials. In the governors' palaces and their political departments, the basic mode of action was to build up a candidate against the RDA's nominee. This happened in Côte d'Ivoire, in Soudan, and in Niger, less prominently in Dahomey and Upper Volta, and finally against the candidates of the CUT in Togo.[35] Habitually, senior colonial officials endorsed the RDA's opponents, lending financial aid and logistical support, and protecting them from physical attacks. Violence against anti-RDA candidates was often a possibility because RDA nominees typically had an entrenched party organization behind them and could mobilize armed supporters, at least in the cities.[36] In territories where the territorial administration was more neutral (often where the RDA was weaker or absent), such as Senegal, opposition movements might still be crushed by the violence of party militants, as was the case in the above-mentioned electoral conflicts in Kaolack.[37]

If elections were one thing, the actions of representatives once elected were another. French territorial governors expected a cooperative attitude from "their deputies" and sometimes tried to impose certain constraints on deputies' behavior after their installation. It soon became apparent that elected politicians were not amenable to such control. A typical example is Sékou Sanogo, whose election as second deputy of Côte d'Ivoire in 1951 the French territorial administration had facilitated in an effort to counteract the RDA's dominance. Much of this official support involved the protection of Sanogo's adherents from attacks and intimidation by RDA followers.[38] Sanogo did not behave as expected after his electoral success, however. He repeatedly criticized the role of the French governor in the territory, and his entire relationship with the territorial administration was antagonistic. Thus confounded, the officials most closely involved in sponsoring Sanogo's election, such as Charles Wilt, police commissioner in Abidjan, expressed mounting frustration at this "betrayal" of old colonial practices.[39]

In Togo Nicolas Grunitzky caused similar headaches to senior colonial minds. Here French administrators worked to strengthen the position of the declared opponent of the allegedly pro-British and pro-Communist CUT candidate Sylvanus Olympio.[40] Indeed, staff of French commissioner Jean Cédile's political affairs directorate did their utmost to bring Olympio's career as a deputy to an end. They evidently had few moral qualms about resorting to illegal means, as illustrated by recurrent debate about the creation and the use of black funds. Take, for example, the handwritten note from Olympio's opponent to a senior French official in the Ministry for Overseas France:

> many thanks for your latest efforts to secure supplementary secret funds for use in the Territory. I understand the difficulties that you've encountered in this matter, but it is deplorable that the Government fails to understand that, here as elsewhere [electoral] success depends on the sums of money that the administration is able to disburse. Our [party] opponents have well stocked treasuries. And my informants advise me that Sylvanus Olympio has recently received substantial sums.[41]

The alleged important sums in the bank accounts of the CUT were mere speculation, but those paid by the French were real. Nonetheless, as in Côte d'Ivoire the recipients proved unreliable. Moreover, Grunitzky's party, the Parti Togolais du Progrès (PTP), took full advantage of French anxiety about Olympio and demanded substantial financial backing from the French authorities to fund extravagant personal expenses and a massive propaganda campaign in their favor. Furthermore, once both the Togo deputyship in the French National Assembly and a majority in the Togolese Territorial Assembly were secured, PTP leaders coaxed the French administration of Togo into helping them consolidate their own ruling position. PTP politicians exploited official fears that support for Olympio's adherents might take off under the cover of a new party, and they demanded extraordinary French subsidies for the territory instead of voting tax rises that threatened to endanger the PTP's popularity with voters. A Ministry for Overseas France record of a 27 July 1954 meeting with Grunitzky illustrated these tactics in practice:

> M. Grunitzky warned that Togo faced the threat of disorder, arising in particular from the creation of a third [political] party, which will cause confusion and facilitate Sylvanus Olympio's return to the scene. He added that it is therefore essential that the Territorial Assembly should not be called upon to vote additional taxes during its next budgetary session. A subvention of metropolitan funds is therefore indispensible.[42]

Angry at being held hostage by their one-time auxiliaries, French officials were highly ambivalent when it came to bolstering the position of the PTP leaders grouped around Grunitzky in the key elected positions in the territory.[43] Many French administrators hesitated to support those they regarded as corrupt profiteers, and their hesitations contributed, in the PTP's case, to its unexpected and spectacular defeat in the 1958 territorial elections.[44]

Between 1950 and 1956 French administrators increasingly turned away from directly underwriting their partners among the new African political elites. One reason was the new modus vivendi struck with the RDA after the party formally severed its ties with the PCF in 1950. RDA leaders were, in general, grudgingly accepted as potential partners as a result.[45] Another reason was a question of style. The Ministry for Overseas France insisted on adherence to a strict legalism even in the case of those African politicians who still seemed sympathetic to Communism. Thus, when the governor of Niger, Paul Bordier, sought to sabotage the electoral campaign of Djibo Bakary, deputy of Niger and member of the supposedly left-leaning Sawaba Party, in the municipal elections for the post of mayor of Niamey, the governor found himself disciplined by Minister Gaston Defferre.[46]

Did the French administrators rediscover old habits and return to manipulative behavior after it became clear in 1958 that African populations would have the opportunity to vote, in principle, over a national future for the African colonies with or without France? The referendum over this question as well as the subsequent elections in the now-autonomous territories would be decisive in this process. Seizing the opportunity presented by de Gaulle's new proposals for a French "Communauté," two deputies, who were also territorial leaders—Djibo Bakary and Sékou Touré in Guinea-Conakry—moved swiftly, announcing their intention to quit the French Union. As there were still several French officials active in the different African territories, a manipulation of the referendum against the leading party's local preference for a no-vote would, at least theoretically, have been possible.[47]

In Guinea-Conakry, the French response to the challenge of Sékou Touré came too late. The "Communist leader," as he was dubbed by many of those officials who encountered him in the period directly before the referendum, made known his intention to leave the empire at the precise moment when the French were unable to react. Moreover, the French administration underestimated the danger that an African leader in a Territoire d'Outre-Mer could really force the pace of independence. When French officials finally grasped that they had to take Touré's claims seriously and that he would indeed leave the French Union, they had already lost the initiative.[48] Plans to neutralize the propaganda of key African political figures within the territory, many of them councilors of the territorial government and quasi-ministers—such as sabotaging the radio stations—came belatedly.[49] The French contented themselves with damaging a future independent Guinea economically by withdrawing from the outset any financial and logistic help after the territory's decisive "no" vote in the referendum.[50] Manipulating voting behavior had become too complex and too costly to be feasible.

Far from France being a neocolonial plotter, French administrators' minds had decisively changed, with many becoming committed to a sort of electoral fairness. Such was even the case in Niger where the then-dominant Sawaba Party had called for a popular vote for independence on the occasion of the referendum. French agents were reluctant to risk a fight with Djibo Bakary, the strongman of the territory.[51] These officials dismissed the notion that electoral manipulation was the sole means to prevent Niger's people from exercising their sovereign rights. Instead, a Sawaba faction, including Issofoye Djermakoye and the conservative and pro-chieftaincy wing of the party, broke with Bakary.[52] The French governor, soon-to-be High Commissioner, Don-Jean Colombani, was relieved, but it is clear from the archival correspondence that the French were not instrumental in Bakary's fall. During the electoral campaign of December 1958, Lafeuille, French administrator of Niamey, was even accused by troops loyal to Hamani Diori and Djermakoye of backing Sawaba supporters in the capital![53] And Bruneton, *cercle* commander of Konni, disciplined the imam of the town of Konni who had mobilized support against Sawaba in his mosque.[54] Finally, high commissioner Colombani insisted that while Bakary was a dangerous individual, employing nondemocratic means to prevent his election was out of the question.[55] French officials were undoubtedly content to see Sawaba contained by the decisions of indigenous chiefs, but they did not manipulate the elections.[56] These actions—or inactions—spoke volumes about the fundamental changes in colonial minds. In the final months of the French Empire in sub-Saharan Africa both the disillusionment of colonial administrations with former manipulative practices and their growing commitment to electoral transparency made it impossible to continue with large-scale interference in the style of the late 1940s.

Conclusion

Although examples of French attempts to manipulate elections in sub-Saharan Africa in the 1940s and 1950s can be found at both local and territorial levels, it was difficult to organize such manipulation as a coherent strategy in what the colonial administration perceived as a battle against African "radicals" and "Communists." As French interference in elections is an established topic in the study of the French late colonial state in Africa, such a result might seem surprising at first glance. However, one has to conclude that the rigging of elections through the backstairs actions of French colonial administrations was a circumscribed process, in which French officials were often reluctant to utilize what room for maneuver remained available to them. Undoubtedly, in the late 1940s French administrators, particularly those in some unruly territories such as Côte d'Ivoire, had persisted in their bad habits. This was obvious in the case of Sékou Sanogo, opponent of Félix Houphouët-Boigny, and similarly apparent in support for Nicolas Grunitzky against Sylvanus Olympio in Togo. Increasingly often, however, local administrators found themselves caught in an ambiguous position between paternalist intervention and new-style reformism, in which it was difficult to decide how to react in contested elections. Racist beliefs and the wish to marginalize Communist activism were still prevalent, and those ideas sometimes prompted officials to intervene, but the moral pressure to foster good governance, combined with the "fair" participation of African representatives in territorial government, first curbed then stifled official enthusiasm for underhand manipulation.

Moreover, administrators quickly became aware of the fact that African deputies once in office were anything but weak-willed puppets. Time and again, opposition candidates supported by the French against more popular but seemingly "radical" politicians proved highly inventive when it came to securing favors from the colonial administration in order to consolidate their political power. French officials responded to such cajoling with frustration and with a growing reluctance to support their erstwhile allies. To the contrary, "traditional rulers" in a way remained cornerstones of the old colonial order. For the chiefs, interference in the electoral process was often a matter of political survival. Fearing that a councilor of an electoral district might become their adversary in relations with both the local population and the territorial administration, influential chiefs worked to foster the electoral success of individuals belonging to their own networks.

As Africans increasingly played an instrumental role in electoral manipulation, the French officials slowly abandoned such behavior. Elections were still not free. Crucially, however, the constraints on electoral behavior no longer derived primarily from the activities of the colonial power, but mainly from what one might call local internal dynamics. Those included the ambitions, patronage networks, and emerging distributions of power among African leaders. Whether they liked it or not, colonial minds finally acquiesced in electoral processes that they could no longer control.

Notes

Alexander Keese's work is funded through ERC Starting Grant no. 240898 within the 7th European Community Framework Program.

    1. Voting rights figure less prominently in some masterly scholarly studies

of African decolonization, however. John Hargreaves, for instance, does not discuss them among the "new imperial dynamics"; see John D. Hargreaves, *Decolonization in Africa* (London: Longman, 1988), 95–107. Frederick Cooper discusses their impact in the French case but only mentions them in passing in the British case; see Frederick Cooper, *Africa since 1940: The Past of the Present* (Cambridge: Cambridge University Press, 2002), 41–42, 51–52, 58.

2. Joseph Roger de Benoist, *L'Afrique occidentale française de 1944 à 1960* (Dakar: Les Nouvelles Editions Africaines, 1982), 73–74, 292, 513–14.

3. G. Wesley Johnson, The Emergence of Black Politics in Senegal: The Struggle for Power in the Four Communes, 1900–1920 (Stanford CA: Stanford University Press, 1971).

4. Iba Der Thiam, "Le combat des populations africaines pour la démocratie, l'égalité et la justice, 1895–1960: L'exemple du Sénégal," 250–63, 257–58; and Alice L. Conklin, "A Force for Civilization: Republican Discourse and French Administration in West Africa, 1895–1930," 283–302, 294–95, both chapters in AOF: *Réalités et héritages: Sociétés ouest-africaines et ordre colonial, 1895–1960*, ed. Charles Becker, Saliou Mbaye, and Ibrahima Thioub (Dakar: Direction des Archives du Sénégal, 1997).

5. Archives Nationales, Paris (AN), AG/5(FPR)/199, Calixte, Administrateur stagiaire de la F.O.M. in Guinea, *Rapport de Stage au Ministère de l'Intérieur* (no number), n.d., spring 1958.

6. Tony Chafer, The End of Empire in French West Africa: France's Successful Decolonization? (Oxford: Berg, 2002), 62–63.

7. Raymond-Marin Lemesle, *La conférence de Brazzaville de 1944: Contexte et repères: Cinquantenaire des prémices de la colonisation* (Paris: CHEAM, 1994); Martin Shipway, "Reformism and the French 'Official Mind': The 1944 Brazzaville Conference and the Legacy of the Popular Front," in *French Colonial Empire and the Popular Front: Hope and Disillusion*, ed. Tony Chafer and Amanda Sackur (Basingstoke UK: Macmillan, 1999), 131–51. On the limitations of the French commitment to mass democracy, personified particularly by the governor-general of French Equatorial Africa, Félix Eboué, see James I. Lewis, "Félix Eboué and Late French Colonial Ideology," *Itinerario* 25:1 (2002), 127–60, particularly 140–42.

8. P.-F. Gonidec, "L'Evolution des Territoires d'Outre-Mer depuis 1946," *Revue Juridique et Politique de l'Union Française* 11:3 (July–September 1957), 429–77, and 11:4 (October–December 1957), 701–28.

9. Alice L. Conklin, *A Mission to Civilize: The Republican Idea of Empire in France and West Africa, 1895–1930* (Stanford CA: Stanford University Press, 1997), 164–68; Conklin, "'Democracy' Rediscovered: Civilization

through Association in French West Africa (1914–1930)," *Cahiers d'etudes africaines* 37:1 (1997), 59–84, especially 75–77.

10. See, for instance, Frederick Cooper, "A Parting of the Ways: Colonial Africa and South Africa, 1946–48," *African Studies* 65:1 (Summer 2006), 27–44.

11. Wolfgang Reinhard, *Geschichte der Europäischen Expansion*, book 4: *Dritte Welt—Afrika* (Stuttgart: Kohlhammer, 1990), 150. The question of elections and of the experience of electoral campaigns is notably absent from the 1,200-page, two-volume Dakar conference proceedings edited by Charles Becker, Saliou Mbaye, and Ibrahima Thioub, AOF: *Réalités et héritages: Sociétés ouest-africaines et ordre colonial, 1895–1960* (Dakar: Direction des Archives du Sénégal, 1997). There are two exceptions: Joseph-Roger Benoist's chapter, "Le Grand Conseil de l'AOF: Ébauche du Parlement fédéral," 75–88; and Peter J. Schraeder, "Les élites africaines et le développement des institutions démocratiques: Quelques leçons tirées de la 'troisième vague' de démocratisation en Afrique," 430–50. But the former fails to address the issue of local participation, and the latter does not discuss the obvious precedent of electoral experiences during the late colonial state in Francophone Africa.

12. Thomas Bierschenk, "The Local Appropriation of Democracy: An Analysis of the Municipal Election in Parakou, Republic of Benin, 2002–03," *Journal of Modern African Studies* 44:4 (2006), 543–71, at 544–55.

13. Kenneth Robinson, "Colonialism French-Style, 1945–55: A Backward Glance," *Journal of Imperial and Commonwealth History* 12 (1984–85), 24–41, at 26.

14. Ahmadou Kourouma, *En attendant le vote des bêtes sauvages* (Paris: Seuil, 2003), 105, 109. All translations are by the author unless otherwise noted. Although the situation described in Kourouma's fiction is certainly closer to the political alliances and intrigues of the first years of independent Dahomey, the character of "Crunet" is modeled on Nicolas Grunitzky, long-standing deputy and later president of Togo, whose case is discussed later in this study. The first quote in the original French reads as follows: "Il se lança dans la politique, créa la ligue du Nord. Le parti fut combattu par les pouvoirs locaux et *par l'administration coloniale française* parce qu'il se prétendait socialiste et réclamait la collectivisation des biens de production." The second quote reads: "Systématiquement, durant quinze ans et au cours de toutes les consultations, l'administration coloniale parvint à donner la victoire au parti de J.-L. Crunet en truquant les élections. Le métis Crunet resta le député de son pays à l'Assemblée nationale française pendant dix ans et devint le Premier Ministre du territoire quand l'autonomie de la colonie fut proclamée."

15. Edward Mortimer, *France and the Africans, 1944–1960: A Political*

History (London: Faber and Faber, 1969), 137–44; Ruth Schachter Morgenthau, *Political Parties in French-Speaking West Africa* (Oxford: Oxford University Press, 1964), 61. This position has only recently been underlined by Elizabeth Schmidt's inspiring new book on grassroots mobilization in Guinea-Conakry under French colonial rule; see Elizabeth Schmidt, *Cold War and Decolonization in Guinea, 1946–1958* (Athens: Ohio University Press, 2007), 6, 52–53, 67, 74, 78, 102–3. While the author claims to have sufficient proof to characterize several elections as "fraudulent," it has at least to be remarked that her oral sources and nationalist politicians appearing with their testimony in the literature—both employed to back her claim—can be expected to make such a statement. This does not prove the opposite, of course, but one wonders if a nationalist leader or a former party militant giving his testimony in retrospect is really a reliable source. Schmidt does not appear to cite any colonial document to substantiate her claims, although if she is correct, hints in the colonial reports and letters would be likely to exist.

16. Gregory Mann, "What Was the *Indigénat*? The 'Empire of Law' in French West Africa," *Journal of African History* 50:2 (2009), 331–53, at 349.

17. Denise Bouche, "L'administration de l'Afrique occidentale française et les libertés démocratiques (1944–1946)," in *Les Chemins de la Décolonisation de l'Empire Colonial Français*, ed. Charles-Robert Ageron (Paris: CNRS Editions, 1986), 467–79, citation at 476.

18. Catherine Atlan, "De la gestion à l'arbitrage: L'Administration du Sénégal face aux premières élections libres de l'après-guerre (1945–1958)," *Outre-Mers* 90:338–39 (2003), 133–52, at 145.

19. Alexander Keese, Living with Ambiguity: Integrating an African Elite in French and Portuguese Africa, 1930–1961 (Stuttgart: Steiner, 2007), 136–44.

20. Mortimer, *France*, 111; Morgenthau, *Parties*, 181–82.

21. Centre des Archives d'Outre-Mer (CAOM), Aix-en-Provence, Fonds Marius Moutet 28/PA/8/168, no. 155/AP/2, AOF Governor-General Barthes to Moutet, 19 October 1946, pp. 1–2.

22. Regarding the close cooperation between the French administration and the Mossi ruling dynasty in what was still called "Upper Côte d'Ivoire," see Archives Nationales Sénégalaises (ANS), Dakar, Senegal, GGAOF 17G 23, no. 228/C, Latrille to Cournarie, 24 April 1945.

23. CAOM, Fonds Moutet 28/PA/8/168, no. 1063, Soudan Governor Louveau to Barthes, 7 December 1946; no. 1202/AP/2, Moutet telegram to Barthes, 20 September 1947; Louveau, "Rapport sur l'Evolution des Partis Politiques-deuxième trimestre 1947," n.d., 1947, p. 3.

24. Chafer, *End of Empire*, 72. The French administration was concerned

that even Senghor might be seduced by Communist propaganda; see the still unexplored report in CAOM, Fonds Moutet 28/PA/8/168, "Rapport Léopold Senghor," no file number or date.

25. At least two curious reports on rumors about armed revolt organized by the CUT survive in the archives; see CAOM, FM 1AffPol/2115/1, no. 11/S, French Military Commander of Togo and Dahomey, Maury, to Secretary-General of Togo, 4 March 1948, 1.; and Ministère des Affaires Etrangères (MAE) Paris, Direction Afrique-Levant (DAL), Togo (1953–1959), 5, no. 29/TC, Renner, French Consul (Accra), to Cédile, French Commissioner of Togo, 15 February 1955.

26. David K. Fieldhouse, "British Merchants and French Decolonization: UAC in Francophone Africa (1945–1960)," in *L'Afrique noire française: L'heure des Indépendances*, ed. Charles-Robert Ageron and Marc Michel (Paris: CNRS Editions, 1992), 489–98.

27. Alexander Keese, "'Quelques Satisfactions d'Amour-Propre': African Elite Integration, the Loi-cadre, and Involuntary Decolonisation of French Tropical Africa," *Itinerario* 26:1 (2003), 33–57, at 49.

28. It was even more essential for the chief to keep the nomination of "traditional chiefs" under close scrutiny, although in the electoral field, too, overt manipulation became more difficult after World War II; see Francis Simonis, *Le Commandant en tournée: Une administration au contact des populations en Afrique Noire coloniale* (Paris: Seli Arslan, 2005), 46–47.

29. ANS, 11D1–1148, no. 605/CK, Kaolack cercle commander to acting Governor of Senegal, Bailly, "Plainte contre Chef Subdivision Nioro-Rip," 20 September 1949.

30. Atlan, "De la gestion," 148.

31. See, for example, ANS, GGAOF 17G 565, Atimon Idogo, Canton Chief of Diaro, Upper Volta, to RDA Secretary-General in Bobo-Dioulasso, 12 May 1950; in same file: Yao Anguemian, Canton Chief of Bini, Côte d'Ivoire, to RDA Executive Committee, Abidjan, 20 May 1950.

32. See, among others, ANS, GGAOF 17G 565, Côte d'Ivoire police intelligence report no. 3150/PS/R/C, "Renseignements: Démission du R.D.A. de trois chefs de quartier musulmans de Bondoukou," 12 June 1950; ANS, GGAOF 17G 565; Atimon Idogo, Canton Chief of Diaro, Upper Volta, to RDA Secretary-General in Bobo-Dioulasso, 12 May 1950; Guinea-Conakry police intelligence report no. 226/1279/C/PS2, "Renseignements: Démissions du RDA," 4 December 1951. Elizabeth Schmidt also highlights the anti-RDA activity of many canton chiefs in Guinea; see Elizabeth Schmidt, "Cold War in Guinea: The Rassemblement Démocratique Africain and the Struggle over Communism, 1950–1958," *Journal of African History* 48:1 (2007), 95–121, at 107.

However, it should be noted that Schmidt relies here on a report of the Conakry section of the Parti Démocratique de Guinée, Guinea's RDA section, which was intended for use as RDA propaganda in the French National Assembly, so this source has to be used with caution.

33. ANS, 11D1-95, Diourbel cercle commander Berthet report, "Appréciations générales du Commandant de Cercle," 2 March 1953.

34. ANS, 11D1-1148, Kaolack security service report, no. 405/C.SU, "Renseignements: Nomination de chef de quartier," 11 June 1949.

35. Benoist, Afrique, 116–21. For Chad, see Bernard Lanne, *Histoire Politique du Tchad de 1945 à 1958: Administration, Partis, Elections* (Paris: Karthala, 1998), 165–67.

36. Bernard Charles illustrated these techniques of violence in the egregious case of Guinea-Conakry; see Charles, "Le rôle de la violence dans la mise en place des pouvoirs en Guinée," in Ageron and Michel, *L'Afrique noire française*, 361–73.

37. ANS, 11D1-1148, Kaolack Commander, Mazou, "Rapport des renseignements sur les incidents survenus entre membres du Bloc et le Parti Indépendant de Kaolack," 19 July 1946.

38. CAOM, FM 1AffPol/2174/2, Wilt to AOF Government *chef de Cabinet*, 12 May 1952.

39. CAOM, FM 1AffPol/2174/2, Wilt report to Côte d'Ivoire Governor, Péchoux, 14 May 1952.

40. Marc Michel, "The Independence of Togo," in *Decolonization and African Independence: The Transfer of Power, 1960–1980*, ed. Prosser Gifford and William Roger Louis (New Haven CT: Yale University Press, 1988), 305–9.

41. CAOM, FM 1AffPol/3322/1, Digo handwritten note to Director of Political Affairs Delteil, 11 April 1951: "Je vous suis reconnaissant de la nouvelle démarche que vous avez faite pour obtenir, au profit du Territoire, un supplément de fonds secrets. Je réalise les difficultés que vous rencontrez à ce sujet, mais je déplore que le Gouvernement ne comprenne pas que le succès est subordonné, ici comme ailleurs, à l'importance des fonds dont disposera l'administration française. Nos adversaires ont des caisses bien approvisionnées. Des informateurs me signalent que Sylvanus Olympio a reçu récemment des sommes importantes."

42. CAOM, FM 1AffPol/1012, "Réunion du 27 Juillet 1954 chez M. de Villelongue," no date, p. 3: "M. Grunitzky indique que des désordres menacent au Togo, en particulier du fait de la création du 3ème parti, qui va créer la confusion et faciliter la rentrée en scène de Sylvanus Olympio. Il ajoute qu'il est essentiel que l'Assemblée territoriale ne soit pas appelée á voter des impôts

nouveaux lors de sa prochaine session budgétaire. Une subvention métropolitaine serait donc indispensable."

43. Michel, "Independence of Togo," 310.

44. CAOM, FM 1AffPol/3322/1, telegram 166, no. 166, Spénale, French Commissioner, Togo, to Minister for Overseas France, Jacquet, n.d., but noted as "1958."

45. Nevertheless, distrust of RDA leaders' "real motives" remained prevalent well into the 1950s; see CAOM, FM 1AffPol/2180/8, Bénilan, Section de Documentation Militaire de l'Union Française, Centre d'Etudes Asiatiques et Africaines, "Evolution du R.D.A. de 1946 à 1951," March 1951, p. 26.

46. CAOM, FM 1AffPol/490, telegram 592/JD/CL, Gaston Defferre, to Governor of Niger Bordier, 27 November 1956, pp. 3–4.

47. Chafer, *End of Empire*, 173–79.

48. Three days before the referendum, French administrators and secret service agents alike still believed that Sékou Touré's propaganda was no more than a great "bluff": see CAOM, 2181/6, Service d'Espionnage et Contre-Espionnage (SDECE), "Bulletin des Renseignements: Guinée Française, prise de position de Sékou Touré," 25 September 1958, p. 2.

49. MAE, DAL, Guinée, 9, telegram 365, Cornut-Gentille to Messmer, 20 September 1958; Telegram 753–5, Messmer reply to Cornut-Gentille, 23 September 1958; Telegram 762–4, Messmer to Cornut-Gentille, 25 September 1958.

50. CAOM, 2181/6, Ministry for Overseas France, Directorate of Political Affairs, "Guinée: Transfert des capitaux, en Guinée, à la suite de l'indépendance envisagée par ce territoire," 22 September 1958.

51. Claude Fluchard, Le PPN-RDA et la décolonisation du Niger, 1946–1960 (Paris: Harmattan, 1996), 233–34.

52. Finn Fuglestad, "Djibo Bakary, the French, and the Referendum of 1958 in Niger," *Journal of African History* 14:2 (1973), 327–29.

53. CAOM, FM 1AffPol/2174/1, Candidates for the Parti de l'Union pour la Communauté Franco-Africaine (UCFA) in Niamey to Colombani, 5 December 1958; Delanne, UCFA member, to Colombani, 8 December 1958; CAOM, FM 1AffPol/2174/1, no. 511/CF, French Administrator, Niamey, Lafeuille, to Colombani, 9 December 1958.

54. CAOM, FM 1AffPol/2174/1, no. 565, Konni cercle commander, Berneton, to El Hadj Assane, Imam of Konni, 8 December 1958.

55. CAOM, FM 1AffPol/2174/1, telegram 152, Colombani to Cornut-Gentille, 9 December 1958.

56. CAOM, FM 1AffPol/2181/1, no. 375/CAB, Colombani to Cornut-Gentille and Messmer, 27 October 1958.

Contributors

TONY CHAFER is professor of contemporary French area studies and director of the Centre for European and International Studies Research at the University of Portsmouth, United Kingdom. He has published widely on Franco-African relations in the late colonial and postcolonial era and is the author of *The End of Empire in French West Africa: France's Successful Decolonization?* (Berg, 2002). He has recently completed a research project on Franco-British cooperation in Africa with Gordon Cumming (Cardiff University), the main findings of which will be published in a book entitled *From Rivalry to Partnership? New Approaches to the Challenges of Africa* (Ashgate, forthcoming 2011).

VÉRONIQUE DIMIER is associate professor of political science at the Université Libre de Bruxelles, Institut d'Études Européennes. She is the author of *Le gouvernement des colonies: Regards croisés franco-britanniques* (Presses Universitaires de Bruxelles, 2004), and she has recently completed a further book, *Recycling Empire: The Invention of a European Aid Bureaucracy, 1998–2008* (Palgrave-Macmillan, 2011).

JENNIFER M. DUECK earned her D.Phil. in modern history at Merton College, Oxford, where she was a senior scholar. Her doctoral thesis on culture and politics in French Mandate Syria and Lebanon was awarded the Leigh Douglas Memorial Prize by the British Society for Middle Eastern Studies. Her book on the same topic, entitled *The Claims of Culture at Empire's End: Syria and Lebanon under French Rule*, was published in 2010 by Oxford University Press. Currently a postdoctoral research fellow at Corpus Christi College, Oxford, she has also held teaching and research appointments at the University of Cambridge and the London School of Economics.

RUTH GINIO is senior lecturer in history at Ben Gurion University of the Negev and a research fellow at the Harry S. Truman Research Institute for the Advancement of Peace in Jerusalem. Her publications include *French Colonialism Unmasked: The Vichy Years in French West Africa* (University of Nebraska Press, 2006), *Violence and Non-Violence in Africa*, coedited with Pal Ahluwalia and Louise Bethlehem (Routledge, 2007), and *Shadows of War: A History of Silence in the Twentieth Century*, coedited with Efrat Ben Ze'ev and Jay Winter (Cambridge University Press, 2010).

ALEXANDER KEESE is an assistant professor at the Centre of African Studies of the University of Porto (Portugal). He is the author of *Living with Ambiguity: Integrating an African Elite in French and Portuguese Africa, 1930–61* (Steiner, 2007) and the editor of *Ethnicity and the Long-Term Perspective: The African Experience* (Peter Lang, 2009).

JAMES D. LE SUEUR is professor of history at the University of Nebraska–Lincoln. He has written extensively on the impact of colonialism on Algeria and, among other works, is author of *Uncivil War: Intellectuals and Identity Politics during the Decolonization of Algeria*, now in a second edition with the University of Nebraska Press. Most recently he published *Algeria since 1989: Between Democracy and Terror* (Zed Books, 2010), and he is currently finishing a documentary on writers from Muslim-majority countries living in exile as a result of political and religious persecution.

PATRICIA M. E. LORCIN is associate professor of history at the University of Minnesota–Twin Cities and editor of *French Historical Studies*. Her publications include *Imperial Identities: Stereotyping, Prejudice and Race in Colonial Algeria* (I. B. Tauris, 1995), an edited volume, *Algeria and France, 1800–2000: Identity, Memory and Nostalgia* (Syracuse University Press, 2006), several coedited volumes, and numerous articles on French colonial history. She is currently completing a monograph on colonial women writers in Algeria and Kenya.

MARÍA DEL MAR LOGROÑO NARBONA is an assistant professor of modern Middle Eastern history at Florida International University. She has conducted a collaborative research and dissemination project on "Islam in Latin America" (2009–11) funded by the Social Science Research Council. As part of this project she has written and coproduced a short educational documentary, *Being Muslim in Latin America* (Oxford Talks, 2010). She has also written "The 'Woman Question' in the Aftermath of the Great Syria Revolt" in *Al-Raida* (May 2007), and "La actividad política transnacional de las comunidades árabes en Argentina: El caso de Jorge Sawaya," in *La Contribución Arabe a los Identidades Iberoamericanas* (Casa Arabe, 2009).

Contributors

KENNETH J. OROSZ is an assistant professor at Buffalo State College, where he teaches European, African, and colonial history. He is the author of several forthcoming articles on missionary activities in colonial Africa and a book entitled *Religious Conflict and the Evolution of Language Policy in German and French Cameroon, 1885–1939* (Peter Lang, American University Studies series, 2008), winner of the French Colonial History Society's Alfred Heggoy Prize.

ANNE RAFFIN is associate professor in the Department of Sociology at the National University of Singapore. She is the author of *Youth Mobilization in Vichy Indochina and Its Legacies, 1940–1970* (Rowman and Littlefield, 2005) and has published widely on aspects of colonialism in French Indochina. She is currently completing a book on communal tensions in French Pondicherry.

TODD SHEPARD is associate professor of history at the Johns Hopkins University. A revised edition of his first book, *The Invention of Decolonization: The Algerian Revolution and the Remaking of France* (Cornell University Press, 2007), appeared in French as *1962: Comment l'indépendence algérienne a transformé la France*. His current project examines the social policies that the French implemented in response to the Algerian War, both in France and Algeria.

MARTIN SHIPWAY is senior lecturer in French studies and head of the Department of European Cultures and Languages, Birkbeck, University of London. He is the author of *Decolonization and Its Impact: A Comparative Approach to the End of the European Empires* (Wiley-Blackwell, 2008) and *The Road to War: France and Vietnam, 1944–47* (Berghahn, 1996). He works on French and comparative decolonization and has also written on French late colonial policy and decolonization in sub-Saharan Africa, Madagascar, and Algeria.

EMMANUELLE SIBEUD is maître de conférences at the University of Paris VIII and is a member of the Institut Universitaire de France. She is a specialist in colonial ethnography in French Africa and is the author of *Une science imperiale pour l'Afrique? La construction des savoirs africanistes en France, 1878–1930* (Editions de l'EHESS, 2002). She is also the coeditor, with Jean-Loup Amselle, of *Maurice Delafosse: Entre orientalisme et ethnographie: L'itinéraire d'un africaniste, 1870–1926* (Maisonneuve and Larose, 1998). She is currently researching imperial encounters and transimperial intellectual networks in the first half of the twentieth century.

Contributors

JOHN STRACHAN is lecturer in history at Lancaster University, United Kingdom. He has published articles and essays in *French History* (2004, 2006), *Social History of Alcohol and Drugs* (2007), and *France's Lost Empires: Fragmentation, Nostalgia, and la fracture coloniale*, (ed. Kate Marsh and Nicola Frith, 2011), and is preparing a monograph on European settlers in colonial Algeria.

MARTIN THOMAS is professor of colonial history and director of the Centre for the Study of War, State, and Society at the University of Exeter. His publications include *The French Empire between the Wars: Imperialism, Politics, and Society* (Manchester University Press, 2005) and *Empires of Intelligence: Security Services and Colonial Disorder after 1914* (University of California Press, 2007). His comparative study of policing and interwar political violence in European colonial empires, *Violence and Colonial Order: Police, Workers, and Protest in the European Colonial Empires, 1918–1940*, will be published by Cambridge University Press.

Index

Abbas, Ferhat, 200
Abduh, Muhammad, 182
acclimatization, xiii
acculturation, 278
Advanced School of Homecrafts. *See* École Supérieure des Arts Ménagers
Affaire des Grottes, 86
Affaire des Sixas, 132
affaire du foulard, 19n4
affirmative action (U.S. policy), 318
Africa and the Victorians (Robinson and Gallagher), 221
Afrikaans language, xxxii, 194
Afrique Occidentale Française AOF. *See* French West Africa (FWA)
Ageron, Charles-Robert, 299
agriculture, 282, 286–87
aid for development. *See* development funds and grants
Akel, Salim, 160
Al-Azhar Mosque, 182
Albert Kahn Travelling Fellowship, 43–44n10
Al-Fatat, 153
Algeria, 5, 12, 13, 15, 222, 298–306, 309–23; Braudel and, xxviii–xxix, 73, 77, 78, 80–84; centenary of French in, 82–83, 84, 85; Cixous and, 79–80; Germany and, 6, 256; "integrationism" in, xxxvi, 298–300, 305–18; language policy and, xxxi–xxxii, 194–216, 312; Laurentie and, 228; "local laws," 301; Monnerville Commission and, 248–49n48; Robert-Houdin in, xxii–xxiv; travel fellowships and, 34; voting rights, 21n17. *See also* Affaire des Grottes; Organic Statute of Algeria (1947)
Algerian War of Independence, 8, 12–13, 15, 298–323; Arabization and, 195, 197–98, 200, 206, 208, 210, 211; bibliography, 21–22n19; Cold War and, 17; Germany and, 6; intellectuals and, 80; *Voice of Algeria* and, 238
al-Hadi, Abd. *See* Hadi, Abd al-
al-Hikma School, 177, 179
al-Husri, Sati. *See* Husri, Sati al-
al-Khuri, Bishara. *See* Khuri, Bishara al-
Allard, Louis, 45n19
Allardt, Helmuth, 256
Alliance française, 8
Alliance Libanaise, 161
Alsace-Lorraine, 9, 11, 130, 205–6
al-Sulh, Riad. *See* Sulh, Riad al-
American University of Beirut, 183, 184
Americans in Cameroon, 125
Amis de l'Orient, 151

351

Annales School (historiography), xvi, xvii, 72, 74, 76, 77, 78, 81, 88
Année sociologique, L', 31, 39
anthropology, xxii, 55, 66, 75, 310, 321n24
anticlericalism, 121, 124, 170, 174
anticolonialism, 13, 32, 80. *See also* resistance to colonialism
anticolonialists, 26–27, 85–86, 89, 294
anti-Communism, 241–42, 243, 290–91, 327, 330–31, 339
anti-Islamism, 201, 204
AOF. *See* French West Africa (FWA)
Arab Congress of 1913, 153
Arabic language, 159, 161, 174, 185; Algeria, xxxi–xxxii, 194–216, 312
Arabization, xxxii, 194–216
Arab nationalism. *See* nationalism: Arab; pan-Arabism
Aragon, Louis, 77, 84
archaeology, 84, 88
Argentina, 144, 145, 147–48, 150, 155, 156, 157, 162–67; dragoman system and, 160, 161
Arida, Antoine Pierre, 176–77, 178, 179
Ariès, Philippe, 74
armed forces, xxv, 8, 97, 98, 100, 311, 316
Armenians, 154
arts, 317
assimilation, 31, 136, 175, 278–79, 285, 288, 292–93; Algeria, 84, 300–302, 306; "integration" and, 307; voting rights and, 306
"association" (concept), 278–79, 285, 307, 326
Association Européenne de Coopération (AEC), 266
Association with Overseas Territories, 251
athletics. *See* sports
atrocities, 40, 41, 47n39, 48n49
Aubert, Louis, 47n38
Auclert, André, 258, 259, 271n34
Austen, Ralph, 123
Australia, 31, 35, 36
"Autour du monde" fellowships, 29–36
Autour du monde par les boursiers de voyage de l'Université de Paris, 30, 37, 39
Auvergne, Jean, 36
Azande people, 58

Bakary, Djibo, 336, 337
Bamako, Mali, 289, 330
Bamum language, 134
banks and banking, 156, 159
Barthes, René, 281, 284, 292, 295n16
Barthes, Roland, xii
Battaglie di Algeri, La (Pontecorvo), 8
Baum, Robert, 59, 61
Bayardelle, Aimé, 231, 240, 241
Bayly, Susan, xi–xii
BDS. *See* Bloc Démocratique Sénégalais (BDS)
Béchard, Paul, 284, 290, 292
Bedouins: surveillance of, 145
Bée, Clotaire, 307
Belgium, xii, 226, 253, 266. *See also* Congo Free State
Bellanger, Robert, 304
Belloff, Max, 308
Ben Bella, Ahmed, xxxii, 196, 198
Berbers, xxxi, 88, 196, 199, 206, 207, 208, 317; Algerian civil status, 301

Bergson, Henri, 29, 74–75
Beynet, Étienne, 186
bicycles and bicycling, 110, 111; races, 107, 109, 111
Bidault, Georges, 233, 242, 243
"bio-power" (Foucault concept), 97–98, 104
Blache, Paul Vidal de la. *See* Vidal de la Blache, Paul
Blachére, Régis, 207, 208–11
The Black Jacobins (James), 80
Bloc Démocratique Sénégalais (BDS), 333
Bloch, Marc, 74, 75
Bloc National, 125
Blum, Léon, 51, 85, 99, 228
Blum-Viollette bill, 13, 21n17
Bodin, Jean, 57, 68–69n21
Boigny, Félix Houphouët, 255
Boisson, Pierre François, 135, 225
Bokassa, Jean-Bédel, 263
Bonnecarrère, Paul, 134–35
Booth, Alan, 69n28
Bordier, Paul, 336
Boumediene, Houari, xxxii, 196, 198, 199
Bounoure, Gabriel, 172–74, 175, 176, 177, 180, 183
Bourde, Paul, 40, 47n48
Bourdieu, Pierre, 90, 198, 211–12, 299
Bourgogne, Lucien, 31, 45n20
Bouteflika, Abelazziz, 198
Braudel, Fernand, xxviii–xxix, 72–78, 80–82, 84, 85, 87–95
Brazil: Braudel and 78, 81; "integration" and, 307; Laurentie in, 226; Ottoman immigrants, 145, 150, 155, 160–61, 162–67
Brazza, Pierre Savorgnan de, 40

Brazzaville Conference (1944), 277, 280, 289; French Union and, 223, 232; Laurentie and, 223, 225, 228, 229, 236; Monnerville Commission and, 230; voting rights and, 326
Breton, André, 77, 84
Britain. *See* Great Britain
British Commonwealth, 224, 268, 307
Brittany, 174
Burke, Peter, 73, 81
Burundi, 227, 272n55

Cahier d'un retour au pays natal (Césaire), 80
Cahiers de la quinzaine, 37, 38, 40–41
Cairo, 182
Cambodia and Cambodians, 101–2
Cambon, Paul, 8
Cameroon, xxx, 9, 121–43, 225, 230–31, 248n38
Cameroun, Le (Labouret), 123
camps, summer. *See* summer camps
Camus, Albert, 76, 80, 87, 312
cannibalism, 51, 52–53, 56, 59–60, 62–66, 69–70n33
Cannibalism and the Colonial World (Hulme), 60
Capdecomme, Laurent, 206
Capdeville, Jean, 305
Capelle, Jean, 281–85, 292
Carde, Jules, 127
Carlier, Omar, 78, 89
Carlin, Murray, xix–xx
Catholic Church, 179. *See also* Maronite Church; nuns
Catholic missionaries, 168–69, 170, 173–74, 175, 180, 185. *See also* Jesuits; Lazarists; Spiritains

Catroux, Georges, 200
caves as redoubts, 86
Cédile, Jean, 335
Cellerier, Michel, 258, 271n31
censorship, 41, 149, 213, 248n41
centenary celebrations, 82–83, 84, 85
Center for Feminine Youth (Saigon), 106
Certeau, Michel de, 79, 83
Césaire, Aimé, 80, 308
Ce Soir en France (radio program), 237
CGT. *See* Confédération Générale du Travail (CGT)
Chad, 225, 226
Challaye, Félicien, xxvii, 26–29, 32, 34–48, 263
Chamberlain, Joseph, 36
Chapperon, Jean, 259, 266, 271n36
Chassigneux, Edmond, 34
Cheysson, Claude, 251
chiefs and headmen, 65, 330, 331–33, 338, 339, 343n28
Chiha, Michel, 172
Chinese-Cambodians, 102
Chirac, Jacques, xxv
Chkeiban, Adib, 179
choreographed spectacles. *See* mass spectacles
Christian missionaries, xxx; Cameroon, 9, 121–43; French Congo, 40; Lebanon, 172, 176, 185; Zimbabwe, 98. *See also* Catholic missionaries; Protestant missionaries
Christian morality, 106
Chronique (radio program), 236–38, 239–40, 241
Churchill, Winston, 222, 241
cinema. *See* films

citizenship, 7; Algerians and, 84, 200, 301, 303, 305, 316; Levantine expatriates and, 147–48; voting and, 230, 326
citizenship laws, 22n20
"civilizing mission," xv, 82–83, 135, 152, 260; Carde and, 127; Marchand and, 129, 132; repackaged as "mission to modernize," 299; as stock phrase, xi
civil rights, 278, 301
civil service "exceptional promotion." *See* "exceptional promotion"
Cixous, Hélène, 79–80
clothing. *See* dress
Cohen, William B., 221
Cold War, 4, 5, 17–18, 238, 263, 290, 291
collective bargaining, 287
Colombani, Don-Jean, 338
colonial administrators, former. *See* ex-colonial officers
colonial administrators' training schools, xxxiii, 220, 221, 228, 235, 258, 259
colonial exhibitions, 39, 77, 82–83, 84
"colonial humanism" (*colonisation altruiste*), 279, 293
Colonial Ministry. *See* Ministry of Colonies
Colonial Party, xxiii, 26, 40, 42, 151–52, 153, 154, 155
"color-blind" policies, 317
Comité Central Syrien, 154, 155, 156
Comité de Défense des Intérêts Françaises en Orient, 152
Comité de l'Asie Française, 151, 152

Comité de l'Orient, 151, 153, 154
Comité d'Union Togolaise (CUT), 331, 334
Comité Supérieur Consultatif de l'Instruction Publique, 281
Commissariat Générale du Plan, 285–86
Commission de Modernisation et d'Équipement aux Territoires d'Outre-Mer, 285
Communauté français, 22n20
Communism and Communists, 18, 32, 85, 335. *See also* anti-Communism; Vietminh
Communist Party of France. *See* Parti Communiste Français (PCF)
Compagnie des Messageries, 33
Confédération Générale du Travail (CGT), 286, 289, 290, 291
confession to crimes, 65–66, 69–70n33
conflict of interest, 249n49
Congo, French. *See* French Congo
Congo Free State, xii, 40, 41
Congregation of the Mission. *See* Lazarists
Conklin, Alice, 279
Connelly, Matthew, 299
Conquête d'Alger (Rousset), 83
conscience, 77
Constituent Assembly, 223, 234, 237, 277; elections, 230; Laurentie and, 238–44
Constitution of France, 22n20, 242, 243
Cooper, Frederick, xv, xviii, 124, 222, 246n15, 286, 287, 309, 326
Cornuel, Paul, 33, 34
corruption, xxxvii, 336
Côte d'Ivoire, 290, 329, 330, 332, 333, 334–35, 338; cases involving witchcraft, 51; Ferrandi and, 263; Prouteaux and, xxviii, 57
Coty, René, 203–4
Coubertin, Pierre de, 113–14
Cournarie, Pierre, 239
court cases: French West Africa, 51, 52–55, 59. *See also* slander cases; trials
courts, native. *See* native courts
criminal confession. *See* confession to crimes
criminal justice: French West Africa, 49–71
crimes, "ritual." *See* "ritual" crimes
crocodile attacks, 53
Croix-de-Feu, 13
Cros, Pierre, 258, 259, 265, 271n31
cruises, 46n33
Cuba, 31, 72
customary law, 56
CUT. *See* Comité d'Union Togolaise (CUT)
Cyprus, 154

Dah, Jonas, 123
Dahomey, 328, 334, 341n14
D'Argenlieu, Georges Thierry, xxiii
Da'uq, Umar, 181–82
Davesne, André, 129
De Caix, Robert, 152, 157–58, 159, 160
Declaration on Indochina (1945), xxxiii, 232, 233–34
decolonization, 4, 6, 13, 17, 80, 195, 212, 223, 224; inability to accept, 297n41; as "inevitable," 222; and reassignment of bureaucrats, 252; "successfulness" of, 275–76
De Coppet, Marcel, 50–51

De Coubertin, Pierre. *See* Coubertin, Pierre de
Decoux, Jean, xxix, 11, 97, 100, 101–2, 104, 112; discipline and, 110; mass spectacles and, 107, 114; Sr. Durand and, 106
Defferre, Gaston, 244, 253, 336
De Gaulle, Charles, 222, 242; Algeria and, 210; Bokassa and, 263; Brazzaville Conference and, 280; "events of May" (1958), 299; French Equatorial Africa and, 277; French West Africa and, 337; Laurentie and, 220, 225, 228, 229, 236–37, 243, 244, 247n33; resignation of, 229
De la Blache, Paul Vidal. *See* Vidal de la Blache, Paul
De la Décolonisation à la révolution culturelle (Taleb-Ibrahimi), 197
Delafosse, Maurice, 51
Delavignette, Robert, 228, 260–61, 278, 280, 295n15
demonstrations, protests, etc., 168, 204
Deniau, Jean François, 259
Déracinement, Le (Bourdieu and Sayad), 299
De Saint-Mart, Pierre, 228
development, economic. *See* economic development
development funds and grants, xxxiii–xxxv, 7, 17, 251–74
Dewald, Jonathan, 77
Dia, Mamadou, 333
dialects: Arabic, 202, 206, 207, 208–10, 213
Dimier, Véronique, 221
Diola people, 61, 65
Diori, Hamani, 330, 338

discipline, 97, 99, 100, 108–9, 110, 113
Discourse on Colonialism (Césaire), 308
"discrimination" (word), 305
disease, xiii, xiv, 98, 103
dissent, 149
Djermakoye, Issofoye, 337, 338
doctors. *See* physicians
Doumer, Paul, 36, 46n34
Doumergue, Gaston, 175
dragoman system, 159–63, 166n48
dress, 19n4, 108–9, 136. *See also* uniforms
Dreyfus Affair, 26, 28, 29, 37, 38, 85
Duala language, 126, 134
Duala people, 123, 126, 133
Du Bois, W. E. B., 308
Ducoroy, Maurice, xxix, 97, 100, 104, 105, 109, 110; on discipline, 108–9, 113; mass spectacles and, 107; racial classification by, 102–3, 110
Dumoutier, E., 36
Durand, Sister, 97, 100, 105–6
Durieux, J., 273
Durkheim, Émile, 30, 31, 51, 97

Éboué, Félix, 225–26, 228, 231, 246n20
EC. *See* European Community (EC)
École française d'Extrême-Orient, 39, 45n19
École nationale de la France d'Outre-Mer (ENFOM) (École Coloniale), xxxiii, 220, 228, 235, 258, 259; historiography and, 221
École Normale Supérieure, 27, 28, 29, 31, 41, 43n6, 45n19

Index

École Supérieure d'Éducation Physique de l'Indochine (ESEPIC), 108, 111
École Supérieure des Arts Ménagers, 106
École Supérieure des Cadres de la Jeunesse Féminine d'Indochine (ESCJFIC), 105, 106
École Supérieure des Monitrices d'Indochine (ESMIC), 105
École William Ponty, 282
écoles ménagères, 106, 129
economic development, 123, 127, 279, 285, 288, 302. *See also* development funds and grants
Écriture de l'histoire, L' (Certeau), 79
Ecstasies (Ginzburg), 58
Eddé, Émile, 168, 171, 176
EDF. *See* European Development Fund (EDF)
education and education policy, xxx, 121; Algeria, 311; bibliography, xlv; Cameroon, 121–43; Egypt and Palestine, 174; FIDES investment statistics, 296n278; French West Africa, 281–85; Lebanon, 168–93. *See also* girls' education and training; higher education; physical education; religious education; schools
EEC. *See* European Economic Community (EEC)
Egypt, 33, 98, 149, 174, 222, 302; Algeria and, xxxii, 210; Challaye in, 35; Lebanese school closures and, 168; Légion d'Orient in, 154; Muslim education in, 182
elections, 230, 239; French West Africa, xxxvi–xxxvii, 324–45; manipulation of results, 7, 325, 327–31, 333–39; quota systems and, 316
electoral college systems, 230, 306, 316, 325
ENFOM. *See* École nationale de la France d'Outre-Mer (ENFOM)
enfranchisement. *See* voting and voting rights
English language, xxxii, 29, 186, 194
environment: humans and, 73
epidemiology, 16–17
ESCJFIC. *See* École Supérieure des Cadres de la Jeunesse Féminine d'Indochine (ESCJFIC)
ESEPIC. *See* École Supérieure d'Éducation Physique de l'Indochine (ESEPIC),
ESMIC. *See* École Supérieure des Monitrices d'Indochine (ESMIC)
Esquer, Gabriel, 82
ethnography, xxii, 39, 51, 55–56
ethnologists, 310–11, 321n24
Étranger, L' (Camus), 76
eugenics, xv, 105
European Commission: Directorate General VIII, 251–74
European Community (EC), 254, 259
European Development Fund (EDF), 255, 256–59, 263, 264
European Development Fund for Overseas Territories, 253–54, 254–55
European Economic Community (EEC), xxxiii–xxxv, 17, 251, 253, 255, 258, 259, 263, 264, 265
Europeans and Indigenous Americans: first contact, 79

European Union, 7
Evans-Pritchard, Edward, 50, 58
Ewondo language, 134
"exceptional promotion," 313–17
ex-colonial officers, 251–74
exhibitions, colonial. *See* colonial exhibitions
expatriate remittances. *See* remittances (by expatriates)
expatriates, Levantine, xxx–xxxi, 144–67
Exposition coloniale internationale (Paris, 1931) 77, 82–83, 84

Fall, Omar Bayo, 333
Fanon, Frantz, 16
farming. *See* agriculture
Fashoda Incident, 17, 33
Fatat, al-. *See* Al-Fatat
Faure, Edgar, 309
Faure, Marcel, 290
Fay, Pierre Émile, 258, 271n30
FCNL. *See* French Committee for National Liberation (FCNL)
Febvre, Lucien, 74, 77, 82
federalism, 308, 309, 310
FERDES. *See* Fonds d'Équipement Rural pour l'Développement Économique et Social (FERDES)
Ferrandi, Jacques, 255–59, 260, 261–68, 270n17
FIDES. *See* Fonds d'Investissement pour le Développement Économique et Social (FIDES)
fieldwork, anthropological, 55, 66, 310, 321n24
films, xxiii, xxiv, 8, 82
Firestone, Ya'akov, 312, 316
First Arab Congress. *See* Arab Congress of 1913

FLN. *See* Front de Libération Nationale FLN
FMAS. *See* "Muslim French citizens from Algeria" (FMAS)
Foncin, Pierre, 8
Fonctions mentales dans les sociétés inférieures, Les (Lévy-Bruhl), 51
Fonds d'Équipement Rural pour l'Développement Économique et Social (FERDES), 286
Fonds d'Investissement pour le Développement Économique et Social (FIDES), xxxv, 252, 255, 256, 285, 286, 288, 291
Fonds Européen de Développpment pour l'Outre-Mer. *See* European Development Fund for Overseas Territories
Fontainebleau peace conference (1946), 243
forced labor, 132
Foreign Ministry. *See* Ministry of Foreign Affairs
former colonial officers. *See* ex-colonial officers
Forster, E. M., 76
Foucault, Michel, 97–98, 113
Fourneau, Lucien, 125–26, 127
Framework Law of 1956, 224, 244, 253
France combattante, 289
La France et l'Agérie (Mélia), 84
Franco-Vietnam War, xxxii–xxxiii, 222
French-Algerian war. *See* Algerian War of Independence
French-British relations, 17, 150, 153–56
French Cameroon. *See* Cameroon
French Committee for National Liberation (FCNL), 225, 228, 232

French Congo, 40, 41, 47n39, 225
French Equatorial Africa (FEA), 225, 230–31, 277, 324. *See also* Cameroon; Chad; French Congo; Gabon
French-German relations, 6–7, 9, 43n4, 96, 99, 132–33, 205–6, 280; economic development and, 256, 263
French Guinea, 52, 53, 225, 265, 332, 337
French Indochina. *See* Indochina
French-Indochina War. *See* Franco-Vietnam War
French Information Service. *See* Service de Renseignements
French language, 8–9, 174, 285; Algeria, xxxi, 198, 200; Cameroon, xxx, 122, 124, 126–48; Lebanon, 178, 186
French Left, 14, 99–100, 176. *See also* Parti Communiste Français PCF
French Revolution, 76, 196–97
French Right, 13, 100, 241
French Sudan. *See* Soudan
French Union, 22n20, 260, 281, 290, 293; Cappelle and, 282, 285; *Chronique* and, 237; Commission de Modernisation and, 285; Giacobbi on, 233–34; Guinea and, 337; integrationism and, 310; Laurentie and, 221, 223–24, 226, 227, 232, 234, 236, 238, 240–43; models for, 307; Monnerville Commission and, 230, 234; Niger and, 337; PCF and, 289
French West Africa (FWA), xxv, xxxv, 275–97; economic development and, 256, 258, 259, 285, 288; education policy, 281–85; elections, xxxvi–xxxvii, 324–45; in fiction, 328; labor policy, 286–88; Monnerville Report and, 230–31; witchcraft and, 49–71. *See also* Côte d'Ivoire; Dahomey; French Guinea; Mauritania; Niger; Senegal; Soudan; Upper Volta
Front de Libération Nationale (FLN), 6, 212, 222, 303; language policy and, xxxii, 195, 196, 197, 198, 207
Front National, 13
Front Popular. *See* Popular Front

Gabon, 272n55
Gafaiti, Hafid, 199, 213
Gallagher, John: *Africa and the Victorians*, 221
Gallicization, 121, 124–28, 136, 298
Gallieni, Joseph, 31–32
Gambetta, Léon, 136
Garnier, Charles-Marie, 31, 45n20
Gaud and Toqué trial, 40, 41, 48n49
Gautier, Émile-Félix, 82, 85, 87
gender, 15–16, 101
general strikes, 287, 289
Gentil, Émile, 41
geography, 73, 75–76, 87, 88
Germany, xxx, 6; Cameroon and, 121, 125; Challaye and, 28; EEC and, 252–53, 255. *See also* French-German relations; Nazis and Nazism; West Germany
Ghanem, Shukri, 151, 153
Ghomsi, Emmanuel, 123
Giacobbi, Paul, 229, 230–31, 233–34, 238
Gibbon, Edward, 73
Ginzburg, Carlo, 58

359

Girardet, Raoul, 83, 110
girls' education and training, 105–6, 108, 129, 141
Gobineau, Arthur, xiv
Gouraud, Henri, 156, 157, 173
Grandsimon, J., 207
grants for development. *See* development funds and grants
Great Britain, 222, 243, 245–46n14; Caribbean colonies, 12; EEC and, 268; imperialism of, 289; India and, 113, 311; Kenya and, 9; Pakistan and, 302; Swaziland and, 69n28; Togo and, 331; travel fellowships and, 26, 30, 31, 33, 36; Uganda and, xix–xx. *See also* British Commonwealth; French-British relations
Greater Syria (Ottoman province), 144, 145, 151, 152, 153
Grégoire, Henri, 197
Groupes d'actions républicaines, 289
Groupes d'études communistes, 289
Grunitzky, Nicolas, 335–36, 338
Gsell, Stéphane, 87, 88
Guèye, Lamine, 242, 330. *See also* Loi Lamine Guèye
Guinea, French. *See* French Guinea
gymnastics, 99, 100, 110

Hadi, Abd al-, 153
Hadj, Messali. *See* Messali Hadj
Hadj-Sad, Mohammed, 207
Hanna, Nakkoul, 160
Hardy, Georges, 129
Hashimoto, Kōhei, 146–47
Hauser, Henri, 82, 86–88
Haut comité méditerranéen, 85
Haydar, Rustum, 153
headmen. *See* chiefs and headmen

head scarves: banning of, 19n4, 136
Hearn, Lafcadio, 47n38
Hébert, Georges, 105
Hendus, Heinrich, 256
Herriot, Édouard, 130, 175, 242
higher education, 284–85, 317
hiring quotas. *See* "exceptional promotion"
Histoire de l'Afrique du Nord (Julien), 78, 84, 85, 86–87, 88–89
Histoire et destin (Roupnel), 76–77
historical time. *See* time, historical
historiography, xvi–xvii, 3–4, 16, 72–95, 123, 222–23, 224, 326; British, 221
Ho Chi Minh, 85, 220, 234, 244–45n3
Hodeir, Catherine, 255
Holland. *See* Netherlands
homemaking schools. *See* écoles ménagères
hommes-panthères. *See* "leopard men" (*hommes-panthères*)
honeycomb model (transnational relations), xviii–xix
Hong Kong, 194
Houphouët-Boigny, Félix, 255, 285, 289, 293, 330, 338
House, Jim, 207
housekeeping schools. *See* écoles ménagères
Hulme, Peter, 60
humanitarianism, 17
Humanité, L', 51
Husri, Sati al-, 178–79

immigration and emigration, xxx, 4, 5, 6; French language and, 8–9. *See also* expatriates, Levantine
indenture, 12

Index

India, 31, 33, 35, 311; in fiction, 76; polo in, 113
Indigenous Americans, 79, 309
Indochina, xxix, xxxiii, xxxiv, 11; Laurentie and, 221, 226, 237, 240, 242; March 1946 Accords, 237, 240, 242; Monnerville Commission and, 230; proposed cruises in, 46n33; sports and physical education in, 96–118; travel fellowships and, 33, 35, 36, 37, 38, 39. *See also* Cambodia and Cambodians; Laos and Laotians; Vietnam
Indochina Advanced School for Feminine Youth Cadres. *See* École Supérieure des Cadres de la Jeunesse Féminine d'Indochine (ESCJFIC)
Indochina Advanced School of Female Instructors. *See* École Supérieure des Monitrices d'Indochine (ESMIC)
Indochina Advanced School of Physical Education. *See* École Supérieure d'Éducation Physique de l'Indochine (ESEPIC)
Indochine, 101, 104
inequality, xxv, 300, 301–2; in economic aid, 272–73n55; in pay, 312
Inspection du travail, xxxv, 286–88, 292
inspectors and inspections, xxix, 104, 266–67, 285
Institut ethnographique international de Paris, 55
Institut français d'anthropologie, 51
"integrationism," xxxvi, 298–300, 305–18

intellectuals, xxvii, 12–13, 26–48; Algeria and, 80
intelligence gathering, 144–51, 155–67
interpreters. *See* translators and translation
Iraq, 154, 168
Islam, 56, 62, 81, 88, 182. *See also* anti-Islamism; Muslims; Shiite Islam; Sunni Islam
Islamic law. *See* Qur'anic law
Islamization, 195, 199, 212
Israel, 84
Ivory Coast. *See* Côte d'Ivoire

Jabal Druze, 145
Jalabert, Louis, 175, 176
James, C. L. R., 80
Japan, 11, 34–35, 37, 96, 112, 114, 234
Jaurès, Jean, 51
Java, 33, 35, 36, 37
Jesuits, xxxi, 9, 173, 174, 175–76, 179, 180, 185, 187
Jews, 19n4, 84, 301
Joan of Arc Day, 107
Jola people. *See* Diola people
Joll, James, xvii, xli(n27)
Joseph, Richard, 123
Jouplain, M.: *La Question du Liban*, 152
Julien, Charles-André, xxviii, 78, 82–83, 84, 85–90

Kahn, Albert, 29, 30, 43–44n10
Kaolack, Senegal, 333
Kenya, 9
Khamla. *See* Princess Khamla
Khuri, Bishara al-, 168, 171–72, 176, 183
King Leopold II. *See* Leopold II

361

King Philip II. *See* Philip II
Konaté, Mamadou, 330
Koran. *See* Qur'an
Koranic Civil Status (Algeria). *See* Qur'anic Civil Status (Algeria)
Koranic law. *See* Qur'anic law
Kourouma, Ahmadou, 327–28, 341n14

labor, xvi, 12, 131, 286–88, 289; hiring quotas, 313–16; stereotypes and, 101, 102. *See also* forced labor; slavery
Labor Inspectorate. *See* Inspection du travail
Labouret, Henri, 123
Lacoste, Robert, 206–7
Lambert, Christian, 329
Lamine Guèye Law. *See* Loi Lamine Guèye
land grants, 133
language dialects. *See* dialects
language policy, 9; Algeria, xxxi–xxxii, 194–216, 312; Cameroon, xxx, 9, 121–43
language translation. *See* translators and translation
Laos and Laotians, 101, 102, 107, 108, 110
Laoust, Henri, 208–9
Latin America, xxx, xxxvi, 7, 307. *See also* Argentina; Brazil; Cuba; Mexico
Latrille, André, 290, 329, 330
Laurent, Jean Petit, 271n33
Laurentie, Henri, xxxii–xxxiii, 219–50
Lausanne, Treaty of. *See* Treaty of Lausanne
Lavisse, Ernest, 31–32, 38, 39

Lazarists, 174, 185
law, customary. *See* customary law
law, Qur'anic. *See* Qur'anic law
laws, local. *See* "local laws"
League of Nations, xvii; Cameroon and, 121, 128, 133, 134, 225; Duala people and, 126, 133; Levant and, 145, 148, 157
Lebanese: in Latin America, xxx, 144–67
Lebanon, xxxi, xlv(n60), 152–53, 168–93
Le Bon, Gustave, xiv
Leenhardt, Maurice, 51
legal cases. *See* court cases
Légion d'Orient, 154–55
Legion of Honor, 106
Lemaignen, Robert, 255, 256, 260, 269–70n16
Léonard, Roger, 302
"leopard men" (*hommes-panthères*), 49, 62, 68n12, 70n39
Leopold II, xii
Le Roy, Alexandre, 125
Le Sueur, James, 299
Le Tourneau, R., 207
Levantine expatriates. *See* expatriates, Levantine
Lévi-Strauss, Claude, 75, 78
Lévy-Bruhl, Lucien, xxviii, 50–54, 60, 63–64, 66, 67
Lewis, Bernard, 166n48
Lewis, James, 222–23
Lewis, Mary, xvii
Liard, Louis, 29, 34, 38, 39
Ligue de l'enseignement libre, 184–85
Ligue des Droits de l'Homme, 27, 41, 42, 47n39, 48n51, 85
Ligue française pour la défense des indigènes, 41

Ligue française pour la défense des indigènes dans le bassin du Congo, 41
Lister, Marjorie, 263
literacy, 324
Livre noir du colonialisme, Un (Challaye), 27, 37
"local laws," 301
Loi Cadre, xxxvi, 22n20
Loi Lamine Guèye, 22n20
Lomé Convention, xxxiv, 251, 253, 262, 268
longue durée (Braudel concept), 73, 74, 75–76, 89
Louveau, Edmond, 329
Lozeray, Henri, 241

MacLean, Nancy, 318
MacMaster, Neil, 207
Madagascar (Malagasy), 220, 221, 226, 241
Magie Noir (Morand), 49
Makerere University, xix–xx
Malagasy. *See* Madagascar (Malagasy)
Malessard, Father, 128, 130
Malley, Robert, 199
mandarins, 111
Manifesto of the Algerian People, 200, 313
Mann, Greg, xx
Maqasid Islamic Charitable Association, 176, 181–83
Marchand, Theodore Paul, 128–30, 131–34
marches, 107, 113
Mardam Bey, Jamil, 155
Maronite Church, xxxi, 9, 168, 169, 171–72, 173, 176–80, 183–87
Marseilles, 203
Marseilles exhibition (1906), 39

Marshall, D. Bruce, 297n41
Marun, Father, 177, 179, 184, 185
Mashnuq, Abdallah, 184
Massignon, Louis, 84, 195, 201–5, 207, 210, 213, 321n24
mass spectacles, 107–8, 113
Mauritania, 231
Mauritius, 56
Mauss, Marcel, 41, 51, 321n24
medicine, 16, 103. *See also* physicians
The Mediterranean and the Mediterranean World in the Age of Philip II (Braudel), 72–74, 75, 76–77, 78, 81–82, 86, 88, 90
Mediterranean Sea, 73–74, 77, 81–82
Mélia, Jean, 84–85
Mendés France, Pierre, 309
Mentalité primitive, La (Lévy-Bruhl), 51–52
Messali Hadj, 304
Messmer, Pierre, 228, 245n5
Métin, Albert, 33, 41
Mexico, 153, 307, 309
Mexico, An Indian Land (Soustelle), 309
Michelet, Jules, 76
militarism, 4, 8, 99, 154–55, 206
military forces. *See* armed forces
Mille, Pierre, 40, 41
Millerand, Alexandre, 150
minimum wage, 312
Ministry for North Africa (proposed), 233
Ministry for Overseas France, 278, 281, 288, 292, 326, 336; African elections and, 329; Capelle and, 282; FIDES and, 285–86; Laurentie and, 221, 226; PCF and, 290

Ministry of Colonies, xxii, 252, 277, 278, 283; Delavignette and, 228; Ferrandi and, 256, 259; Laurentie and, 219, 225, 228–29, 232, 233; propaganda of, 42; renamed Ministry for Overseas France, 221, 278

Ministry of Culture, 317

Ministry of Education, 175, 281, 282–83, 292

Ministry of Foreign Affairs, 146, 156, 157–59, 170, 175, 176, 233, 234

Ministry of the Interior, 233

missionaries, Christian. *See* Christian missionaries

mission civilisatrice. *See* "civilizing mission"

Mission laïque française, 173, 175, 180

Mitchell, Timothy, 98

Mitterrand, François, xxxvi, 275, 302, 303, 306, 311

Mizrahi, Jean-David, 145

"modernity" and "modernization" (concepts), 97, 299–300

Mohammed and Charlemagne (Pirenne), 82

Mollet, Guy, 203, 314

Monnerville, Gaston, 230, 326

Monnerville Commission, 231–32, 233, 234, 239, 248–49n48, 326

Monteil, Vincent-Mansûr, 310, 311, 321n24

morality, Christian. *See* Christian morality

Morand, Paul, 49

Morocco, 82, 202, 233, 234, 240, 311

Mortimer, Edward, 328

Mosry, Magali, 85

Mossi people, 330

Mount Lebanon (Ottoman province), 144, 152, 172

Moutet, Marius, xxxiii, 229, 242, 280, 295n15, 330; Barthes and, 281, 295n16; Delavignette and, 228; Laurentie and, 240, 241; replacement of, 284

Mouvement Républicain Populaire MRP, 241

Mubarak, Ignatius, 176, 185, 185

murder, 56; witchcraft and, 57–58, 61–63, 66, 68n12, 70n37–38

murder trials, 40, 41, 48n49

Mus, Paul, xi

"Muslim French citizens from Algeria" (FMAs), 299, 302–6, 310, 312; "exceptional promotion" and, 313–17; guaranteed electoral seats for, 316

Muslims: Arabic language and, 200, 202, 210–11; assimilation, 136; censorship by, 213; education and, 9, 168, 172–87; French language and, 9; Lebanon, 9, 168, 169, 172–87; Niger, 338. *See also* youth groups, Muslim

Naccache, Georges, 179

Nachabé, Hicham, 183

Najjada, 184, 185

names and naming, 180–81

National Front. *See* Front National

nationalism, 13, 99–100, 308; Arab, 171, 173, 174, 178, 184; language and, 196, 197; Lebanese, 171, 185; Syrian, 184

nation-state model, 307, 308

Native Americans. *See* Indigenous Americans

364

native courts, 50, 51, 56, 59, 62, 301
naturalization: of Algerians, 84; of Syrians and Lebanese, 147–48
Nazis and Nazism, 305, 308
Netherlands, 36, 252–53, 255
New Zealand, 31, 35
Nietzsche, Friedrich, 74, 75
Niger, 329, 330, 334, 336, 337–38
Noguéres, M., 237
nongovernmental organizations (NGOs), 17
North African Star, 304
Nouschi, André, 85, 87
Nujaym, Bulus, 152–53
nuns, 105, 106

Oceania, xxi
OECD. *See* Organisation for Economic Co-operation and Development (OECD)
"official mind," xlvi(n63)
Olympio, Sylvanus, 335–36, 338
orchestrated spectacles. *See* mass spectacles
Organic Statute of Algeria (1947), 200, 306, 310, 311, 312
Organisation for Economic Co-operation and Development (OECD), 257
Orientalism, 79
Other (concept), xii, 79, 83
Ottoman Empire, 144, 147, 151, 169, 172
Ourabah, Abdelmajid, 309
Overseas Reform Act. *See* Loi Cadre

pacifists, 27
Pakistan, 302
Palestine, 154, 155, 174
Palewski, Gaston, 232

pan-Arabism, xxxii, 149, 153, 181, 184, 210, 213
parades, 107, 113, 114, 264
Paris Colonial Exposition (1931). *See* Exposition coloniale internationale (Paris, 1931)
Paris Evangelical Missionary Society, 124, 126
Parti Colonial. *See* Colonial Party
Parti Communiste Français (PCF), 14, 223, 241–42, 329; Algeria and, 14, 304–5; Challaye and, 27; French West Africa and, 276, 288–91, 330, 336; *L'humanité* and, 51
Parti Démocratique de la Côte d'Ivoire (PDCI), 330, 332
Parti Progressiste du Niger (PPN), 330
Parti Social Français, 13
Parti Socialiste. *See* Socialist Party of France
Parti Togolais du Progrès (PTP), 335–36
Passage to India (Forster), 76
paternalism, xxv–xxvi, xxxiv, 221, 260–61
PCF. *See* Parti Communiste Français (PCF)
PDCI. *See* Parti Démocratique de la Côte d'Ivoire (PDCI)
Péguy, Charles, 27, 37, 38, 40, 43n6
Perrot, Georges, 27, 30–31
Peterson, Alan, 103
Peyrouton, Marcel, 200
Philip II, 73, 89
Philippines, 31
physical education: Indochina, 96–118
physicians, 16–17, 98
pieds-noirs, 204, 205

365

Pierre de Coubertin. *See* Coubertin, Pierre de
Pignon, Léon, 226, 228
Pirenne, Henri, 77, 82–83
Pleven, René, 225, 227, 229, 247n34
Poincaré, Raymond, 175
poisoning, 51, 58, 66, 70n37
Poivre, Pierre, 56
police, xxv, xxx, 149, 207, 335
polo, 113
Pontecorvo, Gillo, 8
Popular Front, 99, 109, 177, 198, 228, 229, 279, 280, 287
popular opinion. *See* public opinion
Popular Republican Movement. *See* Mouvement Républicain Populaire MRP
Portuguese language, xxxii, 159
PPN. *See* Parti Progressiste du Niger (PPN)
Pradel, Paule, 81
Presbyterians, 125, 126–27, 128, 130
"primitive mentality," 51–52, 63
Princess Khamla, 108
prisons, 98
private schools, 126, 127, 129, 176, 184
propaganda, 4, 30, 37–38, 42, 101, 235, 236; "integrationism" as, 299; Levant emigrants and, 145, 155, 157–58, 159; Togo, 335
Protestant missionaries, xxx, 124–25, 126, 127, 128, 129, 132, 136
protests, demonstrations, etc. *See* demonstrations, protests, etc.
Prouteaux, Marcel, xxviii, 50, 57–58, 60–62, 63, 66
Provence, Michael, 145

psychiatry, 16
"La psychology génétique et ethnique" (Challaye), 39–40
PTP. *See* Parti Togolais du Progrés (PTP)
Puaux, Gabriel, 173, 181, 183
public opinion, xxiii
punishment, 174

Quai d'Orsay. *See* Ministry of Foreign Affairs
Question du Liban, La (Jouplain), 152–53
Quilici, François, 309
quota systems, 313–17, 318
Qur'an, 182
Qur'anic Civil Status (Algeria), 301, 306, 312, 314–15
Qur'anic law, 205, 301

race and race theory, xv, 103, 317
racism, 13, 32, 98, 239, 308, 317, 339; Algeria, 303–5; of Lucciardi, 160. *See also* state racism
"racism" (word), 305
racist stereotypes. *See* stereotypes
radio programs, 236–38, 239–40, 241
Ranke, Leopold von, 73
Raquez, Alfred, 39
Rassemblement Démocratique Africain (RDA), 289, 290, 291, 329–30, 332, 333, 334
religious education, xxx, 178
remittances (by expatriates), 156, 158–59
repression, 79, 290, 291, 302, 303, 309
resistance to colonialism, xx, 4, 13; French language and, 9; historiography and, 123

Revue Africaine, 81, 87
Revue de Paris, 31, 37, 47n38
Revue du Moi, 41
Revue générale des sciences pures et appliqués, 46n33
Revue historique, 85
Revue indochinoise, 39
"ritual" crimes, 49, 51, 52, 56, 57, 62, 64
Rivet, Paul, 51, 321n24
Robert-Houdin, Jean-Eugéne, xxii–xxiv
Roberts, Hugh, 199
Robinson, Kenneth, xxxvii, 327
Robinson, Ronald: *Africa and the Victorians*, 221
Rochereau, Henri, 259
Roman Catholic Church. *See* Catholic Church
Roman Empire, 73, 84, 88
Rome, Treaty of. *See* Treaty of Rome
Rosenstock-Huessy, Eugen, 75
Roupnel, Gaston, 74, 76–77, 78
Rousset, Camille, 83
Roustan, Désiré, 45n19
Ruanda-Urundi (Rwanda), 226–27
Ruedy, John, 200–201
Rue Oudinot. *See* Ministry for Overseas France; Ministry of Colonies
running races, 109–10, 111
Russia, 35, 37

Saab, Chekri Abi, 161
"Sabbath" (word), 69n22
Said, Edward, 84
Saint Joseph University (Beirut), 175, 183
Saint-Mart, Pierre de. *See* De Saint-Mart, Pierre
Salmon, Guy, 271n33

Samne, Georges, 151
Sanogo, Sékou, 334–35, 338
San Remo conference (1920), 156, 158–59
Sarkozy, Nicolas, xxvi
Sartre, Jean-Paul, 80, 87
Saudi Arabia, 302
Sawaba Party, 336, 337, 338
Sayad, Abdelmalek, 299
Schachter-Morgenthau, Ruth, 328
Schmidt, Elizabeth, 342n15
schools: Algeria, 198; Cameroon, 126, 127, 129, 132, 134; French West Africa, 282; Indochina, 39, 45n19, 105, 106, 108, 111; Lebanon, 168, 173, 175, 176, 179, 180–81, 184, 185, 186; punishment in, 174; Senegal, 282; Syria, 173, 175, 177, 183. *See also* colonial administrators' training schools; écoles ménagères; private schools
secret societies, xxviii, 51, 56, 57, 61
Section Française de l'International Ouvrière (SFIO), 333
Sékou Touré, Ahmed, 337
Senegal, xxv–xxvi, 59, 65, 231, 239, 242, 330, 333; Capelle in, 281; Dakar general strike of 1946, 289; Ferrandi in, 256, 259; FIDES and, 285; schools, 282; voting in, 325
Senghor, Léopold Sédar, 224, 248n41, 253, 293, 330; on assimilation, 307; BDS and, 333; Capelle and, 285; Ferrandi and, 263; Laurentie and, 220, 238–39, 242; proposed education bill of, 283–84
Service de Renseignements, 166n47
servicemen, West Africa. *See* soldiers, West African

Servier, Jean, 310, 321n24
Sèvres, Treaty of. *See* Treaty of Sèvres
sexuality: colonial officials and, xvi
SFIO. *See* Section Française de l'Internationale Ouvrière (SFIO)
Shehadé, Georges, 172
Shiite Islam, 171, 172
shorts (clothing), 108–9
Sibeud, Emmanuelle, 55–56
Sicking, Louis, xxxiv
Siegfried, André, 76
Sikhs, 19n4
Sixas Affair. *See* Affaire des Sixas
slander cases, 132
slavery, 12, 84
snake bites, 53–54
Socialist Party of France, 85, 241
Socialists, 26, 28, 99, 229
Société autour du monde, 30
societies, secret. *See* secret societies
Society of Jesus. *See* Jesuits
soldiers, West African, xxv, 324
sorcery. *See* witchcraft
Soudan, 329, 330, 334
Soustelle, Jacques, xxxvi, 203, 206, 229, 298, 309–14, 321n24
South Africa, Union of. *See* Union of South Africa
Southeast Asia. *See* Indochina
Southern Rhodesia, 246n14
Souvenirs sur la colonisation (Challaye), 38
Soviet Union, 247n33, 290, 307, 329
Spain, 81
Spanish language, 159, 161
Specialized Administrative Services (SAS), 311
spectacles (displays). *See* mass spectacles

Spiritains, xxx, 9, 121–22, 124–43
sports: Indochina, 96–118
stadium events, 107–8, 109
Stanard, Matthew, xxiv
state racism, 31, 318
stereotypes, xxiv, xxviii, 101–3, 110, 112
Stoler, Ann, xii, xiii, 124
strikes, 287, 289
structuralism, 74, 75, 89
subsidies, educational, 126, 129, 174, 175, 177–78, 183
Sudan, 58
Sudan, French. *See* Soudan
suffrage. *See* voting and voting rights
suicide, 65
Sulh, Riad al-, 172, 183
summer camps, 104
Sunni Islam, 170, 171, 172, 181, 182
Surnaturel et nature dans le mentalité primitive, Le (Lévy-Bruhl), 52
surveillance, 145, 155, 157, 207
Swaziland, 69n28
swimming, 110
Sykes-Picot agreement, 154
Syria, 145, 155–56, 171, 177, 178–79; Laurentie and, 225; Lebanese school closures and, 168; schools, 173, 175, 177, 183
Syrians: in Latin America, xxx, 144–67; Légion d'Orient and, 154–55

Tahaluf Lubman/Alliance Libanaise, 161
Taleb-Ibrahimi, Ahmed, 195, 196, 197
Tamazight language, 196, 207
Tauber, Eliezer, 151
Taylorism, 105

taxation, 132, 336
Tchad. *See* Chad
Tebib, Abdallan, 316
Temps, Le, 40, 41
Temps de l'histoire, Le (Ariès), 74
Thailand, 110
Thomas, Albert, 41
Thomas, Keith, 70–71n41
Thomas, Martin, 145, 275
Thomas Cook (travel agency), 33
Thompson, Elizabeth, 176
Tillion, Germaine, 195, 203, 208, 210–11, 310, 311, 321n24
time, historical, 72–73. *See also longue durée* (Braudel concept)
Tixier, Adrien, 248–49n48
tobacco industry, 177
Toby, Jean, 329
Togo, 328, 330–31, 334, 335–36, 338
Toqué, Georges, trial of. *See* Gaud and Toqué trial
torture, 16, 311
Tour de France, 109, 111
Tour d'Indochine, 109, 111
tourism, xxiii, xxiv, 46n33
trade unions. *See* unions
"traditional" societies, 97, 278, 280, 288, 290, 294
translators and translation, 159–61
travel agencies, 33
travel fellowships, 27, 29–37, 43–44n10
Treaty of Friendship with Moscow, 247n33
Treaty of Lausanne, 146–47, 148
Treaty of Rome, xxxiv, 251, 252, 253, 254, 261, 265
Treaty of Sèvres, 146–47
trials, 61, 65. *See also* murder trials

Triste sort des indigènes musulmans d'Algérie, Le (Mélia), 85
Tristes Tropiques (Lévi-Strauss), 75
"tropical neurasthenia," xiv
Trumball, George, xxii
Tunisia, 34, 210, 233, 234
Turkey, 147, 148
Turkish Empire. *See* Ottoman Empire

Uganda, xix–xx
"underdevelopment," 262
uniforms, 108, 113
Union française. *See* French Union
Union of South Africa, 31, 34
unions, 286, 287
Union Sacrée, 124, 130
Union soudanaise, 330
United Kingdom. *See* Great Britain
United Nations, 135, 222, 226, 263, 302, 331
United Nations Relief and Rehabilitation Administration (UNRRA), 226
United States, 8, 31; affirmative action in, 318; discrimination in, 305; imperialism of, 289; "integration" and, 306; Laurentie retirement in, 226; as model for French Union, 307; Ottoman immigrants, 144, 153; travel fellowships and, 30, 35. *See also* Americans in Cameroon
Université Saint-Joseph de Beyrouth. *See* Saint Joseph University (Beirut)
University of Algiers, xxix, 85, 204, 210
University of Dakar, 284–85
University of Laval, 28

University of London, 43n10
Upper Volta, 330, 332, 334
USSR. *See* Soviet Union

veils: banning of, 136
Vespucci, Amerigo, 79
veterans, 324
Vichy empire: Africa and, 277; Indochina and, xxix, 96–118
Vidal de la Blache, Paul, 30, 76
Vietminh, 112, 114, 234
Vietnam, xxi, xxiii, xxix, 5, 98; athletics in, 109, 110, 111; Fontainbleau peace conference and, 243; training of girls in, 105–6. *See also* Franco-Vietnam War
Vietnamese: stereotypes of, 102–3, 110
violence, 4, 8, 12, 13–14; against election candidates, 334; Challaye on, 46n35. *See also* repression; torture
Viollette, Maurice, 21n17, 84
virility, 101, 105, 110
Vogt, F. X., 129, 130–33, 134
Voice of Algeria, 238
voting and voting rights, 243, 326; Algeria, 21n17, 306; French West Africa, 293, 324, 325; Monnerville Commission and, 230–31

Wade, Abdoulaye, xxv
wage, minimum. *See* minimum wage
wars. *See* Algerian War of Independence; Franco-Vietnam War; World War I; World War II
Weber, Max, 97
Weinstein, Brian, 225–26
West Africa, French. *See* French West Africa (FWA)

West African soldiers. *See* soldiers, West African
West Germany, 256
Weil, Simone, 75
Weulersse, Jacques, 32, 45n19
"white man's burden," xv, 35, 102
White Mythologies (Young), 72, 80
Wilder, Gary, 308
Wilt, Charles, 335
Winterbottom, Thomas, 60
witchcraft, xxvii–xxviii, 49–71
women: boarding schools and, 132; dress, 19n4, 108–9, 136; historiography, 15–16; roles, 106; travel fellowships and, 29; voting rights, 306, 312
work. *See* labor
Work Inspectorate. *See* Inspection du Travail
World Bank, 261
world travel fellowships. *See* travel fellowships
World War I, 99, 121, 150, 153–56, 161, 246n17
World War II, 98, 226, 277, 280, 307, 308

Yacine, Kateb, 198
Yaoundé Convention, xxxiv, 251, 253, 262, 265
Young, Robert J. C., 72, 80
youth: physical training of, 96–118
youth groups, Muslim, 184
Yver, Georges, 82

Zamir, Meir, 154–55
Zimmerman, Andrew, xxi–xxii
Zinoman, Peter, 98

In the France Overseas series

To Hell and Back:
The Life of Samira Bellil
Samira Bellil
Translated by Lucy R. McNair
Introduction by Alec G. Hargreaves

Colonial Metropolis:
The Urban Grounds of
Anti-Imperialism and Feminism
in Interwar Paris
Jennifer Anne Boittin

The French Navy and the
Seven Years' War
Jonathan R. Dull

I, Nadia, Wife of a Terrorist
Baya Gacemi

Transnational Spaces and Identities
in the Francophone World
Edited by Hafid Gafaïti,
Patricia M. E. Lorcin, and
David G. Troyansky

French Colonialism Unmasked:
The Vichy Years in
French West Africa
Ruth Ginio

Bourdieu in Algeria:
Colonial Politics, Ethnographic
Practices, Theoretical Developments
Edited and with an introduction
by Jane E. Goodman and
Paul A. Silverstein

Endgame 1758:
The Promise, the Glory, and
the Despair of Louisbourg's
Last Decade
A. J. B. Johnston

Cinema in an Age of Terror:
North Africa, Victimization,
and Colonial History
Michael F. O'Riley

Making the Voyageur World:
Travelers and Traders in the
North American Fur Trade
Carolyn Podruchny

A Workman Is Worthy of His Meat:
Food and Colonialism in Gabon
Jeremy Rich

The Moroccan Soul:
French Education, Colonial
Ethnology, and Muslim
Resistance, 1912–1956
Spencer D. Segalla

Silence Is Death:
The Life and Work of Tahar Djaout
Julija Šukys

*The French Colonial Mind,
Volume 1:
Mental Maps of Empire and
Colonial Encounters*
Edited and with an introduction
by Martin Thomas

*The French Colonial Mind,
Volume 2:
Violence, Military Encounters,
and Colonialism*
Edited and with an introduction
by Martin Thomas

Beyond Papillon:
*The French Overseas
Penal Colonies, 1854–1952*
Stephen A. Toth

*Madah-Sartre:
The Kidnapping, Trial, and
Conver(sat/s)ion of Jean-Paul Sartre
and Simone de Beauvoir*
Written and translated by
Alek Baylee Toumi
With an introduction by
James D. Le Sueur

To order or obtain more information
on these or other University
of Nebraska Press titles, visit
www.nebraskapress.unl.edu.

www.ingramcontent.com/pod-product-compliance
Lightning Source LLC
Chambersburg PA
CBHW021814300426
44114CB00009BA/173